Roth IRA Book

An Investor's Guide

Based on the Taxpayer Relief Act of 1997
and the Technical Corrections Act of 1998

Roth IRA Book

An Investor's Guide

Gobind Daryanani, Ph.D.

including a personal interview with
Senator William V. Roth, Jr. (R-De)
Chairman: U.S. Senate Finance Committee

Edited by Murray Alter
Pricewaterhouse Coopers, N.Y. , New York

Digiqual Inc., NJ
http://www.rothirabook.com

This publication is designed to provide accurate and authoritative information on the subject matter covered. It is sold under the assumption that neither the publisher nor the author is engaged in providing legal, accounting or financial planning services. These services should be obtained from professionals in these areas.

Graphic designs and book layout by Mark Eisenberg
Cover design by Amadeu Dimas

Library of Congress Cataloging-in-Publication Data:

p. cm.

Includes index

ISBN 0-96-653981-8

1.Finance, Personal 2.Retirement-Planning 3.Taxes

Printed in the United States of America

10 9 8 7 6 5 4 3 2

To my daughters Previn and Shana

who inspired me to take on this work

Acknowledgments

The author is grateful to the following persons for their help and encouragement:

Carol, my wife, for believing

Bob Matthews, of Business Technology Inc., Franklin, TN, for contributions to the software used in this book

Richard Franklin for contributions to the chapter on minimum distributions

Larry Cohen, Consumer Financial Decisions, SRI Consulting, Princeton NJ, for the 1996 IRA data use in Chapter 1 and for insights in motivators for savings

Malcolm Hall for artistic directions and marketing advice

Thomas J. Regan, Senior Financial Consultant and Vice President at Merrill Lynch, Florham Park NJ: my personal financial advisor, for his insights on retirement planning and helping me simplify the complexities of the Roth IRA

Jim McCarthy, VP of Next Generation Marketing, Merrill Lynch, for discussions on subtleties of Roth Conversions and prompting my efforts on analyses of Roth Calculators

Jim Morrison an advisor at a full-service brokerage firm in Morristown NJ, for sharing his perspectives on how different people look at the same investment, and for challenging my views

Larry O'Connor, an investment executive and Senior Vice President at PaineWebber Inc., in Florham Park N.J., for suggesting marketing strategies and prompting the Roth Contribution eligibility chart

Joanne Carter, VP of Retirement Account Services at PaineWebber Inc., for prompting the critical audits of the book and for some interesting view points on retirement and calculators

Ellen A. Breslow, Director of Individual Retirement Planning Services, and David R. Hondula at Salomon Smith Barney (Morristown NJ) for prompting the Quick Start, for reading the essence of the book in 15 minutes, and suggesting the reference style of the book

Brian Mattes, of Vanguard Funds, for discussions on drawing assets from an IRA to pay for taxes

Brian Melter of Strong Funds for discussions on effective use of lump sum calculators

Rowena Itchon, of T Rowe Price, for explaining the subtleties of their calculators

Mark Snodgrass, of Money Tree Software, for discussions on automatic tax calculations

Diane Baker, of Adaris Corporation, for her insights in the banking industry, and pointing out some subtle points on eligibility

Acknowledgments (continued)

Ben Norquist, Judy Muehlbauer and the advisory team at Universal Pensions Inc., for clearly explaining the Roth IRA rules and their implications.

Greg Kolojeski, of Brentmark Software, Inc., and editor of the www.rothira.com website, for discussions on the subtleties of the Roth IRA and minimum required distributions

Robert S. Keebler, CPA, MST, author of "A CPA's Guide to Making the Most of the New IRAs", for insights on estate planning and taxes

Natalie B. Choate, author of "Life and Death Planning for Retirement Benefits", for clarifying some subtle issues on estate planning

Seymour Goldberg, author of "Pensions Distributions: Planning Strategies", for advice on tailoring the book to the advisors' markets and for his encouragement

Ed Slott, AICPA faculty member, and editor of "Ed Slott's IRA Advisor" newsletter for his detailed inputs on the chapter on Taxes, and simplification of penalties in the chapter on Rules

Kaye A. Thomas, editor of "Fairmark Press Tax Guide for Investors" at the www.fairmark.com website, for his incisive inputs on the chapter on Rules

Gary Lesser, for his encouragement and explanations of the IRS regs

John Mattoon, a perceptive client, for editing the book

Arun Netravali, for constantly challenging me by raising the bar

Ned and Linda Forbes, for listening

Dan Watter, for helping me through my toughest times

My daughter, Shana, for her insights on me, and

Previn, my daughter, for her humor: (may the Roth be with you).

Contributions

The chapter on "Roth IRA in Estate Planning" was largely written by Mr. Richard S. Franklin, a Florida Bar Board Certified, Trusts and Estate Lawyer in private practice. He is the appointed 1998-1999 Vice Chairperson for the American Bar Association's Probate and Trust Division on Employee benefits.

About the Book

This book is written for individuals who are considering including the Roth IRAs in their retirement and estate plans; and for financial advisors, to help them teach the basics of retirement planning and the Roth IRAs to their clients. In particular it is written for:

- the younger generation, who have not yet started saving
- the middle generation who need to save more for a better future
- the older generation who wish to provide for their children
- the person who understands taxes, does their own taxes or keeps records of their expenses will be able to follow this book.

Financial advisors include:

- brokers
- bankers
- lawyers
- insurers
- tax accountants
- financial planners
- self-advisors

It is assumed that all of the readers, including professionals, have access to professional advisors.

Quick Start: 15 minutes

The following 8 pages will provide a Quick Start to help you assess the value of Roth IRA Contribution and Conversion for your financial profile:

Check the reference tables in Chapter 4 (pages 74 to 89) and Chapter 5 (pages 102 to 119) for the financial profile that most closely matches your case.

For example, a 45 year old person will need to read pages: 78 79 and 102-103

End of Quick Start.

"... what the Roth IRA does is to recognize the great American dream. If you work hard and if you save hard, you can have a good retirement income that allows you to leave something for your children."

Senator William V. Roth Jr. (R-DE) was first elected to the Senate in 1970 and is currently serving his fifth term. He served in the House of Representatives, 1967-71 and was the Delaware State Republican Chairman from 1961-64. He received his M.B.A. from Harvard University in 1947 and the law degree from Harvard School in 1949. He is currently the Chairman of the Senate Finance Committee. He championed the Roth IRA and led it through its becoming law, in July 1998.

Preface

The following is an excerpt from an interview between Senator William V. Roth Jr. and the author, Gobind Daryanani, held on May 15th 1998 in Washington D.C.

I would like to introduce this book with a few words about the circumstances that led me to begin writing it, and then present a most enlightening interview that allowed me to complete this book.

In 1995 I was a manager at AT&T (now Lucent Technologies), responsible for the development of their High Definition Television (HDTV) program. Although my team had made considerable progress, AT&T had then decided that it did not want to proceed further with HDTV products. At this point, I decided to undertake a major entrepreneurial gamble.

I had saved enough money to ensure for my wife's and my retirement and felt reasonably secure financially. So I asked AT&T to give me the rights to develop the HDTV technology further in return for royalties. The company agreed, and I went off on my own.

Within 9 months, constant delays in the process of agreeing upon HDTV standards forced me to close my business. As a result, I had significantly less money than before and also found difficulty in finding a middle management job comparable to the one I had left. For the next year and a half, I struggled to find a new career path. This situation worsened when our 18-year old daughter was diagnosed with a disability that will almost certainly result in her eventually needing long-term care. In mid-1997 I went to Merrill Lynch and asked them to do a retirement analysis. While they were preparing the report, I decided to perform my own analysis. I am, after all, an applied mathematician by training, and creating the software was not a difficult problem. I was pleased when my analysis reproduced their work. However, one reference in the report confused me.

"What's this Roth IRA you mention?" My analyst briefly explained the basics of the new program, but said that it didn't apply to me because of my normal income. However, I realized that since I was still unemployed, I might still qualify. I returned home and began my own analysis.

The results nearly knocked me out of my chair. It seemed that not only would my wife and I be able to establish a trust for our daughter, but also we would have even more funds for our retirement than originally projected. To ensure the soundness of my conclusions, I confirmed my analysis with professional financial analysts. I was surprised to find that many did not understand the Roth IRA, and they certainly did not have adequate software to provide a customized client analysis.

My next step was to evaluate all the Roth IRA software that was available at that time. In all, I looked at software from 25 companies. I ended up writing a 300-page report that I sold to two major full-service brokerage houses and another large corporation. I had also come to realize that many investors as well as their financial advisors did not fully understand the pros and cons of the Roth IRA. Since I had previously written textbooks, I decided to write a tutorial that would help financial advisors explain the Roth IRA to their clients. To ensure that it would also be accessible to self–advised investors, I determined that it would be written in language people could understand, with a minimum of jargon.

Three months later, the manuscript was completed. However, as I reviewed it, I could not help but feel there was a significant omission. I had captured the mechanics of the Roth IRA, but had neglected to establish the spirit or vision behind the program. And this concern has very real practical concerns: many professionals fear that the program is "too good to be true" and that it will be taken away or gravely weakened by legislators unwilling to lose potential tax revenues.

I therefore approached the one man who best understands the intent and future of this legislation, Senator William V. Roth, who graciously agreed to give me an interview and discuss the program that bears his name. What follows is a somewhat abridged account of the interview, which took place in Washington DC on May 15, 1998.

Dr. Daryanani:
> Could you describe the central motivating idea behind the Roth IRA? What does it accomplish?

Senator Roth:
> I think what the Roth IRA does is to recognize the great American dream. If you work hard and if you save hard, you can have a good retirement income

that allows you to leave something to your children. All these are part of the American dream.

DD: Was leaving money to one's children an original legislative goal? Because that is surely one of the major outcomes of the Roth IRA.

SR: Yes. Again, that's part of the American dream. People save so their children can have a better life.

DD: In the course of preparing this book, I've heard it said that it is too easy to pull out money, and that people may withdraw funds prior to their retirement.

SR: I am familiar with that argument. But frankly it seems to me that we needed to provide some flexibility, particularly to attract the young. For example, because part of the American dream is to own your own home, we permitted early withdrawal of up to $10,000 for the purchase of a first home.

The same thing is true for education. The best thing you can give your children is a good education, so I think a withdrawal for educational costs is worthwhile.

I am very much bothered that so many young people are forced to go deeply into debt in order to complete college. As a nation, we do not want our young people getting married and starting families with the burden of a huge debt. So yes, these withdrawals do open up the account, but we think it helps achieve desirable goals.

DD: Another concern I've heard is that the Roth IRA is a win for private individuals but a long-term loss for the government. How do you respond?

SR: It seems to me that the Roth IRA is a win–win. It's good for the family, and it's good for the nation. Alan Greenspan has said on many occasions that the most important problem this country faces is to increase its savings. An example of the extent of this problem is that the typical baby boomer has very little in savings.

That's a major concern when we consider that these people are nearing retirement age. So I felt that something had to be done for them. But there's also the national interest. If you look at the savings rate in Japan, Germany and elsewhere, we're at a tremendous competitive disadvantage. In fact, we've been forced to rely on foreign savings and foreign investment to spark our economy. It's fortunate that these funds have been available in the past, but we don't want to become dependent on them. My point is that it is in the national interest both for the economy and the family that we have significant savings. That's why I perceive the program to be a win-win for both parties.

DD: Do you envision the Roth IRA becoming more or less restrictive in the future?

SR: I'd like to expand the program further. If you look at IRAs when they started in the early 1980s, a maximum $2,000 contribution was permitted. This was not indexed. The same $2,000 has a purchasing power of $1,000 in today's dollars.

DD: Is the Roth IRA indexed?

SR: Not now. But we would like to expand the contribution in many ways. We would like to index it and increase the dollar amount to make up for lost ground. I would also like to expand the eligibility. I was not happy when we had to phase it out to $150,000 for a couple and $95,000 for an individual. But the White House insisted on that.

DD: Do you know why they insisted on a limit?

SR: Their argument is that we were helping the rich. But, as I have said on many occasions, what we are really trying to do is develop a culture of savings. We'd like to see people start off when they're young and every year save whatever they can afford, whether it's $500 or $2000. But when you start placing limitations — "You've made too much money this year" —you take away the ability to plan.

DD: The economic model suggests that the government will make money in the next five years (because of less tax-deferred savings and conversion taxes), but that they would lose money after that (because of tax-exempt withdrawals). And, with the introduction of the recent clause permitting more of the over-70-year-old group to contribute after 2004, the period of losing money may be postponed to 10 years.

Do you see the losing of these monies as a long-term threat to the program, that legislators would be tempted to take it away?

SR: I think the program is already so popular that it would be politically risky for anyone to try to take it away. And it certainly won't be taken away as long as I am Chairman of the Finance Committee. But more important, I think the program will remain in place because we need a *stable* policy to encourage savings.

DD: What other strategies are you considering to help people save?

SR: As you know, we have the Educational IRA. When it went through the Senate last year, a $2000 maximum contribution was allowed. We were forced to cut this back to $500. But it's still a good start. We have legislation in the Senate that would increase the contribution back to $2000.

DD: If you were to look at the two best things that have happened to the Roth IRA, what would they be?

SR: The best is that we got the Roth IRA enacted. The next best thing is that we were able to make it available to a large enough segment of the population that the securities industry will develop products for it and market them. Obviously you need to be able to explain the program to people. The regulations are complex. However, the program is still broad enough that it is receiving strong advertising and sales support.

DD: Finally, I was wondering if you think you've met the goals you had in mind when you first began to advocate these changes.

SR: I'm never satisfied. I always want to do more.

May 15 th, 1998
Washington D.C.

Contents at a Glance

Contents

Chapter 8 Minimum Required Distributions   163

References   269

Index

Chapter 1 Overview of the Roth IRA

This chapter provides an overview of the basics of the Roth IRA: what it is; the retirement benefits it provides; and how it differs from other retirement savings options. These basics are explained at an introductory level for someone new to retirement planning and new to IRAs. We will also provide some background on the objectives of the Roth IRA project and future initiatives that are being considered (as explained to the author by Senator Roth in a personal interview captured in the Preface of this book).

The topics covered are:

- History and highlights of the Roth IRA
- Retirement savings options available today
- Features offered by the Roth IRA and the Education IRA
- What could go wrong and will Congress take it away?

1.1   History and Highlights

Created by the Taxpayer Relief Act of 1997 (TRA-97), and championed by Senate Finance Committee Chairman William V. Roth Jr., (R-De), the Roth IRA provides a new approach to retirement savings. It went into effect January 1, 1998. The Technical Corrections Act of 1998 (TCA '98) provided modifications and clarification on numerous issues. This TCA '98 was signed into law by the President of the United States in July, 1998.

This book is based on the Roth IRA rules enacted by the Taxpayer's Relief Act of 1997 and the modifications made by the Technical Corrections Act of 1998.

The concept behind the Roth IRA is that the money you invest will grow tax-free. When you do pull the money out, you will not pay any taxes (subject to some restrictions).

There are two types of **Roth IRAs:**

Roth Contributions

The Roth Contribution allows an individual to invest up to $2,000 per year. You do not get an income tax deduction, as you would with the deductible Traditional IRA. Thus this is not a deductible account. However,

you will not need to pay income taxes on the growth

Thus you will not need to pay income taxes when the money is ultimately withdrawn from the account (subject to certain restrictions).

Roth Conversions

You are allowed to rollover funds currently held in a Traditional IRA into a Roth IRA account. The Traditional IRA may contain both deductible assets and non-deductible assets.

You **will need to pay up-front income taxes**[1] on the portion of the Traditional IRA rollover that was deductible. The taxable amount is the total Traditional IRA account minus any non-deductible amounts. From then on you will not pay income taxes on the growth, nor will you pay income taxes at the time of the withdrawal (again subject to some restrictions). There is no limit on the amount that can be rolled over.

Other types of qualified retirement accounts (such as 401(k), 403(b) and SIMPLE IRA) may not be converted **directly** to a Roth account. You may rollover these accounts to a Traditional IRA first and then convert the Traditional IRA to a Roth IRA.

A characteristic of the Roth IRA is that the tax advantage is realized in **future** years (at the time of withdrawal). In contrast, the deductible Traditional IRA provides a tax advantage **now, in the year of investment.** These deductible-Traditional IRA

---

[1] In this book, all references to "income taxes" means the Federal income tax, unless otherwise indicated.

investments are not included in the taxable income in the year of investment, which leads to a reduction in the tax dollars owed in the year of the investment. The taxes are due at the time of withdrawal, on both the principal and the growth

> *Thus it can be seen that the deductible Traditional IRA alleviates the tax burden in the year of investment, while the Roth IRA alleviates the tax burden in the future years of withdrawal.*
>
> *Note that with the Roth IRA you never pay taxes on the growth. This is one of the features that makes the Roth IRA financially attractive.*

The **tax-free growth** aspect of these Roth IRA vehicles can provide substantial financial advantages that can significantly enhance your retirement benefits. You may be aware that tax-deferred Traditional IRA accounts provide a greater return than a taxable account (assuming identical investments in each account). The Roth IRA will, in most cases, provide an even greater return than a tax-deferred Traditional IRA account. The typical advantage of a Roth IRA over a Traditional IRA will be shown to be in the range of 10% to 50%, and in some cases the advantage is considerably greater. It is the first time in the recent history of this nation that Congress has offered a tax-free savings vehicle. It is a major step with potentially dramatic implications.

The main criteria in determining whether you will be eligible for the Roth IRAs are explained next.

Eligibility Criteria for Roth Contributions:

If you are single, your modified adjusted gross income (MAGI)[2] needs to be under $95,000, and your earnings need to be at least $2,000, to be eligible for the full $2,000 contribution. Note that interest and dividends are not included in "earnings".

If you are married filing jointly, you and your spouse's combined MAGI needs to be less that $150,000, and your combined earnings need to be at least $4,000, to be eligible for the full $4,000[3].

---

[2] MAGI is generally close to the AGI, adjusted gross income from the IRS 1040 tax Form. See Chapter 3.

Eligibility Criteria for Roth Conversions:

If you are single, your MAGI needs to be less than $100,000.

If you are married, you must file a joint return and your combined MAGI needs to be less than $100,000.

The amount converted is added to your taxable income when you make the conversion. Thus you will be paying taxes on the converted amount up-front. However, if you make the conversion in the year 1998, you will get some tax relief: you may[4] choose to add 1/4th of the amount converted to your taxable income over each of the next four years.

Taxes and Penalties

Generally, to avoid paying taxes and possible early withdrawal penalties, you must leave the money in a Roth IRA account for **at least five years** . Assuming you do so and meet certain other criteria, the withdrawals of these funds will then be tax-free.

The detailed rules for Roth Contributions and Conversions are covered in Chapter 7.

1.2   Retirement Savings Options Available Today

To understand the objectives of the Roth IRA we need to first look at current retirement savings options. There are currently five sources of retirement funds for most Americans:

1. Social Security income
2. Pension income
3. Personal savings in other assets
4. Employer sponsored savings plans e.g.401(k), 403(b)
5. IRA funds: tax deferred and tax-free

The broad objective of all of these approaches is to enhance your retirement savings. This section will validate the commonly held view that the current retirement savings picture in the U.S. is not a rosy one. While it is arguable as to how much more needs to

---

[3] Partial contributions can be made for individuals with MAGI between $95,000 and $110,000; and by married couples with MAGI between $150,000 and $160,000.

[4] This is a Technical Correction. Prior to the correction the rule was that you must spread your income over the four years.

be done, it goes undisputed that something needs to be done. Let us start by looking at each of these retirement savings options.

1.2.1 Social Security

Social Security is:

> *Partially taxable*
> *Continues through your life and*
> *Is tied to inflation (increases each year)*

The maximum Social Security benefit that a worker can receive in 1998 is $16,104. This assumes that the individual has paid the maximum Social Security taxes for 35 working years and that he or she retires at age 65. The average Social Security distribution in 1998, for individuals who have not received disability benefits, is $11,160. A 1994-study report from the Social Security Administration stated that Social Security represented 42% of income for the average retiree.

Consider a couple who receives $24,000 in Social Security benefits. Up to 85% of this Social Security payout is taxable. At a tax rate of 25%, the tax paid will be 25% of 85% of $24,000, which is $5,100. This leaves the retirees with $19,000 after taxes. If the couple needed $60,000 in retirement income, after taxes, this Social Security benefit would represent approximately 32% of their retirement needs. If their after-tax retirement expenses were $70,000 per year this payout would represent 27% of the needs.

The benefits from Social Security are **indexed with inflation**, meaning that as inflation rises, the Social Security benefit received will correspondingly increase. Another way of saying this is that it is not necessary to adjust the Social Security benefits to correct for rising costs due to inflation: the payout received will be adjusted, using a cost-of-living-adjustment (COLA).

The money that the retired person receives from the Social Security Administration comes from the Social Security taxes that working people pay. At the present time the Social Security Administration is taking in more money than it is paying out. This is certainly a stable and healthy situation. However, there are some socio-economic forces that will change this situation. First, people are living longer, so more money will be needed for Social Security benefits per person as time goes on. Second, there are fewer people entering the work force and more people entering retirement. There will be a greater shift in this direction, in 5 to 10 years, as the peak population segment known as the baby boomer population (now ages approximately 35 to 55) start to leave the work force and enter retirement. Then fewer people will be in the work force, and more people will be in the retirement pool. These factors lead to a reasonable projection that Social Security benefits are likely to decrease with time and this source is expected to pay for a smaller a portion of one's retirement needs in the future. Generally it is expected that:

Social Security benefits are likely to decrease with time
In particular, baby boomers, and more so the Generation X population
(ages less than 35) will find that Social Security provides a decreasingly
smaller portion of their retirement needs.

The exact calculation of Social Security benefits is complex. You can get an assessment of your social security benefits from the Social Security benefits office which can be reached through http://www.ssa.gov or by calling 1-800-772-1213.

1.2.2 Employer-Sponsored Pension Funds

This section describes retirement savings plans provided by employers. There are two kinds of employer-sponsored plans. The first is referred to as a **defined benefit** or pension plan and the second is referred to as a **defined contribution** plan (such as the 401(k), 403(b) or the SEP IRA). Many large and some mid-size corporations offer the **defined benefit plan.** These plans typically provide a fixed retirement benefit pension determined by the individual's salary prior to retirement and the total years of service.

Defined Benefit pension plans are:

Taxable and
Pay a fixed amount till death
*The benefits are often **not** increased to keep up with inflation*

A typical pension plan may provide 1.5% of a person's average annual salary over the last five years for each year of service. Thus an employee retiring with 20 years of service would receive 20*1.5 = 30% of her salary. For an individual whose average salary for the last five years of employment was $75,000, this translates to a pension of $22,500 (30% of $75,000) per year. Assuming a 25% tax rate, this yields $16,875 after taxes. If the person needs $60,000 in income after taxes, the pension will provide 28% of this need in the year of retirement. In general this pension is not tied to inflation. Thus, as retirement income needs rise to keep up with inflation, assuming a 3.5% inflation rate, it can be shown that this constant $16,875 will drop to 20% of the growing needs in 10 years, and to 14% of the growing needs in 20 years. The **averaged** percentage of income needs provided by the pension over 20 years is 21%.

In recent years the number of defined corporate pension plans have decreased, due to corporate restructuring and downsizing. A 1994 survey indicated that approximately 45% of the population receive pensions.

Many corporations are replacing pension plans with **defined contribution plans** such as the 401(k), 403(b) and the SEP IRA retirement plans.

Defined contribution plans of the 401(k)-type

> *Are Tax-deferred*
> *Taxes are paid during withdrawal*
> *Sometimes have corporate matching funds*
> *Returns depend on your choice of investment*

Many employers offer a defined contribution plan. In such a plan you contribute either a percentage of your salary or a fixed amount per year. The amounts are automatically subtracted from your paycheck; for this reason it is sometimes referred to as a payroll-reduction plan In some corporations the employer will match the funds you invest up to a certain maximum. For example, if you invest 6% of your salary, an employer may match up to 3% and add that to your retirement savings, generally up to a certain maximum.

> *This matching fund, if provided, is a strong motivator for employees*
> *to contribute to such a plan.*

Typically the employee will have a choice of investments for these savings. Under these plans the return on the investments is determined by the performance of the investments chosen. The total amount that an employee can contribute to the 401(k), 403(b) and the SEP IRA plans in 1998 cannot exceed $10,000 per year. A related rule is that the maximum contribution from an employer plus the employee is 25% of the employee's income or $30,000, whichever is lower. These upper limits are increased to account for inflation.

What these plans have in common is that they are tax-deferred. From that perspective they are similar to the deductible Traditional IRA plans. In both cases the tax advantage is provided in the year of the investment: you do not pay taxes in the year of contribution, nor do you pay taxes during the growth of the accounts. Taxes are paid at the time of withdrawal. These plans are financially equivalent (same rate of return) to the deductible Traditional IRA plans if the employer is not providing any matching funds; they are better than the deductible Traditional IRA plans if the employer does provide matching funds.

Currently 25% of the population have some kind of employer-contribution plan. The average asset size in these plans is $23,000, which is relatively small. Thus these plans, while they are conceptually great, are not widespread. In fact most small companies do not provide such plans, largely because they are expensive.

The percentage of retirement needs that these assets will provide is discussed in Chapter 2. One example is presented here to put the value of these accounts in perspective.

Consider a couple, both age 45, who plan to retire in 20 years. They have $50,000 in their 401(k) account. How much can they expect per year, in today's dollars after taxes, between the ages of 70 and 90 of retirement from this tax deferred account? The account is assumed to grow at 9% and inflation is assumed to be 3.5%.

As we will show in Chapter 2, the $50,000 balance will yield an annual $13,670 payout for 20 years, after taxes in today's dollars. For a couple needing $60,000 after taxes, this represents 23% of their needs.

Note that while a Traditional IRA account may be converted to a Roth IRA, subject to the eligibility requirements, these defined contribution plans cannot be converted directly to Roth IRAs. They will first need to be rolled over to a Traditional IRA, and then the Traditional IRA can be converted to a Roth IRA. However, most defined contribution accounts cannot be converted to the Traditional IRAs at any time of your choosing: You may only have this option if you leave your current employer to change to another job, or when you retire.

1.2.3 Personal Savings and Other Assets

Personal savings and other assets include **fixed assets** (home, car) and **investable assets** such as cash accounts and investments in mutual funds, bonds, and other taxable accounts. The sequence in which money should be drawn in retirement is as follows: first the taxable investable accounts, then the tax-deferred accounts and last the tax-free-withdrawal accounts.

Draw money last from the account that provide the highest return.

Let us illustrate the withdrawal sequence principle using the example from the last section. Assume that the couple needs $60,000 per year during retirement, after taxes, expressed in today's dollars. Assume that Social Security will provide 30% of their needs and that their pension will provide 20%. These assets will provide 50% of their needs through their retirement. The balance of $30,000 needs to come from other investable assets, defined-contribution 401(k)-type plans; tax-deferred and tax-free IRA accounts. They will start by withdrawing funds from their personal investable assets. Let us assume they have $150,000 in these. How long will their non-retirement funds last, if they draw their total balance needs from this account?

Assuming a growth rate of 9%, and a tax rate of 22%, the account will grow by a factor of 2 over 20 years, after correcting for inflation. Thus at retirement, assumed to be 65, their investable asset account will be worth $300,000 in today's dollars. At a spending rate of $30,000 per year, this asset can be shown to last 11 years. After age 76, which is 11 years from retirement, they will need to draw from their tax-deferred and tax-free accounts: in this example these accounts will need to provide 50% of the couple's retirement needs (the remaining 50% assumed to be provided by Social Security and a company pension).

While individual situations will vary, in general we expect that for baby boomers, and more so for the Generation X groups, an even larger percentage of retirement needs will need to come from such tax-advantaged accounts.

Next let us describe these tax-advantaged accounts.

1.2.4 Individual Retirement Accounts IRAs

This section discusses the Individual Retirement Account (IRA) as a retirement vehicle. These are voluntary retirement savings accounts. In the Traditional IRA individuals can invest up to $2,000 per year. Two types of Traditional IRAs have been available: deductible and non-deductible. In a deductible IRA this $2,000 is deducted from taxable income, thereby providing additional income (i.e., the tax savings on the deductions) in the year of the investment. The growth of the IRA account is also not taxed. Taxes are paid at the time of withdrawal typically after retirement, and there is a minimum amount that needs to be withdrawn annually after the required beginning date, which is age 70 1/2. With non-deductible IRAs, the investment is not deductible but the growth is tax deferred. Persons who do not qualify for the deductible Traditional IRA because they exceed the relatively low AGI limits sometimes use the non-deductible IRA instead of a taxable account.

Table 1.1 shows the number of households that have Traditional IRAs relative to the number that qualify for the IRA. Of the 109.7 million households in the U.S., 80 million were eligible for contributing to one of the two types of Traditional IRA in 1996. Of these households only 28% or 30.5 million households have IRA accounts. Of the 30.5 million households only 11.3 million contributed to the IRA in 1996.

Thus only 10% of the population contributed to Traditional IRAs in 1996 even though approximately 80% were eligible.

There has been a definite decrease in the popularity of the Traditional IRAs since they were first introduced. One reason for this low participation is there is an income limit: if an individual makes more than $40,000 he or she could not contribute to the tax deductible Traditional IRA (for a couple, the limit is $60,000). Other possible reasons are that people will prefer to invest in a matching-fund company plan, or that they just do not have the funds to invest. Whatever the reasons, it is clear that

Traditional IRAs represent a relatively small part of the nation's retirement savings.

[5] The data was provided by Consumer Financial Decisions, SRI Consulting.. Their report uses total number of separate economic households. This is slightly higher than the number of households used by the U.S. census since there may be non-related separate households that do not share their finances.

Table 1.1 Traditional IRA Data for 1996

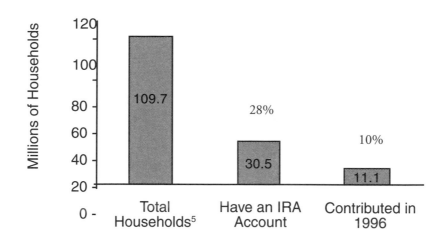

Source for All Charts:
The Macro Monitor
Consumer Financial Decisions
SRI Consulting
Princeton NJ

The percentage of retirement income provided by these Traditional IRAs is analyzed in detail in Chapters 4 and 5 for various financial profiles. One example is presented here: Consider a couple, both 45 years of age, who invest $2,000 each (total $4,000) per year for 20 years in the deductible Traditional IRA. We will assume that the assets grow at 9%, inflation is 3.5% and that the couple retires at age 65 and draw from this account over 20 years. Their withdrawal is increased annually to keep up with inflation. How much will this investment provide per year in today's dollars, after taxes, assuming a tax rate of 25%? The retirement benefit from a deductible Traditional IRA depends on one critical question:

> *What does the couple do with the tax savings in the year of the investment? Do they spend the tax savings or re-invest it?*

Their tax bill did go down by 25% * $4,000 = $1,000. Did they spend that $1,000 or did they take the IRS refund (if that's how the $1,000 showed up) and invest in a taxable account? In most cases the answer is that they spent it. In that case they receive $7,298 per year. This would represent 12% of their retirement need of $60,000 per year.

Suppose, instead, the couple had the discipline and the means to invest this up front tax savings in a taxable account (such as a mutual fund) that, for example, provides a 7% after tax growth. In that case they will receive $8,744 per year.

1.3   The Roth IRAs

This section will broadly quantify the benefits of the Roth IRA and provide some guidelines to aid in the decision to contribute or convert to the Roth IRA. We then discuss the future stability and directions of the Roth IRA: will they take it away? what are the risks and the downsides? what could go wrong? This last section evolved from discussions with Senator Roth.

1.3.1   Quantifying the Benefits of the Roth IRA

How do the Traditional IRAs compare with the new Roth IRA contributions?

Let us look at the results of the above example with the Roth Contribution. Using the same assumptions, the Roth Contribution of $4,000 per year for 20 years will provide the couple with $9,732 per year for the 20 years of retirement. This is 8.4% more than the Traditional IRA case where the couple did reinvest their tax refund and **28% higher** than the Traditional IRA case where the couple did not reinvest their tax refund.

The Roth Contribution IRA is seen to provide three types of advantages:

- **Tax-Free Growth Advantage**: The first advantage is that a tax-free-growth account is generally better than a tax deferred account. The growth is free of taxes.

- **Discipline Advantage**: For some clients there is a second advantage: it does remove the temptation of spending the tax-savings in the year of investment. Of course, this is an advantage only if you can afford to forgo that income.

- **It is available to a larger segment** (approximately 97%) of the population (see Table 1.2).

Table 1.2

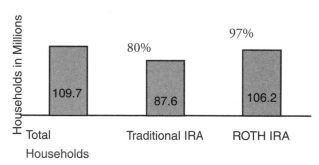

For people seeking retirement benefits, rather than front-end tax savings, the Roth Contribution is a definite win. The retirement benefits are so clear-cut that it would be correct to say that

> *If you meet the eligibility criteria, you should maximize your investment in the Roth Contribution IRA.*

The one retirement option that will do better than the Roth IRA is the employer matched retirement plan, assuming a one for one match (100% match). This means that the employer would invest $1 for each $1 that you invest. We will show in a later chapter that the Roth IRA is not as good as employer plans with greater than 25% match, but that the Roth IRA will generally do better than any plan that has between a 0% and a 25% match.

If you have the means, you may want to contribute more than the maximum allowed **per person** limit of $2,000 . Note that the maximum per family can be a lot higher. All the members in your family could make a contribution if they meet the eligibility condition. The spouse can contribute whether the spouse has earned income or not. Children can invest up to the limit of their earned income. Thus a family of four could **potentially** contribute as much as $8,000 per year to the Roth IRA.

Roth IRA Conversion

The Roth IRA Conversion allows individuals and families to greatly enhance their retirement assets with one step all in one year. The percentage of households eligible for the Roth IRA Conversion (MAGI less than $100,000 and currently own a Traditional IRA) is shown in Table 1.3 to be 23% of the U.S. population.

Table 1.3

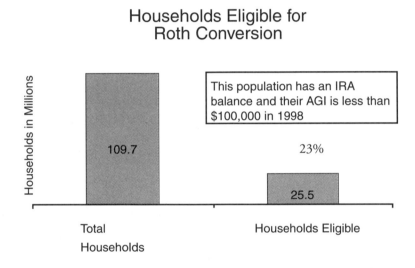

If the eligibility conditions are met there is no limit to the amount that can be converted to the Roth IRA. All or part of the existing Traditional IRA may be converted. This, like the Roth Contribution IRA, is also a tax-free-withdrawal account. The advantage of this Roth Conversion will be seen to range from small to medium to very large, depending on the individual situation. The one factor that moves the advantage from small to very large is the **holding-period**. The longer you leave the funds in the Roth account the larger is the advantage of the Roth IRA.

Let us illustrate this with an example. A 55-year-old couple has $100,000 in a Traditional IRA account. They convert the Traditional IRA to a Roth IRA, paying the tax (assumed to be 25%, or $25,000) over four years. The assets are assumed to grow at 9% and inflation is assumed to be 3.5%. How much will the couple get per year over a 20-year period? How much will they have if they were to start pulling the money out at age 75?[6]

---

[6] We assume that the conversion taxes are paid from outside assets; and that in the Traditional IRA case these tax dollars (called opportunity lost dollars) are invested in a taxable account.

If they started withdrawing at age 75, as we will show in a later chapter, the Roth IRA will provide a 12% advantage over the deductible Traditional IRA, even after considering the taxes that were paid up front. If the withdrawals started later the advantage increases: for instance starting at age 80 raises the advantage to 22%. Now if they are mainly interested in leaving the funds for their children to withdraw, starting after their age 85, the advantage goes up to 31%, and at age 90 the advantage is 43%. The advantage keeps on increasing with later withdrawals[7].

> *Another financial advantage provided by the Roth IRA is that mandatory withdrawals are not imposed during your lifetime. Traditional IRAs, in contrast, require withdrawal after you reach age 701/2. This feature of the Roth IRA provides an increasing benefit over the Traditional IRA, the later you draw from the Roth IRA.*

On the other hand, if the couple will need the money very soon after the conversion date, the Roth Conversion could yield poorer results than the Traditional IRA. In particular if the couple will need to draw the money in the first five years, there may be additional penalties imposed. In that case the couple should not convert to the Roth IRA. Of course if they need some, but not all their money soon after the five years they may want to convert a portion of their IRA to the Roth IRA. The special chapter on Roth Optimal Conversion (Chapter 6) provides guidance on partial Roth Conversions.

While it is difficult to make broad recommendations regarding the Roth Conversions that will apply to all clients, some generalizations can be made:

* The longer you leave your money in the Roth Conversion account the better the account will do.
* If you need your IRA funds only for later years in your retirement then the Roth will provide a very large advantage.
* If you are mainly saving for the next generation, the Roth Conversion is definitely the best approach.
* If you need all the funds in the first five years, do not convert to the Roth IRA.
* If you are in between, needing some funds early on and some later on, consider a partial conversion. Chapter 6 provides guidance on partial conversions.
* If you need to draw from the Traditional IRA funds to pay for the Conversion tax, the advantage of the Roth IRA will be reduced. This is discussed further in Chapter 5.

---

[7]Useful analogy: Roth IRA can be compared to a fast runner who gives his slower opponent a "head start". If the race is short he loses. The longer the race the further ahead he gets.

1.3.2 How the Roth IRA was Born: Pros and Cons of the Roth IRA

From the last sections on current methods for savings, we can draw the framework under which the Roth project was born. We saw that:

• Social Security is a good source for retirement income. However, it is likely to provide a decreasingly smaller portion of retirement needs with time.

• Employer-defined pension plans are on the decrease, and less than 50% of the U.S. population can depend on this source.

• Traditional IRAs have lost popularity, with only 10% of the population contributing to them in 1997.

In most cases these three sources will provide no more than 50% to 60% of people's retirement needs. Currently, the remainder comes from personal savings or work after retirement and, for some people, from employer contribution plans (401(k)-type). It is clear that in the future, the baby boomers, and more so the Generation X population, can depend less on government sponsored benefits and will **need** to rely more on their own savings. In spite of this reality, it appears that the rate of savings among young people in particular is far from what it needs to be. Something needs to be done to remedy this problem; a problem that will grow in size in 5-10 years when the baby boomers start leaving the work force and enter into retirement.

It was against this background that the Roth IRA was conceived The vision of the Roth project, in the words of Senator Roth, was to:

> " *help people meet their dream…the American dream…if you work hard you will be able to save for your retirement, you will be able to provide for your children's education and later needs…*"

People need encouragement, and always have needed encouragement, to save for the future. The encouragement in the case of the Traditional deductible IRA has been the tax deduction in the year of investment: this gives you more money to spend now. The Roth IRA took a different approach: **the tax advantage will be provided in the future, when you use the funds you are saving and the growth will never be taxed.** The advantage provided is a very significant one. With reasonable assumptions, the return on investments are in the order of 50% more than in an equivalent investment in a taxable account, and approximately 25% more than in a Traditional IRA account. Further, the Roth IRA reaches out to a much larger population than the Traditional IRA: the eligibility conditions have been expanded so that 97% of the population can make annual contributions to the Roth IRAs.

> *It is hoped that these motivators will encourage the younger generation to embark on a program to start saving regularly to ensure that they will have sufficient funds for all their future needs.*

But what about those who are already close to retirement? They can benefit by converting existing IRA funds to the Roth IRA. This can happen in one year and can make a dramatic difference to retirement savings. A Roth Conversion can provide 25% to 100% more in retirement funds, depending on when you need to start drawing from these funds. For some people this will mean truly retiring rather than working during retirement; for others it will mean providing for their children; for all (who are eligible) it will mean additional financial assets in the future. Not everyone is eligible for this program. Possibly the program will be expanded in the future to include a wider population segment.

The Roth IRA was structured with awareness that different people have different priorities in their future aspirations. Retirement is one, owning a home is another, providing for children's education is another, and providing for their future needs is yet another. The Roth IRA provides some flexibility in the use of the funds.

> *In particular, the Roth IRA is extremely attractive if you aspire to leave funds for your children after your death. This is because it does not have a required minimum distribution during your lifetime.*
>
> *The Roth IRA should be considered in estate planning.*

This feature lets the Roth IRA grow tax-free for a longer time, and generally results in well over 50% more funds for the next generation.

Younger people in particular may want the flexibility to use their future dollars for such pressing aspirations as owning a home or paying for children's education. The Roth IRA does provide some flexibilityby not imposing a penalty for withdrawals for these needs.

The Education IRA is a related initiative under the umbrella of the Roth project. This IRA allows a savings of $500 per year for funding the education of a child. The eligibility criteria are similar to the Roth Contribution IRA. Each child may receive up to a maximum of $500 per year until age 18; and anyone may contribute funds for the child. Like the Roth IRA, these funds are not deductible, they grow tax free and there is no tax upon withdrawal. This initiative fits in well with the Roth vision. However, the $500 per year savings is relatively small and will fund only a small part of any higher education. It is a beginning that hopefully will be expanded in the near future. It is high on the list of the near-term initiatives for the Senate Finance Committee.

Before we move on to the deficiencies of the Roth IRA, let us revisit its advantages:

- The tax free growth advantage motivator is significant.
- The tax advantage comes in the future, rather than now.
- Addresses retirement needs for the younger as well as for the older population segments.
- Addresses children's needs after their parents' deaths.
- Addresses education needs .
- Addresses home buyers' needs.

Let us now look at the shortfalls of the Roth IRA, keeping in mind that proposed additions and expansions to the Roth IRA may address many of these in the near future.

1. The Roth IRA limits the population segments that can use this vehicle by imposing eligibility constraints based on maximum incomes. It would be desirable to expand the program to a **broader population.** The limits on income were not indexed to inflation. Thus with rising inflation and increases in salaries, a smaller and smaller segment of the population will be eligible. Thus people would be squeezed out of the program. It would be desirable to **index the maximum income levels.**

2. The annual contributions are also not indexed. Consider that with reasonable assumptions a $2,000 investment today will be equivalent to a $1,200 investment in 15 years. This begs for an **indexing of the annual contribution**.

3. Imagine a hypothetical couple whose combined income is $140,000. After three years the wife receives a promotion and a $25,000 raise. They are now ineligible for the Roth IRA and must reformat their retirement strategy. The limits on income **make it difficult to plan a lifetime strategy of savings**.

4. The Education IRA is a good step toward encouraging young people to save toward the future. However, the $500 per year un-indexed saving will result in a small part

of college needs. The **$500 limit should be raised and indexed** if the Education IRA is to be a meaningful way of saving for higher education.

5.   The flexibility provided in allowing withdrawal of funds for college education and first-time home buyers is viewed by some as a negative: providing too much flexibility will make the funds too accessible and will draw funds away from retirement savings.

6.   There is one other potentially negative aspect of the Roth IRA proposal. Congress will certainly receive extra funds in the early years (from conversion taxes); however, in later years when people start withdrawing tax-exempt money, Congress will be losing revenues. This raises the frequently voiced question:

> *Could these lost revenues induce Congress to change the rules or take the Roth IRA away?*

This topic is addressed in the next section.

1.3.3 What Could Go Wrong and Will Congress Take it Away?

The Roth IRA provides significant tax advantages to the people of America. A tax advantage for the people means a tax disadvantage for the U.S. Treasury.

In the first five years of the program, the U.S. Treasury will gain money because of conversion tax dollars that will come in. Since there is a significant penalty we can safely assume that there will not be any significant withdrawals in these five years.

While it is true that people should keep funds in the Roth IRA as long as they can, and that this should be the **last** account to draw from, some people fear that there may be a significant withdrawal of funds from the Roth IRAs soon after the five years.

The 1998 Technical Corrections Act provided that after the year 2004, people over 70 1/2 will not need to include their minimum required distributions from a Traditional IRA in their MAGI for computing eligibility for Roth Conversions. This will allow a segment of this population to convert their Traditional IRA accounts (which is relatively large) to a Roth IRA. Thus there will be some new monies in the form of conversion taxes coming in starting in 2005: these monies also will most likely not be withdrawn for at least five years (to avoid the penalties).

After the second five year period, in 10 years, it is possible that there will be significant net tax-exempt withdrawals from the Roth IRA accounts, and a consequent loss in revenues for the U.S. Treasury. From a national standpoint, however, these losses in revenues will need to be weighed against the positive impact of the infusion of funds into the economy (by the people who are withdrawing funds).

The fear in some people's minds is that these lost revenues (because of taxes not paid) may prompt a new administration to reverse the current law and either disallow future Roth accounts or require taxes to be paid on all Roth IRA accounts going forward.

However, making the reasonable assumption that such a reversal happens no sooner than in 10 years, those who have converted in 1998 will already be ahead of the no-conversion scenario by a significant amount. For them there will not be a loss, only not as large a gain.

In additions, in 10 years or so it is reasonable to project that the Roth IRA will have gained enough momentum, and popularity, that canceling of such a program would most likely result in great political risk to the proponents of such a move.

> *The other powerful factor to consider is that the Roth project is setting out to change American culture by encouraging the younger generations to save money on a regular basis, to make a habit of this saving. If this is indeed what transpires, it is hard to imagine a reversal of such a positive force.*

In the unlikely event that changes were brought in, the first step that may be considered is to disallow future Roth IRA accounts; the next (more unlikely) step will be to require payments of taxes on future growth on existing Roth IRA accounts. It would be unreasonable to expect that Congress will require payment of taxes on past growth.

1.4 The Next Steps for the Roth Project

We have shown that the Roth IRA can greatly enhance the retirement assets for a large percentage of the population. Over 97% of the population are eligible for the Roth Contributions. Approximately 30% of the population currently own an IRA: 84% of this population will be eligible to convert their assets to the Roth IRA. These potential conversions and the contributions would represent a significant shift in assets to Roth IRAs. One can project that:

With sufficient marketing effort from the securities industry the Roth IRA will become a dominant vehicle for retirement planning in the future.

The marketing effort is crucial. Without marketing, without advertisement, without an adequate training program, the best ideas in the world fall by the wayside. This is true of any new innovation. So far, it appears that the financial industries have bought in to these new concepts as being winners. They are advertising the products well and are seeing impressive results from the programs.

The Roth IRA is a good program and a win-win all the way around: for the individual, for the family, for the financial community, and even (for now) for the U.S. Treasury.

What about the next steps of expanding the Roth project? Based on inputs from the Finance Committee and Senator Roth, the next initiatives will be to:

* Increase the Education IRA limit
* Index the annual contribution of $2,000 per year, and increase the limits.
* Index the Roth Conversion eligibility limits, and increase the limits.

An additional high-priority initiative that the author would recommend is to:

* Foster a program for providing an automatic payroll deduction for Roth Contributions to encourage the habit of saving.

1.5 Conclusions

The Roth IRA is a great retirement vehicle. There are many positives and few negatives. For many people it can make a profound difference in their long-term savings program. I hope this book will help you understand the program and help you make the best decisions for both the Roth IRA Contribution and the Roth IRA Conversion.

Chapter 2 Basics of Retirement Planning

The Roth IRA is one of the elements that will help you meet your retirement needs. To understand the relative value of the Roth IRA, you will need to address your total retirement picture, with all the elements.

This chapter will help you prepare a retirement plan. It will provide you with a simple way of relating your retirement and other future needs with the various sources of retirement income. In this and the following chapter it is assumed that you have an advisor, or more than one advisor: broker, banker, accountant, lawyer, insurer, yourself (if you have experience in all aspects of financial planning), or a knowledgeable friend who has the experience to address your special needs.

In particular, you will:

- Understand the meaning of inflation, present value, future value.
- Understand the meaning of compounding and growth.
- Understand tax-advantaged assets and terms such as "tax-deferred," "deductible," "nondeductible," and "tax-free" assets.
- Be able to lay out a step-by-step approach for your retirement plans.
- Understand the concept of sequence of withdrawals (which accounts you should draw money from first and last).

These are the basics of retirement planning. They will give you a start. They do not replace the need for a good advisor or a high-end software program. You will need both to prepare a more detailed plan. And you also will need to revisit the plan as your goals change and when there are significant changes in your financial picture.

Easy look-up tables are provided for you to look up your personal financial situation.

The sections in this chapter are:

- Sources for retirement income
- Steps for assessing retirement income
- Client profiles described in this book
- Aids in understanding basic concepts
- Summary and preview of next chapters

2.1 Sources of Retirement Income

The sources of retirement income for most individuals can be grouped into the following classes:

1. Social Security
2. Earned Income (if you will be working during retirement)
3. Pension and Annuities
4. Non-retirement assets (these include investable assets—such as stocks, bonds and cash, and non-investable assets such as your home and car. For retirement planning we consider only investable-assets)
5. Tax-advantaged assets (these include Traditional and Roth IRAs, and employer defined-contribution plans such as the 401(k) and the 403(b) plans).

2.2.1 Steps for Assessing Retirement Income

In this section we will describe a step-by-step procedure that will tell you how much each of these asset classes will provide during retirement.

Retirement Planning Steps

Step 1: Recurring Indexed Income

Determine the recurring income that keeps up with inflation. This is income that continues through your life. Calculate this income after taxes.

Step 2: Recurring Non-indexed Income

Determine the amount of income that is recurring but is not indexed with inflation. This is income that is a constant dollar amount each year. Calculate this income after taxes. Subtract these from your total retirement needs to obtain the balance required from other personal investable-assets accounts and from tax-advantaged sources.

Step 3: Investable Assets

First make withdrawals from the investable-assets accounts. Determine how many years these assets will last.

Steps 4 and 5: Tax-advantaged Assets

For the balance of the years of retirement you will need to make withdrawals from the tax-advantaged accounts, which include tax-deferred IRAs, 401(k)-type plans, and tax-free-withdrawal Roth IRA accounts. Step 4 addresses annual contributions, and Step 5 addresses existing assets that you may have in a tax-advantaged account. The payout from these tax-advantaged assets will be discussed in the next few chapters.

*We will leave this chapter with the following information: **how much you will need** from the tax-advantaged assets and **how many years after retirement** you will need to start withdrawing from the tax-advantaged assets.*

2.2.2 Step 1: Recurring Indexed Income (e.g. Social Security)

The first step in the planning process is to determine the amount that you will receive from recurring income that is indexed with inflation. This is income that continues through your life. The term "indexed with inflation" means that the income from the assets is increased each year to keep up with rising costs due to inflation. The term COLA (cost of living adjustment) is often used to describe this increase. Social Security falls into this category: these benefits increase each year to keep up with inflation. You can obtain your projected Social Security benefits by contacting the Social Security Administration through http://www.ssa.gov. If you do not have the information on your benefits from Social Security, refer to Table 2.1 on maximum and average pay-outs in 1998 to estimate this income.

Table 2.1 Social Security Benefits 1998 Retirement Age 65		
	Per Month	Per Year
Maximum for a Single	$1,342	$16,104
Maximum for Couple	$2,684	$32,208
Average for Single	$925	$11,100
Average for Couple	$1,850	$22,200

You may also have established a payout annuity (from a trust, for example) that provides a monthly or annual amount that is increased each year to keep up with inflation. This is called an indexed annuity. Such annuities should be included in this recurring-indexed-annuity category. In addition, if you are planning to work through your retirement, the income you will earn is likely indexed with inflation, so it should also be included in this category. Thus

> *Annual inflation indexed recurring funds consist of the following:*
> *Social Security + indexed annuity + earned income*

Add the items that relate to your case to get the total annual inflation-indexed recurring funds. To calculate the tax on this income, you will need to estimate your post-retirement average tax rate (Federal plus State). A conservative estimate of the average tax rate is the total taxes paid in 1998 divided by your taxable income. Typically, retirement tax rates will be 2 to 5 percentage points lower. Subtract the tax to get the after-tax income.

Let us take an example and carry it through this chapter. Assume that Mr. and Ms. Example A will receive $20,000 per year in Social Security distributions and that they do not receive any other inflation-indexed annuities. Their income from the recurring indexed category will be $20,000 before any taxes are paid. They estimate an average post-retirement tax rate (Federal plus State) of 25%. The tax on their recurring inflation-indexed funds is $5,000 (25% of $20,000). So the after-tax recurring income for Mr. and Ms. A is $15,000. This is expressed in 1998 dollars, and will be indexed with inflation.

We are now ready for Step 2.

2.2.3 Step 2: Recurring Un-indexed Income (e.g. Pensions)

This category includes income that is a constant dollar amount that continues through your lifetime. Many pension funds provided by corporations fall into this category. Typically the pension will be based on the number of years of work and your salary over the last few (typically 5) years of employment.

> *Your needs will increase each year with inflation, but the payouts from pension funds may be fixed: so the buying power or value of the payout decreases with time.*

Since we are assuming that your required retirement income will increase annually with inflation, we need to somehow relate this type of pension income to your needs. One simplified way of translating this pension to an indexed annuity is to use the **averaged value** of the pension through your lifetime. This is illustrated in the following example:

Consider the case of Ms. Example A. Her current income in 1998 is $60,000. Assume that she plans to retire in 20 years and that her salary will just keep up with inflation for the 20 years of service. Thus her salary at retirement, expressed in 1998 dollars, will be exactly $60,000. The corporation she works for provides a pension that is 1.5% times this salary for each year of service. If she will have worked for a total of 20 years, her pension will be 1.5*20 = 30% of $60,000 = $18,000, expressed in today's dollars. That is the amount in the year of retirement. With no indexing this is exactly the amount she will receive each year through retirement.

Table 2.2   Present Worth of $1,000

Years	Inflation Rate							
	0.0%	2.5%	3.0%	3.5%	4.0%	5.0%	6.0%	10.0%
0	$1,000	$1,000	$1,000	$1,000	$1,000	$1,000	$1,000	$1,000
1	$1,000	$976	$971	$966	$962	$952	$943	$909
2	$1,000	$952	$943	$934	$925	$907	$890	$826
3	$1,000	$929	$915	$902	$889	$864	$840	$751
4	$1,000	$906	$888	$871	$855	$823	$792	$683
5	$1,000	$884	$863	$842	$822	$784	$747	$621
6	$1,000	$862	$837	$814	$790	$746	$705	$564
7	$1,000	$841	$813	$786	$760	$711	$665	$513
8	$1,000	$821	$789	$759	$731	$677	$627	$467
9	$1,000	$801	$766	$734	$703	$645	$592	$424
10	$1,000	$781	$744	$709	$676	$614	$558	$386
11	$1,000	$762	$722	$685	$650	$585	$527	$350
12	$1,000	$744	$701	$662	$625	$557	$497	$319
13	$1,000	$725	$681	$639	$601	$530	$469	$290
14	$1,000	$708	$661	$618	$577	$505	$442	$263
15	$1,000	$690	$642	$597	$555	$481	$417	$239
16	$1,000	$674	$623	$577	$534	$458	$394	$218
17	$1,000	$657	$605	$557	$513	$436	$371	$198
18	$1,000	$641	$587	$538	$494	$416	$350	$180
19	$1,000	$626	$570	$520	$475	$396	$331	$164
20	$1,000	$610	$554	$503	$456	$377	$312	$149
30	$1,000	$477	$412	$356	$308	$231	$174	$57
40	$1,000	$372	$307	$253	$208	$142	$97	$22
50	$1,000	$291	$228	$179	$141	$87	$54	$8.52
60	$1,000	$227	$170	$127	$95	$54	$30	$3.28
70	$1,000	$178	$126	$90	$64	$33	$17	$1.27
80	$1,000	$139	$94	$64	$43	$20	$9.45	$0.49
90	$1,000	$108	$70	$45	$29	$12	$5.28	$0.19
100	$1,000	$85	$52	$32	$20	$7.60	$2.95	$0.07

Example: In   20   years,   at   3.5%   inflation, $18,000   will   have   a   Present Worth of $503 x 18 = $9,054

At the end of her retirement the buying power of the $18,000 will be less, and can be obtained from Table 2.2. For instance, if the retirement period is 20 years, the $18,000 will be worth $9,054 at the end of the retirement, based on an inflation rate of 3.5%. The averaged value of the pension payout through retirement in today's dollars is therefore $13,527 ($18,000+$9,054 =27,054 / 2= $13,527), which is about two-thirds of the starting pension.

> *An approximate rule of thumb is that the averaged value of a non-inflation-indexed pension that will last 20 years is two-thirds of the starting pension.*

The tax on $13,527, at a 25% rate is $3,381. Thus the averaged after-tax income from the pension , expressed in today's dollars as an inflation-adjusted income, is $10,145 per year.

Another category of income that you may have is a fixed annuity. One example is a trust fund that pays a fixed amount each year. In this case also, you will need to compute the start and end value of the annuity in today's dollars and use the average value for the annual payout in today's dollars.

> In our continuing example we will assume Example A will receive an averaged pension of $10,145. This together with the $15,000 in Social Security benefits provides Mr. and Ms. Example A with a total recurring income of $25,145 per year through their lifetime. Let us assume that Mr. and Ms. Example A need a total of $50,000 per year after taxes in today's dollars. Subtracting the recurring income from their needs leaves a shortfall of $24,855 per year. This is the amount needed from investable-accounts and tax-advantaged accounts.

Remember that all of these are expressed as after-tax 1998 dollars. Let's move to the next step of withdrawals.

2.2.4 Step 3 Personal Investable-Assets (e.g. Stocks)

The remaining funds you require will need to be drawn from investable accounts and tax-advantaged accounts. The order in which you should draw these funds is:

First:	*taxable assets (personal investable accounts)*
Second:	*tax-deferred balances (401(k)/403(b), tax-deferred IRAs)*
Third and last:	*tax-free IRAs (Roth IRA)*

The reason for this sequence is that tax-free Roth IRAs will yield a higher return than tax-deferred IRAs, and tax-deferred IRAs will yield a higher return than taxable accounts, assuming that these are invested in the same type of investments.

> *The principle to follow is that the highest yielding accounts should be the last ones that you should draw money from.*[1]

The needed retirement funds will be withdrawn until they are used up. This section will provide a method for calculating the **number of years** that these funds will last. After they have been used up, the next step will be to withdraw funds from the tax-advantaged accounts: that is covered in Steps 4 and 5 and is discussed in the next few chapters.

> Let us assume that Mr. and Ms Example A currently have $100,000 in investable-assets, which consists of mutual funds, bonds, stocks, and some cash. Assume that this portfolio grows at 9%, that the tax rate is 25%, and that inflation is at 3.5%. Recall that Mr. and Ms. Example A are 45 years of age and plan to retire in 20 years. They have recurring income of $25,145 and need an additional $24,855 per year through their retirement. How many years of income will the current $100,000 in investable accounts provide?
>
> The first step in the calculation is to compute the value of this asset in the year of retirement. This can be read off from Table 2.10 which shows that the value of a $100,000 investment 20 years from now (expressed in today's dollars), growing at 9% with inflation at 3.5% and a tax rate of 25%, will be $185,588. The next calculation needed is the number of years that this

---

[1] If, however, the investments have different rates of return to start with, the problem becomes much more complicated. You will need to consult with your financial advisor or use a high-end software package to find the best sequence of withdrawal.

$185,588 will last. Recall that Example A needs to withdraw the full balance of their needs, which was $24,855, from this account. The answer is obtained from Table 2.5, which shows the number of years that $185,588 will provide an indexed payout annuity of $24,855. This amount is 13.4% of the starting balance, so it will last 8 years. Since they retired at age 65, they will be out of these funds by age 73. Then, for the remainder of the retirement years they will need to withdraw from their tax-deferred and their tax-free accounts.

2.2.5 Step 4 and 5 Tax-Advantaged Accounts (e.g. IRAs , 401(k))

The balance of their retirement funds will need to come from their existing tax-advantaged accounts and from additional contributions that they make to the tax-advantaged accounts.

We are using the term tax-advantaged to include tax-deferred, non-deferred, and tax-free accounts. These include the 401(k), 403(b), SEP IRA, SIMPLE IRA, SAR SEP IRA, Keogh, Traditional IRA (deductible and non-deductible), Roth IRAs, and other qualified retirement tax-advantaged plans.

For the Roth IRA options they will need to address the value of converting their existing Traditional IRA to a Roth IRA, and to assess the relative merit of making annual contributions to a Roth IRA versus to a Traditional IRA. These topics will be discussed in the next few chapters.

2.3 Eleven Client Profiles Ages 25 to 85

This section will describe the client profiles that we will be examining in the rest of this book. The profiles (shown in Table 2.4) were selected as typical examples based on input from financial advisors in major brokerage companies.

These profiles have been selected to illustrate the principles of Roth IRA contribution and conversion. They are not meant to be demographic averages.

The names of the profiles indicate the age of the individuals. For instance, EX45A refers to a 45-year-old couple. We have selected the two Generation X examples (age less than 35) to have no investment assets. In their cases we will be illustrating the retirement assets that could be achieved by using annual contributions alone. The baby-boomers (ages 35 to 55) and the near-retired profiles (age 60) have varying amounts of other-investable assets. They may benefit from Roth annual contributions and from Roth conversions. In our examples we assume that the annual contributions will stop at age 65, so the over 65 profiles will be candidates for the Roth conversions IRAs only.

In all the cases we will assume a retirement age of 65 years, and a death age of 90 years. In profiles involving spouses, they are assumed to be the same age, and the beneficiary (e.g., a child) is assumed to be 30 years younger. We will assume inflation to be 3.5%, and the rate of return to be 9% for all investments.

As we go through the analyses, we will change some of these assumptions to study how that affects the resulting outcomes.

Table 2.4A Profiles Used in Analysis

	CONTRIBUTION ONLY (Genex)		CONTRIBUTION & CONVERSION (Baby Boomer)					CONVERSION ONLY			
								Near Retirement	Early Retired	Late Retired	
Example Name	EX 25A	EX35A	EX45A	EX55A	EX55B	EX55SNGL	EX55C	EX60A	EX65A	EX75A	EX85A
Age	25	35	45	55	55	55	55	60	65	75	85
Current Income	$35,000	$40,000	$90,000	$100,000	$100,000	$100,000	$200,000	$100,000	$100,000	$100,000	$100,000
Desired Retirement Income After taxes	$30,000	$35,000	$65,040	$55,020	$70,780	$66,700	$134,250	$71,000	$71,000	$71,000	$71,000
Other Investible Assets	$0	$0	$75,000	$75,000	$200,000	$200,000	$2,000,000	$100,000	$500,000	$250,000	$250,000
Planned Savings per Year	$2,000	$4,000	$8,000	$6,000	$6,000	$10,000	$6,000	$10,000	$0	$0	$0
Traditional IRA Existing Balance	$0	$0	$40,000	$100,000	$120,000	$150,000	$2,000,000	$225,000	$500,000	$300,000	$300,000
STEP 1 Recurring Indexed : Soc. Sec.											
Social Security Income	$12,000	$12,000	$24,000	$15,000	$24,000	$15,000	$24,000	$24,000	$24,000	$24,000	$24,000
Social Security After Taxes	$9,920	$9,920	$18,410	$12,150	$18,050	$10,800	$16,680	$18,000	$18,000	$18,000	$18,000
STEP 2 Recurring Unindexed : Pension											
Service years	20	20	20	20	20	20	20	20	20	20	20
Pension % of Income	30%	30%	30%	30%	30%	30%	30%	30%	30%	30%	30%
Pension at age 65	$10,500	$12,000	$27,000	$30,000	$30,000	$30,000	$60,000	$30,000	$30,000	$30,000	$30,000
Pension averaged	$6,930	$7,920	$17,820	$19,800	$19,800	$19,800	$39,600	$20,000	$20,000	$20,000	$20,000
Pension Averaged After Taxes	$5,730	$6,550	$13,670	$16,040	$14,890	$14,260	$27,520	$15,000	$15,000	$15,000	$15,000
Total Recurring Income After Tax	$15,650	$16,470	$32,080	$28,190	$32,940	$25,060	$44,200	$33,000	$33,000	$33,000	$33,000
Bal. from investable & tax-advantaged	$14,350	$18,530	$32,960	$26,830	$37,840	$41,640	$90,050	$38,000	$38,000	$38,000	$38,000
STEP 3 Investible Assets											
Years till retirement	40	30	20	10	10	10	10	5	0	0	0
Value of investible assets at age 65	$0	$0	$139,190	$107,500	$273,000	$265,600	$2,600,000	$120,000	$500,000	$250,000	$250,000
Bal. Required + Investable Assets at 65	0.0%	0.0%	24.0%	25.0%	14.0%	16.0%	3.0%	32.0%	8.0%	15.0%	15.0%
Years invesaible assets will last	0	0	4	4	8	6	31	4	15	7	7
Age for starting tax-adv. withdrawals	65	65	70	70	74	72	97	70	81	83	93
Balance req'd from tax-advantaged	$14,350	$18,530	$32,960	$26,830	$37,840	$41,640	$90,050	$38,000	$38,000	$38,000	$38,000
Step 4 Annuity from Contributions											
Planned annual contributions	$2,000	$4,000	$8,000	$6,000	$6,000	$10,000	$6,000	$10,000			
Step 5: Annuity from Existing IRA									$0	$0	$0
Percentage Contributions											
Indexed recurring [Social Security]	33%	28%	28%	22%	26%	16%	12%	25%	25%	25%	25%
Non-indexed recurring [Pension]	19%	19%	21%	29%	21%	21%	20%	21%	21%	21%	21%
% Bal. required from tax-advantaged	48%	53%	51%	49%	53%	62%	67%	54%	54%	54%	54%
TAX RATES											
Retirement Income	$31,500	$36,000	$81,000	$65,000	$90,000	$90,000	$180,000	$90,000	$90,000	$90,000	$90,000
% Income for Retirement	90.0%	90.0%	90.0%	65.0%	90.0%	90.0%	90.0%	90.0%	90.0%	90.0%	90.0%
Exemptions / deductions	$12,500	$12,500	$12,500	$12,500	$7,500	$6,800	$30,000	$12,500	$12,500	$12,500	$12,500
Retirement Taxable Income	$19,000	$23,500	$68,500	$52,500	$82,500	$83,200	$150,000	$77,500	$77,500	$77,500	$77,500
Current Avg. Tax rates	17%	17%	25%	21%	26%	30%	32%	26%	26%	26%	26%
Retirement Avg. Tax rate	17%	17%	23%	19%	25%	28%	31%	25%	25%	25%	25%
Conversion Tax rate			26%	25%	30%	32%	42%	28%	33%	30%	30%
Conversion Tax	$0	$0	$10,400	$18,750	$75,000	$48,000	$840,000	$63,000	$165,000	$90,000	$90,000

Table 2.4 B Profiles Used in Analyses EX45A

Profile description	
Age	45
Current Income	$90,000
Desired Retirement Income After taxes	$65,040
Other Investable Assets	$75,000
Planned Savings per Year	$8,000
Traditional IRA existing balance	$40,000
STEP 1 Recurring Indexed : Soc. Sec.	
Social Security Income	$24,000
Social Security After Taxes	$18,410
STEP 2 Recurring Unindexed : Pension	
Service years	20
Pension % of Income	30%
Pension at age 65	$27,000
Pension averaged	$17,820
Pension Averaged After Taxes	$13,670
Total Recurring Income After Tax	$32,080
Balance req'd from investable & tax-advantaged	$32,960
STEP 3 Investable Assets	
Years till retirement	20
Value of investable assets at age 65	$139,190
Balance Required ÷ investable Assets at 65	24.0%
Years investable assets will last	4
Age for starting tax-advantaged withdrawals	70
Balance req'd from tax-advantaged	$32,960
Step 4 Indexed annuity from Annual Contributions	
planned contributions	$8,000
Step 5: Annuity from Existing IRA starting age A1	
Existing Traditional IRA Assets. Convert?	$40,000
Percentage Contributions from All Sources	
Indexed recurring [Social Security]	28%
Non-indexed recurring [Pension]	21%
Annual Contributions	?
Roth Conversion	?
% from Social Security	28%
% from Pension	21%
Total Recurring Income	49%
% Balance required from tax-advantaged	51%
TAX RATES Federal plus State	
Retirement Income	$81,000
% Income for Retirement	90.0%
Exemptions / deductions	$12,500
Retirement Taxable Income	$68,500
Current Avg. Tax rates	25%
Retirement Avg. Tax rate	23%
Conversion Tax rate	26%

Let us consider at EX45A for the purpose of explaining Table 2.4. In this profile the couple's current income is $90,000. Consider retirement steps 1 through 3 for this case:

Step 1:   Recurring Indexed Income

Their recurring inflation-indexed-income consists entirely of Social Security benefits assumed to be $24,000 per year. After paying 23% retirement taxes, this becomes $18,410.

Step 2:   Non-recurring Indexed Income

Their pension, based on 20 years of service, is assumed to be 30% of their salary: this is $27,000 in the year of retirement. Assuming this is not indexed, we find the average indexed pension, using the two-thirds rule of thumb. This averaged indexed pension is 2/3*$27,000 = $17,820.

After paying 23% taxes, this becomes $13,670.

Their total recurring income is therefore: $18,410 + $13,670 = $32,080 after taxes in today's dollars.

They would like 90% of their current income after retirement: this is $81,000. Subtracting income adjustments of $12,500 (for exemptions and deductions) gives a taxable income of $68,500. After paying 23% taxes of $15,960 they are left with $81,000-$15,960=$65,040. This is their retirement need, after taxes, in today's dollars. Subtracting the recurring income from this results in a balance of $65,040-$32,080 = $32,960 that must be provided by other non-retirement and tax-advantaged balances. Thus 51% of their retirement needs must be met from nonrecurring income.

Step 3:   Investable-accounts

They have $75,000 in other investable assets today. At a 9% growth rate, with a 25% tax rate, and assuming a 3.5% inflation rate, we see from Table 2.10 that in 20 years this will grow to 75,000*1.85588=$139,191 after taxes in today's dollars. The money required, $32,960 per year, is 23% of the total asset base of $139,191. From Table 2.5, we see that this will last 4 years.

Thus they will have to start making withdrawals from their tax-advantaged account at age 70, and the amount that they will need to withdraw annually is $32,960.

This is the end of Step 3. The amounts they can expect from Roth contributions and conversions will be discussed in the next chapters.

For the examples we are investigating, we see that approximately 55% of retirement expenses will need to come from tax-advantaged accounts.

For these clients, Social Security will provide an average of about 25% and pensions will provide an average of 20% of retirement needs.

You may want to study the profile list to see which of these profiles is the closest to your own case. Alternately you may want to calculate your needs following the same procedure.

2.4 Understanding Finances: Basic Concepts

This section provides a tutorial on some concepts that we have used in this chapter and will be referring to throughout the book. We will discuss the following

Inflation, Present Value and Future Value
Compounding and Growth

Table 2.3		Inflation Rates							
1988	1989	1990	1991	1992	1993	1994	1995	1996	1997
4.4%	4.6%	6.1%	3.1%	2.9%	2.7%	2.7%	2.5%	3.3%	1.7%
5 year average	2.6%								
10 year average	3.4%								

Source: Department of Labor Statistics

2.4.1 Inflation

Let us consider the following examples. How much will your expenses increase 20 years from now due to inflation? Table 2.6 shows that if the inflation rate per year is 3.5%, then you will need to multiply your current expenses by a factor of 2 to obtain the expenses in 20 years. The multiplying factors for different inflation rates over different number of years is shown in Table 2.6. The actual dollar expenses you will need, assuming a 3.5% inflation rate, is shown in Table 2.7.

Another way of looking at inflation is to ask what $1,000 in today's dollars will be worth in the future. Table 2.2 provides this information. For example, with an inflation rate of 3.5%, in 10 years the buying power of $1,000 will be $709.

While we cannot predict the future, we can look at the past to learn how inflation has changed over the years. The average inflation over the last 10 years has been 3.41% This is shown in Table 2.3. In assessing any change in financial planning, such as the Roth conversion, you would be well advised to consider the effects of inflation on the end results. A range of inflation from 2% to 5% will be used in the analyses in this book.

2.4.2 Asset Growth Rates and Compounding

How much does rate of growth affect the value of an investment? Tables 2.8 through 2.10 provide future values for various growth rates. It is not only the principal in your assets that is growing, but the growth on the assets is also growing: That is what is meant by the term "compounding."

Small differences in growth rates can make a big difference in asset values over time. Consider, for example, an investment of $10,000 growing at 8%. Its value in 25 years would be $68,484 (see Table 2.8). If it grew at 9%, the value would be $86,231, which is 26% more. Let's go out further in time. In 50 years the asset would grow to $469,020 at 8% and $743,580 at 9%: a difference of 57%. Just to emphasize the effect of time, let's go to 100 years. At 8%, the asset would be worth $2,199,760 and at 9% it would be worth $5,529,040: a difference of 151%.

> *It is clear that compounding makes an increasingly bigger percentage difference as the time interval increases.*

These numbers start to get so large that it becomes hard to comprehend their value. Remember that these are future dollars and they will not have the same buying power as today's dollars due to the rising costs of goods with inflation. To assess the buying power of future dollars, we can adjust them to remove the effect of inflation. This is done in Table 2.9, which shows the present value, or buying power, of these assets after inflation has been corrected for. This inflation-adjusted number is called the "present worth" of the future dollars. So the present worth of a $10,000 investment growing for 20 years at 7% will be $19,447, and at 8% the present worth will be $23,424. These numbers show your buying power. We will express all our results through the book in today's dollars, as present worth dollars. Occasionally you will see the terms "net present value." It has the same meaning, expressing the value of future dollars in today's buying power.

> *Net Present Value and Present Worth are terms used to express the value of future dollars in today's buying power.*

It is clear that the rate of growth makes a difference to the end result that keeps increasing with time. What growth rates should you assume for your investments? As you know, the growth rates depend on the kinds of investments. With more aggressive investments, the growth rates can be higher than with more conservative investments. However, there is a risk with all investments, and higher growth rate investments tend to carry a higher risk, which also means that they have a greater chance of doing poorly in bad market times. Selection of assets to be consistent with your risk tolerance should not be treated lightly, and this should be done with the help of a financial advisor.

2.5 Summary and Preview of Next Chapters

This chapter discussed the various sources of income during retirement and how you can determine the amount of funds each of these sources can provide. The steps for determining retirement benefits from Social Security, pensions, and other annuities were explained. The balance of your needs will come from your investable accounts and from tax-advantaged assets in retirement accounts. The first withdrawals need to come from the investable accounts, which are taxable. This chapter showed you how to calculate he number of years these assets will last. That establishes the start date of withdrawals from the tax-advantaged assets. The withdrawals from these assets are the subject of the rest of this book. You may want to go through the steps so far to assess **when you will need to start** these withdrawals and **how much you will need**. Recall that the amount of tax-advantaged funds you need to withdraw is the difference between your need and the amount provided by the recurring income.

In the next chapter we will address retirement savings resulting from annual contributions, and will compare the relative merits of such savings in taxable, tax-deferred and tax-free accounts. This will be followed by an assessment of the value of any pre-existing tax-advantaged balances you may have, and a study of the value of converting these to a Roth IRA (Chapter 5). Optimum (or partial) Roth IRA conversions will be discussed in Chapter 6. The remaining chapters will discuss the rules (Ch. 7), minimum required distributions (Ch. 8), estate planning consideration (Ch. 9) and finally the role of the Education IRA in planning your future savings.

Table 2.5   Number of Years Assets Will Last

Asumptions :
Tax Rate 25% & Inflation 3.5%

% Of Assets Drawn	Growth Rate			
	7%	8%	9%	10%
5%	24	27	31	38
6%	19	21	23	26
7%	16	17	18	20
8%	14	14	15	16
9%	12	12	13	14
10%	10	11	11	12
11%	9	10	10	11
12%	8	9	9	9
13%	8	8	8	8
14%	7	7	8	4
15%	7	7	7	7
16%	6	6	6	7
17%	6	6	6	6
18%	5	5	6	6
19%	5	5	5	5
20%	5	5	5	5
21%	4	5	5	5
22%	4	4	4	4
23%	4	4	4	4
24%	4	4	4	4
25%	4	4	4	4

Example: *If the assets growth rate is 9%, and the average tax rate is 25%, and if you withdraw 13% of your total assets in the first year, and this amount is increased each year by 3.5%, then these assets will last 8 years.*

Table 2.6   Multiplication Factor for Current Expenses

Inflation Rate

YRS	0.0%	2.5%	3.0%	3.5%	4.0%	5.0%	6.0%	10.0%
0	1.0	1.0	1.0	1.0	1.0	1.0	1.0	1.0
1	1.0	1.0	1.0	1.0	1.0	1.1	1.1	1.1
2	1.0	1.1	1.1	1.1	1.1	1.1	1.1	1.2
3	1.0	1.1	1.1	1.1	1.1	1.2	1.2	1.3
4	1.0	1.1	1.1	1.1	1.2	1.2	1.3	1.5
5	1.0	1.1	1.2	1.2	1.2	1.3	1.3	1.6
6	1.0	1.2	1.2	1.2	1.3	1.3	1.4	1.8
7	1.0	1.2	1.2	1.3	1.3	1.4	1.5	1.9
8	1.0	1.2	1.3	1.3	1.4	1.5	1.6	2.1
9	1.0	1.2	1.3	1.4	1.4	1.6	1.7	2.4
10	1.0	1.3	1.3	1.4	1.5	1.6	1.8	2.6
11	1.0	1.3	1.4	1.5	1.5	1.7	1.9	2.9
12	1.0	1.3	1.4	1.5	1.6	1.8	2.0	3.1
13	1.0	1.4	1.5	1.6	1.7	1.9	2.1	3.5
14	1.0	1.4	1.5	1.6	1.7	2.0	2.3	3.8
15	1.0	1.4	1.6	1.7	1.8	2.1	2.4	4.2
16	1.0	1.5	1.6	1.7	1.9	2.2	2.5	4.6
17	1.0	1.5	1.7	1.8	1.9	2.3	2.7	5.1
18	1.0	1.6	1.7	1.9	2.0	2.4	2.9	5.6
19	1.0	1.6	1.8	1.9	2.1	2.5	3.0	6.1
20	1.0	1.6	1.8	2.0	2.2	2.7	3.2	6.7
21	1.0	1.7	1.9	2.1	2.3	2.8	3.4	7.4
22	1.0	1.7	1.9	2.1	2.4	2.9	3.6	8.1
23	1.0	1.8	2.0	2.2	2.5	3.1	3.8	9.0
24	1.0	1.8	2.0	2.3	2.6	3.2	4.0	9.8
25	1.0	1.9	2.1	2.4	2.7	3.4	4.3	10.8
26	1.0	1.9	2.2	2.4	2.8	3.6	4.5	11.9
27	1.0	1.9	2.2	2.5	2.9	3.7	4.8	13.1
28	1.0	2.0	2.3	2.6	3.0	3.9	5.1	14.4
29	1.0	2.0	2.4	2.7	3.1	4.1	5.4	15.9
30	1.0	2.1	2.4	2.8	3.2	4.3	5.7	17.4
40	1.0	2.7	3.3	4.0	4.8	7.0	10.3	45.3
50	1.0	3.4	4.4	5.6	7.1	11.5	18.4	117.4
60	1.0	4.4	5.9	7.9	10.5	18.7	33.0	304.5
70	1.0	5.6	7.9	11.1	15.6	30.4	59.1	789.7
80	1.0	7.2	10.6	15.7	23.0	49.6	105.8	2048.4
90	1.0	9.2	14.3	22.1	34.1	80.7	189.5	5313.0

Example: *If the inflation rate is 3.5%, your future expenses 20 years from today can be obtained by multiplying your current expenses by 2.0*

Table 2.7   Projecting Future Expenses

Assumptions:
Inflation 3.50%

	Curent Expenses						
Years	$50,000	$75,000	$100,000	$125,000	$150,000	$200,000	$300,000
1	$51,750	$77,625	$103,500	$129,375	$155,250	$207,000	$310,500
2	$53,561	$80,342	$107,123	$133,903	$160,684	$214,245	$321,368
3	$55,436	$83,154	$110,872	$138,590	$166,308	$221,744	$332,615
4	$57,376	$86,064	$114,752	$143,440	$172,128	$229,505	$344,257
5	$59,384	$89,076	$118,769	$148,461	$178,153	$237,537	$356,306
6	$61,463	$92,194	$122,926	$153,657	$184,388	$245,851	$368,777
7	$63,614	$95,421	$127,228	$159,035	$190,842	$254,456	$381,684
8	$65,840	$98,761	$131,681	$164,601	$197,521	$263,362	$395,043
9	$68,145	$102,217	$136,290	$170,362	$204,435	$272,579	$408,869
10	$70,530	$105,795	$141,060	$176,325	$211,590	$282,120	$423,180
11	$72,998	$109,498	$145,997	$182,496	$218,995	$291,994	$437,991
12	$75,553	$113,330	$151,107	$188,884	$226,660	$302,214	$453,321
13	$78,198	$117,297	$156,396	$195,495	$234,593	$312,791	$469,187
14	$80,935	$121,402	$161,869	$202,337	$242,804	$323,739	$485,608
15	$83,767	$125,651	$167,535	$209,419	$251,302	$335,070	$502,605
16	$86,699	$130,049	$173,399	$216,748	$260,098	$346,797	$520,196
17	$89,734	$134,601	$179,468	$224,334	$269,201	$358,935	$538,403
18	$92,874	$139,312	$185,749	$232,186	$278,623	$371,498	$557,247
19	$96,125	$144,188	$192,250	$240,313	$288,375	$384,500	$576,750
20	$99,489	$149,234	$198,979	$248,724	$298,468	$397,958	$596,937
30	$140,340	$210,510	$280,679	$350,849	$421,019	$561,359	$842,038
40	$197,963	$296,944	$395,926	$494,907	$593,889	$791,852	$1,187,778
50	$279,246	$418,870	$558,493	$698,116	$837,739	$1,116,985	$1,675,478
100	$1,559,570	$2,339,356	$3,119,141	$3,898,926	$4,678,711	$6,238,282	$9,357,422

Example: If the inflation rate is 3.5%, and your curent expenses are $75,000 then 20 years from today your expenses will be $149,234

Table 2.8   Compounding $1 Annually: no taxes, no inflation

Assumptions:
Tax Rate   0.0%
Inflation Rate 0.0%

				Growth Rate					
Years	2%	5%	7%	8.0%	8.5%	9.0%	10%	12%	15%
0	1.00000	1.00000	1.00000	1.00000	1.00000	1.00000	1.00000	1.00000	1.00000
1	1.02000	1.05000	1.07000	1.08000	1.08500	1.09000	1.10000	1.12000	1.15000
2	1.04040	1.10250	1.14490	1.16640	1.17723	1.18810	1.21000	1.25440	1.32250
3	1.06121	1.15763	1.22504	1.25971	1.27729	1.29503	1.33100	1.40493	1.52088
4	1.08243	1.21551	1.31080	1.36049	1.38586	1.41158	1.46410	1.57352	1.74901
5	1.10408	1.27628	1.40255	1.46933	1.50366	1.53862	1.61051	1.76234	2.01136
6	1.12616	1.34010	1.50073	1.58687	1.63147	1.67710	1.77156	1.97382	2.31306
7	1.14869	1.40710	1.60578	1.71382	1.77014	1.82804	1.94872	2.21068	2.66002
8	1.17166	1.47746	1.71819	1.85093	1.92060	1.99256	2.14359	2.47596	3.05902
9	1.19509	1.55133	1.83846	1.99900	2.08386	2.17189	2.35795	2.77308	3.51788
10	1.21899	1.62889	1.96715	2.15892	2.26098	2.36736	2.59374	3.10585	4.04556
11	1.24337	1.71034	2.10485	2.33164	2.45317	2.58043	2.85312	3.47855	4.65239
12	1.26824	1.79586	2.25219	2.51817	2.66169	2.81266	3.13843	3.89598	5.35025
13	1.29361	1.88565	2.40985	2.71962	2.88793	3.06580	3.45227	4.36349	6.15279
14	1.31948	1.97993	2.57853	2.93719	3.13340	3.34173	3.79750	4.88711	7.07571
15	1.34587	2.07893	2.75903	3.17217	3.39974	3.64248	4.17725	5.47067	8.13706
10	1.37279	2.18287	2.95216	3.42594	3.68872	3.97031	4.59497	6.13039	9.35762
17	1.40024	2.29202	3.15882	3.70002	4.00226	4.32763	5.05447	6.86604	10.7613
18	1.42825	2.40662	3.37993	3.99602	4.34245	4.71712	5.55992	7.68997	12.3755
19	1.45681	2.52695	3.61653	4.31570	4.71156	5.14166	6.11591	8.61276	14.2318
20	1.48595	2.65330	3.86968	4.66096	5.11205	5.60441	6.72750	9.64629	16.3665
21	1.51567	2.78596	4.14056	5.03383	5.54657	6.10881	7.40025	10.8038	18.8215
22	1.54598	2.92526	4.43040	5.43654	6.01803	6.65860	8.14027	12.1003	21.6447
23	1.57690	3.07152	4.74053	5.87146	6.52956	7.25787	8.95430	13.5523	24.8915
24	1.60844	3.22510	5.07237	6.34118	7.08457	7.91108	9.84973	15.1786	28.6252
25	1.64061	3.38635	5.42743	6.84848	7.68676	8.62308	10.8347	17.0001	32.9190
26	1.67342	3.55567	5.80735	7.39635	8.34014	9.39916	11.9182	19.0401	37.8568
27	1.70689	3.73346	6.21387	7.98806	9.04905	10.2451	13.1100	21.3249	43.5353
28	1.74102	3.92013	6.64884	8.62711	9.81822	11.1671	14.4210	23.8839	50.0656
29	1.77584	4.11614	7.11426	9.31727	10.6528	12.1722	15.8631	26.7499	57.5755
30	1.81136	4.32194	7.61226	10.0627	11.5583	13.2677	17.4494	29.9599	66.2118
40	2.20804	7.03999	14.9745	21.7245	26.1330	31.4094	45.2593	93.0510	267.864
50	2.69159	11.4674	29.4570	46.9016	59.0863	74.3575	117.391	289.002	1083.66
60	3.28103	18.6792	57.9464	101.257	133.593	176.031	304.482	897.597	4384.00
70	3.99956	30.4264	113.989	218.606	302.052	416.730	789.747	2787.80	17735.7
80	4.87544	49.5614	224.234	471.955	682.935	986.552	2048.40	8658.48	71750.9
90	5.94313	80.7304	441.103	1018.92	1544.10	2335.53	5313.02	26891.9	290272
100	7.24465	131.501	867.716	2199.76	3491.19	5529.04	13780.6	83522.3	1174313

Example: *At 8% growth rate, in 25 years, $10,000 will grow to $68,484*
At 9% growth rate, in 25 years, $10,000 will grow to $86,231

Table 2.9   Compounding $1 Annually: no taxes, inflation 3.5%

Assumptions:
Tax Rate   0.0%
Inflation Rate 3.5%

				Growth Rate					
ears	2%	5%	7%	8.0%	8.5%	9.0%	10%	12%	15%
0	1.00000	1.00000	1.00000	1.00000	1.00000	1.00000	1.00000	1.00000	1.00000
1	0.98551	1.01449	1.03382	1.04348	1.04831	1.05314	1.06280	1.08213	1.11111
2	0.97122	1.02920	1.06878	1.08885	1.09895	1.10910	1.12955	1.17100	1.23457
3	0.95715	1.04411	1.10492	1.13619	1.15204	1.16804	1.20049	1.26716	1.37174
4	0.94328	1.05924	1.14228	1.18559	1.20770	1.23011	1.27588	1.37123	1.52416
5	0.92961	1.07459	1.18091	1.23713	1.26604	1.29548	1.35601	1.48384	1.69351
6	0.91613	1.09017	1.22085	1.29092	1.32720	1.36432	1.44117	1.60571	1.88168
7	0.90286	1.10597	1.26213	1.34705	1.39132	1.43682	1.53167	1.73758	2.09075
8	0.88977	1.12200	1.30481	1.40562	1.45853	1.51318	1.62787	1.88028	2.32306
9	0.87688	1.13826	1.34893	1.46673	1.52899	1.59359	1.73010	2.03469	2.58117
10	0.86417	1.15475	1.39455	1.53050	1.60285	1.67827	1.83875	2.20179	2.86797
11	0.85164	1.17149	1.44171	1.59705	1.68029	1.76745	1.95423	2.38262	3.18664
12	0.83930	1.18847	1.49046	1.66648	1.76146	1.86137	2.07696	2.57829	3.54071
13	0.82714	1.20569	1.54086	1.73894	1.84655	1.96029	2.20740	2.79004	3.93412
14	0.81515	1.22317	1.59297	1.81454	1.93576	2.06446	2.34603	3.01917	4.37124
15	0.80334	1.24089	1.64684	1.89344	2.02927	2.17416	2.49336	3.26712	4.85694
16	0.79169	1.25888	1.70253	1.97576	2.12731	2.28970	2.64995	3.53543	5.39660
17	0.78022	1.27712	1.76010	2.06166	2.23008	2.41137	2.81637	3.82578	5.99622
18	0.76891	1.29563	1.81962	2.15130	2.33781	2.53951	2.99324	4.13998	6.66246
19	0.75777	1.31441	1.88116	2.24484	2.45075	2.67446	3.18122	4.47998	7.40274
20	0.74679	1.33346	1.94477	2.34244	2.56914	2.81659	3.38101	4.84790	8.22526
21	0.73596	1.35278	2.01054	2.44428	2.69325	2.96626	3.59335	5.24603	9.13918
22	0.72530	1.37239	2.07853	2.55056	2.82336	3.12389	3.81902	5.67687	10.1546
23	0.71479	1.39228	2.14881	2.66145	2.95976	3.28989	4.05886	6.14308	11.2829
24	0.70443	1.41246	2.22148	2.77717	3.10274	3.46472	4.31376	6.64759	12.5366
25	0.69422	1.43293	2.29660	2.89791	3.25263	3.64883	4.5847	7.19353	13.9296
26	0.68416	1.45369	2.37426	3.02391	3.40976	3.84273	4.8726	7.78430	15.4773
27	0.67424	1.47476	2.45455	3.15538	3.57449	4.0469	5.1786	8.42359	17.1970
28	0.66447	1.49613	2.53756	3.29257	3.74717	4.2620	5.5038	9.11538	19.1078
29	0.65484	1.51782	2.62337	3.43573	3.9282	4.4885	5.8495	9.86399	21.2308
30	0.64535	1.53981	2.71208	3.5851	4.1180	4.7270	6.2168	10.6741	23.5898
40	0.55769	1.77811	3.7821	5.4870	6.6005	7.9332	11.4312	23.5021	67.6550
50	0.48194	2.0533	5.2744	8.3979	10.5796	13.314	21.019	51.7468	194.033
60	0.41648	2.3710	7.3554	12.853	16.958	22.344	38.649	113.94	556.480
70	0.35990	2.7380	10.257	19.672	27.180	37.500	71.066	250.86	1595.97
80	0.31102	3.1617	14.305	30.107	43.566	62.935	130.67	552.35	4577.19
90	0.26877	3.6509	19.948	46.079	69.830	105.62	240.28	1216.2	13127.3
100	0.23226	4.216	27.819	70.525	111.93	177.26	441.81	2677.7	37648.6

Example: If inflation rate is 3.5%, and after-tax growth rate is 7%, then in 20 years $10,000 will grow to $ 19,447 (in todays dollars)

Table 2.10   Compounding $1 Annually: tax rate 25%, inflation 3.5%

Assumptions:
Tax Rate   25%
Inflation Rate 3.5%

				Growth Rate					
Years	2%	5%	7%	8.0%	8.5%	9.0%	10%	12%	15%
0	1.00000	1.00000	1.00000	1.00000	1.00000	1.00000	1.00000	1.00000	1.00000
1	0.98068	1.00242	1.01691	1.02415	1.02778	1.03140	1.03865	1.05314	1.07488
2	0.96173	1.00484	1.03410	1.04889	1.05633	1.06379	1.07879	1.10910	1.15537
3	0.94314	1.00726	1.05159	1.07423	1.08567	1.09719	1.12048	1.16804	1.24188
4	0.92492	1.00970	1.06937	1.10018	1.11583	1.13164	1.16378	1.23011	1.33487
5	0.90704	1.01214	1.08745	1.12675	1.14682	1.16718	1.20876	1.29548	1.43482
6	0.88952	1.01458	1.10584	1.15397	1.17868	1.20383	1.25548	1.36432	1.54226
7	0.87233	1.01703	1.12453	1.18184	1.21142	1.24163	1.30400	1.43682	1.65774
8	0.85547	1.01949	1.14355	1.21039	1.24507	1.28062	1.35439	1.51318	1.78188
9	0.83894	1.02195	1.16288	1.23962	1.27966	1.32083	1.40674	1.59359	1.91530
10	0.82273	1.02442	1.18254	1.26957	1.31520	1.36231	1.46110	1.67827	2.05872
11	0.80683	1.02689	1.20254	1.30023	1.35173	1.40509	1.51757	1.76745	2.21287
12	0.79124	1.02937	1.22287	1.33164	1.38928	1.44921	1.57622	1.86137	2.37857
13	0.77595	1.03186	1.24355	1.36380	1.42787	1.49471	1.63714	1.96029	2.55668
14	0.76096	1.03435	1.26457	1.39675	1.46754	1.54165	1.70041	2.06446	2.74812
15	0.74625	1.03685	1.28596	1.43048	1.50830	1.59006	1.76612	2.17410	2.95389
16	0.73183	1.03936	1.30770	1.46504	1.55020	1.63999	1.83438	2.28970	3.17508
17	0.71769	1.04187	1.32981	1.50042	1.59326	1.69148	1.90528	2.41137	3.4128
18	0.70382	1.04438	1.35230	1.53667	1.63752	1.74460	1.97891	2.53951	3.6684
19	0.69022	1.04691	1.37516	1.57378	1.68300	1.79938	2.05539	2.67446	3.9431
20	0.67688	1.04943	1.39841	1.61180	1.72975	1.85588	2.13483	2.81659	4.2383
21	0.66380	1.05197	1.42206	1.65073	1.77780	1.91416	2.21733	2.96626	4.5557
22	0.65098	1.05451	1.44610	1.69060	1.82719	1.97427	2.30302	3.12389	4.8968
23	0.63840	1.05706	1.47055	1.73144	1.87794	2.03626	2.39203	3.2899	5.2635
24	0.62606	1.05961	1.49542	1.77326	1.93011	2.10020	2.48448	3.4647	5.6576
25	0.61396	1.06217	1.52070	1.81609	1.98372	2.16615	2.5805	3.6488	6.0812
26	0.60210	1.06474	1.54641	1.85996	2.03882	2.23417	2.6802	3.8427	6.5366
27	0.59046	1.06731	1.57256	1.90489	2.09546	2.3043	2.7838	4.0469	7.0260
28	0.57905	1.06989	1.59915	1.95090	2.15367	2.3767	2.8914	4.2620	7.5522
29	0.56786	1.07247	1.62619	1.99802	2.2135	2.4513	3.0031	4.4885	8.1177
30	0.55689	1.07506	1.65368	2.0463	2.2750	2.5283	3.1192	4.7270	8.7255
40	0.45817	1.10131	1.9556	2.5979	2.9921	3.4443	4.5575	7.9332	17.963
50	0.37695	1.1282	2.3125	3.2982	3.9351	4.6922	6.6589	13.314	36.9814
60	0.31013	1.1558	2.7347	4.1873	5.1755	6.3922	9.7294	22.344	76.1343
70	0.25515	1.1840	3.2339	5.3160	6.8068	8.7082	14.216	37.4999	156.739
80	0.20992	1.2129	3.8242	6.7490	8.9524	11.863	20.7706	62.9349	322.681
90	0.17271	1.2425	4.5223	8.5683	11.7742	16.1614	30.3480	105.622	664.31
100	0.14209	1.2728	5.3478	10.8781	15.4854	22.0168	44.342	177.262	1367.62

Example: If the average tax rate is 25% and inflation rate is 3.5: then in 20 years, with a growth rate of 9%, $75,000 will grow to $139,190 (in today's $ after-taxes)

Chapter 3 Taxes

"... the best thing is that we got the Roth IRA enacted... the next best thing is that we were able to make it available to a large enough segment of the population..." Senator Roth

This chapter deals with taxes. One of the main criteria for determining eligibility for Roth Contributions and Conversions is based on the taxpayer's modified adjusted gross income (MAGI). The MAGI is derived from the adjusted gross income for Federal tax calculations. If the MAGI exceeds a certain amount, the client will not be eligible for these Roth IRA investments. It is important to fully understand the distinction between income, adjusted gross income, modified adjusted gross income, and taxable income. Further, the benefits of tax-advantaged investments versus taxable investments are closely tied with your tax rates. Thus it is important to correctly assess the tax rates both prior to retirement and after retirement, and to understand the differences between marginal tax rates and effective or average tax rates. This chapter walks you through the process of tax computation, explaining the principles, and provides tables for estimating taxes. The topics covered are:

- Overview of the Federal Tax Form 1040
- Income
- Adjusted Gross Income
- Modified Adjusted Gross Income
- Taxable Income
- Tax Rates: Marginal versus Average
- Summary

3.1 Overview of Federal Form 1040

The IRS Form 1040 used to compute Federal taxes is shown the next two pages. There are three major sections leading up to the tax due. These are:

- Income
- Adjusted Gross Income
- Tax Computation

The first section in Form 1040[1] addresses the total income and losses. The second section[2] includes the adjustments to income used in calculating the adjusted gross income (AGI), which is the last entry at the bottom of the first page on Form 1040. Tax computations are detailed in the next section. In these lines[3] exemptions and deductions (standard or itemized) are subtracted from the AGI, and the result is the taxable income. The tax on the taxable income is calculated using tables, Form 8814, Form 4972 or the tax schedule. The last item in this section[4] is the total tax. Each of these sections is discussed below.

The sections in italics relate to items that could reduce an individual's AGI.

3.2 Income

This section details the items to be included in the **income** section of the Federal Form 1040.

Wages, salaries, tips, etc.

The income to be reported on this line item includes the total of all wages, salaries and tips. For joint returns the income from the spouse is also included. First, the amounts shown in W-2 forms will be included. In addition, other income, including tip income, dependent care benefits, adoption benefits provided by an employer, scholarship and fellowship grants, salary deferrals and disability pensions, will also need to be included.

---

[1] Lines 7 to 22 in the 1997 Form 1040
[2] Lines 23 to 32 in the 1997 Form 1040
[3] Lines 33 to 39 in the 1997 Form 1040
[4] Line 39 in the 1997 Form 1040.

Form
1040A

Department of the Treasury—Internal Revenue Service

U.S. Individual Income Tax Return **1998** IRS Use Only—Do not write or staple in this space.

OMB No. 1545-0085

Label

(See page 18.)

Use the IRS label.

Otherwise, please print or type.

L A B E L

H E R E

Your first name and initial	Last name		Your social security number
If a joint return, spouse's first name and initial	Last name		Spouse's social security number
Home address (number and street). If you have a P.O. box, see page 19.		Apt. no.	**▲ IMPORTANT! ▲**
City, town or post office, state, and ZIP code. If you have a foreign address, see page 19.			You **must** enter your SSN(s) above.

Presidential Election Campaign Fund (See page 19.)
Do you want $3 to go to this fund? . . . .
If a joint return, does your spouse want $3 to go to this fund?

Yes	No

Note: *Checking "Yes" will not change your tax or reduce your refund.*

Filing status

Check only one box.

1 ☐ Single
2 ☐ Married filing joint return (even if only one had income)
3 ☐ Married filing separate return. Enter spouse's social security number above and full name here. ▶ _____
4 ☐ Head of household (with qualifying person). (See page 20.) If the qualifying person is a child but not your dependent, enter this child's name here. ▶ _____
5 ☐ Qualifying widow(er) with dependent child (year spouse died ▶ 19___). (See page 21.)

Exemptions

If more than seven dependents, see page 21.

6a ☐ **Yourself.** If your parent (or someone else) can claim you as a dependent on his or her tax return, **do not** check box 6a.

b ☐ **Spouse**

c **Dependents:**

(1) First name Last name	(2) Dependent's social security number	(3) Dependent's relationship to you	(4) ✓ if qualified child for child tax credit (see page 22)
_____			☐
_____			☐
_____			☐
_____			☐
_____			☐
_____			☐
_____			☐

No. of boxes checked on 6a and 6b _____

No. of your children on 6c who:
• lived with you _____
• did not live with you due to divorce or separation (see page 23) _____

Dependents on 6c not entered above _____

Add numbers entered on lines above ☐

d Total number of exemptions claimed.

Income

Attach Copy B of your Forms W-2 and 1099-R here.

If you did not get a W-2, see page 24.

Enclose, but do not staple, any payment.

7 Wages, salaries, tips, etc. Attach Form(s) W-2. 7 _____

8a **Taxable** interest. Attach Schedule 1 if required. 8a _____
b Tax-exempt interest. DO NOT include on line 8a. 8b _____

9 Ordinary dividends. Attach Schedule 1 if required. 9 _____

10a Total IRA distributions. 10a _____ 10b Taxable amount (see page 24). 10b _____

11a Total pensions and annuities. 11a _____ 11b Taxable amount (see page 25). 11b _____

12 Unemployment compensation. 12 _____

13a Social security benefits. 13a _____ 13b Taxable amount (see page 27). 13b _____

14 Add lines 7 through 13b (far right column). This is your **total income.** ▶ 14 _____

Adjusted gross income

15 IRA deduction (see page 28). 15 _____

16 Student loan interest deduction (see page 28). 16 _____

17 Add lines 15 and 16. These are your **total adjustments.** 17 _____

18 Subtract line 17 from line 14. This is your **adjusted gross income.**
If under $30,095 (under $10,030 if a child did not live with you), see the EIC instructions on page 36. ▶ 18 _____

For Disclosure, Privacy Act, and Paperwork Reduction Act Notice, see page 49. Cat. No. 11327A **1998 Form 1040A**

1998 Form 1040A page 2

Taxable income	**19**	Enter the amount from line 18.	19	

20a Check { □ **You** were 65 or older □ Blind } **Enter number of**
if: { □ **Spouse** was 65 or older □ Blind } **boxes checked ▶** 20a [ ]

b If you are married filing separately and your spouse itemizes deductions, see page 30 and check here . . . . **▶** 20b □

21 Enter the **standard deduction** for your filing status. **But** see page 31 if you checked any box on line 20a or 20b **OR** if someone can claim you as a dependent.
- Single—$4,250 • Married filing jointly or Qualifying widow(er)—$7,100
- Head of household—$6,250 • Married filing separately—$3,550   21

22 Subtract line 21 from line 19. If line 21 is more than line 19, enter -0-.   22

23 Multiply $2,700 by the total number of exemptions claimed on line 6d.   23

24 Subtract line 23 from line 22. If line 23 is more than line 22, enter -0-. This is your **taxable income.** **▶** 24

Tax, credits, and payments	**25**	Find the tax on the amount on line 24 (see page 31).	25	

26 Credit for child and dependent care expenses. Attach Schedule 2.   26

27 Credit for the elderly or the disabled. Attach Schedule 3.   27

28 Child tax credit (see page 32).   28

29 Education credits. Attach Form 8863.   29

30 Adoption credit. Attach Form 8839.   30

31 Add lines 26 through 30. These are your **total credits.**   31

32 Subtract line 31 from line 25. If line 31 is more than line 25, enter -0-.   32

33 Advance earned income credit payments from Form(s) W-2.   33

34 Add lines 32 and 33. This is your **total tax.** **▶** 34

35 Total Federal income tax withheld from Forms W-2 and 1099.   35

36 1998 estimated tax payments and amount applied from 1997 return.   36

37a **Earned income credit.** Attach Schedule EIC if you have a qualifying child.   37a

b Nontaxable earned income:
amount ▶ | and type ▶

38 Additional child tax credit. Attach Form 8812.   38

39 Add lines 35, 36, 37a, and 38. These are your **total payments.** **▶** 39

Refund	**40**	If line 39 is more than line 34, subtract line 34 from line 39. This is the amount you **overpaid.**	40

Have it directly deposited! See page 43 and fill in 41b, 41c, and 41d.

41a Amount of line 40 you want **refunded to you.**   41a

b Routing number [ ][ ][ ][ ][ ][ ][ ][ ][ ]   **c** Type: □ Checking □ Savings

d Account number [ ][ ][ ][ ][ ][ ][ ][ ][ ][ ][ ][ ][ ][ ][ ][ ][ ]

42 Amount of line 40 you want **applied to your 1999 estimated tax.**   42

Amount you owe	**43**	If line 34 is more than line 39, subtract line 39 from line 34. This is the **amount you owe.** For details on how to pay, see page 44.	43
	44	Estimated tax penalty (see page 44).	44

Sign here	Under penalties of perjury, I declare that I have examined this return and accompanying schedules and statements, and to the best of my knowledge and belief, they are true, correct, and accurately list all amounts and sources of income I received during the tax year. Declaration of preparer (other than the taxpayer) is based on all information of which the preparer has any knowledge.

Joint return?
See page 19.
Keep a copy for your records.

Your signature	Date	Your occupation	Daytime telephone number (optional)
Spouse's signature. If joint return, BOTH must sign.	Date	Spouse's occupation	( )

Paid preparer's use only	

Preparer's signature	Date	Check if self-employed □	Preparer's social security no.
Firm's name (or yours if self-employed) and address		EIN	
			ZIP code

✪

If you have been considering a sabbatical from work or leave without pay, you may want to consider this in 1998 or in later years to get below the $100,000 MAGI limit to be eligible for Roth Conversions. The increase in retirement assets from a conversion can be big enough to give this serious consideration.

Taxable interest, tax-exempt interest and dividends

Include all taxable income from interest, dividend and capital gain distributions.

You may want to consider moving some taxable assets to tax-free investments such as tax-free bonds to reduce your AGI. Again if you are trying to reduce your MAGI, to be eligible for the Roth IRA conversion, such a temporary shift may be justifiable for the year in which you intend to exercise the Roth IRA conversion. This should be discussed with your tax or other advisor.

Taxable refunds, credits, or offsets of state and local income taxes

Include refunds, credits, or offsets of state or local income taxes.

Note that none of the refund is taxable if you did not itemize these as deductions in a previous year.

Alimony received

Include the amount received as alimony or separate maintenance.

Business income or (loss)

If you operated a business or practiced your business as a sole proprietor, the income and expenses are to be included in Schedule C or C-EZ.

All "ordinary and necessary expenses" paid or incurred by you during your taxable year in carrying on any trade or business are allowed on Schedule C or C-EZ, which can reduce the AGI in Form 1040. The words "ordinary and necessary" can be interpreted as "reasonable and customary," an interpretation accepted by the IRS. Check with your tax or other advisor for specific considerations.

Capital gain (or loss)

Capital gains are calculated on Schedule D and reported here. You may want to consider harvesting some losses to reduce your AGI.

> *Capital losses may be taken up to a maximum of $3,000 against ordinary income, but excess losses can be carried over to future years.*

Other gains (or losses) from Form 4797

Any other gains from sale or exchange of assets are reported in this line.

The following, are permitted:

> *Worthless securities (up to a maximum of $3,000 per year). Again excess losses can be carried forward.*
>
> *Losses from Section 1244 stock (investment in companies with less than $1,000,000 in assets). The maximum loss that can be taken is $50,000 for a single individual, and $100,000 for married filing jointly. Certain restrictions apply: check with your tax or other financial advisor.*
>
> *Business bad debts. Proof is required.*

Total IRA distributions

Include the distributions from your Individual Retirement Arrangement. For the 1998 to 2004 tax filing year required minimum distributions need to be included

IRA distributions that were rolled over to another IRA are not taxable and therefore do not affect AGI.

However, amounts rolled over to a Roth IRA will need to be included. Note that, for a 1998 Roth IRA Conversion, you may elect to either include all of the rollover in this one year, or include 1/4th of the rollover in each of the years 1998, 1999, 2000 and 2001. This election, once made, cannot be reversed (see Chapter 7 for the detailed rules).

Total pensions and annuities

All pensions and annuities as reported on Form 1099-R are to be included.

> *Amounts rolled over from one qualified plan to another qualified plan either directly or within 60 days of a distribution will be subtracted out and will not be included in the total income.*

Rental real estate, royalties, S corporations, trusts, etc. from Schedule E

Schedule E is used to include gains and losses from rents, royalties and S corporations.

> *If you participate actively in real estate activities, up to $25,000 of losses may be taken if your adjusted gross income is under $100,000. If the AGI is above $100,000, this deduction is reduced by 50% of the amount above $100,000. Passive losses cannot be taken as losses to offset earned income. But suspended passive losses become deductible in the year the investment is sold or otherwise disposed of. Theses losses can be used to offset any type of ordinary loss. Certain types of oil and gas investments are deductible. Check with your tax or other advisor on detailed rulings.*

Farm income or (loss)

Farm income will need to be reported using Schedule F.

> *Losses from operating a farm may be included here. This must be a business, not a hobby.*

Unemployment compensation

Unemployment compensation as shown on form 1099-G is to be included here.

Social security benefits

Social security benefits as shown on Form SSA-1099 are to be included here. Not all of the income from Social security benefits will be taxable. You will need to calculate your adjusted gross income then use the Social Security benefits worksheet provided by the IRS to calculate the amount that is taxable.

Other income

This line is a catch-all for other income. Some examples of items to be included here are:prizes and awards, gambling and lottery winnings, jury duty fees, reimbursements received for items deducted in earlier years, rental of personal property, and income from activities not engaged in for profit.

> *You may include losses from certain corrective distributions of excess deferrals. You do not need to include nontaxable income such as child support; money or property that was inherited, willed to you, or received as a gift; or life insurance collected when a person died.*

The total of this first major section is called "total income"

We will next discuss the adjustments to the total income that will result in the adjusted gross income to be used for your tax calculations. This AGI will also be used as a starting point to calculate the MAGI (modified adjusted gross income), which is used to check your eligibility for Roth Contributions and Conversions.

3.3 Adjusted Gross Income

This major section is used to calculate the adjusted gross income to be used for calculating the federal taxable income.

IRA deduction

Contributions to deductible IRAs are included here.

> *The maximum amount that can be contributed to a deductible IRA (**deductible Traditional IRA**) is $2,000 per individual. See Chapter 7 for eligibility rules.*

Contributions to a Roth IRA or a non-deductible IRA are not included here and will not reduce your AGI.

Medical savings account deduction

> *If you made a contribution to a medical savings account for 1998, you may be able to take this deduction. The maximum deduction depends on a variety of factors. Check with your tax advisor.*

> *Some employers offer flexible spending plans, such as to pay medical or dependent care expenses on a pre-tax basis. The AGI will be reduced by the amount put in such a plan. Form 8853 is required.*

Moving expenses

> *Moving expenses incurred if you change job locations or if you start a new job are generally deductible. Your new job must be at least 50 miles from your former job location and you must make the move within one year from the date you start your new job. Form 3903 or 3903-F is required.*

One-half of self-employment tax

> *One half of the self-employment tax from Schedule SE is deductible.*

Self-employed health insurance deduction

> *Self-employed individuals may deduct 50% of payments for health insurance for themselves, their spouses, and their dependents, for the 1998 tax-filing year.*

Part of the amount paid for long-term care may be deductible.

Keogh and self-employed SEP and SIMPLE plans

If you are self employed, include your contribution to Keogh, SEP and SIMPLE IRA plans.

Penalty on early withdrawal of savings

Any penalties you were charged on early withdrawals from savings accounts or certificates of deposit are deductible.

Alimony paid

Certain payments that constitute "alimony" payments may be taken. Such payments may be made from husband to wife or from wife to husband. There are definitive conditions that must be met (check with your financial advisor). If these conditions are met, the payments (without limit) are AGI deductible by the spouse who is providing the payments, and are to be included as income by the receiving spouse.

The sum of the amounts from this section are subtracted from "total income" to obtain your "adjusted gross income". It is the last entry at the bottom of the first page of the Form 1040.

We will next consider the modified adjusted gross income that is used to check your eligibility for Roth Conversions and Contributions.

3.4 Modified Adjusted Gross Income

The starting point in computing the MAGI is the AGI from Form 1040. The following items need to be **added** to the IRS AGI:

1. Any foreign earned income exclusion.
2. Any foreign housing exclusion.
3. Any interest exclusion on U.S. savings bonds used to pay for higher education.
4. Any adoption-assistance program exclusions.
5. Any deduction taken for investments in Traditional IRAs

The following items need to be **subtracted** from the result:

1. Any income produced by rolling over or converting a Traditional IRA to a Roth IRA.
2. In the 1998 to 2004 tax years, required minimum distributions from IRA plans may **not** be subtracted. After year 2004 you will be allowed to subtract the minimum required distributions to determine MAGI.

Thus the amount converted to a Roth IRA *is* included in the calculation of the IRS AGI, and therefore *is* taxed.

However, the converted amount *is not* included in the MAGI, and therefore is not included in assessing your eligibility to convert or contribute to the Roth IRA.

Let us return to the IRS Form 1040 and consider the section on Tax Computation.

3.5 Tax Computation

The third major section is called "Tax Computation" in the IRS Form 1040. This section is used for computing your taxable income and the corresponding tax. We will describe the exemptions and deductions that are subtracted from the AGI to give the taxable income.

While the exemptions and deductions will decrease the tax owed, they have no effect on your eligibility to use the Roth investments.

> *Itemized deductions have no impact on your MAGI and therefore will not affect your eligibility for the Roth investments.*

Standard and Itemized Deductions

You are permitted to take the larger of these two: itemized deductions shown on Schedule A or the standard deduction. Note that a Roth IRA Conversion will increase your AGI and therefore raise the thresholds for some itemized deductions.

In 1998, the standard deduction for married filing jointly is $7,100; and the standard deduction for single filers is $4,250.

The deduction is subtracted from the AGI.

Deduction for Exemptions

The next step is determining the reduction in your taxable income based on the number of exemptions claimed. In addition to claiming a personal exemption for yourself and your spouse (on a joint return), you may claim an exemption for each of your other dependents.

In 1998 the exemption amount is $2,700. For married filing jointly, the exemption is reduced by 2% for each $2,500 or fraction thereof by which your AGI exceeds $186,800. This exemption is reduced to $0 if your AGI exceeds $309,300.

For single filers, the exemption amount is reduced by 2% for each $2,500 or fraction thereof by which your AGI exceeds $124,500. This exemption is reduced to $0 if your AGI exceeds $247,000.

---

[5] The IRS requires that the tax tables be used if your taxable income is less than $100,000. The difference between the tax table and the tax schedule, which we will be using, is less than $10.

Table 3.1 1998 IRS 1040 Tax Schedule

Married Filing Jointly
Taxable Income

Over	But Not Over	Amount of Tax	+ Rate on Excess	Of the Amount Over
$0	$42,350		15.0%	
$42,350	$102,300	$6,353	28.0%	$42,350
$102,300	$155,950	$23,139	31.0%	$102,300
$155,950	$278,450	$39,770	36.0%	$155,950
$278,450		$83,870	39.6%	$278,450

Single
Taxable Income

Over	But Not Over	Amount of Tax	+ Rate on Excess	Of the Amount Over
$0	$25,350		15.0%	
$25,350	$51,400	$3,803	28.0%	$25,350
$61,400	$128,100	$13,897	31.0%	$61,400
$128,100	$278,450	$34,574	36.0%	$128,100
$278,450		$88,700	39.6%	$278,450

Taxable Income

Subtract the exemption deduction and the Standard / Itemized deduction from the AGI to determine your taxable income.

Tax

The tax on your taxable income is calculated using tax tables, Form 8814 or Form 4972 or the tax schedule provided by the IRS. We will use the tax schedule (shown in Table 3.1) for the discussions in this book.[5]

3.6 Marginal Versus Average Tax Rates

In this section we will explain the difference between marginal and average tax rates, and provide a table for estimating your average tax, including federal and state. This average rate will be needed in the calculations of the projected asset values of the Traditional and Roth IRA accounts to be discussed in the next few chapters. The average tax rate is also the tax rate that you should use with any of the Roth IRA calculators that are currently available in the marketplace.

TABLE 3.2 Tax Calulation	A	B
AGI	$90,000	$90,100
Standard Deduction	$7,100	$7,100
Deduction for 2 exemptions	$5,400	$5,400
Total Adjustments	$12,500	$12,500
Taxable Income	$77,500	$77,600
Federal Tax	$16,195	$16,223
Avg. Tax = Fed. Tax / Taxable	21%	21%
Increase in Fed Tax (B-A)		$28
Percentage increase		28%

Let us start with an example. Let us assume Mr. and Mrs. Example B have calculated their adjusted gross income from line 32 to be $90,000. What is their federal tax? We are now in the third of the federal Form 1040. The first step in this section is to determine their deduction, which is the larger of these two: Schedule A for itemized deductions or the standard deductions. We will assume that they are married filing jointly, that they use the standard deduction of $7,100, and that they can claim two exemptions. The following Table 3.2 shows their taxable income.

The tax on $77,500 may be obtained from the following tax schedule:

The tax that Mr. and Mrs. Example B will pay on $77,500 is $16,195. This tax of $16,195 is 21% of the taxable income of $77,500. We will refer to this tax percentage as the **average tax rate.** It is sometimes referred to as the **effective tax** rate.

The average or effective tax rate is determined by dividing total tax by taxable income.

Now if they receive an additional income of $100, their tax will increase to $16,223, which is an increase of $28. Thus the tax rate on the increase is 28%. This **tax rate on the last dollars of your taxable income is referred to as the marginal tax**.

The average tax rate is less than the marginal tax rate (21% as compared with 28%). In this book we will be focusing on the total tax and not make a distinction between which dollars were taxed first or last.

The relationship between average and marginal tax rates is shown in the Table 3.3. The difference between the two rates is shown for a range of taxable incomes for a couple filing jointly. Observe that the rates are the same for taxable incomes of less than $42,350. Above $42,350 the average tax is lower than the marginal tax rate. To pay close to the maximum marginal tax rate of say 39.5%, your taxable income would need to be over $2,000,000. The average tax rate increases gradually with no jumps while the marginal tax rate has jumps in it. The two tax rates have been drawn in Table 3.3.

State taxes have a similar marginal tax rate structure. To compute your total average tax, including federal plus state, see Tables 3.4. To use this table you will first need to calculate your taxable income: Recall that this is the AGI minus exemptions and deductions. Then look up the average tax rate for your state using the closest taxable income.

Table 3.3

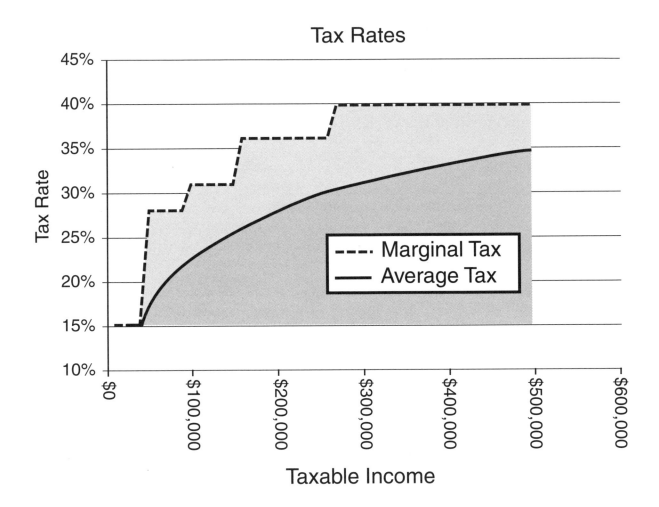

Table 3.4 Federal Plus State Average Tax Rates

Taxable Income	MFJ Federal Marginal Tax	MFJ Federal Average Tax	MFJ Federal Plus Avg. of States Tax	SNGL Federal Plus Avg. Of States Tax
$10,000	15.0%	15.0%	17%	18%
$20,000	15.0%	15.0%	17%	18%
$30,000	15.0%	15.0%	18%	21%
$40,000	15.0%	15.0%	19%	24%
$50,000	28.0%	17.0%	21%	26%
$60,000	28.0%	19.0%	23%	27%
$70,000	28.0%	20.0%	25%	29%
$80,000	28.0%	21.0%	26%	30%
$90,000	28.0%	22.0%	27%	30%
$100,000	28.0%	22.0%	27%	31%
$110,000	31.0%	23.0%	28%	32%
$120,000	31.0%	24.0%	29%	32%
$130,000	31.0%	24.5%	30%	33%
$140,000	31.0%	25.0%	30%	33%
$150,000	31.0%	25.5%	31%	34%
$160,000	36.0%	26.0%	31%	34%
$170,000	36.0%	26.5%	32%	35%
$180,000	36.0%	27.0%	32%	35%
$190,000	36.0%	27.5%	33%	36%
$200,000	36.0%	28.0%	33%	36%
$250,000	36.0%	29.5%	35%	37%
$300,000	39.6%	31.0%	37%	38%
$400,000	39.6%	33.0%	39%	40%
$500,000	39.6%	34.5%	40%	41%
$750,000	39.6%	36.0%	42%	43%
$1,000,000	39.6%	37.0%	43%	43%
$2,000,000	39.6%	38.5%	44%	44%
$5,000,000	39.6%	39.0%	45%	45%
$10,000,000	39.6%	39.3%	45%	45%

Example: If your taxable income is $100,000, then for Married Filing Jontly, the average tax rate (Federal plus State) is 22%. Note that State taxes was calculated by averaging the tax for all 50 states in the U.S.

3.7 Summary

In this chapter we discussed the concepts of adjusted gross income, modified adjusted gross income, marginal tax rates, and average tax rates. We will be using average tax rates for the examples in this book and will refer to Table 3.4 to compute the average federal-plus-state tax rates. As we will show in later chapters, the relative advantage of taxable, tax-deferred and tax-free investments is closely related to the tax rates. Thus it will be important to get an accurate estimate of your current and post-retirement tax rates.

Chapter 4 Roth IRA and Other Annual Contributions

".. what we're really trying to do is develop a culture of savings. We'd like people to start off when they're young and every year save whatever they can afford, whether it's $500 or $2,000. …" Senator Roth

This chapter deals with annual contributions. Specifically we will address the relative advantages of **annual** contributions (typically $2,000 per year) in the following investments:

- Tax-deferred deductible IRA
- Non-deductible IRA
- Roth IRA
- Taxable account
- Employee tax-deferred savings plans with matching funds (e.g. 401(k) and 403(b))

The sections in this chapter are:

- Principles of tax-advantaged investments
- Case studies for contribution accounts ($2000 per year)
- Non-deductible Traditional IRAs and capital gains taxable accounts
- Employee-sponsored defined contribution plans 401(k)-type
- Summary

4.1 Principles of Tax-Advantaged Investments

This section explains the basic principles underlying tax-deductible IRAs, non-deductible IRAs, the Roth IRA, and accounts subject to capital gains taxes, such as those containing mutual funds and individual stocks. The eligibility rules for investing in these accounts are described in detail in Chapter 7. We will refer to these rules as needed.

Let us assume that you want to invest $2,000 in some account in 1998. Assume that you have already paid taxes on the $2,000. The various options for this investment are described below.

4.1.1 Taxable Account

Examples of taxable accounts are individual stocks, mutual funds, money market funds, checking and savings accounts. Individual stocks and stock mutual funds are subject to capital gains tax, while money market funds, checking, and savings accounts are subject to ordinary income taxes. In both cases, you pay taxes on the growth each year. Thus, if the investment grows at 9%, and your tax rate is 22.22%, the net growth will be 9% - 9%*22.22% = 7%. Thus the after-tax growth rate you realize is 7%. The remaining 2% goes to pay the taxes each year. Referring to Table 2.8, we see that in 8 years, at a growth rate of 7%, the $2,000 will grow to $3,436. Thus you will receive $3,436 after all taxes have been paid.

With a taxable account:

      There are no income restrictions on the amount you can invest

      Example balance $3,436

      The principal is taxed in the year of investment

      The growth is taxed each year (as it is realized)

4.1.2 Non-Deductible Traditional IRA

The maximum an individual can invest per year in a non-deductible IRA is $2,000. You may invest in this account no matter how high your income is. This is a non-deductible investment, which means that it must be included in your taxable income in the year of investment. However the **taxes on the growth are deferred** so you do not pay taxes each year. You will pay these taxes when you finally withdraw the funds. For example, if the account grew at the rate of 9% per year, the account value at the end of 8 years would be $3,985 (from Table 2.8). The growth portion of the account ($3,985-$2,000 =$1,985) is taxable. At a 22.22% tax rate the tax is $441. So the balance that you will receive after taxes is $3,985-$441 = $3,544.

If your tax rate happens to be lower than 22.22% at the time of withdrawal, the account will do better.

With a Non-deductible-Traditional IRA

> The investment is included in your taxable income

> There is no income restriction

> The maximum an individual can invest is $2,000 per year

> The accounts do better if the tax rates arc lower at withdrawal

> Example balance: $3,544

> *The principal is taxed in the year of investment*

> *The growth is taxed upon withdrawal*

4.1.3 Deductible-Traditional IRA (or Traditional IRA)

This type of investment is also referred to as a Deductible IRA or simply a Traditional IRA. You do **not** include this investment in your taxable income in the year of investment. At a tax rate of 22.22% you will get a tax advantage in the form of reduced taxes paid (or a refund) of $2000*22.22% = $445. At a growth rate of 9% the account will grow to $3,985 in 8 years. Upon withdrawal you will need to pay taxes on the full $3,985. At a 22.22% tax rate this tax is $885. So the balance that you receive is $3,985-$885 = $3,100. But remember you did get a tax rebate of $445 in the first year. Now, if you had invested this $445 in a taxable account, it would have grown at an after-tax 7% rate to 1.72*$445 = $764 (the factor 1.72 is obtained from Table 2.8). The total balance to you, if you did reinvest the tax rebate, would then be $3,100 + $764 = $3,864.

This account, like the non-deductible IRA, will do better if the withdrawal tax rate is lower than 22.22%. For instance, if your average tax rate drops to 15%, you would only pay $3,985*15% = $598 in taxes and receive $3985 - $598 = $3,387. Including the growth in the reinvested amount of $754, you would then receive $4,141. With a tax-deferred IRA:

> You get a tax rebate in the year of investment

> You pay taxes on the the full withdrawal

> The maximum contribution is $2,000 per year.

> Your modified adjusted gross income cannot exceed $150,000 (if you are married filing jointly) and $95,000 (if you are single) per year to be eligible to contribute the full $2,000.

> In the example:

> If you do not reinvest the tax rebate, the balance is $3,100
> If you do reinvest the tax rebate, the balance is $3,864
> The account does better if the tax rate at withdrawal is lower

> *The principal is taxed upon withdrawal*

> *The growth is taxed upon withdrawal*

4.1.4 Roth IRA

This type of investment is sometimes referred to as a tax-free IRA. This investment is included in your taxable income in the year of investment. The growth on the account is not taxed. At the time of withdrawal you do not pay any taxes: no taxes on the growth, no taxes on the initial investment. As mentioned before, it is outside the Federal Income Tax system. In the example we have been considering the $2,000 initial account would grow to $3,985 in 8 years at a 9% rate of return. Thus you would receive the full $3,985.

With a Roth IRA:

You do not get a tax rebate in the year of investment. The investment is included in your taxable income

You do not pay taxes on the growth, nor do you pay taxes at the time of withdrawal

The maximum annual contribution is $2,000 per year for individuals, and $4,000 per year for married couples filing jointly

Your adjusted gross income cannot exceed $150,000 (if you are married filing jointly) or $95,000 (if you are single) per year to be eligible to contribute the full $2,000

In the example you would receive $3,985

In this account, the tax rate during withdrawal does not matter since you will not be paying any taxes

The principal is taxed in the year of investment

The growth is never taxed

4.2 Case Studies for Contribution Accounts ($2,000 per year)

In this section we will study the relative benefits of annual contribution investments in IRA and taxable accounts for a range of financial profiles. We will explore the effect of early and later withdrawals, one-shot lump sum withdrawals, and multi-year withdrawals (which we call an indexed payout annuity).

If you are taking a lump sum withdrawal, you will be receiving the entire balance of your account in the withdrawal year, and will pay taxes on the entire amount. This is generally **not** the way most individuals will withdraw from the accounts. Note that many of the software programs available in the marketplace make this very assumption[3]. Unless you are planning to take such a lump sum withdrawal, be wary of using results from calculators that use this method in evaluating the benefits of the Roth IRA.

Most people will want to withdraw their retirement balance over a number of years. We will assume that the withdrawals are increased each year to keep up with inflation. This is called an **indexed payout annuity.**

The start date for the withdrawal will vary for different people, depending on the value of their investable accounts. Recall that the recommended sequence for withdrawals is: first from your investable accounts, then from the tax-deferred accounts, and finally from the tax-free Roth accounts. Thus if your investable accounts are relatively large, they will last a relatively longer time, and you will not need to withdraw from the tax-advantaged accounts until the other accounts are used up. The examples will illustrate the values of the accounts for different start dates for these annuity withdrawals.

---

[3] *Many software programs use Net Assets After Taxes (NAT) as the metric for comparing assets. This implies that the monies are withdrawn from the account in one lump sum and all the taxes paid in one installment. Such a lump sum withdrawal is unusual: most individuals will not withdraw all their funds in one year. However, if you do use a lump sum withdrawal, you will need to enter a retirement tax rate that corresponds to the relatively large withdrawal. The alternate metric of a multi-year withdrawal represented as a payout annuity is much more realistic. An indexed annuity is what most people will want, and that is the recommended metric.*

The assumptions in our analyses are as follows:

Spouses are the same age

Contingent beneficiary is	30 years younger than spouses
Spouses' life expectancy is	90 years
Rate of return for all accounts	9%
Inflation	3.5%
Tax Rates on investable accounts	28%
Number of years for annuity	1, 10, and 20
Start age for drawing annuity	60, 65, 70, 75, 80, 85, 90
Withdrawal method for IRAs	Joint Term Certain

All monies are expressed in today's dollars after taxes.

The subject of withdrawal methods will be discussed in detail in Chapter 8. For the analyses in this chapter, we will assume the "Joint Term Certain" method. This is briefly introduced here.

4.2.1 Introduction to the Joint Term Certain Withdrawal Method

For Traditional IRAs you are required to withdraw a certain amount called the "minimum required distribution" starting the year after you reach age 70 1/2. With the Term Certain method, for a couple who are both the same age, this minimum in the first year of withdrawal is 1/20.6 times the balance as of December 31 of the prior year. Thus if the balance was $100,000, the amount that *must* be withdrawn is $4,854. If the amount that you want to withdraw as a payout annuity is greater than $4,854, you will have met the minimum required distribution rule. However, suppose that your retirement needs were such that you did not need to withdraw any amount, or needed to withdraw less than the minimum required, from the Traditional IRA account. In that case you would withdraw the required minimum and immediately reinvest the unneeded amount in a taxable account. The growth rate in the taxable account will be less than in a tax-advantaged account. This is the model used in the analyses presented in this chapter.

What happens at age 72? During the year you are 71, you will have withdrawn a certain amount, and the remaining account balance will have grown at some rate (we assume 9% in our examples). The minimum required withdrawal in the second year will be

1/19.6 of the balance as of December 31 of the prior year. In the following years the amounts that need to be withdrawn will be 1/18.6, 1/17.6, 1/16.6 (and so on) of the prior year-end balance. This divisor decreases by one each year, in the Term Certain method. After 21 years the divisor will be 0.6, and thus all of the remaining balance will need to be withdrawn in that year. This example assumes that the couple is the same age. The starting divisor, which was 20.6 in this example, will be different for couples whose ages are different, and will also be different for single individuals. The general discussion of these other cases and the discussion of other withdrawal methods (such as the Recalculation and the Hybrid methods) are deferred to Chapter 8.

The withdrawal rules for the Roth IRA accounts are more lenient than those for Traditional IRA accounts. There is no required minimum withdrawal during the person's lifetime, however withdrawals are required after both spouses die. In our examples we are assuming that the couple will die at age 90. The next or contingent beneficiary is the child, assumed to be 60 when the couple dies. Thus the child must start withdrawing from the Roth IRA at a certain minimum rate. With the Term Certain method, which actually is the only option for the child, the minimum withdrawal in the first year is 1/24.2 of the prior year's balance. In the following years, the divisors are 23.2, 22.2, 21.2 and so on. This account will be totally withdrawn in 25 years. Again, these are the divisors for a child who is 30 years younger than the parents are. The more general cases are discussed in Chapter 8.

In the following sections, we will go through the retirement planning steps described in Chapter 2 for a range of financial profiles and age groups corresponding to the Generation X (under 35), early and late baby boomers (36 to 55), pre-retirement (56 to 64) and retired (65 to 85) groups. You need to read only the section that most closely matches your profile. The profiles are summarized in Table 4.1

Table 4.1 Profiles Used in Analyses

	CONTRIBUTION ONLY Genex			CONTRIBUTION & CONVERSION Baby Boomer				Near Retirement
Example Name	EX 25A	EX35A	EX45A	EX55A	EX55B	EX55SNGL	EX55C	EX60A
Age	25	35	45	55	55	55	55	60
Current Income	$35,000	$40,000	$90,000	$100,000	$100,000	$100,000	$200,000	$100,000
Desired Retirement Income After taxes	$30,000	$35,000	$65,040	$55,020	$70,780	$66,700	$134,250	$71,000
Other Investible Assets	$0	$0	$75,000	$75,000	$200,000	$200,000	$2,000,000	$100,000
Planned Savings per Year	$2,000	$4,000	$8,000	$6,000	$6,000	$10,000	$6,000	$10,000
Traditional IRA Existing Balance	$0	$0	$40,000	$100,000	$120,000	$150,000	$2,000,000	$225,000
STEP 1 Recurring Indexed : Soc. Sec.								
Social Security After Taxes	$9,920	$9,920	$18,410	$12,150	$18,050	$10,800	$16,680	$18,000
STEP 2 Recurring Unindexed : Pension								
Pension Averaged After Taxes	$5,730	$6,550	$13,670	$16,040	$14,890	$14,260	$27,520	$15,000
Total Recurring Income After Tax	$15,650	$16,470	$32,080	$28,190	$32,940	$25,060	$44,200	$33,000
Balance req'd	$14,350	$18,530	$32,960	$26,830	$37,840	$41,640	$90,050	$38,000
STEP 3 Investible Assets								
Age for starting tax-advantaged withdrawals	65	65	70	70	74	72	97	70
Balance req'd from tax-advantaged	$14,350	$18,530	$32,960	$26,830	$37,840	$41,640	$90,050	$38,000
Step 4 Annuity from Annual Contributions								
Annuity from $2,000 in Roth IRA	$15,908	$9,029	$6,303	$2,751	$3,383	$3,051	$4,989	$1,400
Annuity from $2,000 in tax-deductible	$13,204	$7,544	$4,853	$2,255	$2,397	$2,150	$1,940	$1,050
Annuity from $2,000 in taxable	$9,225	$5,964	$3,604	$1,944	$2,056	$1,827	$2,029	$985
Savings per year in Roth IRA	$2,000	$4,000	$4,000	$4,000	$4,000	$2,000	$4,000	$4,000
Savings in tax-deductible plan	$0	$0	$0	$0	$0	$0	$0	$0
Savings in taxable accounts	$0	$0	$4,000	$2,000	$2,000	$8,000	$2,000	$6,000
Annuity from Roth IRA	$15,908	$18,058	$12,606	$5,502	$6,766	$3,051	$9,978	$2,800
Annuity from tax-deductible	$0	$0	$0	$0	$0	$0	$0	$0
Annuity from taxable	$0	$0	$7,208	$1,944	$2,056	$7,308	$2,029	$2,955
Total Annuity from annual savings	$15,908	$18,058	$19,814	$7,446	$8,822	$10,359	$12,007	$5,755
Balance req'd from existing tax advantaged	($1,558)	$472	$13,146	$19,384	$29,018	$31,281	$78,043	$32,245
Step 5: Annuity from Existing IRA								
Percentage Contributions								
Indexed recurring [Social Security]	33%	28%	28%	22%	26%	16%	12%	25%
Non-indexed recurring [Pension]	19%	19%	21%	29%	21%	21%	20%	21%
Annual contributions	53%	52%	30%	14%	12%	16%	9%	8%
% Balance required from existing IRAs	-5%	1%	20%	35%	41%	47%	58%	45%
TAX RATES								
Current Avg. ax rates	17%	17%	25%	21%	26%	30%	32%	26%
Retirement Avg. Tax rate	17%	17%	23%	19%	25%	28%	31%	25%

4.2.2 Example 25A

This age 25 Generation X couple has no retirment savings. They plan on saving $2,000 per year till age 65. They do not have any assets for conversion. From Table 4.1 we see that the recurring income for this couple was $15,650, and their retirement need was $30,000, after taxes in today's dollars. They will need $14,350 from tax-advantaged accounts starting at age 65.

The top part of the adjacent table lists the basic assumptions made for this profile. The middle Reference part of the table shows how various accounts would do if $2,000 were invested annually in them. The results are shown for a taxable account [A] ; the Traditional IRA tax-deductible account assuming the tax deduction received in the year of investment is used up (**not reinvested**) [B]; the Traditional tax-deductible IRA assuming the tax-deduction in the year of the investment **is reinvested** [B1], and the Roth IRA [C]. The account values are shown for withdrawals over 20, 10, and one year periods. Note that the average tax rate will increase as the withdrawal period decreases. These tax rates were derived from the tax tables in Chapter 3. The withdrawals are shown starting at ages ranging from 60 to 90. From the Reference section the following general observations can be made:

- The Roth IRA does better than the Traditional IRA.
- The Traditional IRA, even without reinvestment, does better than a taxable account.
- The later you start the withdrawals, the greater the advantage of the Roth IRA. If you withdraw the full amount in one year at age 90 the benefit is 53%.

The effect of retirement tax rate, inflation rate, and rate of return for Example 25A are shown at the bottom of the table. We see that:

- If retirement tax rates drop, the Traditional IRA result improves, while the Roth IRA result is unchanged. This is expected since no taxes are paid on the Roth IRA. Thus, in the case of the Roth IRA, it does not matter what the tax rates do during retirement.
- Inflation affects both the Traditional and the Roth IRA.
- Rate of return affects both the Traditional and the Roth IRA accounts. The Roth account does better with a higher rate of return, since you get more tax free growth.

Referring to the Reference line (the first line under "Sensitivity to Variables"), we see that:
$2,000 in a Roth IRA provides an indexed payout annuity of $15,908 per year for 20 years

| Annual annuity from $2,000 in Roth account | $15,908 |
| Balance needed | $0 |

Thus a savings of $2,000 per year in a Roth IRA will provided the couple with the balance that they need.

We see that, for Example 25A, the Roth IRA is 21% better than the Traditional IRA with no reinvestments, and 8% better than a Traditional IRA with reinvestment of the up-front tax deduction. Investing in the Roth contribution IRA is definitely recommended. Annual contributions provide 53% of their retirement needs.

CONTRIBUTIONS

EXAMPLE 25A

ASSUMPTIONS

Age	25	Inflation	3.50%
Spouse's Age	25	Pre-Retirement Tax Rate	17%
Beneficiary's Age	1	Retirement tax rate	17%
Check Out Age	90	Other assets tax rate	17%
Annual Contribution	$2,000	Rate of Return	9%
Save $2,000 per year till age	65	Withdrawal Method	Joint Term Certain

REFERENCE TABLE

	WITHDRAWALS		INDEXED ANNUITY PER YEAR				ROTH ADVANTAGE	
	Start Withdr'l At Age	Withdr'l Tax Rate	**A** Taxable Assets Tax 28%	**B** Trad'l IRA without Re-Invest Tax Savings	**B1** Trad'l IRA with Re-Invest Tax Savings	**C** ROTH IRA	ROTH % Adv. Over B	ROTH % Adv. Over B1
Withdrawal Period 20 Years	60	17%	$7,643	$10,192	$11,401	$12,280	20%	7.7%
	65	17%	$9,225	$13,204	$14,663	$15,908	20%	8.5%
	70	17%	$11,136	$17,105	$18,867	$20,608	**20%**	**9.2%**
	75	17%	$13,442	$21,064	$23,190	$26,698	27%	15.1%
	80	17%	$16,225	$25,676	$28,242	$34,587	35%	22.5%
	85	17%	$19,585	$31,267	$34,365	$44,806	43%	30.4%
	90	17%	$23,641	$37,898	$41,637	$58,046	53%	39.4%
Withdrawal Period 10 Years	60	17%	$12,888	$16,265	$18,304	$19,596	20%	7.1%
	65	17%	$15,557	$21,071	$23,532	$25,387	20%	7.9%
	70	17%	$18,779	$27,297	$30,268	$32,888	20%	8.7%
	75	17%	$22,667	$34,380	$37,965	$42,606	24%	12.2%
	80	17%	$27,361	$42,675	$47,003	$55,195	**29%**	**17.4%**
	85	17%	$33,027	$52,507	$57,731	$71,504	36%	23.9%
	90	17%	$39,866	$63,908	$70,214	$92,632	45%	31.9%
Withdrawal Period 1 Year	60	21%	$106,827	$121,987	$138,885	$154,414	27%	11.2%
	65	27%	$132,100	$148,435	$169,331	$203,335	37%	20.1%
	70	28%	$159,454	$189,660	$214,883	$263,417	39%	22.6%
	75	30%	$192,473	$237,354	$267,800	$341,251	44%	27.4%
	80	32%	$232,330	$292,039	$328,789	$442,084	51%	34.5%
	85	33%	$280,440	$358,388	$402,749	$572,711	60%	42.2%
	90	34%	$338,512	$431,511	$485,058	$741,935	**72%**	**53.0%**

SENSITIVITY TO VARIABLES

Withdrawal Period 20 Years								
Reference	65	17%	$9,225	$13,204	$14,663	$15,908	20%	8.5%
Ret Tax	65	15%	$9,225	$13,522	$14,981	$15,908	18%	6.2%
Ret Tax	65	21%	$9,225	$12,567	$14,027	$15,908	27%	13.4%
Inflation 2%	65	17%	$18,599	$26,446	$29,388	$31,863	20%	8.4%
Inflation 5%	65	17%	$4,591	$6,615	$7,341	$7,970	20%	8.6%
Rate of return 11%	65	17%	$16,664	$27,004	$29,600	$32,535	20%	9.9%
Rate of return 7%	65	17%	$5,137	$6,483	$7,308	$7,810	20%	6.9%
Rate of Return 4%	65	17%	$2,177	$2,278	$2,636	$2,744	20%	4.1%

Average Benefit of ROTH IRA   **21%**   **8%**

4.2.2 Example 35A

This age-35 Generation X couple has no savings and they plan to save $4,000 per year till age 65. They do not have any assets for Roth Conversion. From Table 4.1 we see that the recurring income for this couple was $16,470, and their retirement need was $35,000,after taxes in today's dollars. They will need $18,530 from tax-advantaged accounts starting at age 65.

The top part of the adjacent table lists the basic assumptions made for this profile. The middle Reference part of the table shows how various accounts would do if $2,000 were invested annually in them. The results are shown for a taxable account [A] ; the Traditional IRA tax-deductible account assuming the tax deduction received in the year of investment is used up (**not reinvested**) [B]; the Traditional tax-deductible IRA assuming the tax-deduction in the year of the investment **is reinvested** [B1], and the Roth IRA [C]. The account values are shown for withdrawals over 20, 10, and one year periods. Note that the average tax rate will increase as the withdrawal period decreases. These tax rates were derived from the tax tables in Chapter 3. The withdrawals are shown starting at ages ranging from 60 to 90. From the Reference section the following general observations can be made:

- The Roth IRA does better than the Traditional IRA.
- The Traditional IRA, even without reinvestment, does better than a taxable account.
- The later you start the withdrawals, the greater the advantage of the Roth IRA. If you withdraw the full amount in one year at age 90 the benefit is 45%.

The effect of retirement tax rate, inflation rate, and rate of return for Example 35A are shown at the bottom of the table. We see that:

- If retirement tax rates drop, the Traditional IRA result improves, while the Roth IRA result is unchanged. This is expected since no taxes are paid on the Roth IRA. Thus, in the case of the Roth IRA, it does not matter what the tax rates do during retirement.
- Inflation affects both the Traditional and the Roth IRA.
- Rate of return affects both the Traditional and the Roth IRA accounts. The Roth account does better with a higher rate of return, since you get more tax free growth.

Referring to the Reference line (the first line under "Sensitivity to Variables"), we see that:
$2,000 in a Roth IRA provides an indexed payout annuity of $9,089 per year for 20 years
Annual annuity from $4,000 in Roth account $18,058
Balance needed $472

We see that, for Example 35A, the Roth IRA is 21% better than the Traditional IRA with no reinvestments, and approximately 8% better than a Traditional IRA with reinvestment of the up-front tax deduction. Investing in the Roth contribution IRA is definitely recommended. Annual contributions provide 52% of their retirement needs.

CONTRIBUTIONS

ASSUMPTIONS

Age	35	Inflation	3.50%
Spouse's Age	35	Pre-Retirement Tax Rate	17%
Beneficiary's Age	5	Retirement tax rate	17%
Check Out Age	90	Other assets tax rate	17%
Annual Contribution	$2,000	Rate of Return	9%
Save $2,000 per year till age	65	Withdrawal Method	Joint Term Certain

REFERENCE TABLE

		WITHDRAWALS	A	INDEXED ANNUITY PER YEAR B	B1	C	ROTH ADVANTAGE	
	Start Withdr'l At Age	Withdr'l Tax Rate	Taxable Assets Tax 28%	Trad'l IRA without Re-Invest Tax Savings	Trad'l IRA with Re-Invest Tax Savings	ROTH IRA	ROTH % Adv. Over B	ROTH % Adv. Over B1
Withdrawal Period 20 Years	60	17%	$4,941	$5,823	$6,605	$7,016	20%	6.2%
	65	17%	$5,964	$7,544	$8,487	$9,089	20%	7.1%
	70	17%	$7,199	$9,773	$10,912	$11,774	**20%**	**7.9%**
	75	17%	$8,690	$12,035	$13,409	$15,254	27%	13.8%
	80	17%	$10,489	$14,670	$16,329	$19,761	35%	21.0%
	85	17%	$12,661	$17,864	$19,867	$25,600	43%	28.9%
	90	17%	$15,283	$21,652	$24,070	$33,164	53%	37.0%
Withdrawal Period 10 Years	60	17%	$6,932	$9,293	$10,611	$11,196	20%	5.5%
	65	17%	$10,057	$12,039	$13,630	$14,504	20%	6.4%
	70	17%	$12,140	$15,596	$17,516	$18,790	20%	7.3%
	75	17%	$14,654	$19,642	$21,960	$24,342	24%	10.8%
	80	17%	$17,688	$24,382	$27,180	$31,535	**29%**	**16.0%**
	85	17%	$21,351	$29,999	$33,377	$40,853	36%	22.4%
	90	17%	$25,772	$36,513	$40,590	$52,924	45%	30.4%
Withdrawal Period 1 Year	60	21%	$67,067	$68,009	$78,618	$86,088	27%	9.5%
	65	22%	$85,400	$90,615	$104,124	$116,173	28%	11.6%
	70	24%	$103,084	$114,380	$130,686	$150,500	32%	15.2%
	75	26%	$124,430	$143,358	$163,041	$194,970	36%	19.6%
	80	28%	$150,197	$176,668	$200,426	$252,579	43%	26.0%
	85	29%	$181,299	$216,985	$245,664	$327,212	51%	33.2%
	90	31%	$218,841	$257,745	$292,363	$423,896	**64%**	**45.0%**

SENSITIVITY TO VARIABLES

Withdrawal Period 20 Years								
Reference	65	17%	$5,964	$7,544	$8,487	$9,089	20%	7.1%
Ret Tax	65	15%	$5,964	$7,726	$8,669	$9,089	18%	4.8%
Ret Tax	65	21%	$5,964	$7,180	$8,124	$9,089	27%	11.9%
Inflation 2%	65	17%	$10,390	$13,057	$14,701	$15,732	20%	7.0%
Inflation 5%	65	17%	$3,428	$4,364	$4,906	$5,258	20%	7.2%
Rate of return 11%	65	17%	$9,420	$13,069	$14,536	$15,745	20%	8.3%
Rate of return 7%	65	17%	$3,777	$4,349	$4,956	$5,240	20%	5.7%
Rate of Return 4%	65	17%	$1,911	$1,909	$2,224	$2,300	20%	3.4%
Average Benefit of ROTH IRA							**21%**	**8%**

4.2.2 Example 45A

This age-45 couple has $75,000 in investable assets, and $40,000 in existing IRA accounts. They plan to save $8,000 per year. From Table 4.1 we see that the recurring income for this couple was $32,080, and their retirement need was $65,040. They will need $32,960 from tax-advantaged accounts starting at age 70.

The top part of the adjacent table lists the basic assumptions made for this profile. The middle Reference part of the table shows how various accounts would do if $2,000 were invested annually in them. The results are shown for a taxable account [A] ; the Traditional IRA tax-deductible account assuming the tax deduction received in the year of investment is used up (**not reinvested**) [B]; the Traditional tax-deductible IRA assuming the tax-deduction in the year of the investment **is reinvested** [B1], and the Roth IRA [C]. The account values are shown for withdrawals over 20, 10, and one year periods. Note that the average tax rate will increase as the withdrawal period decreases. These tax rates were derived from the tax tables in Chapter 3. The withdrawals are shown starting at ages ranging from 60 to 90. From the Reference section the following general observations can be made:

- The Roth IRA does better than the Traditional IRA.
- The Traditional IRA, even without reinvestment, does better than a taxable account.
- The later you start the withdrawals, the greater the advantage of the Roth IRA. If you withdraw the full amount in one year at age 90 the benefit is 51.6%.

The effect of retirement tax rate, inflation rate, and rate of return for Example 45A are shown at the bottom of the table. We see that:

- If retirement tax rates drop, the Traditional IRA result improves, while the Roth IRA result is unchanged. This is expected since no taxes are paid on the Roth IRA. Thus, in the case of the Roth IRA, it does not matter what the tax rates do during retirement.
- Inflation affects both the Traditional and the Roth IRA.
- Rate of return affects both the Traditional and the Roth IRA accounts. The Roth account does better with a higher rate of return, since you get more tax free growth.

Referring to the Reference line (the first line under "Sensitivity to Variables"), we see that:
$2,000 in a Roth IRA provides an indexed payout annuity of $6,303 per year for 20 years

Annual annuity from $4,000 in Roth account	$12,606
Annual annuity from $4,000 in taxable account	$7,208
Total indexed payout annuity	$19,814
Balance needed	$13,146

The balance will need to come from investable accounts and in tax-deferred plans: the 401(k)-type), and the existing IRAs, which may be convertible to a Roth IRA.

We see that, for Example 45A, the Roth IRA is 30% better than the Traditional IRA with no reinvestments, and 10% better than a Traditional IRA with reinvestment of the up-front tax deduction. Investing in the Roth contribution IRA is definitely recommended. Annual contributions provide 30% of their retirement needs.

CONTRIBUTIONS

EXAMPLE 45A

REFERENCE

Age	45	Inflation	3.50%	
Spouse's Age	45	Pre-Retirement Tax Rate	25%	
Beneficiary's Age	15	Retirement tax rate	23%	
Check Out Age	90	Other assets tax rate	25%	
Annual Contribution	$2,000	Rate of Return	9%	
Save $2,000 per year till age	65	Withdrawal Method	Joint Term Certain	

REFERENCE TABLE

	Withdrawals		Indexed Annuity Per Year				Roth Advantage	
			A	B	B1	C		
	Start Withdr'l At Age	Withdr'l Tax Rate	Taxable Assets Re-Invest	Trad'l IRA without Re-Invest	Trad'l IRA with Over B Tax Savings	ROTH IRA Over B1 Tax Savings	ROTH% Adv	ROTH% Adv
Withdrawal Period 20 Years	60	25%	$2,645	$2,817	$3,436	$3,756	33%	9.3%
	65	25%	$3,087	$3,649	$4,372	$4,866	33%	11.3%
	70	25%	$3,604	$4,727	$5,571	$6,303	**33%**	**13.1%**
	75	25%	$4,206	$5,680	$6,665	$8,166	44%	22.5%
	80	25%	$4,909	$6,726	$7,875	$10,578	57%	34.3%
	85	25%	$5,730	$7,955	$9,297	$13,704	72%	47.4%
	90	25%	$6,688	$9,345	$10,911	$17,753	90%	61.7%
Withdrawal Period 10 Years	60	25%	$4,587	$4,495	$5,569	$5,994	33%	7.6%
	65	25%	$5,354	$5,823	$7,077	$7,765	33%	9.7%
	70	25%	$6,249	$7,544	$9,008	$10,059	33%	11.7%
	75	25%	$7,293	$9,376	$11,084	$13,031	39%	17.6%
	80	25%	$8,513	$11,409	$13,402	$16,882	**48%**	**26.0%**
	85	25%	$9,936	$13,707	$16,034	$21,870	60%	36.4%
	90	25%	$11,597	$16,204	$18,920	$28,332	75%	49.7%
Withdrawal Period 1 Year	60	27%	$34,808	$31,350	$39,501	$42,945	37%	8.7%
	65	29%	$46,767	$44,156	$55,108	$62,191	41%	12.9%
	70	29%	$54,586	$57,203	$69,986	$80,567	41%	15.1%
	75	30%	$63,711	$72,381	$87,302	$104,373	44%	19.6%
	80	32%	$74,363	$88,152	$105,567	$135,213	53%	28.1%
	85	33%	$86,795	$106,278	$126,604	$175,166	65%	38.4%
	90	33%	$101,305	$126,452	$150,177	$226,924	**79%**	**51.1%**

SENSITIVITY TO VARIABLES

Withdrawal Period 20 Years								
Reference	70	23%	$3,604	$4,853	$5,697	$6,303	30%	10.6%
Ret Tax	70	18%	$3,604	$5,169	$6,013	$6,303	22%	4.8%
Ret Tax	72	28%	$3,604	$4,538	$5,382	$6,303	39%	17.1%
Inflation 2%	72	23%	$5,855	$7,809	$9,180	$10,142	30%	10.5%
Inflation 5%	70	23%	$2,218	$3,017	$3,537	$3,918	30%	10.8%
Rate of return 11%	70	23%	$5,238	$7,901	$9,111	$10,262	30%	12.6%
Rate of return 7%	70	23%	$2,466	$2,954	$3,540	$3,837	30%	8.4%
Rate of Return 4%	70	23%	$1,383	$1,379	$1,715	$1,791	30%	4.4%
Average Benefit of ROTH IRA							**30%**	**10%**

4.2.3 Example 55A

This age -55 couple has $75,000 in investable assets, and $100,000 in existing IRA accounts. They plan on saving $6,000 per year till age 65. From Table 4.1 we see that the recurring income for this couple was $28,190, and their retirement need was $55,020. They need $26,830 from tax-advantaged accounts starting at age 70.

The top part of the adjacent table lists the basic assumptions made for this profile. The middle Reference part of the table shows how various accounts would do if $2,000 were invested annually in them. The results are shown for a taxable account [A] ; the Traditional IRA tax-deductible account assuming the tax deduction received in the year of investment is used up (**not reinvested**) [B]; the Traditional tax-deductible IRA assuming the tax-deduction in the year of the investment **is reinvested** [B1], and the Roth IRA [C]. The account values are shown for withdrawals over 20, 10, and one year periods. Note that the average tax rate will increase as the withdrawal period decreases. These tax rates were derived from Table 3.4. The withdrawals are shown starting at ages ranging from 60 to 90. From the Reference section the following general observations can be made:

- The Roth IRA does better than Traditional IRA when the up-front tax-deduction is not reinvested.
- The Traditional IRA, with reinvestment, does better than a taxable account.
- The later you start withdrawals, the greater the advantage of the Roth IRA. This couple has enough investable accounts to last four years, and must start withdrawals at age 70. If you withdraw the full amount in one year at age 90 the benefit is 36%.

The effect of retirement tax rate, inflation rate, and rate of return for Example 55A are:

- If retirement tax rates drop, the Traditional IRA result improves, while the Roth IRA result is unchanged. This is expected since no taxes are paid on the Roth IRA. Thus, in the case of the Roth IRA, it does not matter what the tax rates do during retirement.
- Inflation affects both the Traditional and the Roth IRA.
- Rate of return affects both the Traditional and the Roth IRA accounts. The Roth account does better with a higher rate of return, since you get more tax free growth.

Referring to the Reference line (the first line under "Sensitivity to Variables"), we see that:
$2,000 in a Roth IRA provides an indexed payout annuity of $2,751 per year for 20 years .

Annual annuity from $4,000 in Roth account	$5,502
Annual annuity from $2,000 in taxable account	$1,944
Total annuity	$7,446
Balance needed	$19,384

The balance will need to come from investable accounts and in tax-deferred plans: the 401(k)-type, and the existing IRAs, which may be convertible to a Roth IRA.

We see that, for Example 55A, the Roth IRA is 22% better than the Traditional IRA with no reinvestments, and is 4% better than the Traditional IRA with reinvestment. The Roth IRA will also provide a hedge against rising tax rates. Annual contributions provide 14% of their retirement needs.

CONTRIBUTIONS

EXAMPLE 55A

ASSUMPTIONS

Age	55	Inflation	3.5%
Spouse's Age	55	Pre-Retirement Tax Rate	21%
Beneficiary's Age	25	Retirement tax rate	18%
Check Out Age	90	Other assets tax rate	21%
Annual Contribution	$2,000	Rate of Return	9%
Save $2,000 per year till age	65	Withdrawal Method	Joint Term Certain

REFERENCE TABLE

	Start Withdr'l At Age	Withdr'l Tax Rate	A Taxable Assets Tax 28%	B Trad'l IRA without Re-Invest	B1 Trad'l IRA with Re-Invest Tax Savings	C ROTH IRA Tax Savings	ROTH% Adv Over B	ROTH% Adv Over B1
Withdrawal Period 20 Years	60	21%	$1,379	$1,295	$1,565	$1,639	27%	4.7%
	65	21%	$1,637	$1,677	$1,998	$2,123	27%	6.2%
	70	21%	$1,944	$2,173	$2,554	$2,751	**27%**	**7.7%**
	75	21%	$2,307	$2,643	$3,096	$3,563	35%	15.1%
	80	21%	$2,738	$3,176	$3,713	$4,616	45%	24.3%
	85	21%	$3,251	$3,811	$4,449	$5,980	57%	34.4%
	90	21%	$3,858	$4,548	$5,304	$7,747	70%	46.1%
Withdrawal Period 10 Years	60	21%	$2,359	$2,066	$2,529	$2,615	27%	3.4%
	65	21%	$2,800	$2,677	$3,226	$3,388	27%	5.0%
	70	21%	$3,323	$3,468	$4,119	$4,389	27%	6.6%
	75	21%	$3,944	$4,338	$5,112	$5,686	31%	11.2%
	80	21%	$4,682	$5,332	$6,250	$7,367	**38%**	**17.9%**
	85	21%	$5,558	$6,482	$7,572	$9,543	47%	26.0%
	90	21%	$6,597	$7,776	$9,069	$12,363	59%	36.3%
Withdrawal Period 1 Year	60	21%	$12,938	$10,909	$13,446	$13,809	27%	2.7%
	65	23%	$24,110	$20,897	$25,624	$27,138	30%	5.9%
	70	25%	$28,618	$26,368	$31,979	$35,157	33%	9.9%
	75	26%	$33,970	$33,439	$40,099	$45,546	36%	13.6%
	80	27%	$40,322	$41,567	$49,473	$59,003	42%	19.3%
	85	27%	$47,862	$51,312	$60,696	$76,438	49%	25.9%
	90	28%	$56,812	$61,029	$72,168	$99,024	**62%**	**37.2%**

SENSITIVITY TO VARIABLES

Withdrawal Period 20 Years								
Reference	70	18%	$1,944	$2,255	$2,637	$2,751	22%	4.3%
Ret Tax	70	15%	$1,944	$2,338	$2,719	$2,751	18%	1.2%
Ret Tax	70	23%	$1,944	$2,118	$2,499	$2,751	30%	10.1%
Inflation 2%	70	18%	$2,724	$3,136	$3,670	$3,825	22%	4.2%
Inflation 5%	70	18%	$1,384	$1,619	$1,890	$1,975	22%	4.4%
Rate of return 11%	70	18%	$2,601	$3,213	$3,715	$3,918	22%	5.5%
Rate of return 7%	70	18%	$1,439	$1,561	$1,848	$1,904	22%	3.0%
Rate of Return 4%	70	18%	$900	$874	$1,057	$1,066	22%	0.8%
Average Benefit of ROTH IRA							**22%**	**4%**

4.2.4 Example 55B

This age-55 couple has $200,000 in investable assets, and $120,000 in existing IRA funds. They plan on saving $6,000 per year till age 65. From Table 4.1 we see that the recurring income for this couple was $32,940, and their retirement need was $70,780. Tax-advantaged accounts need to provide $37,840 starting at age 74.

The top part of the adjacent table lists the basic assumptions made for this profile. The middle Reference part of the table shows how various accounts would do if $2,000 were invested annually in them. The results are shown for a taxable account [A] ; the Traditional IRA tax-deductible account assuming the tax deduction received in the year of investment is used up (**not reinvested**) [B]; the Traditional tax-deductible IRA assuming the tax-deduction in the year of the investment **is reinvested** [B1], and the Roth IRA [C]. The account values are shown for withdrawals over 20, 10, and one year periods. Note that the average tax rate will increase as the withdrawal period decreases. These tax rates were derived from Table 3.4. The withdrawals are shown starting at ages ranging from 60 to 90. From the Reference section the following general observations can be made:

- The Roth IRA does better than the Traditional IRA, with or without reinvestment of the tax deduction received in the investment year.
- The Traditional IRA, even without reinvestment, does better than a taxable account.
- The later you start the withdrawals, the greater the advantage of the Roth IRA. If you withdraw the full amount in one year at age 90 the benefit is 41%.

The effect of retirement tax rate, inflation rate, and rate of return for Example 55B are shown at the bottom of the table. We see that:

- If retirement tax rates drop, the Traditional IRA result improves, while the Roth IRA result is unchanged. This is expected since no taxes are paid on the Roth IRA. Thus, in the case of the Roth IRA, it does not matter what the tax rates do during retirement.
- Inflation affects both the Traditional and the Roth IRA. A
- Rate of return affects both the Traditional and the Roth IRA accounts. The Roth account does better with a higher rate of return, since you get more tax free growth.

Referring to the Reference line (the first line under "Sensitivity to Variables"), we see that:
$2,000 in a Roth IRA provides an annuity of $3,383 per year for 20 years

Annual annuity from $4,000 in Roth account	$6,766
Annual annuity from $2,000 in taxable account	$2,056
Total annuity	$8,822
Balance needed (rounded to $1,000)	$29,018

The balance will need to come from investable accounts and in tax-deferred plans: the 401(k)-type), and the existing IRAs, which may be convertible to a Roth IRA. We see that, for Example 55B, the Roth IRA is 41% better than the Traditional IRA with no reinvestments, and 16% better than a Traditional IRA with reinvestment of the up-front tax deduction. Investing in the Roth contribution IRA is definitely recommended. The annual contributions provide 12% of their retirement needs.

CONTRIBUTIONS

EXAMPLE 55B

REFERENCE

Age	55	Inflation	3.50%
Spouse's Age	55	Pre-Retirement Tax Rate	26%
Beneficiary's Age	15	Retirement tax rate	25%
Check Out Age	90	Other assets tax rate	26%
Annual Contribution	$2,000	Rate of Return	9%
Save $2,000 per year till age	65	Withdrawal Method	Joint Term Certain

REFERENCE TABLE

	WITHDRAWALS		INDEXED ANNUITY PER YEAR				ROTH ADVANTAGE	
			A	B	B1	C		
	Start Withdr'l At Age	Withdr'l Tax Rate	Taxable Assets Tax 28%	Trad'l IRA without Re-Invest	Trad'l IRA with Re-Invest Tax Savings	ROTH IRA Tax Savings	ROTH% Adv Over B	ROTH% Adv Over B1
Withdrawal Period 20 Years	60	26%	$1,333	$1,213	$1,538	$1,639	35%	6.6%
	65	26%	$1,556	$1,571	$1,950	$2,123	35%	8.9%
	70	26%	$1,817	$2,035	$2,478	$2,751	**35%**	**11.0%**
	75	26%	$2,120	$2,445	$2,962	$3,563	46%	20.3%
	80	26%	$2,475	$2,896	$3,499	$4,616	59%	31.9%
	85	26%	$2,888	$3,425	$4,129	$5,980	75%	44.8%
	90	26%	$3,371	$4,023	$4,845	$7,747	93%	59.9%
Withdrawal Period 10 Years	60	26%	$2,312	$1,935	$2,499	$2,615	35%	4.7%
	65	26%	$2,699	$2,507	$3,165	$3,388	35%	7.1%
	70	26%	$3,150	$3,248	$4,015	$4,389	35%	9.3%
	75	26%	$3,677	$4,037	$4,932	$5,686	41%	15.3%
	80	26%	$4,291	$4,912	$5,957	$7,367	**50%**	**23.7%**
	85	26%	$5,009	$5,902	$7,122	$9,543	62%	34.0%
	90	26%	$5,846	$6,977	$8,401	$12,363	77%	47.2%
Withdrawal Period 1 Year	60	27%	$12,778	$10,081	$13,193	$13,809	37%	4.7%
	65	27%	$23,575	$19,811	$25,553	$27,138	37%	6.2%
	70	27%	$27,516	$25,665	$32,367	$35,157	37%	8.6%
	75	28%	$32,116	$32,488	$40,310	$45,546	40%	13.0%
	80	29%	$37,486	$40,164	$49,294	$59,003	47%	19.7%
	85	29%	$43,752	$49,146	$59,802	$76,438	56%	27.8%
	90	30%	$51,067	$57,651	$70,089	$99,024	**72%**	**41.3%**

SENSITIVITY TO VARIABLES

Withdrawal Period 20 Years								
Reference	74	25%	$2,056	$2,397	$2,898	$3,383	41%	16.8%
Ret Tax 20%	74	20%	$2,056	$2,557	$3,058	$3,383	32%	10.7%
Ret Tax 30%	74	30%	$2,056	$2,237	$2,738	$3,383	51%	23.6%
Inflation 2%	74	25%	$3,060	$3,536	$4,281	$4,988	41%	16.5%
Inflation 5%	74	25%	$1,380	$1,624	$1,960	$2,293	41%	17.0%
Rate of return 11%	74	25%	$2,872	$3,636	$4,326	$5,183	43%	19.8%
Rate of return 7%	74	25%	$1,458	$1,558	$1,918	$2,175	40%	13.4%
Rate of Return 4%	74	25%	$855	$792	$1,008	$1,087	37%	7.8%
Average Benefit of ROTH IRA							**41%**	**16%**

4.2.5 Example 55SNGL

This age-55 individual has $200,000 in investable assets, and $150,000 in existing IRA accounts. He plans on saving $10,000 per year till age 65. From Table 4.1 we see that the recurring income for this individual was $25,060, and the total retirement need was $66,700. Tax-advantaged accounts need to provide $41,640 starting at age 72.

The top part of the adjacent table lists the basic assumptions made for this profile. The middle Reference part of the table shows how various accounts would do if $2,000 were invested annually in them. The results are shown for a taxable account [A] ; the Traditional IRA tax-deductible account assuming the tax deduction received in the year of investment is used up (**not reinvested**) [B]; the Traditional tax-deductible IRA assuming the tax-deduction in the year of the investment **is reinvested** [B1], and the Roth IRA [C]. The account values are shown for withdrawals over 20, 10, and one year periods. Note that the average tax rate will increase as the withdrawal period decreases. These tax rates were derived from Table 3.4. From the Reference section we see that:

- The Roth IRA does better than the Traditional IRA, with or without reinvestment of the tax deduction received in the investment year.
- The Traditional IRA, even without reinvestment, does better than a taxable account.
- The later you start the withdrawals, the greater the advantage of the Roth IRA. If you withdraw the full amount in one year at age 90 the benefit is 51%.

The effect of retirement tax rate, inflation rate, and rate of return for Example 55SNGL are shown in the bottom of the table. We see that:

- If retirement tax rates drop, the Traditional IRA result improves, while the Roth IRA result is unchanged. This is expected since no taxes are paid on the Roth IRA. Thus, in the case of the Roth IRA, it does not matter what the tax rates do during retirement.
- Inflation affects both the Traditional and the Roth IRA.
- Rate of return affects both the Traditional and the Roth IRA accounts. The Roth account does better with a higher rate of return, since you are get more tax free growth.

Referring to the Reference line (the first line under "sensitivity to variables"), we see that:$2,000 in a Roth IRA provides an annuity of $3,051 per year for 20 years (in today's dollars after taxes)
Assume the individual invests $2,000 in the Roth IRA.

Annual annuity from $2,,000 in Roth account	$3,051
Annual annuity from $6,000 in taxable account	$7,308
Total annuity	$10,359
Balance needed (rounded to $1,000)	$31,281

The balance will need to come from investable accounts and in tax-deferred plans: the 401(k)-type), and the existing IRAs, which may be convertible to a Roth IRA. We see that, for Example 55SNGL, the Roth IRA is pproximately 42% better than the Traditional IRA with no reinvestments, and 15% better than a Traditional IRA with reinvestment of the up-front tax deduction. Investing in the Roth contribution IRA is definitely recommended. The annual contributions provide 16% of the individual's needs.

CONTRIBUTIONS

EXAMPLE 55SNGL

REFERENCE

Age	55	Inflation	3.50%
Spouse's Age	55	Pre-Retirement Tax Rate	28%
Beneficiary's Age	25	Retirement tax rate	28%
Check Out Age	90	Other assets tax rate	28%
Annual Contribution	$2,000	Rate of Return	9%
Save $2,000 per year till age	65	Withdrawal Method	Joint Term Certain

REFERENCE TABLE

	WITHDRAWALS		INDEXED ANNUITY PER YEAR				ROTH ADVANTAGE	
			A	B	B1	C		
	Start Withdr'l At Age	Withdr'l Tax Rate	Taxable Assets Tax 28%	Trad'l IRA without Re-Invest	Trad'l IRA with Re-Invest Tax Savings	ROTH IRA Tax Savings	ROTH% Adv Over B	ROTH% Adv Over B1
Withdrawal Period 20 Years	60	28%	$1,300	$1,180	$1,522	$1,639	39%	7.7%
	65	28%	$1,498	$1,529	$1,923	$2,123	39%	10.4%
	70	28%	$1,726	$1,980	$2,434	$2,751	**39%**	**13.0%**
	75	28%	$1,989	$2,357	$2,880	$3,563	51%	23.7%
	80	28%	$2,293	$2,761	$3,364	$4,616	67%	37.2%
	85	28%	$2,642	$3,230	$3,925	$5,980	85%	52.4%
	90	28%	$3,045	$3,750	$4,551	$7,747	107%	70.2%
Withdrawal Period 10 Years	60	28%	$2,278	$1,883	$2,482	$2,615	39%	5.4%
	65	28%	$2,625	$2,440	$3,130	$3,388	39%	8.3%
	70	28%	$3,026	$3,160	$3,956	$4,389	39%	11.0%
	75	28%	$3,487	$3,908	$4,825	$5,686	46%	17.9%
	80	28%	$4,019	$4,720	$5,777	$7,367	**56%**	**27.5%**
	85	28%	$4,632	$5,621	$6,839	$9,543	70%	39.5%
	90	28%	$5,338	$6,573	$7,977	$12,363	88%	55.0%
Withdrawal Period 1 Year	60	30%	$12,659	$9,666	$12,995	$13,809	43%	6.3%
	65	31%	$23,182	$18,726	$24,822	$27,138	45%	9.3%
	70	31%	$26,717	$24,259	$31,284	$35,157	45%	12.4%
	75	31%	$30,791	$31,100	$39,197	$45,546	46%	16.2%
	80	31%	$35,487	$38,844	$48,175	$59,003	52%	22.5%
	85	32%	$40,899	$46,536	$57,290	$76,438	64%	33.4%
	90	34%	$47,135	$53,206	$65,601	$99,024	**86%**	**50.9%**

SENSITIVITY TO VARIABLES

Withdrawal Period 20 Years								
Reference	72	28%	$1,827	$2,150	$2,631	$3,051	42%	16.0%
Ret Tax	72	23%	$1,827	$2,300	$2,780	$3,051	33%	9.7%
Ret Tax	72	33%	$1,827	$2,001	$2,481	$3,051	52%	22.9%
Inflation 2%	72	28%	$2,644	$3,078	$3,774	$4,368	42%	15.7%
Inflation 5%	72	28%	$1,260	$1,500	$1,831	$2,128	42%	16.2%
Rate of return 11%	72	28%	$2,456	$3,163	$3,801	$4,507	42%	18.6%
Rate of return 7%	72	28%	$1,348	$1,441	$1,800	$2,035	41%	13.1%
Rate of Return 4%	72	28%	$840	$767	$996	$1,076	40%	8.1%

Average Benefit of ROTH IRA **42%** **15%**

4.2.6 Example 55C

This age-55 couple has $2,000,000 in investable assets and $2,000,000 in existing IRA assets. Since they have significant investable accounts, withdrawals from the tax-advantaged accounts are not needed during their lifetime. Their investable accounts will last 31 years, after which withdrawals from the tax-advantaged accounts will be required. We assume that the couple's beneficiaries will be using these funds. From Table 4.1 we see that that the recurring income for this couple was $44,200, and their total retirement need was $134,250. They plan on saving $6,000 per year.

The top part of the adjacent table lists the basic assumptions made for this profile. The middle Reference part of the table shows how various accounts would do if $2,000 were invested annually in them. The results are shown for a taxable account [A] ; the Traditional IRA tax-deductible account assuming the tax deduction received in the year of investment is used up (**not reinvested**) [B]; the Traditional tax-deductible IRA assuming the tax-deduction in the year of the investment **is reinvested** [B1], and the Roth IRA [C]. The account values are shown for withdrawals over 20, 10, and one year periods. Note that the average tax rate will increase as the withdrawal period decreases. These tax rates were derived from Table 3.4. From the Reference section the following general observations can be made:

- The Roth IRA does better than the Traditional IRA, with or without reinvestment of the tax deduction received in the investment year.
- The Traditional IRA, even without reinvestment, does better than a taxable account.
- The later you start the withdrawals, the greater the advantage of the Roth IRA. If you withdraw the full amount in one year at age 90 the benefit is 66%.

The effect of retirement tax rate, inflation rate, and rate of return for Example 55C are shown at the bottom of the table. We see that:

- If retirement tax rates drop, the Traditional IRA result improves, while the Roth IRA result is unchanged. This is expected since no taxes are paid on the Roth IRA. Thus, in the case of the Roth IRA, it does not matter what the tax rates do during retirement.
- Inflation affects both the Traditional and the Roth IRA.
- Rate of return affects both the Traditional and the Roth IRA accounts. The Roth account does better with a higher rate of return, since you get more tax free growth.

Referring to the Reference line (the first line under "Sensitivity to Variables"), we see that:
$2,000 in a Roth IRA provides an annuity of $4,989 per year for 20 years (in today's dollars after taxes)

Annual annuity from $4,000 in Roth account	$9,978
Annuity from $2,000 invested in a taxable fund.	$2,029
Total annuity starting at beneficiaries' age 67	$12,007
Balance needed during their lifetime	none

We see that, for Example 55C, the Roth IRA is 151% better than the Traditional IRA with no reinvestments, and approximately 90% better than a Traditional IRA with reinvestment of the up-front tax-deduction. Investing in the Roth contribution IRA is definitely recommended.

CONTRIBUTION S

EXAMPLE 55C

ASSUMPTIONS

Age	55	Inflation	3.50%
Spouse's Age	55	Pre-Retirement Tax Rate	32%
Beneficiary's Age	25	Retirement tax rate	32%
Check Out Age	90	Other assets tax rate	28%
Annual Contribution	$2,000	Rate of Return	9%
Save $2,000 per year till age	65	Withdrawal Method	Joint Term Certain

REFERENCE TABLE

	WITHDRAWALS		INDEXED ANNUITY PER YEAR				ROTH ADVANTAGE	
			A	B	B1	C		
	Start Withdr'l At Age	Withdr'l Tax Rate	Taxable Assets Tax 28%	Trad'l IRA without Re-Invest	Trad'l IRA with Re-Invest Tax Savings	ROTH IRA Tax Savings	ROTH% Adv Over B	ROTH% Adv Over B1
Withdrawal Period 20 Years	65	32%	$818	$735	$980	$1,080	47%	10.2%
	70	32%	$943	$952	$1,235	$1,400	**47%**	**13.3%**
	75	32%	$1,086	$1,133	$1,459	$1,813	60%	24.2%
	80	32%	$1,252	$1,327	$1,703	$2,349	77%	37.9%
	85	32%	$1,443	$1,552	$1,986	$3,043	96%	53.2%
	90	32%	$1,663	$1,802	$2,302	$3,942	119%	71.3%
Withdrawal Period 10 Years	65	32%	$1,434	$1,172	$1,603	$1,724	47%	7.5%
	70	32%	$1,652	$1,519	$2,015	$2,234	47%	10.8%
	75	32%	$1,904	$1,878	$2,450	$2,893	54%	18.1%
	80	32%	$2,195	$2,268	$2,928	$3,748	**65%**	**28.0%**
	85	32%	$2,529	$2,701	$3,461	$4,856	80%	40.3%
	90	32%	$2,915	$3,159	$4,035	$6,291	99%	55.9%
Withdrawal Period 1 Year	65	40%	$12,659	$8,285	$12,090	$13,809	67%	14.2%
	70	42%	$14,590	$10,376	$14,760	$17,889	72%	21.2%
	75	42%	$16,815	$13,302	$18,355	$23,175	74%	26.3%
	80	43%	$19,379	$16,328	$22,152	$30,023	84%	35.5%
	85	43%	$22,334	$19,849	$26,561	$38,894	96%	46.4%
	90	45%	$25,740	$22,561	$30,296	$50,387	**123%**	**66.3%**

SENSITIVITY TO VARIABLES

Withdrawal Period 20 Years								
Reference	97	40%	$2,029	$1,940	$2,549	$4,989	157%	95.7%
Ret Tax	97	35%	$2,029	$2,101	$2,711	$4,989	137%	84.0%
Ret Tax	97	45%	$2,029	$1,778	$2,388	$4,989	181%	108.9%
Inflation 2%	97	40%	$3,931	$3,759	$4,941	$9,591	155%	94.1%
Inflation 5%	97	40%	$1,050	$1,004	$1,319	$2,604	159%	97.4%
Rate of return 11%	97	40%	$3,665	$3,878	$4,965	$10,744	177%	116.4%
Rate of return 7%	97	40%	$1,107	$956	$1,294	$2,267	137%	75.3%
Rate of Return 4%	97	40%	$435	$322	$457	$665	107%	45.5%
Average Benefit of ROTH IRA							**151%**	**90%**

4.2.7 Example 60A

This near-retirement couple has $100,000 in other investable assets and $225,000 in existing IRA assets. From Table 4.1 we see that the recurring income for this couple was $33,000, and their total retirement need was $71,000. They will need to start withdrawing from their tax-advantaged accounts starting at age 70. They plan on saving $10,000 per year till age 65.

The top part of the adjacent table lists the basic assumptions made for this profile. The middle Reference part of the table shows how various accounts would do if $2,000 were invested annually in them. The results are shown for a taxable account [A] ; the Traditional IRA tax-deductible account assuming the tax deduction received in the year of investment is used up (**not reinvested**) [B]; the Traditional tax-deductible IRA assuming the tax-deduction in the year of the investment **is reinvested** [B1], and the Roth IRA [C]. The account values are shown for withdrawals over 20, 10, and one year periods. Note that the average tax rate will increase as the withdrawal period decreases. These tax rates were derived from Table 3.4. From the Reference section the following general observations can be made:

• The Roth IRA does better than the Traditional IRA.
• The Traditional IRA, even without reinvestment, does better than a taxable account.
• The later you start the withdrawals, the greater the advantage of the Roth IRA. If you withdraw the full amount in one year at age 90 the benefit is 36%.

The effect of retirement tax rate, inflation rate, and rate of return for Example 60A are shown at the bottom of the table. We see that:

• If retirement tax rates drop, the Traditional IRA result improves, while the Roth IRA result is unchanged. This is expected since no taxes are paid on the Roth IRA. Thus, in the case of the Roth IRA, it does not matter what the tax rates do during retirement.
• Inflation affects both the Traditional and the Roth IRA.
• Rate of return affects both the Traditional and the Roth IRA accounts. The Roth account does better with a higher rate of return, since you get more tax free growth.

Referring to the Reference line (the first line under "Sensitivity to Variables"), we see that:
$2,000 in a Roth IRA invested until age 65 provides an annuity of $1,400 per year (in today's dollars after taxes) for 20 years.

Annual annuity from $4,000 in Roth account	
The annual annuity from $4,000 in Roth accounts	$2,800
Annuity from $6,000 in a taxable account	$2,955
Total annuity starting at beneficiaries' age 51 is	$5,755
Balance needed during their lifetime (rounded):	$32,245

Later in this chapter we will discuss the benefits from their 401(k)-type or existing IRA, which may be converted to a Roth IRA. We see that, for Example 60A, the Roth IRA is approximately 33% better than the Traditional IRA with no reinvestments, and approximately 8% better than a Traditional IRA with reinvestment of the up-front tax-deduction. Investing in the Roth contribution IRA is definitely recommended. Annual contributions will provide 8% of retirement needs.

CONTRIBUTIONS

EXAMPLE 60A

ASSUMPTIONS

Age	60	Inflation	3.50%
Spouse's Age	60	Pre-Retirement Tax Rate	26%
Beneficiary's Age	30	Retirement tax rate	25%
Check Out Age	90	Other assets tax rate	25%
Annual Contribution	$2,000	Rate of Return	9%
Save $2,000 per year till age	65	Withdrawal Method	Joint Term Certain

REFERENCE TABLE

	WITHDRAWALS		INDEXED ANNUITY PER YEAR				ROTH ADVANTAGE	
			A	B	B1	C		
	Start	Withdr'l	Taxable	Trad'l IRA	Trad'l IRA	ROTH	ROTH%	ROTH%
	Withdr'l	Tax	Assets	without	with	IRA	Adv	Adv
	At Age	Rate	Tax 28%	Re-Invest	Re-Invest		Over B	Over B1
					Tax Savings	Tax Savings		
Withdrawal Period 20 Years								
	65	26%	$844	$799	$1,005	$1,080	35%	7.5%
	70	26%	$985	$1,036	$1,275	$1,400	**35%**	**9.7%**
	75	26%	$1,149	$1,244	$1,524	$1,813	46%	19.0%
	80	26%	$1,341	$1,473	$1,800	$2,349	59%	30.5%
	85	26%	$1,566	$1,743	$2,124	$3,043	75%	43.2%
	90	26%	$1,827	$2,047	$2,492	$3,942	93%	58.2%
Withdrawal Period 10 Years								
	65	26%	$1,463	$1,276	$1,632	$1,724	35%	5.6%
	70	26%	$1,707	$1,653	$2,069	$2,234	35%	8.0%
	75	26%	$1,993	$2,054	$2,539	$2,893	41%	13.9%
	80	26%	$2,326	$2,499	$3,066	$3,748	**50%**	**22.3%**
	85	26%	$2,715	$3,003	$3,664	$4,856	62%	32.5%
	90	26%	$3,169	$3,550	$4,322	$6,291	77%	45.6%
Withdrawal Period 1 Year								
	65	27%	$12,778	$10,081	$13,193	$13,809	37%	4.7%
	70	27%	$14,914	$13,059	$16,692	$17,889	37%	7.2%
	75	27%	$17,408	$16,761	$21,000	$23,175	38%	10.4%
	80	27%	$20,318	$21,013	$25,962	$30,023	43%	15.6%
	85	28%	$23,715	$25,359	$31,135	$38,894	53%	24.9%
	90	28%	$27,679	$30,173	$36,915	$50,387	**67%**	**36.5%**

SENSITIVITY TO VARIABLES

Withdrawal Period 20 Years								
Reference	81	25%	$985	$1,050	$1,289	$1,400	33%	8.5%
Ret Tax 20%	81	20%	$985	$1,120	$1,359	$1,400	25%	3.0%
Ret Tax 30%	81	30%	$985	$980	$1,220	$1,400	43%	14.8%
Inflation 2%	81	25%	$1,285	$1,357	$1,670	$1,809	33%	8.3%
Inflation 5%	81	25%	$752	$810	$993	$1,080	33%	8.7%
Rate of return 11%	81	25%	$1,248	$1,412	$1,711	$1,882	33%	10.0%
Rate of return 7%	81	25%	$770	$769	$959	$1,025	33%	6.9%
Rate of Return 4%	81	25%	$523	$467	$599	$623	33%	4.0%
Average Benefit of ROTH IRA							**33%**	**8%**

4.3 Conclusions on Roth Contributions from Profile Analyses

This section summarizes the main conclusions that can be drawn from the contribution case studies. The following conclusions were seen to hold for the full range of financial profiles studied in Section 4.2 (see Table 4.1).

1. The Roth IRA will do significantly better than a Traditional IRA if the tax deduction from the Traditional IRA is not reinvested. In fact, most people do not reinvest this deduction, but rather use it for other expenses in the year of investment. The average advantage of the Roth IRA over all the variations considered was approximately 45%. This advantage in future benefits from the Roth IRA will need to be weighed against the loss of the current year tax deduction that the Traditional IRA provides.

2. The Roth will usually do better than the Traditional IRA if the Traditional IRA deduction is reinvested in another taxable account. In the examples, the average advantage of the Roth IRA in this case was 20%.

3. The value of the Roth IRA is independent of tax rates during retirement, because no taxes are being paid.

4. The value of a Traditional IRA increases as the retirement tax rates drop, and the value declines as the tax rates go up.

5. Inflation rate affects the Roth IRA and the Traditional IRA almost equally.

6. Higher rates of return increase the benefit of the Roth IRA.

7. If one assumes conservative rates of return, lower than 4% for example, the benefit of the Roth is greatly minimized.

8. The longer you wait to withdraw from the account, the greater the benefit of the Roth IRA. The amount of time one can wait to withdraw these funds depends on how much one has in investable accounts (see Table 4.2).

9. The Roth IRA asset should be the last one to draw retirement needs from. This will maximize the benefit of the Roth IRA and will provide the maximum retirement funds.

Table 4.2 Summary of Roth Contribution Profiles

REFERENCE TABLES									
Age **Advantage of Roth IRA** over Trad'l with no reinvest of tax savings	25A	35A	45A	55A	55B	55SNGL	55C	60A	Averages
withdrawal age 60 over 20 years	20%	20%	33%	27%	35%	39%			29%
withdrawal age 65 over 20 years	20%	20%	33%	27%	35%	39%	47%		32%
withdrawal age 70 over 20 years	20%	20%	33%	27%	35%	39%	47%	35%	32%
withdrawal age 80 over 10 years	29%	29%	48%	38%	60%	58%	65%	50%	46%
withdrawal age 90 over 1 years	72%	64%	79%	62%	72%	86%	123%	67%	78%

Table 4.2a

Advantage of Roth IRA
over Trad'l with reinvest of tax savings

	25A	35A	45A	55A	55B	55SNGL	55C	60A	
withdrawal age 70 over 20 years	9%	8%	13%	8%	11%	13%	13%	10%	11%
withdrawal age 80 over 10 years	17%	16%	26%	18%	24%	27%	28%	22%	22%
withdrawal age 90 over 1 years	53%	45%	51%	37%	41%	51%	66%	36%	48%

Advantage of Roth IRA
over taxable account

withdrawal age 70 over 20 years	85%	64%	75%	42%	51%	59%	48%	42%	58%
withdrawal age 80 over 10 years	102%	78%	98%	57%	72%	83%	71%	61%	78%
withdrawal age 90 over 1 years	119%	94%	124%	74%	94%	110%	96%	82%	99%

EXAMPLE PROFILES

Age for starting tax-advantaged withdrawals	65	65	70	70	74	72	97	70	
Advantage of Roth Contribution over									
Trad'l IRA reinvest savings	21%	21%	30%	22%	41%	42%	151%	33%	45%
Trad'l IRA no-reinvest savings	8%	8%	10%	4%	16%	15%	90%	8%	20%
Taxable	72%	52%	75%	42%	65%	67%	146%	42%	70%

The above overview compares the Traditional IRA with the Roth IRA. In the next sections we will show how the Roth IRA compares with some other investment possibilities: a non-deductible IRA, 401(k) / 403(b) accounts with employer matching funds, and taxable accounts with capital gains taxes that range from 15% to 28%.

4.4 Non-deductible IRAs and Capital Gains Taxable Accounts

In this section we will compare contributions to the Roth IRA with a non-deductible Traditional IRA's and to accounts taxed at capital gains tax rates.

Clients may contribute up to a maximum of $2,000 per year to a non-deductible IRA. This IRA does not allow a tax deduction in the year of investment; however, the annual growth on this account is not taxed. The taxes on the growth are paid at the time of withdrawal. There is no maximum AGI (adjusted gross income) restriction with this

Table 4.3

Maximum Capital Gains Tax Rates (1998)

Assets Held	Capital Gains Tax Rates
12 months or less	39.60%*
More than 12 months	20%
More than 5 years acquired after year 2000	18%

* (or marginal tax rate)

IRA. Thus people who exceed the AGI limits of the Roth and Traditional IRA may want to consider the non-deductible IRA.

There are two general classes of taxable accounts. In one class the ordinary income tax rates are applicable: examples are cash checking, savings and money market accounts. The second class of taxable account is subject to capital gains tax: examples include individual stocks, stock mutual funds, and bond funds. The capital gains tax rate depends on how long the assets are held. The rates are detailed in Table 4.3. This is the type of account that you will need to use after you are fully invested in the tax-advantaged accounts.

The following financial profile will be used to illustrate the relative value of the accounts:

Example G

Client age	45
Spouse age	45
Beneficiary's age	15
Annual investment per year	$2,000
Investment stops at age	65
Rate of return	9%
Life expectancy	90
Withdrawal algorithm	Joint Term Certain
Pre-retirement tax rate	25%
Post-retirement tax rate	23%
Capital Gains Tax Rates	18%, 20%, 28%
Annual realized gain	100%

The results are shown in Table 4.4. The amounts shown for ages 45 through 80 are in future dollars. The row labeled NPV (net present value) translates the future values at age 80 to today's dollars, assuming an inflation rate of 3.5%. For instance, with the Roth IRA the asset value at age 80, expressed in today's dollars, is $135,213. The very last row shows the percentage differences, using the 28% capital gains (last column) as a reference. The following conclusions may be drawn from this example:

Table 4.4 Example G: Comparison of Roth with Non-Deductible IRA and capital gainsbased investments

Client age	45		Annual Contribution			$2,000
Spouse age	45		Rate of return			9%
Retirement Age	65		Pre-retirement tax rate			25%
Beneficiary age	15		Retirement tax rate			23%
Life Exp	90		Withdrawal		Joint Term Certain	
Contribute till age	65					

Age	ROTH IRA	IRA with Reinvest	IRA without Reinvest	Non-ded IRA	TXBL ORD TAX	TXBL RATE 18%	TXBL RATE 20%	TXBL RATE 28%
45	$2,180	$2,135	$1,635	$2,135	$2,135	$2,148	$2,144	$2,130
46	$4,556	$4,451	$3,417	$4,417	$4,414	$4,454	$4,442	$4,397
47	$7,146	$6,963	$5,360	$6,860	$6,847	$6,930	$6,906	$6,812
48	$9,969	$9,689	$7,477	$9,477	$9,444	$9,589	$9,547	$9,383
49	$13,047	$12,646	$9,785	$12,285	$12,217	$12,444	$12,379	$12,120
50	$16,401	$15,855	$12,301	$15,301	$15,176	$15,510	$15,414	$15,035
51	$20,057	$19,337	$15,043	$18,543	$18,336	$18,803	$18,668	$18,139
52	$24,042	$23,115	$18,032	$22,032	$21,708	$22,338	$22,156	$21,444
53	$28,386	$27,217	$21,289	$25,789	$25,309	$26,134	$25,895	$24,963
54	$33,121	$31,668	$24,840	$29,840	$29,152	$30,210	$29,904	$28,711
55	$38,281	$36,499	$28,711	$34,211	$33,255	$34,587	$34,201	$32,701
56	$43,907	$41,744	$32,930	$38,930	$37,635	$39,287	$38,807	$36,949
57	$50,038	$47,437	$37,529	$44,029	$42,310	$44,334	$43,745	$41,473
58	$56,722	$53,619	$42,541	$49,541	$47,301	$49,754	$49,039	$46,290
59	$64,007	$60,330	$48,005	$55,505	$52,629	$55,573	$54,714	$51,420
60	$71,947	$67,618	$53,961	$61,961	$58,316	$61,822	$60,797	$56,881
61	$80,603	$75,531	$60,452	$68,952	$64,387	$68,532	$67,319	$62,697
62	$90,037	$84,125	$67,528	$76,528	$70,869	$75,738	$74,310	$68,889
63	$100,320	$93,457	$75,240	$84,740	$77,787	$83,475	$81,804	$75,483
64	$111,529	$103,594	$83,647	$93,647	$85,173	$91,783	$89,838	$82,503
65	$123,747	$117,074	$95,285	$103,310	$93,214	$100,704	$98,450	$89,979
66	$134,884	$127,160	$103,861	$113,521	$99,674	$110,283	$107,683	$97,939
67	$147,023	$138,122	$113,208	$122,868	$106,581	$118,422	$115,436	$104,286
68	$160,256	$150,037	$123,397	$133,057	$113,967	$127,162	$123,747	$111,044
69	$174,679	$162,989	$134,502	$144,162	$121,865	$136,546	$132,657	$118,239
70	$190,400	$177,068	$146,608	$157,010	$130,310	$146,624	$142,208	$125,901
71	$207,536	$199,984	$167,412	$170,857	$139,341	$157,444	$152,447	$134,060
72	$226,214	$218,111	$183,283	$185,789	$148,997	$169,064	$163,423	$142,747
73	$246,573	$237,352	$200,110	$201,879	$159,322	$181,541	$175,190	$151,997
74	$268,765	$258,101	$218,277	$219,203	$170,363	$194,938	$187,804	$161,846
75	$292,953	$280,478	$237,895	$237,840	$182,170	$209,325	$201,325	$172,334
76	$319,319	$304,598	$259,064	$257,875	$194,794	$224,773	$215,821	$183,501
77	$348,058	$330,580	$281,891	$279,392	$208,293	$241,361	$231,360	$195,392
78	$379,383	$358,549	$306,485	$302,485	$222,728	$259,174	$248,018	$208,053
79	$413,528	$388,636	$332,965	$327,249	$238,163	$278,301	$265,875	$221,535
80	$450,745	$420,982	$361,452	$353,782	$254,668	$298,839	$285,018	$235,890

NPV @ Age 80								
	$135,213	$126,285	$108,427	$106,126	$76,394	$89,645	$85,499	$70,762
% difference	91%	78%	53%	50%	8%	27%	21%	0%

- A taxable asset that is held for more than five years and cashed after year 2005 will be subject to a capital gains tax rate as low as 18%. This will yield a NPV that is 27% greater than the reference.
- Taxable assets subject to capital gains tax will approach the yield of a non-deductible IRA asset, as the amount of gain realized annually decrease[2].
- All of the tax-deferred investments do better than any taxable asset.
- The non-deductible Traditional IRA produces almost the same yield as the deductible IRA, assuming no reinvestment of deductible funds. It is preferred over any taxable asset, even with capital gains tax rates as low as 18%.
- The Roth IRA provides the highest return.

It is clear that tax-advantaged assets should be the first choice. However, there is a maximum amount that can be invested in tax-deferred assets, depending on your income. Further investments will then need to be invested in taxable assets.

4.5 Employee-Sponsored Defined-Contribution Plans 401(k), 403(b)

This section will compare investments in a Roth IRA with those in an employer-sponsored defined-contribution plan with matching funds. Examples of such plans are the 401(k) and the 403(b). These plans are tax deferred, and therefore provide tax savings in the year of investment. The maximum that can be invested in 401(k), 403(b) and Simple IRA plans in total in 1998 is $10,000. Many employers will match a part of the employer's contribution, which means that for every dollar the employee invests, the employer will invest a certain percentage. We will compare such a plan with the Roth IRA in this section.

Like a deductible Traditional IRA, the defined-contribution plan is a tax-deferred plan. With both types of investment, taxes are paid upon withdrawal, the funds will need to be withdrawn after age 701/2, and the same minimum distributions will apply. Thus we can use the tables generated in Section 4.2 to derive the benefit of such plans. This suggests a simple method of comparing such matching-fund plans with the Roth IRA.

We will illustrate the method with an example, and then provide a general procedure for the comparison. In Example EX45A with, for example $2,000 annual investment, the Roth IRA was shown to provide an annuity of $6,303, while the Traditional IRA without reinvestment provided an annuity of $4,853. If there were no matching funds, we would get the same result of $4,853 with the 401(k) investment.

Now consider the case of a matching fund. If for example the employer will match the $2,000 dollar-for-dollar (a 100% match), then the employee will effectively have invested $4,000. This will grow like a Traditional tax-deferred account to 2*$4,853 = $9,706, which is considerably higher than with any other account we have looked at, including the Roth IRA.

> *An employer matching tax-deferred, with a 100% match, provides the highest yield of any investment. This is definitely the first place to place any savings.*

But what if the employer only matched 50% of your contribution. In that case, for EX45A, the annuity from the 401(k) would be 1.5*$4,853 = $7,279, which is still slightly better than a Roth IRA investment. If the match were only 25%, the 401(k) would provide 1.25*$4,853 = $6,065 and the Roth IRA would be the better choice.

Some employers will fully match the employer's contribution up to a maximum of a certain percentage of their salary, but there would be no match beyond that amount. As an example consider an employee earning $100,000 per year. The employee wants to contribute $10,000 to some tax-advantaged account in 1998. His employer will match the 401(k) contribution up to 3% of his salary, but there will be no match beyond that. Thus $3,000 will be matched with another $3,000 from the employer. What is the best investment strategy for this employee? He certainly should take full advantage and invest the first $3,000 in the 401(k). The next dollars will do better in a Roth IRA. If he is married he should invest the maximum $4,000 for a couple in the Roth IRA. The balance that he has available is $3,000: this should be invested in the 401(k).

> *Thus of the total $10,000 that he has available, $6,000 should be invested in the 401(k): the employer's match will raise that to a total of $9,000. The balance of $4,000 should be invested in the Roth IRA. This employee will then be investing 60% of his available assets in the 401(k) and 40% in the Roth IRA.*

4.6 Summary

In this chapter we showed that the average benefit of annual contributions to a Roth IRA over those to a Traditional IRA was 40% if we assumed that the Traditional IRA deductions were not invested, and the average advantage was 20% if these deductions were invested. The 401(k) 100% matching case was the best of all the investments. We also showed that in all cases, tax-advantaged accounts would do better than taxable accounts.

Chapter 5 Roth IRA Conversions

"...it seems to me that the Roth IRA is a win-win. It is good for the family, and it's good for the nation ..." Senator Roth

This chapter deals with the Roth IRA Conversion IRA. You are permitted to roll your Traditional IRA accounts into a Roth IRA, if you meet the eligibility conditions.[1] Depending on how soon you need to withdraw funds, the advantages of such a rollover can be small, large, or very large. This conversion can make a very significant difference to your retirement plans. We will address the advantages of a rollover, and demonstrate the effect of time of withdrawal, inflation, tax rates, and rate of return on the results. The financial profiles identified in Chapter 2 will be discussed in detail. For those of you who are keeping track of your own profile, we assume that you have established **when** you need to start withdrawing funds and **how much** you will need per year (following Steps 1, 2, 3, and 4 from Chapters 2 and 3). For those who have skipped these prior chapters, we will review these steps in the first section of this chapter.

The chapter will help you to assess whether you should convert, and will provide a close answer to the benefits of conversion, assuming a 100% conversion. It will not address partial conversions, which is the subject of Chapter 6 on Optimal Conversion. The sections in the chapter are:

- Introduction to Roth IRA Conversions
- Review of Retirement Planning Steps
- Case Studies for Roth IRA Conversion Analyses
- Summary of Client Examples for Conversions
- Paying Conversion Taxes from the IRA
- Borrowing money to pay for Roth IRA Conversion taxes
- Understanding why the Roth IRA provides an advantage
- Should you borrow money to pay for Roth IRA taxes
- Summary and Conclusions

---

[1] Modified Adjusted Gross income less than $100,000; if married you must file a joint return. See Chapter 7.

5.1 Introduction to Roth IRA Conversions

You may roll over a part or all of your Traditional IRA funds to a Roth IRA. This will entail paying up-front taxes, since any amount withdrawn from a Traditional IRA[2] is subject to taxes at the time of withdrawal. A special tax relief has been made available only to those who choose to convert in 1998: you may choose to spread this income over the next four years. Chapter 7 provides details for all the rules.

To be eligible for the Roth IRA Conversion, your modified adjusted gross income must be less than $100,000 in the year you choose to convert. Further discussion on the relationship between total income, modified adjusted gross income, adjusted gross income, and taxable income can be found in Chapter 3.

Once the up-front tax for conversion has been paid, the Roth IRA Conversion IRA account goes outside the domain of the Federal Tax System: no taxes on growth, no taxes on withdrawal[3]. This account will not be affected by future tax rates going up or down. Further, there is no requirement that you must withdraw any funds during your lifetime.

Conversions from other qualified tax-deferred plans, such as a 401(k), 401(b) or SIMPLE IRA[4] may not be made directly: You will first need to transfer these to a Traditional IRA, then convert the Traditional IRA to a Roth IRA.

---

[2] In this book if the Traditional IRA [without a prefix] refers to a "deductible Traditional IRA". The non-deductible Traditional IRA will always include the descriptive suffix "nondeductible".
[3] These are subject to estate taxes
[4] SEP IRAs may be converted directly

5.2 Review of Retirement Planning Steps

To put the relative advantage of the Roth IRA Conversion in perspective, we need to review the overall retirement planning picture as described in Chapter 2. The steps are reviewed here:

Step 1: Calculate your recurring income (through your lifetime) that is indexed with inflation. These include Social Security, earned income and other indexed annuities you may have.

Step 2: Calculate your recurring income that is not indexed with inflation. These include some pensions and flat annuities. Compare these two recurring incomes with your retirement needs to establish the balance needed.

Step 3: The first withdrawals are made from taxable other investible-assets. Calculate how many years that these will last. At this point you will know the amount you need to withdraw from tax-advantaged accounts and when these withdrawals need to start.

Step 4: Calculate the amount that annual contributions will provide. This topic was covered in Chapter 3.

The balance of your retirement needs will come from pre-existing retirement funds, such as IRA and 401(k)-type accounts. The results, through Step 4, for the client profiles identified in Chapter 2 are shown in Table 5.1.

All monies need to be expressed in today's dollars after taxes. The balance of your retirement needs will come from other retirement funds, such as IRA and 401(k)-type accounts. The results, through Step 4, for the profiles identified in Chapter 2, are shown in Table 5.1.

We are now ready for Step 5: determining how much you will get each year from your pre-existing IRA funds. We will provide this information for two cases: A) if you leave all monies in the Traditional IRA and B) if you convert all monies to a Roth IRA.

5.3 Case Studies for Roth IRA Conversion Analyses

The assumptions that we are using for the analyses are:

Spouses are the same age

Contingent beneficiary is 30 years younger than spouses

Spouses' life expectancy is	90 years
Rate of return	9%
Tax rates on investible accounts	28%
Start age for withdrawal of funds	60, 65, 70, 75, 80, 85, and 90
Method of withdrawal (after age 701/2) for IRAs	Joint Term Certain

Taxes for Roth IRA Conversion are paid from an **outside asset**. Since these funds are not used[5] if you do not convert, we will add these funds and their taxable growth to the Traditional IRA assets when comparing the Roth IRA with the Traditional IRA. That makes the comparison a fair one.

The next subsections will detail the Roth IRA Conversion analyses for the financial profiles introduced in Chapter 2. Profiles EX25A and EX35A (the Gen X profiles) did not have any pre-existing IRA assets: so these cases are not included in the analyses. You need only read the section that relates to your case.

---

[5] They are often referred to as opportunity lost dollars

Table 5.1 Profiles Used in Analyses

	CONTRIBUTION & CONVERSION Baby Boomer					CONVERSION ONLY			
Example Name	EX45A	EX55A	EX55B	EX55SNGL	EX55C	Near Retirement EX60A	Early Retired EX65A	Late Retired EX75A	Late Retired EX85A
Age	45	55	55	55	55	60	65	75	85
Current Income	$90,000	$100,000	$100,000	$100,000	$200,000	$100,000	$100,000	$100,000	$100,000
Desired Retirement Income After taxes	$65,040	$55,020	$70,780	$66,700	$134,250	$71,000	$71,000	$71,000	$71,000
Other Investible Assets	$75,000	$75,000	$200,000	$200,000	$2,000,000	$100,000	$500,000	$250,000	$250,000
Planned Savings per Year	$8,000	$6,000	$5,000	$10,000	$6,000	$10,000	$0	$0	$0
Traditional IRA Existing Balance	$40,000	$100,000	$120,000	$150,000	$2,000,000	$225,000	$500,000	$300,000	$300,000
STEP 1 Recurring Indexed : Soc. Sec.									
Social Security After Taxes	$18,410	$12,150	$18,050	$10,800	$16,680	$18,000	$18,000	$18,000	$18,000
STEP 2 Recurring Unindexed : Pension									
Pension Averaged After Taxes	$13,670	$16,040	$14,890	$14,260	$27,520	$15,000	$15,000	$15,000	$15,000
Total Recurring Income After Tax	$32,080	$28,190	$32,940	$25,060	$44,200	$33,000	$33,000	$33,000	$33,000
Balance req'd	$32,960	$26,830	$37,840	$41,640	$90,050	$38,000	$38,000	$38,000	$38,000
STEP 3 Investible Assets									
Age for starting withdrawals	70	70	74	72	67	70	81	83	93
Balance req'd from tax-advantaged	$32,960	$26,830	$37,340	$41,640	$90,050	$38,000	$38,000	$38,000	$38,000
Step 4 Annuity from Annual Contributions									
Total Annuity from annual savings	$19,814	$7,446	$8,822	$10,359	$12,007	$5,755	$0	$0	$0
Balance req'd from existing tax advantaged	$13,146	$19,384	$29,018	$31,281	$78,043	$32,245	$38,000	$38,000	$38,000
Step 5: Annuity from Existing IRA									
Existing Traditional IRA Assets	$40,000	$100,000	$120,000	$150,000	$2,000,000	$225,000	$500,000	$300,000	$300,000
Annuity from 100% Roth Conversion of IRA	$12,446	$18,039	$27,338	$30,845	$1,321,766	$32,201	$97,629	$38,712	$36,798
Total Income	$64,340	$54,177	$69,120	$66,264	$1,377,973	$70,956	$130,629	$71,712	$69,798
Retirement Expenses	$65,040	$55,020	$70,780	$66,700	$134,250	$71,000	$71,000	$71,000	$71,000
Excess (shortfall)	($700)	($843)	($1,660)	($436)	$1,243,723	($44)	$59,629	$712	($1,202)
Percentage Contributions from All Sources									
Indexed recurring [Social Security]	28%	22%	26%	16%	12%	25%	25%	25%	25%
Non-indexed recurring [Pension]	21%	29%	21%	21%	20%	21%	21%	21%	21%
Annual contributions	30%	14%	12%	16%	3%	8%	0%	0%	0%
Roth Conversion	19%	34%	39%	46%	98.3%	45%	138%	55%	52%
Total	99%	98%	98%	99%	102.6%	100%	184%	101%	98%
TAX RATES									
Current Avg. ax rates	25%	21%	26%	30%	32%	26%	26%	26%	26%
Retirement Avg. Tax rate	23%	19%	25%	28%	31%	25%	25%	25%	25%
Conversion tax rate	26%	25%	30%	32%	42%	28%	33%	30%	30%
Conversion tax	$10,400	$25,000	$36,000	$48,000	$840,000	$63,000	$165,000	$90,000	$90,000

5.3.1 Example 45A

This age-45 couple has $40,000 in IRA assets that can be converted to a Roth IRA. From Table 5.1 we see that the couple's recurring income, per year in today's dollars, was $32,080 and their total after tax retirement need was $65,040. Thus, they needed a balance of $32,960 of which $19,538 would be provided from a planned savings of $8,000 per year. The remaining balance of $13,146 would need to be provided from their existing IRA assets, which currently amount to $40,000. Step 5 of the retirement analysis compares the indexed annuity amounts that would be produced by two types of accounts: an existing IRA converted to a Roth IRA and an existing IRA not converted.

The top part of the adjacent table lists the assumptions. The middle part is a general reference for this set of assumptions, **based on a reference $10,000** IRA asset conversion. We use $10,000 only as a reference: actual asset values can be derived from this reference table. We show the value of this asset if it stays in the Traditional IRA, which can be compared with the value if it is converted to a Roth IRA in 1998. The conversion tax of $10,400 (26% of $40,000) required for the Roth IRA is paid from an additional asset that the client is assumed to have. In the Traditional IRA case this $10,400 is assumed to grow in a taxable account. The indexed annuity (a payout that keeps up with 3.5% inflation) for withdrawals starting at different ages is shown. We also show the value of this indexed annuity for different withdrawal intervals. Note that the retirement tax rate will be higher for the shorter withdrawal periods. These average tax rates were taken from the tax tables in Chapter 3, which gives the Federal Tax plus average State Tax for all states in the U.S., for a given income, assuming standard deductions and two exemptions. Note that all monies are expressed in today's dollars, and that these are after-tax dollars (what the couple receives after paying taxes). General observations that can be made from the table are:

- The Roth IRA Conversion always provides an advantage, over the full range of scenarios considered.
- The conversion advantage increases the longer one can wait to make withdrawals from these assets. If the couple had sufficient investible-assets to last their lifetime, the Roth IRA conversion would provide a 59.9% advantage (check age 90, one year annuity in the reference section of the table).
- If the client needs to make withdrawals for these funds before age 70, the benefit is relatively small: around 10%.
- The Traditional IRA's proceeds are dependent on the post-retirement tax rate.
- The Roth IRA asset is not affected by retirement tax rates. So the Roth IRA will provide a hedge against rising tax rates.
- The relative advantage does not change if inflation goes up or down (both the Roth IRA and the Traditional IRA are affected equally).
- The Roth IRA advantage will increase with more aggressive portfolios that provide a higher rate of return. However, the risk of a more aggressive portfolio needs to be taken into consideration.

The specific results for the profile for Example 45A are shown at the bottom of the table. Roth IRA conversion provides $12,446 per year, which is 13% more than the Traditional IRA would provide.

This couple's retirement assets are as follows: recurring income (Social Security, pension) is $32,080[49% of needs]; annual savings of $8,000 per year provides $19,814 per year [30% of needs]; and the Roth IRA Conversion of $40,000 provides $12,446 per year [19% of needs], for a total of $65,064 per year. This is close to their total needs.

CONVERSIONS

EXAMPLE 45A

Assumptions

Age	45	Inflation	3.50%
Spouse's Age	45	Tax in Conversion Years	26%
Beneficiary's Age	15	Pre-Retirement Tax Rate	25%
Check Out Age	90	Retirement tax rate	23%
Conversion Amount	$10,000	Other assets tax rate	25%
Withdrawal Method	Joint Term Certain	Rate of Return	9%

Reference Table

	Start Withd'rl At Age	Withd'rl Tax Trate	Trad'l IRA	ROTH IRA	ROTH Advantage
Withdrawal Period 20 years	60	23%	$1,676	$1,854	10.6%
	65	23%	$2,139	$2,402	12.3%
	70	23%	$2,734	$3,112	**13.8%**
	75	23%	$3,273	$4,031	23.2%
	80	23%	$3,869	$5,222	35.0%
	85	23%	$4,569	$6,765	48.1%
	90	23%	$5,363	$8,764	63.4%
Withdrawal Period 10 years	60	23%	$2,709	$2,959	9.2%
	65	23%	$3,454	$3,833	11.0%
	70	23%	$4,410	$4,966	12.6%
	75	23%	$5,436	$6,433	18.3%
	80	23%	$6,581	$8,334	**26.6%**
	85	23%	$7,879	$10,796	37.0%
	90	23%	$9,300	$13,986	50.4%
Withdrawal Period 1 year	60	30%	$20,443	$23,098	16.0%
	65	30%	$25,844	$30,701	18.8%
	70	31%	$32,509	$39,772	22.3%
	75	33%	$40,265	$51,524	28.0%
	80	33%	$49,852	$66,749	33.9%
	85	33%	$60,390	$86,471	43.2%
	90	35%	$70,073	$112,022	**59.9%**

SENSITIVITY TO VARIABLES

EXAMPLE 45A		Conversion	$40,000	Taxes	$10,400
Reference	70	23%	$10,936	$12,446	13.8%
Ret Tax 18%	70	18%	$11,558	$12,446	7.7%
Ret Tax 28%	70	28%	$10,313	$12,446	20.7%
Inflation 2%	70	23%	$17,617	$20,027	13.7%
Inflation 5%	70	23%	$6,790	$7,737	14.0%
Rate of return 11%	70	23%	$19,739	$22,897	16.0%
Rate of return 7%	70	23%	$5,952	$6,618	11.2%
Rate of Return 4%	70	23%	$2,312	$2,455	6.2%
Average Benefit of ROTH IRA					**13.0%**

5.3.2 Example 55A

This age-55 couple has $100,000 in existing IRA assets that can be converted to a Roth IRA. They have an additional $100,000 investable assets which will last till age 69. From Table 5.1 we see that the couple's recurring income, per year in today's dollars, was $28,190 and their total after-tax retirement need was $55,020. Thus, they needed a balance of $26,830 per year of which $7,446 would be provided from planned savings of $6,000 per year. The remaining balance of $19,384 would need to be provided from existing IRA assets, which amount to $100,000. Step 5 of the retirement analysis compares the indexed annuity amounts that would be produced by two types of account: an existing IRA converted to a Roth IRA and an existing IRA not converted.

The top part of the adjacent table lists the assumptions. The middle part is a general reference for this set of assumptions, based on a reference $10,000 IRA asset conversion. We show the value of this asset if it stays in the Traditional IRA, which can be compared with the value if it is converted to a Roth IRA in 1998. The conversion tax of $25,000(25% of $100,000) required for the Roth IRA comes from an additional asset that the client is assumed to have. In the Traditional IRA case this $25,000 is assumed to grow in a taxable account. The indexed annuity (a payout that keeps up with 3.5% inflation) for withdrawals starting at different ages is shown. We also show the value of this indexed annuity for different withdrawal intervals. Note that the retirement tax rate will be higher for the shorter withdrawal periods. These average tax rates were taken from the tax tables in Chapter 3, which gives the Federal Tax plus average State Tax for all states in the U.S., for a given income, assuming standard deductions and two exemptions. Note that all dollars are expressed in today's dollars, and that these are after-tax dollars (what the couple receives after paying taxes). General observations that can be made from the table are:

- The Roth IRA Conversion provides only a small benefit (2.4%) if the client needs to draw funds from this asset as early as age 60. It is never worse than the Traditional IRA.
- If the Roth IRA assets were not needed during their lifetime, the estate (at age 90) would be 61% greater with a Roth IRA Conversion [assuming a one-year lump sum withdrawal].
- The Traditional IRA is dependent on the post-retirement tax rate.
- The Roth IRA asset is not affected by retirement tax rates. So the Roth IRA will provide a hedge against rising tax rates.
- The relative advantage does not change if inflation goes up or down (both the Roth IRA and the Traditional IRA are affected equally).
- The Roth IRA advantage will increase with more aggressive portfolios that provide a higher rate of return. However, the risk of a more aggressive portfolio needs to be taken into consideration.

The specific results for the profile for Example 55A are shown at the bottom of the table. Roth IRA conversion provides $18,039 per year, which is 5% more than the Traditional IRA would provide. If the couple has more investible assets than assumed for Example 55A, the conversion will provide an increasing advantage.

This couple's retirement assets, are as follows: recurring income (Social Security, pension) is $28,190 [51% of needs]; annual savings of $6,000 per year provides $7,446 per year [14%]; and the Roth IRA Conversion of $100,000 provides $18,039 per year [34%], for a total of $54,177 per year. This is close to their needs.

CONVERSIONS

EXAMPLE 55A

Assumptions

Age	55	Inflation	3.50%
Spouse's Age	55	Tax in Conversion Years	25%
Beneficiary's Age	25	Pre-Retirement Tax Rate	21%
Check Out Age	90	Retirement tax rate	19%
Conversion Amount	$10,000	Other assets tax rate	21%
Withdrawal Method	Joint Term Certain	Rate of Return	9%

Reference Table

	Start Withd'rl At Age	Withd'rl Tax Trate	Trad'l IRA	ROTH IRA	ROTH Advantage
Withdrawal Period 20 years	60	19%	$1,079	$1,105	2.4%
	65	19%	$1,378	$1,431	3.8%
	70	19%	$1,762	$1,854	**5.2%**
	75	19%	$2,134	$2,402	12.5%
	80	19%	$2,558	$3,112	21.7%
	85	19%	$3,062	$4,031	31.6%
	90	19%	$3,648	$5,222	43.2%
Withdrawal Period 10 years	60	19%	$1,743	$1,763	1.1%
	65	19%	$2,224	$2,284	2.7%
	70	19%	$2,841	$2,959	4.1%
	75	19%	$3,525	$3,833	8.7%
	80	19%	$4,308	$4,966	**15.3%**
	85	19%	$5,216	$6,433	23.3%
	90	19%	$6,242	$8,334	33.5%
Withdrawal Period 1 year	60	33%	$12,070	$14,121	16.9%
	65	33%	$15,357	$18,293	19.1%
	70	35%	$19,143	$23,698	23.8%
	75	36%	$23,776	$30,701	29.1%
	80	37%	$29,425	$39,772	35.2%
	85	39%	$35,230	$51,524	46.2%
	90	40%	$41,559	$66,749	**60.6%**

SENSITIVITY TO VARIABLES

EXAMPLE 55A		Conversion	$100,000	Taxes	$25,000
Reference	70	19%	$17,130	$18,039	5.3%
Ret Tax	70	15%	$17,782	$18,039	1.4%
Ret Tax	70	23%	$16,339	$18,039	10.4%
Inflation 2%	70	19%	$23,957	$25,196	5.2%
Inflation 5%	70	19%	$12,219	$12,884	5.4%
Rate of return 11%	70	19%	$26,023	$27,822	6.9%
Rate of return 7%	70	19%	$11,084	$11,468	3.5%
Rate of Return 4%	70	19%	$5,578	$5,584	0.1%
Average Benefit of ROTH IRA					**5.0%**

5.3.3 Example 55B

This age-55 couple has $120,000 in existing IRA assets that can be converted to a Roth IRA. Their investable assets of $200,000 last them until age 73. From Table 5.1 we see that the couple's recurring income, per year in today's dollars, was $32,940, and their total after-tax retirement need was $70,780. Thus, they needed a balance of $37,840 per year of which $8,822 would be provided from planned savings of $6,000 per year ($4,000 in a Roth IRA contribution and $2,000 in a taxable account). The remaining balance of $29,018 would need to be provided from their existing IRA assets. Step 5 of the retirement analysis compares the indexed annuity amounts that would be produced by two types of account: an existing IRA converted to a Roth IRA and an existing IRA not converted.

The top part of the adjacent table lists the assumptions. The middle part is a general reference for this set of assumptions, based on a $10,000 IRA asset conversion. We show the value of this asset if it stays in the Traditional IRA, which can be compared with the value if it is converted to a Roth IRA in 1998. The conversion tax of $36,000 (30% of $120,000) required for the Roth IRA is paid from an additional asset that the client is assumed to have. In the Traditional IRA case this $36,000 is assumed to grow in a taxable account. The indexed annuity (a payout that keeps up with 3.5% inflation) for withdrawals starting at different ages is shown. We also show the value of this indexed annuity for different withdrawal intervals. Note that the retirement tax rate will be higher for the shorter withdrawal periods. These average tax rates were taken from tax tables in Chapter 3, which gives the Federal Tax plus average State Tax for all states in the U.S., for a given income, assuming standard deductions and two exemptions. Note that all dollars are expressed in today's dollars, and that these are after-tax dollars (what the couple receives after paying taxes). General observations that can be made from the table are:

- The Roth IRA Conversion provides a definite benefit over all scenarios considered.
- If the Roth IRA assets were not needed during the couple's lifetime, their estate (at age 90) would be 69.8% greater with a Roth IRA Conversion [assuming a one-year lump sum withdrawal].
- The Traditional IRA is dependent on the post-retirement tax rate.
- The Roth IRA asset is not affected by retirement tax rates. So the Roth IRA will provide a hedge against rising tax rates.
- The relative advantage does not change if inflation goes up or down (both the Roth IRA and the Traditional IRA are affected equally).
- The Roth IRA advantage will increase with more aggressive portfolios that provide a higher rate of return. However, the risk of a more aggressive portfolio needs to be taken into consideration.

The specific results for the profile for Example 55B are shown at the bottom of the table. Roth IRA conversion provides $27,368 per year, which is 17% more than the Traditional IRA would provide. If the couple has more assets in investible accounts than assumed for EX55B the conversion will provide an increasing advantage.

This couple's retirement assets, are as follows: recurring income (Social Security, pension) is $32,940 [47% of needs] annual savings of $6,000 per year; provides $8,822 per year [12% of needs]; and the Roth IRA Conversion of $120,000 provides $27,368 [39% of needs], for a total of $69,130 per year. This is close to their needs.

CONVERSIONS

EXAMPLE 55B

Assumptions

Age	55	Inflation	3.50%
Spouse's Age	55	Tax in Conversion Years	30%
Beneficiary's Age	25	Pre-Retirement Tax Rate	26%
Check Out Age	90	Retirement tax rate	25%
Conversion Amount	$10,000	Other assets tax rate	26%
Withdrawal Method	Joint Term Certain	Rate of Return	9%

Reference Table

	Start Withd'rl At Age	Withd'rl Tax Trate	Trad'l IRA	ROTH IRA	ROTH Advantage
Withdrawal Period 20 years	60	25%	$1,037	$1,105	6.6%
	65	25%	$1,316	$1,431	8.8%
	70	25%	$1,673	$1,854	**10.8%**
	75	25%	$1,995	$2,402	20.4%
	80	25%	$2,349	$3,112	32.5%
	85	25%	$2,763	$4,031	45.9%
	90	25%	$3,231	$5,222	61.6%
Withdrawal Period 10 years	60	25%	$1,684	$1,763	4.7%
	65	25%	$2,134	$2,204	7.0%
	70	25%	$2,709	$2,959	9.2%
	75	25%	$3,325	$3,833	15.3%
	80	25%	$4,008	$4,966	**23.9%**
	85	25%	$4,780	$6,433	34.6%
	90	25%	$5,621	$8,334	48.3%
Withdrawal Period 1 year	60	39%	$11,783	$14,121	10.0%
	65	40%	$14,003	$18,203	25.3%
	70	40%	$18,435	$23,698	28.6%
	75	42%	$22,596	$30,701	35.9%
	80	43%	$27,514	$39,772	44.6%
	85	43%	$33,268	$51,524	54.9%
	90	43%	$39,312	$66,749	**69.8%**

SENSITIVITY TO VARIABLES

EXAMPLE 55B		Conversion	$120,000	Taxes	$36,000
Reference	74	25%	$23,175	$27,368	18.1%
Ret Tax	74	20%	$24,404	$27,368	12.1%
Ret Tax	74	30%	$21,824	$27,368	25.4%
Inflation 2%	74	25%	$34,235	$40,344	17.8%
Inflation 5%	74	25%	$15,674	$18,548	18.3%
Rate of return 11%	74	25%	$37,066	$45,144	21.8%
Rate of return 7%	74	25%	$14,270	$16,264	14.0%
Rate of Return 4%	74	25%	$6,695	$7,156	6.9%
Average Benefit of ROTH IRA					**17.0%**

5.3.4 Example 55SNGL

This single individual has $150,000 in IRA assets that can be converted to a Roth IRA. His investable assets of $200,000 will last till age 71. From Table 5.1 we see that his recurring income, per year in today's dollars, was $25,060, and his total after-tax retirement need was $66,700. Thus, he needed a balance of $41,640 per year of which $10,359 would be provided from planned savings of $10,000 per year ($2,000 in a Roth IRA contribution and $8,000 in a taxable account). The remaining balance of 31,281 would need to be provided from their existing IRA assets. Step 5 of the retirement analysis compares the indexed annuity amounts that would be produced by two types of account: an existing IRA converted to a Roth IRA and an existing IRA not converted.

The top part of the adjacent table lists the assumptions. The middle part is a general reference for this set of assumptions, based on a reference $10,000 IRA asset conversion. We show the value of this asset if it stays in the Traditional IRA, which can be compared with the value if it is converted to a Roth IRA in 1998. The conversion tax of $48,000 (32% of $150,000) required for the Roth IRA is paid from an additional asset that the client is assumed to have. In the Traditional IRA case this $48,000 is assumed to grow in a taxable account. The indexed annuity (a payout that keeps up with 3.5% inflation) for withdrawals starting at different ages is shown. We also show the value of this indexed annuity for different withdrawal intervals. Note that the retirement tax rate will be higher for the shorter withdrawal periods. These average tax rates were taken from the tax tables in Chapter 3, which gives the Federal Tax plus average State Tax for all states in the U.S., for a given income, assuming standard deductions and one exemption. Note that all dollars are expressed in today's dollars, and that these are after-tax dollars (what the person receives after paying taxes). General observations that can be made from the table are:

- The Roth IRA Conversion provides a definite benefit over all scenarios considered.
- If the Roth IRA assets were not needed during the person's lifetime, the estate (at age 90) would be 71.7% greater with a Roth IRA Conversion [assuming a lump sum at age 90].
- The Traditional IRA is dependent on the post-retirement tax rate.
- The Roth IRA asset is not affected by retirement tax rates. So the Roth IRA will provide a hedge against rising tax rates.
- The relative advantage does not change if inflation goes up or down (both the Roth IRA and the Traditional IRA are affected equally).
- The Roth IRA advantage will increase with more aggressive portfolios that provide a higher rate of return. However, the risk of a more aggressive portfolio needs to be taken into consideration.

The specific results for Example 55SNGL are shown at the bottom of the table. Roth IRA conversion provides $30,845 per year, which is 16% more than the Traditional IRA would provide. If the person has more investible assets than assumed for EX55SNGL the conversion will provide an increasing advantage.

This person's retirement assets, are as follows: recurring income (Social Security, pension) is $25,060 [37% of needs]; annual savings of $10,000 per year provides $10,359 per year [16% of needs]; and the Roth IRA Conversion of $150,000 provides $30,845, for a total of $62,264 per year, which is close to the retirement needs.

CONVERSIONS

Assumptions

Age	55	Inflation	3.5%
Spouse's Age	55	Tax in Conversion Years	32%
Beneficiary's Age	25	Pre-Retirement Tax Rate	30%
Check Out Age	90	Retirement tax rate	28%
Conversion Amount	$10,000	Other assets tax rate	28%
Withdrawal Method	Joint Term Certain	Rate of Return	9%

Reference Table

	Start Withd'rl At Age	Withd'rl Tax Trate	Trad'l IRA	ROTH IRA	ROTH Advantage
Withdrawal Period 20 years	60	28%	$1,013	$1,105	9.0%
	65	28%	$1,282	$1,431	11.7%
	70	28%	$1,624	$1,854	**14.1%**
	75	28%	$1,922	$2,402	24.9%
	80	28%	$2,245	$3,112	38.6%
	85	28%	$2,621	$4,031	53.8%
	90	28%	$3,038	$5,222	71.9%
Withdrawal Period 10 years	60	28%	$1,651	$1,763	6.8%
	65	28%	$2,085	$2,284	9.6%
	70	28%	$2,638	$2,960	12.2%
	75	28%	$3,219	$3,833	19.1%
	80	28%	$3,856	$4,966	**28.8%**
	85	28%	$4,566	$6,433	40.9%
	90	28%	$5,326	$8,334	56.5%
Withdrawal Period 1 year	60	39%	$11,987	$14,121	17.8%
	65	40%	$14,863	$18,293	20.1%
	70	41%	$18,462	$23,698	28.4%
	75	43%	$22,481	$30,701	36.6%
	80	43%	$27,580	$39,772	44.2%
	85	43%	$33,152	$51,524	55.4%
	90	43%	$38,878	$66,749	**71.7%**

SENSITIVITY TO VARIABLES

EXAMPLE 55SNGL		Conversion	$150,000	Taxes	$48,000
Reference	72	28%	$26,338	$30,845	17.1%
Ret Tax	72	23%	$27,848	$30,845	10.8%
Ret Tax	72	33%	$24,828	$30,845	24.2%
Inflation 2%	72	28%	$37,776	$44,160	16.9%
Inflation 5%	72	28%	$18,337	$21,514	17.3%
Rate of return 11%	72	28%	$40,778	$49,062	20.3%
Rate of return 7%	72	28%	$16,763	$19,021	13.5%
Rate of Return 4%	72	28%	$8,276	$8,859	7.0%
Average Benefit of ROTH IRA					**16.0%**

5.3.5 Example 55C

This age-55 couple has $2,000,000 in existing IRA assets that can be converted to a Roth IRA. This couple has sufficient outside assets to last them their lifetime: they do not need to withdraw from their tax-advantaged accounts. Their goal is to maximize the estate that they are able to leave to their beneficiaries (children and grandchildren). Example 55C is described in Table 5.1. The recurring income, per year in today's dollars, for this couple was $44,200, and their total after-tax retirement need was $134,250. The analysis will show the effect of two types of accounts: an existing IRA converted to a Roth IRA and an existing IRA not converted.

The top part of the adjacent table lists the assumptions. The middle part is a general reference for this set of assumptions, based on a $10,000 IRA asset conversion. We show the value of this asset if it stays in the Traditional IRA, which can be compared with the value if it is converted to a Roth IRA in 1998. The conversion tax of $840,000 (42% of $2,000,000) required for the Roth IRA is paid from an additional asset that the client is assumed to have. In the Traditional IRA case this $840,000 is assumed to stay in a taxable account. The indexed annuity (a payout that keeps up with 3.5% inflation) for withdrawals starting at different ages is shown. We also show the value of this indexed annuity for different withdrawal intervals. Note that the retirement tax rate will be higher for the shorter withdrawal periods. These average tax rates were taken from the tax tables in Chapter 3, which gives the Federal Tax plus average State Tax for all states in the U.S., for a given income, assuming standard deductions and two exemptions. Note that all dollars are expressed in today's dollars, and that these are after-tax dollars (what the couple receives after paying taxes). General observations that can be made are:

- The Roth IRA Conversion provides a very large benefit over all scenarios considered.
- This couple will not need to draw any money from the Roth IRA accounts during their lifetime.
- They do need to come up with $840,000 in additional taxes over the next four years. After considering the loss of these assets, the Roth IRA Conversion will provide an estate that is 66.2% greater than it would be with no conversion [age 90 assuming a lump sum withdrawal].
- The relative advantage does not change if inflation goes up or down (both the Roth IRA and the Traditional IRA are affected equally).
- The Roth IRA advantage will increase with more aggressive portfolios that provide a higher rate of return. However, the risk of a more aggressive portfolio needs to be taken into consideration. On the other hand, an ultraconservative investment (say a 4% money market fund) drops the advantage of the Roth IRA to 26%. Thus the choice of investments is critical.

The specific results for the client profile for Example 55C are shown in the bottom of the table.

If the assets were left in a trust fund to be used over 20 years, the annual payout after taxes in today's dollars would be $1,321,766, which is 69% more than with no conversion. This analysis assumes that the couple has found a strategy to reduce their adjusted gross income in 1998 to less than $100,000 (see Chapter 3 for a discussion of this topic). The couple will need to weigh this advantage against the pain of paying $840,000 in additional taxes over the next four years.

Estate planning issues will be critical to this client. Chapter 9 provides a thorough assessment of estate planning issues.

CONVERSIONS

EXAMPLE 55C

Assumptions

Age	55	Inflation	3.50%
Spouse's Age	55	Tax in Conversion Years	42%
Beneficiary's Age	25	Pre-Retirement Tax Rate	32%
Check Out Age	90	Retirement tax rate	31%
Conversion Amount	$10,000	Other assets tax rate	28%
Withdrawal Method	Joint Term Certain	Rate of Return	9%

Reference Table

	Start Withd'rl At Age	Withd'rl Tax Trate	Trad'l IRA	ROTH IRA	ROTH Advantage
Withdrawal Period 20 years	60	31%	$1,048	$1,105	5.5%
	65	31%	$1,316	$1,431	8.7%
	70	31%	$1,658	$1,854	**11.8%**
	75	31%	$1,959	$2,402	22.6%
	80	31%	$2,286	$3,112	36.1%
	85	31%	$2,666	$4,031	51.2%
	90	31%	$3,090	$5,222	69.0%
Withdrawal Period 10 years	60	31%	$1,717	$1,763	2.7%
	65	31%	$2,152	$2,284	6.1%
	70	31%	$2,705	$2,959	9.4%
	75	31%	$3,289	$3,833	16.5%
	80	31%	$3,930	$4,966	**26.3%**
	85	31%	$4,646	$6,433	38.5%
	90	31%	$5,416	$8,334	53.9%
Withdrawal Period 1 year	60	44%	$12,328	$14,121	14.5%
	65	45%	$15,187	$18,293	20.5%
	70	45%	$18,940	$23,698	25.1%
	75	45%	$23,521	$30,701	30.5%
	80	45%	$28,621	$39,772	39.0%
	85	45%	$34,298	$51,524	50.2%
	90	45%	$40,172	$66,749	**66.2%**

SENSITIVITY TO VARIABLES

EXAMPLE 55C		Conversion	$2,000,000	Taxes	$840,000
Reference	97	31%	$753,786	$1,321,766	75.4%
Ret Tax	97	28%	$780,642	$1,321,766	69.3%
Ret Tax	97	35%	$720,688	$1,321,766	83.4%
Inflation 2%	97	31%	$1,571,484	$2,733,626	74.0%
Inflation 5%	97	31%	$362,924	$641,907	76.9%
Rate of return 11%	97	31%	$1,661,332	$3,246,216	95.4%
Rate of return 7%	97	31%	$337,776	$524,960	55.4%
Rate of Return 4%	97	31%	$99,010	$124,967	26.2%
Average Benefit of ROTH IRA					**69.0%**

5.3.6 Example 60 A

This age-60 couple plans to retire at age 65. They have $225,000 in IRA assets that can be converted to a Roth IRA. Their investable assets of $100,000 will last till age 69. From Table 5.1 we see that the couple's recurring income, per year in today's dollars, was $33,000, and their total after-tax retirement need was $71,000. Thus, they needed a balance of $38,000 per year of which $5,755 would be provided from planned savings of $10,000 per year ($4,000 in a Roth IRA contribution and $6,000 in a taxable account). The remaining balance of $32,245 would need to be provided from their existing IRA assets.. Step 5 of the retirement analysis compares the indexed annuity amounts that would be produced by two types of account: an existing IRA converted to a Roth IRA and an existing IRA not converted.

The top part of the adjacent table lists the assumptions. The middle part is a general reference for this set of assumptions, based on a reference $10,000 IRA asset conversion. We show the value of this asset if it stays in the Traditional IRA, which can be compared with the value if it is converted to a Roth IRA in 1998. The conversion tax of $63,000 (28% of $225,000) required for the Roth IRA is paid from an additional asset that the client is assumed to have. In the Traditional IRA case this $63,000 is assumed to grow in a taxable account. The indexed annuity (a payout that keeps up with 3.5% inflation) for withdrawals starting at different ages is shown. We also show the value of this indexed annuity for different withdrawal intervals. Note that the retirement tax rate will be higher for the shorter withdrawal periods. These average tax rates were taken from the tax tables in Chapter 3, which gives the Federal Tax plus average State Tax for all states in the U.S., for a given income, assuming standard deductions and two exemptions. Note that all dollars are expressed in today's dollars, and that these are after-tax dollars (what the client receives after paying taxes). General observations that can be made from the table are:

- The Roth IRA Conversion provides a substantial benefit over all scenarios considered.
- If the Roth IRA assets were not needed during the couple's lifetime, the estate (at age 90) would be 65.6% greater with a Roth IRA Conversion [at age 90 assuming a lump sum withdrawal].
- The Traditional IRA is dependent on the post-retirement tax rate.
- The Roth IRA asset is not affected by retirement tax rates. So the Roth IRA will provide a hedge against rising tax rates.
- The relative advantage does not change if inflation goes up or down (both the Roth IRA and the Traditional IRA are affected equally).
- The Roth IRA advantage will increase with more aggressive portfolios that provide a higher rate of return. However, the risk of a more aggressive portfolio needs to be taken into consideration.

The specific results for Example 60A are shown at the bottom of the table., Roth IRA conversion provides $32,201 per year, which is 9% more than the Traditional IRA would provide.

This couple's retirement assets are as follows: recurring income (Social Security, pension) is $33,000 [46% of needs] ; annual savings of $10,000 per year provides $5,755 per year [8% of needs]; and the Roth IRA Conversion of $225,000 provides $32,201 [45% of needs], for a total of $70,956 per year, which is close to their needs.

CONVERSIONS   EXAMPLE 60A

Assumptions

Age	60	Inflation	3.50%
Spouse's Age	60	Tax in Conversion Years	28%
Beneficiary's Age	30	Pre-Retirement Tax Rate	26%
Check Out Age	90	Retirement tax rate	25%
Conversion Amount	$10,000	Other assets tax rate	25%
Withdrawal Method	Joint Term Certain	Rate of Return	9%

Reference Table

	Start Withd'rl At Age	Withd'rl Tax Trate	Trad'l IRA	ROTH IRA	ROTH Advantage
Withdrawal Period 20 years	65	25%	$1,028	$1,105	7.5%
	70	25%	$1,305	$1,431	**9.7%**
	75	25%	$1,556	$1,854	19.2%
	80	25%	$1,832	$2,402	31.1%
	85	25%	$2,155	$3,112	44.4%
	90	25%	$2,520	$4,031	60.0%
Withdrawal Period 10 years	65	25%	$1,668	$1,763	5.7%
	70	25%	$2,116	$2,284	8.0%
	75	25%	$2,594	$2,959	14.0%
	80	25%	$3,127	$3,833	**22.6%**
	85	25%	$3,728	$4,966	33.2%
	90	25%	$4,383	$6,433	46.8%
Withdrawal Period 1 year	65	36%	$11,963	$14,121	18.0%
	70	39%	$14,009	$18,293	24.5%
	75	39%	$18,428	$23,698	28.6%
	80	40%	$22,319	$30,701	37.6%
	85	40%	$26,983	$39,772	47.4%
	90	42%	$31,117	$51,524	**65.6%**

SENSITIVITY TO VARIABLES

EXAMPLE 60A		**Conversion**	**$225,000**	**Taxes**	**$63,000**
Reference	70	25%	$29,367	$32,201	9.7%
Ret Tax	70	20%	$30,901	$32,201	4.2%
Ret Tax	70	30%	$27,680	$32,201	16.3%
Inflation 2%	70	25%	$38,027	$41,623	9.5%
Inflation 5%	70	25%	$22,614	$24,840	9.8%
Rate of return 11%	70	25%	$40,418	$45,098	11.6%
Rate of return 7%	70	25%	$21,042	$22,606	7.4%
Rate of Return 4%	70	25%	$12,420	$12,848	3.4%
Average Benefit of ROTH IRA					**9.0%**

5.3.7 Example 65A

This age-65 couple has just retired. They have $500,000 in IRA assets that can be converted to a Roth IRA. In addition they have $another $500,000 investable assets which will last till age 80. From Table 5.1 we see that the couple's recurring income, per year in today's dollars, was $33,000, and their total after-tax retirement need was $71,000. Thus, they needed a balance of $38,000 per year, all of which would need to be provided from their existing IRA assets. We are assuming that they do not make annual contributions after age 65[6]. Step 5 of the retirement analysis compares the indexed annuity amounts that would be produced by two types of account: an existing IRA converted to a Roth IRA and an existing IRA not converted.

The top part of the adjacent table lists the assumptions. The middle part is a general reference for this set of assumptions, based on a reference $10,000 IRA asset conversion. We show the value of this asset if it stays in the Traditional IRA, which can be compared with the value if it is converted to a Roth IRA in 1998. The conversion tax of $165,000 (33% of $500,000) required for the Roth IRA is paid from an additional asset that the client is assumed to have. In the Traditional IRA case this $165,000 is assumed to grow in a taxable account. The indexed annuity (a payout that keeps up with 3.5% inflation) for withdrawals starting at different ages is shown. We also show the value of this indexed annuity for different withdrawal intervals. Note that the retirement tax rate will be higher for the shorter withdrawal periods. These average tax rates were taken from the tax tables in Chapter 3, which gives the Federal Tax plus average State Tax for all states in the U.S., for a given income, assuming standard deductions and two exemptions. Note that all dollars are expressed in today's dollars, and that these are after-tax dollars (what the client receives after paying taxes). General observations that can be made from the table are:

- The Roth IRA Conversion provides a benefit over all scenarios considered.
- If the Roth IRA assets were not needed during couple's lifetime, the estate (at age 90) would be 60.3% greater with a Roth IRA Conversion, assuming a one year lump sum withdrawal.
- The Traditional IRA is dependent on the post-retirement tax rate.
- The Roth IRA asset is not affected by retirement tax rates. So the Roth IRA will provide a hedge against rising tax rates.
- The relative advantage does not change if inflation goes up or down (both the Roth IRA and the Traditional IRA are affected equally).
- The Roth IRA advantage will increase with more aggressive portfolios that provide a higher rate of return. However, the risk of a more aggressive portfolio needs to be taken into consideration.

The specific results for Example 65A are shown at the bottom of the table. Roth IRA conversion provides $97,629 per year, which is 25% more than the Traditional IRA would provide.

This client's retirement assets, in round numbers, are as follows: recurring income (Social Security, pension) is $33,000 [46% of needs], and the Roth IRA Conversion of $500,000 provides $97,629, which is significantly greater then their needs.

---

[6] Individuals are permitted to contribute up to $2,000 per year till age 70 to a Traditional IRA. Contributions to a Roth IRA may continue after age 70 through the full lifetime of the individual.

CONVERSIONS

EXAMPLE 65A

Assumptions

Age	65	Inflation	3.50%
Spouse's Age	65	Tax in Conversion Years	33%
Beneficiary's Age	35	Pre-Retirement Tax Rate	26%
Check Out Age	90	Retirement tax rate	25%
Conversion Amount	$10,000	Other assets tax rate	26%
Withdrawal Method	Joint Term Certain	Rate of Return	9%

Reference Table

Start Withd'rl At Age	Withd'rl Tax Trate	Trad'l IRA	ROTH IRA	ROTH Advantage
Withdrawal Period 20 years				
70	25%	$1,062	$1,105	**4.0%**
75	25%	$1,265	$1,431	13.2%
80	25%	$1,488	$1,854	24.6%
85	25%	$1,749	$2,402	37.3%
90	25%	$2,045	$3,112	52.1%
Withdrawal Period 10 years				
70	25%	$1,728	$1,769	L.0%
75	25%	$2,113	$2,284	8.1%
80	25%	$2,542	$2,959	**16.4%**
85	25%	$3,027	$3,833	26.6%
90	25%	$3,558	$4,966	39.6%
Withdrawal Period 1 year				
70	43%	$11,601	$14,121	21.7%
75	44%	$14,216	$18,293	28.7%
80	44%	$17,437	$23,698	35.9%
85	44%	$21,018	$30,701	46.1%
90	44%	$24,805	$39,772	**60.3%**

SENSITIVITY TO VARIABLES

EXAMPLE 65 A		Conversion	$500,000	Taxes	$165,000
Reference	81	25%	$76,865	$97,629	27.0%
Ret Tax	81	20%	$80,711	$97,629	21.0%
Ret Tax	81	30%	$72,635	$97,629	34.4%
Inflation 2%	81	25%	$109,181	$137,748	26.2%
Inflation 5%	81	25%	$54,053	$69,083	27.8%
Rate of return 11%	81	25%	$114,372	$152,491	33.3%
Rate of return 7%	81	25%	$51,068	$61,330	20.1%
Rate of Return 4%	81	25%	$27,021	$29,388	8.8%
Average Benefit of ROTH IRA					**25.0%**

5.3.8 Example 75A

This couple has $300,000 in their IRA balance, which can be converted to a Roth IRA. Their remaining IRA balance of $250,000 will last them till age 82. From Table 5.1 we see that the couple's recurring income, per year in today's dollars, was $33,000, and their total after-tax retirement need was $71,000. Thus, they needed a balance of $38,000 per year, all of which would need to be provided from their existing IRA assets. Step 5 of the retirement analysis compares the indexed annuity amounts that would be produced by two types of account: an existing IRA converted to a Roth IRA and an existing IRA not converted.

The top part of the adjacent table lists the assumptions. The middle part is a general reference for this set of assumptions, based on a $10,000 IRA asset conversion. We show the value of this asset if it stays in the Traditional IRA, which can be compared with the value if it is converted to a Roth IRA in 1998. The conversion tax of $90,000 (30% of $300,000) required for the Roth IRA is paid from an additional asset that the client is assumed to have. In the Traditional IRA case this $90,000 is assumed to stay in a taxable account. The indexed annuity (a payout that keeps up with 3.5% inflation) for withdrawals starting at different ages is shown. We also show the value of this indexed annuity for different withdrawal intervals. Note that the retirement tax rate will be higher for the shorter withdrawal periods. These average tax rates were taken from Table 3.4, which gives the Federal Tax plus average State Tax for all states in the U.S., for a given income, assuming standard deductions and two exemptions. Note that all dollars are expressed in today's dollars, and that these are after-tax dollars (what the client receives after paying taxes). General observations that can be made from the table are:

- The Roth IRA Conversion provides a substantial benefit over all scenarios considered.
- If the Roth IRA assets were not needed during the couple's lifetime, the estate (at age 90) would be 47% greater with a Roth IRA Conversion [assuming a one-year lump sum withdrawal].
- The Traditional IRA is dependent on the post-retirement tax rate.
- The Roth IRA asset is not affected by retirement tax rates. So the Roth IRA will provide a hedge against rising tax rates.
- The relative advantage does not change if inflation goes up or down (both the Roth IRA and the Traditional IRA are affected equally).
- The Roth IRA advantage will increase with more aggressive portfolios that provide a higher rate of return. However, the risk of a more aggressive portfolio needs to be taken into consideration.

The specific results for Example 75A are shown at the bottom of the table. Roth IRA conversion provides $38,712 per year, which is 21% more than the Traditional IRA would provide.

This couple's retirement assets are as follows: recurring income (Social Security, pension) is $33,000 [46% of needs], and the Roth IRA Conversion of $300,000 provides $38,712 [55% of needs], for a total of $71,712 per year, which is close to their needs.

CONVERSIONS

EXAMPLE 75 A

Assumptions

Age	75	Inflation	3.50%
Spouse's Age	75	Tax in Conversion Years	30%
Beneficiary's Age	45	Pre-Retirement Tax Rate	26%
Check Out Age	90	Retirement tax rate	25%
Conversion Amount	$10,000	Other assets tax rate	26%
Withdrawal Method	Joint Term Certain	Rate of Return	9%

Reference Table

	Start Withd'rl At Age	Withd'rl Tax Trate	Trad'l IRA	ROTH IRA	ROTH Advantage
Withdrawal Period 20 years					
	80	25%	$959	$1,105	15.2%
	85	25%	$1,118	$1,431	28.1%
	90	25%	$1,301	$1,854	42.5%
Withdrawal Period 10 years					
	80	25%	$1,622	$1,763	**8.7%**
	85	25%	$1,928	$2,284	18.5%
	90	25%	$2,263	$2,959	30.7%
Withdrawal Period 1 year					
	80	43%	$11,201	$14,121	26.1%
	85	43%	$13,617	$18,293	34.3%
	90	43%	$16,126	$23,698	**47.0%**

SENSITIVITY TO VARIABLES

EXAMPLE 75A Conversion		$300,000	Taxes	$90,000	
Reference	83	25%	$31,541	$38,712	22.7%
Ret Tax	83	20%	$33,098	$38,712	17.0%
Ret Tax	83	30%	$29,830	$38,712	29.8%
Inflation 2%	83	25%	$39,894	$48,599	21.8%
Inflation 5%	83	25%	$24,829	$30,734	23.8%
Rate of return 11%	83	25%	$40,978	$52,280	27.6%
Rate of return 7%	83	25%	$23,999	$28,202	17.5%
Rate of Return 4%	83	25%	$15,617	$16,966	8.6%
Average Benefit of ROTH IRA					**21.0%**

5.3.9 Example 85A

This couple has $300,000 in their retirement assets that can be converted to a Roth IRA. They also have $250,000 investable assets that will last till age 92. From Table 5.1 we see that couple's recurring income, per year in today's dollars, was $33,000, and their total after-tax retirement need was $71,000. Thus, they needed a balance of $38,000 per year, all of which would need to be provided from their IRA assets. This couple wishes to maximize their estate and will leave the Roth IRA assets in a trust account that will provide an annual indexed payout. Estate Tax issues will need to be considered: see Chapter 9. Step 5 of the retirement analysis compares the indexed annuity amounts that would be produced by two types of account: an existing IRA converted to a Roth IRA and an existing IRA not converted.

The top part of the adjacent table lists the assumptions. The middle part is a general reference for this set of assumptions, based on a $10,000 IRA asset conversion. We show the value of this asset if it stays in the Traditional IRA, which can be compared with the value if it is converted to a Roth IRA in 1998. The conversion tax of $90,000 (30% of $300,000) required for the Roth IRA is paid from an additional asset that the client is assumed to have. In the Traditional IRA case this $90,000 is assumed to stay in a taxable account. The indexed annuity (a payout that keeps up with 3.5% inflation) for withdrawals starting at different ages is shown. We also show the value of this indexed annuity for different withdrawal intervals. Note that the retirement tax rate will be higher for the shorter withdrawal periods. These average tax rates were taken from Table 3.4, which gives the Federal Tax plus average State Tax for all states in the U.S., for a given income, assuming standard deductions and two exemptions. Note that all dollars are expressed in today's dollars, and that these are after-tax dollars (what the client receives after paying taxes).

General observations that can be made from the table are:

- The Roth IRA Conversion provides a substantial benefit over all scenarios considered.
- The estate (at age 90) is 28.6% greater with a Roth IRA Conversion.
- The Traditional IRA is dependent on the post-retirement tax rate.
- The Roth IRA asset is not affected by retirement tax rates. So the Roth IRA will provide a hedge against rising tax rates.
- The relative advantage does not change if inflation goes up or down (both the Roth IRA and the Traditional IRA are affected equally).
- The Roth IRA advantage will increase with more aggressive portfolios that provide a higher rate of return. However, the risk of a more aggressive portfolio needs to be taken into consideration.

The specific results for Example 85A are shown at the bottom of the table.

Roth IRA conversion provides $36,798 per year, which is 25% more than the Traditional IRA would provide. These will be provided as an annuitized trust fund to the beneficiary. Estate Tax considerations are provided in Chapter 9.

CONVERSIONS

Assumptions

Age	85	Inflation	3.50%
Spouse's Age	85	Tax in Conversion Years	30%
Beneficiary's Age	55	Pre-Retirement Tax Rate	26%
Check Out Age	90	Retirement tax rate	25%
Conversion Amount	$10,000	Other assets tax rate	26%
Withdrawal Method	Joint Term Certain	Rate of Return	9%

Reference Table

	Start Withd'rl At Age	Withd'rl Tax Trate	Trad'l IRA	ROTH IRA	ROTH Advantage
Withdrawal Period 20 years					
	90	25%	$881	$1,105	25.4%
Withdrawal Period 10 years					
	90	25%	$1,532	$1,763	15.1%
Withdrawal Period 1 year					
	90	43%	$10.983	$14,121	**28.6%**

Sensitivity to Variables

EXAMPLE 85 AConversion $300,000 Taxes$ 140,000

Reference	93	25%	$28,931	$36,798	27.2%
Ret Tax	93	20%	$30,322	$36,798	21.4%
Ret Tax	93	30%	$27,400	$36,798	34.3%
Inflation 2%	93	25%	$36,685	$46,215	26.0%
Inflation 5%	93	25%	$22,738	$29,207	28.4%
Rate of return 11%	93	25%	$36,967	$49,246	33.2%
Rate of return 7%	93	25%	$22,433	$27,072	20.7%
Rate of Return 4%	93	25%	$15,041	$16,552	10.0%
Average Benefit of ROTH IRA					**25.0%**

5.4 Summary of Client Examples for Roth Conversion

Table 5.3 summarizes the results for the nine client cases that we have examined in this chapter. As can be seen, the Roth IRA conversion provides a benefit in all cases. However, the benefit can range from small (around 2%) to almost 72%.

1. One major factor that determines the advantage of a Roth IRA Conversion is when the money is withdrawn from the account. This in turn depends on how much the client has in investible accounts.
2. In the examples, if there were sufficient outside assets in investible accounts, so that no withdrawals were needed from the Roth IRA account, the estate that would be left at age 90 would be an average of 59% greater with a Roth IRA Conversion than with no conversion.
3. If withdrawals needed to start at age 60 (or five years after conversion for those who are over 60), the average advantage would be around 06%.
4. The Roth IRA and the Traditional IRA are equally affected by inflation.
5. The Traditional IRA assets depend on the tax rate at retirement.
6. The Roth IRA account does not care what the taxes will be at retirement.
7. The Roth IRA assets will do better relative to the Traditional IRA with a portfolio that provides a higher rate of return. You may wish to consider more aggressive investments for the Roth IRA because the risk of holding a given asset decreases as the time period it is held increases, and because higher yielding investments will increase the relative value of the Roth. You should discuss this with a good professional financial adviser.
8. In contrast, an investment in a conservative account with a low rate of return, such as a money market fund, will minimize the benefit of the Roth IRA account.
9. The Roth IRA account should be the last asset from which withdrawals are made.
10. The Roth IRA account can benefit the young as well as the not- so- young. It is an incorrect myth that the Roth IRA Conversion is only for the young.

Reduction of Risk Over Time

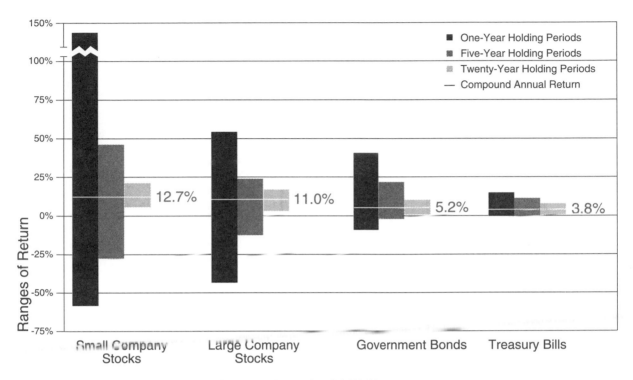

Each bar shows the range of compound annual returns for each asset class over the period 1926-1997.
* The 1933 Small Company Stock total return was 142.9%.
Past performance is no guarantee of future results.
© Copyright Ibbotson Associates 1998

IbbotsonAssociates

Table 5.3 Summary of Roth Conversions for Profiles

REFERENCE TABLES Advantage of Roth IRA over Trad'l IRA	45A	55A	55B	55SNGL	55C	60A	65A	75A	85A	Averages
Withdrawal age 60 over 20 years	10%	2%	6%	9%	5%					6%
Withdrawal age 65 over 20 years	12%	4%	8%	11%	8%	7%				8%
Withdrawal age 70 over 20 years	14%	5%	11%	14%	12%	10%	4%			10%
Withdrawal age 80 over 10 years	27%	15%	24%	29%	26%	22%	16%	8%		21%
Withdrawal age 90 over 1 year	60%	60%	70%	72%	66%	65%	60%	47%	28%	59%

EXAMPLE PROFILES										
Age for starting withdrawals	70	70	74	72	97	70	81	83	93	
Advantage of Roth over Trad'l IRA	13%	5%	17%	16%	69%	9%	25%	21%	25%	21%

121

5.5 Paying Conversion Taxes From the Traditional IRA Account

One of the main considerations in converting to a Roth IRA is that conversion taxes need to be paid up front. If you can pay these with assets in investible accounts, you should always do so. But what if you do not have outside assets? Should you consider paying the taxes from the Traditional IRA balance itself? Then you would be converting most of the IRA, and withdrawing the remainder to pay the conversion taxes (and penalties, if any). The discussions in this section will shed some light on ways to think about the Roth IRA. The factors that come into play are your tax rates, how soon you need to withdraw the funds, and penalties that may be imposed for such withdrawals. These are discussed below.

We will consider two client profiles, one age 58 [labeled EX58A], the other age 70 [labeled EX70A]. The following assumptions are made for both client profiles:

- Amount in the Traditional IRA $10,000
- Rate of Return   9%
- Roth Conversion Tax Rate   25%
- Retirement Tax Rate   21%
- Penalty for withdrawal before 59 1/2   10% [applicable to EX 58A only]
- Withdrawal Algorithm   Term Certain
- Life expectancy at age 70   16 [see Chapter 8 for details]

Example 58A

Three cases are analyzed:

A. Leave all funds in the Traditional IRA
B. Convert to Roth IRA using Traditional IRA funds to pay taxes and penalty for pre-591/2 withdrawal.
C. Convert to Roth IRA using funds from an outside source.

In case A the EX 58 A will have $71,216 after taxes at age 85. These are future dollars, after taxes, but not corrected for inflation. Let us use this as the reference case to compare with cases B and C.

In Case B, EX 58A is able to convert $7,223 to the Roth IRA. This is obtained from the following calculation. The tax due on withdrawal of $10,000 from the Traditional IRA is .25*$10,000 = $2,500. The penalty due (an iterative calculation) is $277, which is 10% of the amount that was not converted [10% of $10,000-$7,223 = .1*2,777 = 277]. This amount grows tax free to $74,000 by age 85.

In case C, the amount in the Roth IRA account is $10,000. The conversion tax of $2,500 is paid from an outside asset. To provide a fair comparison with Cases B and C (in which case there was no such outside asset) we subtract out this additional outside asset from the Roth IRA account.[7] The net result in this account is $88,789 at age 85.

The following will generally hold for individuals under age 59 1/2 who are subject to the pre 591/2 10% withdrawal tax:

> *If you need your funds during your lifetime, then leaving the funds in the Traditional IRA will do better than a conversion that requires payment of the pre-59 1/2 10% penalty.*

Next let us consider Example EX70A

The key difference in this case is that the pre-59 1/2 10% withdrawal penalty will not be applied. The results are shown in Table 5.5.

In this case Case B is seen to provide an advantage over leaving the funds in the Traditional IRA for later withdrawal years. Thus if you need all your funds within the first 10 years, the funds should be left in the Traditional IRA; if the funds are needed after 10 years conversion to the Roth IRA will provide a benefit. In the most general case, for withdrawals extending before and after the 10-year zone, a partial conversion will provide the maximum assets. Thus a guideline that will be generally be true is that:

> *If you are over 59 1/2 [not subject to a 10% withdrawal penalty] a partial conversion with taxes paid from the IRA will provide a small advantage over not converting. It is worth exploring.*
>
> *We repeat again that the maximum advantage is always attained by paying the taxes from outside assets.*

---

[7] An alternate is to add the opportunity lost $ to the Traditional IRA assets. That is the preferred representation. However the subtraction method makes the presentation of this example a little easier to follow. The difference in the two methods is small.

Table 5.4 Roth Conversion Tax Payments

a) from outside assets   b) from the IRA account

Client Age	58	
conv_tax	25%	Conversion $ $10,000
preret_tax	25%	pre 591/2 penalty 10%
ret_tax	21%	Rate of Return 9%
Withdrawal Algorithm	JTC	ROTH Tax $2,500
LE at age 70	16	

	TRADITIONAL IRA WITH MINIMUM DISTRIBUTIONS							ROTH IRA: Tax from outside assets				ROTH IRA: Tax from IRA	
Age	Reference Traditional Pretax	LE at age 70	MRD pre_tax	Reference Traditional After Tax	MRD After_tax	MRD in Taxable Acct	A Trad'l IRA Plus MRD	ROTH IRA	Outside Assets Opp. Lost	B ROTH Minus Opp. Lost	ROTH Tax from Outside vs Trad'l B vs A	C ROTH Tax from IRA	ROTH Tax from IRA vs Trad'l C vs A
58	$10,000		$0	$7,900	$0	$0	$7,900	$10,000	$2,500	$7,500	-5%	$7,223	-9%
59	$10,900		$0	$8,611	$0	$0	$8,611	$10,900	$2,669	$8,231	-4%	$7,873	-9%
60	$11,881		$0	$9,386	$0	$0	$9,386	$11,881	$2,849	$9,212	-2%	$8,582	-9%
61	$12,950		$0	$10,231	$0	$0	$10,231	$12,950	$3,041	$10,101	-1%	$9,354	-9%
62	$14,116		$0	$11,151	$0	$0	$11,151	$14,116	$3,246	$11,075	-1%	$10,196	-9%
63	$15,386		$0	$12,155	$0	$0	$12,155	$15,386	$3,466	$12,140	0%	$11,113	-9%
64	$16,771		$0	$13,249	$0	$0	$13,249	$16,771	$3,700	$13,305	0%	$12,114	-9%
65	$18,280		$0	$14,442	$0	$0	$14,442	$18,280	$3,949	$14,581	1%	$13,204	-9%
66	$19,926		$0	$15,741	$0	$0	$15,741	$19,926	$4,216	$15,976	1%	$14,392	-9%
67	$21,719		$0	$17,158	$0	$0	$17,158	$21,719	$4,500	$17,503	2%	$15,688	-9%
68	$23,674		$0	$18,702	$0	$0	$18,702	$23,674	$4,804	$19,173	3%	$17,099	-9%
69	$25,804		$0	$20,385	$0	$0	$20,385	$25,804	$5,128	$21,000	3%	$18,638	-9%
70	$28,127	16	$1,758	$22,220	$1,389	$0	$22,220	$28,127	$5,475	$22,998	4%	$20,316	-9%
71	$28,742	15	$1,916	$22,706	$1,514	$1,487	$24,194	$30,658	$5,844	$25,183	4%	$22,144	-8%
72	$29,240	14	$2,089	$23,100	$1,650	$3,215	$26,314	$33,417	$6,239	$27,573	5%	$24,137	-8%
73	$29,595	13	$2,277	$23,380	$1,798	$5,210	$28,591	$36,425	$6,660	$30,186	6%	$26,310	-8%
74	$29,777	12	$2,481	$23,524	$1,960	$7,507	$31,031	$39,703	$7,109	$33,043	6%	$28,678	-8%
75	$29,752	11	$2,705	$23,504	$2,137	$10,141	$33,645	$43,276	$7,589	$36,167	7%	$31,258	-7%
76	$29,482	10	$2,948	$23,291	$2,329	$13,150	$36,441	$47,171	$8,101	$39,582	9%	$34,072	-7%
77	$28,922	9	$3,214	$22,848	$2,539	$16,580	$39,428	$51,417	$8,648	$43,315	10%	$37,138	-6%
78	$28,022	8	$3,503	$22,137	$2,767	$20,478	$42,616	$56,044	$9,232	$47,396	11%	$40,481	-5%
79	$26,726	7	$3,818	$21,114	$3,016	$24,898	$46,012	$61,088	$9,855	$51,856	13%	$44,124	-4%
80	$24,970	6	$4,162	$19,726	$3,288	$29,899	$49,625	$66,586	$10,520	$56,731	14%	$48,095	-3%
81	$22,681	5	$4,536	$17,918	$3,584	$35,546	$53,464	$72,579	$11,231	$62,058	16%	$52,424	-2%
82	$19,778	4	$4,944	$15,624	$3,906	$41,912	$57,536	$79,111	$11,989	$67,880	18%	$57,142	-1%
83	$16,168	3	$5,389	$12,773	$4,258	$49,076	$61,849	$86,231	$12,798	$74,242	20%	$62,285	1%
84	$11,749	2	$5,874	$9,282	$4,641	$57,125	$66,407	$93,992	$13,662	$81,194	22%	$67,890	2%
85	$6,403	1	$6,403	$5,059	$5,059	$66,158	$71,216	$102,451	$14,584	$88,789	25%	$74,000	4%

Table 5.5 Roth Conversion Tax Payment

a) from outside assets   **b) from the IRA account**

Age 70		
conv_tax	25%	Conversion $ $10,000
preret_tax	25%	pre 591/2 penalty 0%
ret_tax	21%	Rate of Return 9%
Withdrawal Algorithm$	JTC	LE at age 70 16
ROTH Tax	$2,500	

	TRADITIONAL IRA WITH MINIMUM DISTRIBUTIONS							ROTH IRA: Tax from outside Assets				ROTH IRA: Tax from IRA	
Age	Reference Traditional Pretax	LE at age 70	MRD pre_tax	Reference Traditional After Tax	MRD After-tax	A MRD in Taxable Acct	Trad'l IRA Plus VRD	ROTH IRA	Outside Assets Opp. Lost	B ROTH Minus Opp. Lost B vs A	ROTH Tax from Outside vs Trad'l C vs A	C ROTH Tax from IRA	ROTH Tax from IRA vs Trad'l
70	$10,000	16	$625	$7,900	$494	$0	$7,900	$10,000	$2,500	$7,500	-5%	$7,500	-5%
71	$10,219	15	$681	$8,073	$538	$529	$8,602	$10,900	$2,669	$8,231	-4%	$8,175	-5%
72	$10,396	14	$743	$8,213	$587	$1,143	$9,356	$11,881	$2,849	$9,032	-3%	$8,911	-5%
73	$10,522	13	$809	$8,312	$639	$1,853	$10,165	$12,950	$3,041	$9,909	-3%	$9,713	-4%
74	$10,587	12	$882	$8,364	$697	$2,669	$11,033	$14,116	$3,246	$10,869	-1%	$10,587	-4%
75	$10,578	11	$962	$8,357	$760	$3,605	$11,962	$15,386	$3,466	$11,921	0%	$11,540	-4%
76	$10,482	10	$1,048	$8,281	$828	$4,675	$12,956	$16,771	$3,700	$13,071	1%	$12,578	-3%
77	$10,283	9	$1,143	$8,123	$903	$5,895	$14,018	$18,280	$3,949	$14,331	2%	$13,710	-2%
78	$9,963	8	$1,245	$7,871	$984	$7,281	$15,151	$19,926	$4,216	$15,710	4%	$14,944	-1%
79	$9,502	7	$1,357	$7,507	$1,072	$8,852	$16,359	$21,719	$4,500	$17,219	5%	$16,289	0%
80	$8,878	6	$1,480	$7,013	$1,169	$10,630	$17,643	$23,674	$4,804	$18,869	7%	$17,755	1%
81	$8,064	5	$1,613	$6,370	$1,274	$12,638	$19,008	$25,804	$5,128	$20,676	9%	$19,353	2%
82	$7,032	4	$1,758	$5,555	$1,389	$14,901	$20,456	$28,127	$5,475	$22,652	11%	$21,095	3%
83	$5,748	3	$1,916	$4,541	$1,514	$17,448	$21,989	$30,658	$5,844	$24,814	13%	$22,994	5%
84	$4,177	2	$2,089	$3,300	$1,650	$20,310	$23,610	$33,417	$6,239	$27,179	15%	$25,063	6%
85	$2,277	1	$2,277	$1,798	$1,798	$23,521	$25,320	$36,425	$6,660	$29,765	18%	$27,319	8%

Table 5.6 Roth Conversion Taxes [ignoring MRD's]

a) pay from outside   b) pay from IRA

Example illustrating what happens if you (incorrectly) ignore minimum distributions (compared with Table 5.5)

Client Age	70		Conversion $	$10,000
conv_tax	25%		pre 591/2 penalty	0%
preret_tax	25%		Rate of Return	9%
ret_tax	21%		ROTH Tax	$2,500
Withdrawal Algorithm	None			
LE at age 70	Infinity			

	TRADITIONAL IRA WITH MINIMUM DISTRIBUTIONS						ROTH IRA: Tax from outside assets				ROTH IRA: Tax from IRA		
Age	Reference Traditional Pretax	LE at age 70	MRD pre_tax	Reference Traditional After Tax	MRD After_tax	MRD in Taxable Acct	A Trad'l IRA Plus MRD	ROTH IRA	Outside Assets Opp. Lost	B ROTH Minus Opp. Lost	ROTH Tax from Outside vs Trad'l B vs A	C ROTH Tax from IRA	ROTH Tax from IRA vs Trad'l C vs A
70	$10,000	N.A.	$0	$7,900	$0	$0	$7,900	$10,000	$2,500	$7,500	-5%	$7,500	-5%
71	$10,900	N.A.	$0	$8,611	$0	$0	$8,611	$10,900	$2,669	$8,231	-4%	$8,175	-5%
72	$11,881	N.A.	$0	$9,386	$0	$0	$9,386	$11,881	$2,849	$9,212	-2%	$8,911	-5%
73	$12,950	N.A.	$0	$10,231	$0	$0	$10,231	$12,950	$3,041	$10,101	-1%	$9,713	-5%
74	$14,116	N.A.	$0	$11,151	$0	$0	$11,151	$14,116	$3,246	$11,075	-1%	$10,587	-5%
75	$15,386	N.A.	$0	$12,155	$0	$0	$12,155	$15,386	$3,466	$12,140	0%	$11,540	-5%
76	$16,771	N.A.	$0	$13,249	$0	$0	$13,249	$16,771	$3,700	$13,305	0%	$12,578	-5%
77	$18,280	N.A.	$0	$14,442	$0	$0	$14,442	$18,280	$3,949	$14,581	1%	$13,710	-5%
78	$19,926	N.A.	$0	$15,741	$0	$0	$15,741	$19,926	$4,216	$15,976	1%	$14,944	-5%
79	$21,719	N.A.	$0	$17,158	$0	$0	$17,158	$21,719	$4,500	$17,503	2%	$16,289	-5%
80	$23,674	N.A.	$0	$18,702	$0	$0	$18,702	$23,674	$4,804	$19,173	3%	$17,755	-5%
81	$25,804	N.A.	$0	$20,385	$0	$0	$20,385	$25,804	$5,128	$21,000	3%	$19,353	-5%
82	$28,127	N.A.	$0	$22,220	$0	$0	$22,220	$28,127	$5,475	$22,998	4%	$21,095	-5%
83	$30,658	N.A.	$0	$24,220	$0	$0	$24,220	$30,658	$5,844	$25,183	4%	$22,994	-5%
84	$33,417	N.A.	$0	$26,400	$0	$0	$26,400	$33,417	$6,239	$27,573	4%	$25,063	-5%
85	$36,425	N.A.	$0	$28,776	$0	$0	$28,776	$36,425	$6,660	$30,186	5%	$27,319	-5%

It should be noted that the conclusions on paying taxes from the Traditional IRA are dependent on the critical assumption that minimum distributions are mandated for the Traditional IRAs after age 70 1/2. There are several calculators that ignore the effects of minimum required distributions, leading to incorrect conclusions. To illustrate this we repeated Example 70A ignoring the minimum distributions, leading to the results as shown in Table 5.6. The conclusion that one would draw from such a calculation would be that paying taxes from an IRA is always worse than leaving the funds in the Traditional IRA! Further paying taxes from outside funds appears to provide a relatively small advantage (approximately 5% by age 85). The more complete analysis with minimum distributions shows an advantage of 19% at age 85.

> *In general ignoring minimum required distributions in your calculations will lead to conservative results, making the Traditional IRAs look much better than the real situation.*

5.6 Should You Borrow Money to Pay for Roth IRA Conversion Taxes

In the last section we showed that paying the conversion taxes from outside assets did make sense in some cases. Does it make any sense to borrow money to pay the taxes? This will depend on why you are borrowing the money.

We have clearly demonstrated that paying taxes from outside assets provides the greatest advantage. Now, if you do have outside assets but they are not readily available (not liquid), you may want to consider a loan. We will assume that you will be borrowing money for a short time, until your assets become liquid, at which time you will pay off the loan. By borrowing money, you will have allowed yourself to take advantage of the general rule with Roth IRAs that it is better to pay from outside assets.

> *Assuming you will be paying the loan off soon, borrowing money will most often be a better approach than paying conversion taxes from your IRA account.*

We are assuming that the interest rate on the loan is comparable with the growth rate of the Roth IRA account (within 1 to 2 percentage points). Check with your advisor on loans against a mortgage, that may be deductible for Federal tax purposes.

If, however, you do not have any assets in investible accounts to start with, then borrowing money cannot be recommended. Let us examine why. If all your assets are in the Traditional IRA and you have no assets outside, you will most likely have to start withdrawals as soon as you retire, say at age 65. The advantage of a Roth IRA Conversion is very small in this situation. Looking back at our profiles, Example 55A, in which the couple had some outside assets ($75,000), showed an advantage of only 5%. With no outside assets this advantage could drop to zero or become a disadvantage. Now if on top of that you are going to have to pay off a loan starting at retirement, you will be even worse off with the Roth IRA Conversion. That means you would be better off staying with the Traditional IRA. Thus we can say that:

> *If you do not have any assets outside the Traditional IRA, you should not borrow money to pay for a conversion to the Roth IRA. Stay with the Traditional IRA.*

There is one other scenario that will justify a loan. If you do not have outside funds, but you plan on generating funds by savings in the next few years, you will be availing of the pay-from-outside benefit of the Roth IRA account.

> *Indeed the advantage of the Roth IRA is so very impressive that a few years of extra saving to pay these taxes is certainly worth considering.*

If after reading this section you have decided that a loan is worth considering, you would be well advised to engage the services of a knowledgeable accountant to work through the calculations for your specific situation. Each case will be very different, and broad generalizations are difficult to come by.

5.7 Conclusions and Summary

In this chapter we showed that a conversion to the Roth IRA will definitely provide an advantage if the taxpayer can pay conversion taxes from outside assets. The advantage improves the later he or she needs to withdraw from the account. It is reasonable to take a temporary loan to pay the conversion taxes. The Roth IRA conversion is not recommended for clients who do not have outside assets and will have much lower tax rates after retirement. There are scenarios where it is better to convert not all, but a portion of, the Traditional IRA. This is discussed in Chapter 6 on optimal conversion. The detailed rules for Roth IRA conversions, eligibility, withdrawals and possible penalties are described in Chapter 7.

In Chapter 8 we will show the effect that the minimum-withdrawal method used has on the size of the Roth IRA advantage. The steps that need to be taken to maximize the after-death assets with a Roth IRA account are discussed in Chapter 9.

Chapter 6 Optimal Roth Conversions

In Chapter 5 we examined the relative benefits of a Roth Conversions assuming a full conversion of Traditional IRA funds i.e. a 100% conversion. In this chapter we will demonstrate that income cases a partial conversion, which requires lower conversion taxes, will result in the greatest retirement income.

There are many possible reasons for not converting the full balance of your IRA. Among them are: a) you do not have sufficient outside assets to pay for the conversion taxes, b) you may need to withdraw some emergency funds from the Roth IRA within the next five years c) you want to guard against unforeseen events and are not comfortable putting all your eggs in one basket, and d) **you want to maximize your retirement assets.** This chapter will not address the first three reasons, which are very individual and are better discussed with your personal financial advisor. The focus of the chapter is to **establish the percentage of conversion that will provide the maximum in retirement assets, known as the optimal conversion**. This optimum can be calculated using a high-end software program. This chapter will:

- Explain why 100% conversion does not always lead to the greatest retirement benefits
- Provide some guidelines for determining the optimum
- Describe a method, based on a high-end software algorithm, that can be used for establishing the optimal conversion

6.1 Why There is an Optimum

If the Roth IRA always provided an advantage over all other options, you would always convert 100% of your assets. But we have seen some examples where the Traditional IRA does better than the Roth IRA. In particular, the conditions that lead to the Traditional IRA doing better than the Roth IRA are:

a)   The tax rate during retirement is much lower than during the Roth Conversion years, and

b)   Significant withdrawals are needed in the earlier part of retirement.

To illustrate the concept let us consider two artificially selected extreme cases. Suppose you need to withdraw **all** your funds 2 years after conversion (ignore penalties for the moment), and your tax rate is projected to be lower 2 years from now. Then you will be better off not converting any of your Traditional IRA funds to the Roth: this is a **0% conversion.** On the other hand, if you need to withdraw **all** your funds 20 years from now, you will maximize your return by converting all of the Traditional IRA funds to a Roth IRA: this is a **100% conversion**. But what if you need to withdraw some funds in 2 years and the rest in year 20? You would want to convert the funds you need in 20 years to a Roth IRA and leave the funds you need 2 years from now in a Traditional IRA: this is a **partial conversion**.

The logic can be easily extended to a practical real-world case where you need a payout annuity: some amount each year. If the annuity starts late (say, 15 or more years from the date of conversion), you will benefit most by converting 100%. If the annuity starts sooner, you may need to consider a partial conversion.

In the discussions so far, we have not addressed penalties on funds withdrawn within the first 5 years of conversion, because this really is a separate issue. There will generally be taxes and a 10% penalty[1] on withdrawals within 5 years of the conversion. Because of these negative factors we can say that if you need all your funds within 5 years, you should definitely not convert. Further, if you need part of your funds within the 5 years, you should leave this part in the Traditional IRA. For the rest of this chapter we will only discuss withdrawals made after 5 years, so that penalties are not a consideration in our analysis. In the next section we will explain the different factors that influence .

6.2 Factors Influencing Optimal Conversion

In this section we will discuss the conditions under which a partial conversion, which will require **reduced conversion taxes**, provides the **maximum retirement benefits**. The percentage conversion that maximizes retirement income, called the optimal conversion, depends on tax rates, asset growth rates, and the number of years before the withdrawals begin. We will start by discussing effect of retirement tax rates.

---

[1] See chapter 7 for exceptions to this rule.

We have seen in previous chapters that lower retirement tax rates favor the Traditional IRA. This is exemplified in Table 6.1. From this table we see that if the retirement tax rate is equal to or greater than the tax rate during the conversion years, then the Roth IRA is always better. In this case a 100% conversion to the Roth IRA is indicated. On the other hand, if the retirement tax rate is lower than the conversion tax rate, then the Traditional IRA will be the better choice for early withdrawals (shaded zone in the figure) while the Roth IRA will be better (white zone) for the later withdrawals. The breakeven age, (which is the year in which the two IRAs are equivalent) is seen to shift out in time as the retirement tax rate drops. For instance if the average retirement tax rate drops to 16%, for withdrawals in years 10 through 20 from the year of conversion, the Traditional IRA is always better and no conversion is indicated. If the average retirement tax rate is 19%, the breakeven age is 13 years out, so the Traditional IRA should be used for retirement needs from year 10 through 13, and the Roth IRA should be used to meet the retirement needs from years 14 through 20. That split will provide the maximum retirement income. It can be shown that the breakeven age N is given by the equation

$$N = \log(Tc/Tr)/\log[(1+ror)/1+ror(1-Tother)]$$

where Tc is the conversion tax rate, Tr is the retirement tax rate, Tother is the tax rate for other assets, and ror is the rate of return. This equation verifies our observation that the breakeven age will be further out as the conversion tax rate increases, and as the retirement tax rate decreases. A guideline for optimal conversion that follows from this is that

> *the optimum percentage conversion decreases (convert less) as the conversion tax increases and as the retirement tax rate decreases.*

The next factor that we will study is rate of return. Recall that the key advantage of the Roth IRA is that all growth is tax free. From this simple observation one can easily see that the Roth IRA will fare better that larger the growth i.e. the greater the rate of return. This is validated in the above equation. The guideline this leads to is that the

> *greater the assumed rate of return the more you should convert; and conversely, the lower the assumed rate of return the less you should convert.*

TABLE 6.2 Comparison of Roth vs Traditional IRA for Different Tax Rates

Growth Rate 9%
Amount $10,000

Year	ROTH IRA PreRet Tax 25%	Traditional Rettax 25%	Traditional Rettax 22%	Traditional Rettax 19%	Traditional Rettax 16%	Traditional Rettax 12%	Traditional Rettax 10%	Traditional Rettax 5%	Traditional Rettax 0%
Start	$10,000	$10,000	$10,000	$10,000	$10,000	$10,000	$10,000	$10,000	$10,000
1	$8,231	$8,175	$8,502	$8,829	$9,156	$9,592	$9,810	$10,355	$10,900
2	$9,032	$8,911	$9,267	$9,624	$9,980	$10,455	$10,693	$11,287	$11,881
3	$9,909	$9,713	$10,101	$10,490	$10,878	$11,396	$11,655	$12,303	$12,950
4	$10,869	$10,587	$11,010	$11,434	$11,857	$12,422	$12,704	$13,410	$14,116
5	$11,921	$11,540	$12,001	$12,463	$12,924	$13,540	$13,848	$14,617	$15,386
6	$13,071	$12,578	$13,081	$13,585	$14,088	$14,758	$15,094	$15,932	$16,771
7	$14,331	$13,710	$14,259	$14,807	$15,356	$16,087	$16,452	$17,366	$18,280
8	$15,710	$14,944	$15,542	$16,140	$16,738	$17,535	$17,933	$18,929	$19,926
9	$17,219	$16,289	$16,941	$17,592	$18,244	$19,113	$19,547	$20,633	$21,719
10	$18,869	$17,755	$18,465	$19,176	$19,886	$20,833	$21,306	$22,490	$23,674
11	$20,676	$19,353	$20,127	$20,901	$21,676	$22,708	$23,224	$24,514	$25,804
12	$22,652	$21,095	$21,939	$22,783	$23,626	$24,751	$25,314	$26,720	$28,127
13	$24,814	$22,994	$23,913	$24,833	$25,753	$26,979	$27,592	$29,125	$30,658
14	$27,179	$25,063	$26,065	$27,068	$28,071	$29,407	$30,076	$31,746	$33,417
15	$29,765	$27,319	$28,411	$29,504	$30,597	$32,054	$32,782	$34,604	$36,425
16	$32,594	$29,777	$30,968	$32,159	$33,351	$34,939	$35,733	$37,718	$39,703
17	$35,687	$32,457	$33,756	$35,054	$36,352	$38,083	$38,949	$41,113	$43,276
18	$39,070	$35,378	$36,794	$38,209	$39,624	$41,511	$42,454	$44,813	$47,171
19	$42,768	$38,562	$40,105	$41,647	$43,190	$45,247	$46,275	$48,846	$51,417
20	$46,812	$42,033	$43,714	$45,396	$47,077	$49,319	$50,440	$53,242	$56,044
21	$51,233	$45,816	$47,649	$49,481	$51,314	$53,758	$54,979	$58,034	$61,088
22	$56,066	$49,940	$51,937	$53,935	$55,932	$58,596	$59,927	$63,257	$66,586
23	$61,348	$54,434	$56,611	$58,789	$60,966	$63,869	$65,321	$68,950	$72,579
24	$67,122	$59,333	$61,706	$64,080	$66,453	$69,618	$71,200	$75,155	$79,111
25	$73,433	$64,673	$67,260	$69,847	$72,434	$75,883	$77,608	$81,919	$86,231
50	$678,061	$557,681	$579,989	$602,296	$624,603	$654,346	$669,218	$706,396	$743,575
75	$6,076,533	$4,808,932	$5,001,289	$5,193,646	$5,386,004	$5,642,480	$5,770,718	$6,091,313	$6,411,909
100	$53,573,574	$41,467,806	$43,126,518	$44,785,230	$46,443,943	$48,655,559	$49,761,367	$52,525,888	$55,290,408

Traditional IRA is better

Roth IRA is better

Year Start	ROTH Conversion Tax rate 25%	TRAD'L Retirement Tax rate 18%	TRAD'L Versus ROTH Difference		
1	$8,231	$8,938	8.6%		
2	$9,032	$9,742	7.9%		
3	$9,909	$10,619	7.2%		
4	$10,869	$11,575	6.5%		
5	$11,921	$12,617	5.8%		
6	$13,071	$13,752	5.2%		
7	$14,331	$14,990	4.6%	*Leave all in Trad'l IRA*	
8	$15,710	$16,339	4.0%		
9	$17,219	$17,810	3.4%		
10	$18,869	$19,412	2.9%		
11	$20,676	$21,159	2.3%		*Partial Convert to ROTH*
12	$22,652	$23,064	1.8%		
13	$24,814	$25,140	1.3%		
14	$27,179	$27,402	0.8%		
15	$29,765	$29,868	0.3%		
16	$32,594	$32,557	-0.1%		
17	$35,687	$35,487	-0.6%		
18	$39,070	$38,000	-1.0%		
19	$42,768	$42,162	-1.4%		*Full Convert to ROTH*
20	$46,812	$45,956	-1.8%		
21	$51,233	$50,092	-2.2%		
22	$56,066	$54,601	-2.6%		
23	$61,348	$59,515	-3.0%		
24	$67,122	$64,871	-3.4%		
25	$73,433	$70,709	-3.7%		

Next let us consider the effect of your age on the optimum percentage conversion. Your age is a factor in that it determines how soon you will need to start withdrawing from the retirement accounts. For instance, a person who converts at age 45 will typically leave the funds in retirement accounts for 15 to 20 years. The tax free growth benefit provided by the Roth IRA in this long time will warrant a full 100% conversion. On the other hand, a 60 year old person who needs to withdraw funds in 5 years is more likely to benefit by leaving some funds in the Traditional IRA, so a partial conversion will maximize retirement income.

> *In most cases (assuming withdrawals start at age 65) individuals who are under age 50 will benefit from a 100% conversion, and those who are over 60 will benefit most from a partial conversion.*

Specific situations can vary depending on the assumed tax rates and growth rates. The calculation of the optimum percentage conversion is described in the following section.

6.3 Calculating the Optimal Conversion

Calculation of the percentage conversion for an optimal conversion is very complex and requires a high-end software package. The software model must take the following factors into consideration:

- The software must have a way of varying the percentage of the Traditional IRA that is converted and the program must be capable of modelling sequential withdrawals: draw funds from the other taxable assets first, then from the Traditional IRA and last from the Roth IRA.
- The software program must model minimum required distributions.
- The program needs to include an optimization algorithm.

One such program is the ***Roth Optimizer***[1], developed by DQI Inc. An example, real-world case, analyzed by the Roth Optimizer, is described here.

Example: Mr. and Ms. Bojangles, ages 61, will need to withdraw funds from their retirement assets starting at age 65 till age 88. Their conversion tax bracket (Federal plus State) is 40% and their anticipated tax bracket during retirement years is 25%. They have $600,000 in IRA assets, assumed to grow at 9% per year. In addition they have $300,000 in other investable assets. They will receive $30,000 per year in Social Security income, and will need an additional $50,000 per year in retirement income. What percentage conversion will maximize their annual withdrawals from the retirement assets? It is assumed that the retirement income needs to be increased by 3.0% each year to keep up with inflation. The Recalculation Method model is assumed for post 70 1/2 Traditional IRA minimum required distributions.

The Roth Optimizer software was used to show that the optimum conversion percentage. A graph of the retirement withdrawals versus percentage converted is shown in Table

---

[1] For more information on this program contact DQI, Inc. at http://www.rothirabook.com or 1-877-ROTH911

6.3. The optimum percentage conversion is seen to be 70%. Any more or less conversion will decrease the annual income received. Note that the optimum is reasonably broad, which means that any conversion within, for instance, 10 percentage points of the optimum results in a relatively small difference in the withdrawal amount (this is called a low-Q optimal in mathematical terms). In addition to maximizing the additional benefit provided by the optimum conversion that the **conversion taxes due at the time of conversion will correspondingly be reduced.**

Let us consider some what-if scenarios to further illustrate the concepts underlying optimal conversions. If their retirement tax rate increased to 30%, the optimum

TABLE 6.3 Optimum Conversion

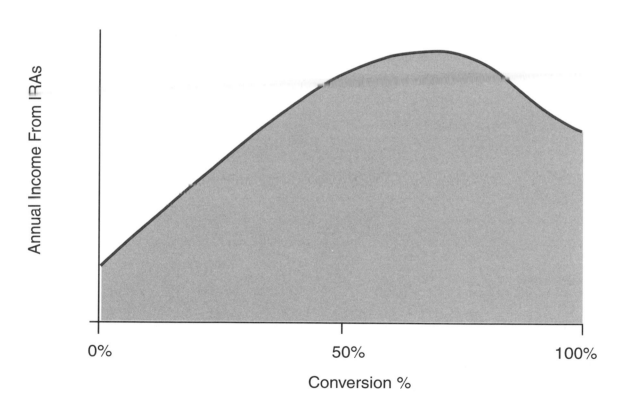

Converting 70% of Traditional IRA gives maximum retirement income

conversion would increase to 90%. On the other hand a decrease in retirement taxes to, for example, 20%, would decrease the optimum to 50%.

If their retirement withdrawals decreased from $50,000 to $30,000, the optimum would increase to 85%; an increase of the retirement withdrawals to $75,000 per year would decrease the optimum to 65%.

If the rate of assumed return of return increased to 11% the optimum would be at 75% conversion, while a drop in the assumed rate of return to 5% would indicate a 45% conversion.

If their other investable assets were lower, say at $150,000, the optimum would drop to 60%; if these assets were at $450,000 the optimum would increase to 80%. If these assets were as high as $600,000 the optimum would be at 100% i.e. a full conversion would be indicated.

In the above analyses we had assumed that the conversion taxes would be paid from outside assets. What if the Bojangles did not have outside assets and they chose to withdraw funds from the Roth IRA to pay the taxes? In this case the advantage of the Roth IRA will be greatly reduced and the optimum conversion, calculated by the Roth Optimizer, was found to be 20%.

6.4 Conclusions on Partial or Optimal Conversion

The calculation of the optimal conversion is a complex problem, depending on many variables. This will require the help of an experienced financial advisor, and /or a high-end program. The basic concepts suggest the following guideline:

Assuming your tax rate is lower during retirement, if you need to start withdrawing funds from a tax-advantaged IRA starting within 15 years of the conversion date, consider a partial conversion. If the withdrawals from these funds will start more than 15 years from the conversion date a full conversion is generally indicated. On the other hand, if you will need all your funds within 5 years of the conversion, Roth conversion is not recommended.

We repeat that these are the mathematical results based on maximizing assets. Other personal factors may enter into the decision of a full or partial conversion: these should be discussed with your financial advisor.

Chapter 7 The Rules for Roth IRA

"…we would like to expand the program in many ways… to index the contributions, and increase the dollar amount, to make up for lost ground [previous IRAs have not been indexed]… and to expand the eligibility for contributions and conversions…"

Senator Roth

The Roth IRA is a new type of IRA that has been made available as of January 1, 1998. It is named after Senate Finance Committee Chairman William V. Roth Jr., (R-De). Its distinguishing characteristic is that it provides tax free growth with tax free withdrawals, in contrast with the deductible Traditional IRAs, which provide tax advantages in the year of investment. The relative advantages of the Roth IRA have been described in this book. In this chapter we will detail the rules related to Roth Contribution and Roth Conversion IRAs. Since you may wish to consider other tax-advantaged options, we will also include appropriate comparisons with the Traditional IRAs (deductible and non-deductible).

The topics that will be included in this chapter are:

- Eligibility (for the Roth and Traditional IRAs)
- Distributions: qualified and non-qualified
- Penalties
- Taxes
- Investment Restrictions
- Transfers
- Deadlines
- Required Minimum Distributions
- Estate and Gift tax
- State Laws
- Forms

7.1 Taxpayer Relief Act of 97 & Technical Corrections Act of 98

The Roth IRA came into existence as a part of the Taxpayer Relief Act of 1997 (TRA '97). While the Roth IRA went into effect on January 1, 1998, some of the rules were finalized in July 1998. The Technical Corrections Act of 1998 (TCA '98) provided clarifications and amendments on numerous issues. The TCA '98 was signed into law by the President of United States in July 1998.

This chapter summarizes the rules applicable to the Roth IRA as enacted by the Taxpayer Relief Act of 1997, including all the modifications made by the Technical Corrections Act of 1998. Thus it reflects current law.

The reader is referred to the web site at http://www.senate.gov/~finance for updates following the Technical Corrections Act and http://www.irs.gov for any regulations or administrative guidance from the Internal Revenue Service. Other informative web sites are listed in Appendix C.

7.2 Roth IRA Contributions

This section will address the rules governing Roth IRA contributions. The Roth Contribution IRAs permit contributions of up to a maximum of $2,000 per year for each individual. These contributions are not tax-deductible (unlike the deductible Traditional IRA); instead they provide tax-free growth and tax-free withdrawals, provided certain conditions are met. The detailed rules are described in this section:

7.2.1 Eligibility: Who Can Contribute

Earned Income:

The annual contribution is limited to $2,000 but cannot be more than your **taxable compensation**. This taxable compensation must be earned from personal services.[1] The types of compensation that can be included are salaries, self-employment income, fees, bonuses, tips, and commissions. Alimony is also included, if it is included in the individual's gross income under a separation instrument or a divorce decree.

---

[1] For example, if your compensation is $1,500 for the year 1998, the maximum that you can contribute will be $1,500.

You may **not include** the following in the definition of taxable compensation: disability payments, Social Security benefits, pensions, deferred compensation, income from interest and dividends, rents, foreign earned income and housing allowances that are excluded from income, and any other amounts not included in your gross income.

Age Restriction:

There is no maximum age: you may contribute even after age 701/2, through your entire lifetime. This is in contrast with Traditional IRAs, which you cannot contribute to after age 701/2.

7.2.2 How Much Can Be Contributed

The amount that can be contributed depends on your filing status and your modified adjusted gross income. Chapter 3 detailed the steps for computing your modified adjusted gross income (MAGI). The MAGI is derived from the adjusted gross income (AGI) from the IRS Form 1040. This AGI is modified by **adding** to it: foreign earned income, foreign housing allowances, interest on U.S. savings bonds used for higher education, adoption-assistance program credits; and deduction claimed for a Traditional IRA; and **subtracting** income derived from rolling over or converting a Traditional IRA to a Roth IRA.

A detailed discussion of Income, Adjusted Gross Income, Modified Gross Income and Taxable Income is presented in Chapter 3.

> *As part of the TCA '98, Congress specifically provided that, after Dec 31. 2004, minimum required distributions (from Traditional IRAs and other qualified plans that begin after age 701/2) need not be included in the MAGI for purposes of determining eligibility.*

In the years 1998 through 2004, however, these required minimum distributions (described in Chapter 8 in detail) will need to be included in the MAGI.

Table 7.1 shows that the amount that can be contributed depends on your tax filing status and your MAGI. The maximum is $2,000 per individual and $4,000 per couple ($2,000 for the husband and $2,000 for the wife). If your MAGI exceeds certain levels, you cannot contribute to the Roth IRA.

Specifically, married couples filing jointly can contribute $4,000 if their combined MAGI is less than $150,000; they can make a partial contribution if their MAGI is between $150,000 and $160,000; and they cannot contribute if their MAGI exceeds $160,000. Individuals with a filing status of single or qualifying widow (er), head of household can contribute $2,000 if their MAGI is less than $95,000; they can make a partial contribution if their MAGI is between $95,000 and $110,000; they cannot make a contribution if their MAGI exceeds $110,000. This same rule applies to individuals who are married filing separately if they live apart from their spouse throughout the year. The general rule for married filing separately (assuming that they did not live apart for the full year) is more restrictive: the phase out occurs between $0 and $10,000.

The partial level contributions are described at the bottom of Table 7.1. Note that the maximum combined (total) contribution to all IRAs is $2,000 per individual.

Note that the $2,000 is not indexed to keep up with inflation

Table 7.1 also shows the eligibility criteria for the deductible and non-deductible Traditional IRAs.

Table 7.2 shows the amounts that can be contributed for individuals whose earned income exceeds $2,000 and couples whose combined earned income exceeds $4,000.

Note 7.2.2.1: You may fund both a Roth IRA and a Traditional IRA, but the total amount must be less than the $2,000 limit. Thus if your MAGI is over the Traditional IRA limit and within the phase-out range for a Roth IRA, you have the option of funding as much as the phase-out rules allow in a Roth IRA, and the balance (to sum to $2,000) in a non-deductible Traditional IRA.

Note 7.2.2.2: You may fund both a Roth IRA and a company sponsored plan such as the 401(k), 403(b) and SEP IRA.

Note 7.2.2.3: Companies may set up an automatic Roth IRA payroll deduction plan. This certainly will provide individuals with the discipline to save as a habit.

Note 7.2.2.4: Companies may not use the Roth IRA to fund a SEP or SIMPLE IRA. (It is possible that these rules will be expanded in the future: it would certainly be consistent with the Roth project initiatives).

Table 7.1 Eligibility for IRA Contributions

BLK	AGE	Filing Status		Participate in Qual Plan		Adjusted Gross Income		Deductible Traditional IRA	ROTH IRA	Non-Ded Traditional IRA
		Single QW	Married Filing Jointly	You	Spouse	More Than	Less Than			
1	under 70	Yes		Yes		$0	$30,000	$2,000	$2,000	
	under 70	Yes		Yes		$30,000	$40,000	Partial (1)	$2,000	
	under 70	Yes		Yes		$40,000	$95,000		$2,000	
	under 70	Yes		Yes		$95,000	$110,000		Partial (2)	$2,000
	under 70	Yes		Yes		$110,000	no limit			$2,000
2	under 70	Yes		No		$0	$95,000	$2,000	$2,000	
	under 70	Yes		No		$95,000	$110,000	$2,000	Partial (2)	$2,000
	under 70	Yes		No		$110,000	no limit	$2,000		$2,000
3	under 70		Yes	Yes		$0	$50,000	$4,000	$4,000	
	under 70		Yes	Yes		$50,000	$60,000	Partial (3)	$4,000	
	under 70		Yes	Yes		$60,000	$150,000		$4,000	
	under 70		Yes	Yes		$150,000	$160,000		Partial (4)	$4,000
	under 70		Yes	Yes		$160,000	no limit			$4,000
4	under 70		Yes	No		$0	$150,000	$4,000	$4,000	
	under 70		Yes	No	Yes	$150,000	$160,000	Partial (4)	Partial (4)	$4,000
	under 70		Yes	No	No	$150,000	$160,000	$4,000	Partial (4)	$4,000
	under 70		Yes	No	Yes	$160,000	no limit			$4,000
	under 70		Yes	No	No	$160,000	no limit	$4,000		$4,000
5	70 & over	Yes				$0	$95,000		$2,000	
	70 & over	Yes				$95,000	$110,000		Partial (4)	
6	70 & over		Yes			$0	$160,000		$4,000	
	70 & over		Yes			$150,000	$160,000		Partial (4)	

Note:
Partial (1) $10 for each $50 over $30,000 minimum of $200
Partial (2) $10 for each $75 over $95,000 minimum of $200
Partial (3) $10 for each $50 over $50,000 minimum of $200
Partial (4) $10 for each $50 over $150,000 minimum of $200
Round up to the next $10

Example: If your age is under 70 [blocks 1,2,3, or 4]
and you are married filling jointly [block 3 or 4]
and you participate in a qualified plan [block 3]
then you should check MAGI in block 3 for eligibility,
e.g. if MAGI is more than $60,000 and less than $150,000
the couple is eligible to contribute $2,000 each [total $4,000]
in the Roth IRA.

Table 7.2 Roth IRA Contribution Limits

Assumptions

Contributions to other Traditional IRAs None

- Married filing jointly
- Earned Income Greater Than $4,000

- Single
- Married Filing Separately
- Head of Household
- Qualifying Widow(er)
- Earned Income Greater Than $2,000

MAGI	Max Contrib	MAGI	Max Contrib	MAGI	Max Contrib	MAGI	Max Contrib
$0	4000	$156,600	1360	$0	2000	$104,500	740
$150,000	4000	$156,700	1320	$96,000	2000	$104,750	700
$150,100	3960	$156,800	1280	$96,250	2000	$105,000	670
$150,200	3920	$156,900	1240	$96,500	1800	$105,250	640
$150,300	3880	$157,000	1200	$96,750	1770	$105,500	600
$150,400	3840	$157,100	1160	$97,000	1740	$105,750	570
$150,500	3800	$157,200	1120	$97,250	1700	$106,000	540
$150,600	3760	$157,300	1080	$97,500	1670	$106,250	500
$150,700	3720	$157,400	1040	$97,750	1640	$106,500	470
$150,800	3680	$157,500	1000	$98,000	1600	$106,750	440
$150,900	3640	$157,600	960	$98,250	1570	$107,000	400
$151,000	3600	$157,700	920	$98,500	1540	$107,250	370
$151,100	3560	$157,800	880	$98,750	1500	$107,500	340
$151,200	3520	$157,900	840	$99,000	1470	$107,750	300
$151,300	3480	$158,000	800	$99,250	1440	$108,000	270
$151,400	3440	$158,100	760	$99,500	1400	$108,250	240
$151,500	3400	$158,200	720	$99,750	1370	$108,500	200
$151,600	3360	$158,300	680	$100,000	1340	$108,750	200
$151,700	3320	$158,400	640	$100,250	1300	$109,000	200
$151,800	3280	$158,500	600	$100,500	1270	$109,250	200
$151,900	3240	$158,600	560	$100,750	1240	$109,500	200
$152,000	3200	$158,700	520	$101,000	1200	$109,750	200
$152,500	3000	$158,800	480	$101,250	1170	$110,000	0
$153,000	2800	$158,900	440	$101,500	1140	$110,250	0
$153,500	2600	$159,000	400	$101,750	1100	$110,500	0
$154,000	2400	$159,100	360	$102,000	1070	$110,750	0
$154,500	2200	$159,200	320	$102,250	1040	$111,000	0
$155,000	2000	$159,300	280	$102,500	1000	$111,250	0
$155,500	1800	$159,400	240	$102,750	970	$111,500	0
$156,000	1600	$159,500	200	$103,000	940	$111,750	0
$156,100	1560	$159,600	200	$103,250	900	$112,000	0
$156,200	1520	$159,700	200	$103,500	870	$112,250	0
$156,300	1480	$159,800	200	$103,750	840	$112,500	0
$156,400	1440	$159,900	200	$104,000	800	$112,750	0
$156,500	1400	$160,000	0	$104,250	770	$113,000	0

Example: If you are married filing jointly and your combined earned income is $151,000, you may contribute up to as total of $3,600

Each individual is limited to $2,000. Thus you may contribute $2,000 for one spouse and $1,600 for the other spouse (for example).

Note 7.2.2.5   Contributions to a Roth IRA are not affected by your participation in an employer retirement plan.

Note 7.2.2.6   The amount you can contribute to a Roth IRA is reduced dollar for dollar for any contribution you also make to a Traditional deductible or Traditional non-deductible IRA.

Note 7.2.2.7   While a couple may contribute a total of $4,000, they must not exceed $2,000 for each of their contributions. Their contributions must be held in separate accounts.

Note 7.2.2.7   The amount you can contribute to a Roth IRA is also reduced dollar for dollar for any contribution you make to a 501(c)(18) plan. This is a pension plan created before June 25 1959 that is funded entirely by employee contributions.

Note 7.2.2.8   All provisions are effective January 1 1998.

7.2.3 Spousal IRA

Spousal contributions are permitted. To be eligible, taxable compensation may be earned by **either spouse.** Thus even if only one spouse has earned income, the maximum of $4,000 may be contributed, assuming the MAGI limits described in Section 7.2.2 are met. The couple must file a joint return.

7.2.4 Deadlines for Contribution

The 1998 contribution may be made any time in 1998 and any time until April 15, 1999. In general, the contribution for a year can be made in the year or in the next year before the federal income tax return deadline (generally April 15).

Note 7.2.4.1   If you make a contribution on or before April 15 of any year, you will need to specify if the contribution is for that year or the previous year.

Note 7.2.4.2   You may file your tax return before making the contribution.

7.2.5 Non-deductible

You may not deduct your contributions to a Roth IRA on your Federal Income tax return.

7.2.6 Taxes

There are no taxes on the growth and there are no taxes upon withdrawal, provided the withdrawals follow the rules stated in Section 7.4 below.

7.2.6 Excess Contributions

Any contribution to the Roth IRA that exceeds the permissible limits is considered an **excess contribution**. You can correct this by withdrawing the excess before the due date of the federal tax return (including extensions: which is an automatic 4 months, and can be extended another 2 months) for the taxable year in which the excess contribution is made.

If you do not correct this mistake and leave the excess contribution in the Roth IRA, you will be subject to a 6% tax (called an excise tax) for **each year** that you leave the excess in.

You can avoid the reapplication of the excise tax in the next year by making a contribution that is equal to your maximum allowable amount **less** the excess from the previous year.

7.2.7 Cash Contributions

The annual contributions must be in cash. You are not permitted to contribute with stocks or other non-cash assets.

7.3 Roth Conversions

This section will detail the rules for the Roth Conversion. You may roll over some or all of the assets from a Traditional IRA to a Roth IRA provided you meet the eligibility conditions.

7.3.1 Eligibility: Who Is Eligible

To be eligible for a Roth Conversion, the individual's modified adjusted gross income (in the year of Conversion) must not exceed **$100,000.** There are no age restrictions.

If a married couple files separate returns (and lived with your spouse at any time during the year) , **neither spouse may roll over any Traditional IRA funds.** Note that if you did not live with your spouse at any time during the year, you are eligible for a Roth Conversion (provided you meet the MAGI condition).

For a 1998 Conversion the MAGI must be equal to or less than $100,000 for the calendar year ending in December 1998. The conversion amounts are not included in the MAGI for assessing eligibility. We also reemphasize that the required minimum distributions are included in the MAGI until the year 2004, but are not included in the MAGI from 2005 and on.

> *An important initiative in the Roth project is to index the eligibility limits This would greatly add to the attractiveness of the Roth IRAs.*

Note 7.3.1.1 The $100,000 MAGI limit applies only to the specific year of conversion. Thus if you make a 1998 conversion, your MAGI in future years (1999 on) may exceed $100,000. This is true even if you have selected to spread your taxable income over 4 years.

Note 7.3.1.2 You may not convert an inherited IRA, unless it is a spousal rollover. Thus it is best for your non-spousal beneficiary if you convert to a Roth IRA before you die. This is discussed further in Chapter 9 on estate planning.

7.3.2 How Much Can Be Converted

Any amount may be rolled over. There is no minimum. There is no maximum.

The early withdrawal 10% penalty tax does not apply for the amounts rolled over from the Traditional IRA, even if you are under 59 1/2. Thus amounts rolled over are considered qualified distributions from the Traditional IRA.

Note 7.3.2.1   If you use some of the IRA assets to pay for the conversion taxes, that amount will be subject to early withdrawal penalty tax. The reason is that the amount withdrawn for taxes is not considered a qualified distribution.

Note 7.3.2.2   The percentage of non-deductible IRA converted must be equal to non-deductible percentage in all of your IRAs put together. Thus you may not convert only the non-deductible portion of your IRA.

7.3.3 Deadline for Conversion

For a 1998 Conversion, the distribution from the Traditional IRA must occur by December 31, 1998. This can be directly transferred to a Roth IRA: making this a direct transfer from trustee to trustee.

Alternatively, while this is not a recommended practice, you may withdraw the Traditional IRA by December 31st, and roll it over to a Roth IRA account within 60 days.

7.3.4 Exceeding the AGI: Reversing the Conversion

If you have rolled your funds over from a Traditional IRA to a Roth IRA, but later find that your MAGI exceeds $100,000, you will need to reverse the rollover.

> *You are permitted to transfer the funds (and earnings) from the Roth IRA account to a Traditional IRA account. This must be done by the due date for the taxpayer's return (including extensions). This must be a direct trustee-to-trustee transfer.*

Some of you may be concerned that you may misjudge your expected MAGI in 1998, convert to a Roth IRA, and later realize that you have exceeded the $100,000 limit. What are the consequences of such an error? You will be able to direct-transfer the funds back from the Roth account to a Traditional IRA account if you act by April 15, 1999 (or by October 15 1999 if you file for a six month extension). The full amount in the opened Roth account will need to be transferred back into the Traditional IRA account: this includes the principal and the growth. There is no penalty imposed.

7.3.5 Taxes

Taxes must be paid on the amount that is rolled over from the Traditional IRA to the Roth IRA, except for any portion that was a non-deductible contribution to the Traditional IRA. For instance, if your Traditional IRA includes some non-deductible amounts, you may roll over that amount but will not need to pay taxes on that amount.

If the rollover occurs by December 31, 1998, the individual has two choices on how the tax is paid.

> *The first choice is to include all of the rolled-over amount as part of the 1998 taxable income. The second choice is to include one-fourth of the rolled-over amount in the income for each of these four years: 1998, 1999, 2000 and 2001.*

Most individuals will benefit from the four-year spread.[2]

If the rollover occurs in any year after 1998, the individual has only one choice: the full amount must be included in that year's taxable income.

Note 7.3.5.1: Note that it is the income that is spread over the 4 years, not the tax on the income.

Note 7.3.5.2:   Not all the IRA funds need to be converted at the same time. Further, you are permitted to have multiple Roth IRA accounts (e.g. with different designated beneficiaries)

Note 7.3.5.3:   If you die before the 4 years are completed, the remaining balance is included in the taxable income in the year of the death. If the Roth IRA is rolled over by your spouse, however, he / she may continue your schedule for including the amount in the income.

Note 7.3.5.4:   Once you elect a method, either to use the 4-year spread or not, you may not change the elected method after the due date for filing the income tax return for the year of conversion (including extensions).

Note 7.3.5.5:   The conversion amount is subtracted from MAGI for determining the MAGI used to determine eligibility. Thus the MAGI-based phase out of the exemption from the disallowance for passive activity losses from rental real estate activities would be applied taking into account the amount of the conversion that is includable in the MAGI, and then the amount of the conversion would be subtracted from the MAGI in determining whether you are eligible to convert into a Roth IRA or not.

Note 7.3.5.6:   The MAGI must include the income of both spouses in determining eligibility. It is not true that if one spouse has a MAGI that is less than $100,000 then that spouse may convert his / her Traditional IRA.

Note 7.3.5.7:   Hardship distributions from a 401(k) or other qualified plan may not be used to pay for Roth conversion taxes.

Note 7.3.5.8   Critical conversion dates: to be eligible for the 4-year-spread, you must withdraw rollover funds from the Traditional IRA by December 31, 1998. It is advisable that you do a direct transfer of these funds to a Roth account (a trustee to trustee transfer). The 5-year clock penalty-free withdrawal starts on January 1 1998, if you open the Roth account by December 31 1998. This means that, with a December 31 opening, you really need only 4 years plus 1 day before you can make a penalty-free withdrawal: not 5 full years.

You do have the option of withdrawing funds from the Traditional IRA account and later (within 60 days) opening the Roth IRA account. Sixty days after December 31 is March 6 1999. If, for some reason, you need to elect this option, the 5-year clock for penalty free withdrawals will start on January 1 1999.

7.3.5 Rollovers from Roth IRAs

Rollovers from one Roth IRA to another Roth IRA are permitted. In such a rollover you receive funds from one Roth IRA account, then you deposit this fund in another Roth IRA account. Such rollovers are limited to one per year, beginning on the date you receive the assets. The rollover must take place within 60 days of distribution from the original Roth IRA.

The rollover must be distinguished from the direct transfer, which is described in the next section.

Note 7.3.5.1   Generally you are permitted only one rollover per year from an IRA to another IRA. The Roth IRA rollover is an exception to this rule: the rollover from a Traditional to a Roth IRA is not included in this one-time-per-year-rule.

7.3.6 Direct Transfers from Roth IRAs

In a direct transfer, you do not receive the funds. Direct transfers occur between custodians or trustees (e.g., banks, brokerage firms). These direct transfers may be made as often as you wish.

7.3.7 Spousal Rollover

A surviving spouse who is the beneficiary can make a tax-free rollover of the deceased spouse's Roth IRA to his or her own Roth IRA. The rollover may or may not be automatic, depending on how the institution you are working with sets up the Roth account. If it is not automatic, you will have to request such a rollover. See Chapter 9 for more on this issue.

[2] If you expect your income to be much greater than $100,000 in 1999, 2000, and 2001, you may be better off including the entire income in 1998. This requires some very careful and detailed analysis.

7.3.8 Non-Spousal Rollover

If you are a non-spouse beneficiary, distributions from an inherited Roth IRA may not be rolled over into a Roth IRA owned by you. See Chapter 9 for the post-death payout options and account titling institutions.

7.3.9 Rollovers from 401(k), 403(b)

You may not make a direct rollover of amounts from employer retirement plans, such as the 401(k) and 403 (b), to the Roth IRA.

However, the rollover may be made in an indirect way. These amounts may first be transferred over to a Traditional IRA . Then the Traditional IRA may be rolled over to a Roth IRA. In general, employees have the option of rolling over from a 401(k)-type plan to a Traditional IRA only after they retire or terminate service with the employer sponsoring the plan.

7.4 Distributions

This section will explain the rules on withdrawals from the Roth IRA account. It applies to both Contribution and Conversion Roth IRA accounts. When you withdraw money it is called a distribution. You will not pay taxes or penalties on this distribution if you meet certain conditions, which will make the distribution a qualified distribution. If you do not meet these conditions, the distribution is called a non-qualified distribution and you will have to pay taxes (on the earnings, not the basis) and you may have to pay a penalty. Thus

For qualified distributions: no taxes, no penalties

For non-qualified distributions: pay taxes; may pay penalties

The specifics are described in the following sections.

7.4.1 Qualified Distributions

We start by describing a qualified distribution. A distribution is qualified if **any one** of the following is true:

a) You have held a Roth IRA for five years and you have reached age 59 1/2
b) You have held a Roth IRA for five years and you are totally and permanently disabled
c) You have held a Roth IRA for five years and you die
d) You have held a Roth IRA for five years and are a qualified first-time home-buyer

Now, let us elaborate on the specific definitions of some of the terms that have been used.

What is meant by "held assets for five years" ?

> For contributions or conversions made in 1998, the five-year period ends on December 31, 2002. In general, the five-year period starts with the first day of the year for which the contribution or conversion was made; and it ends on the last day of the fourth year after this date. This makes the period exactly 365*5 days or five years from the first day of the year in which you converted. However, if you convert as late as December 31 of any year, the 5-year period will end 4 years and 1 day after that date. Note that a subsequent conversion will not trigger a new 5-year period. However, for purposes of calculating pre-59 1/2 penalties on Roth Conversion withdrawals, the five year period starts in the year of that conversion.

Note 7.4.1.1   This ruling suggests that if you convert in 1998, the 5 year clock starts on January 1 1998. If this is followed by a subsequent conversion in a later year, say 2000, the 5 year clock for this latter conversion is still January 1 1998 (not Jan 1 2000). Thus both conversions may be withdrawn after December 31 2002 as qualified distributions.

Note 7.4.1.2   Roth IRA contributions and conversions may be held in the same account.

What is meant by totally and permanently disabled?

This means that you have a medically determinable physical or mental impairment that can be expected to result in death or be long-continued and of indefinite duration.

What is a "qualified first-time home-buyer," and how much can one withdraw?

These are costs for acquiring, constructing, or reconstructing your or your spouse's principal residence or the principal residence of your spouse's child, grandchild, or ancestor, provided that the individual for whom the house is being acquired is a first-time home-buyer. The term "first-time home-buyer" means that the individual did not have ownership interest in a principal residence during the two-year period ending on the date a binding contract to purchase a principal residence is executed or the date when construction or reconstruction of a principal residence begins.

The distribution has a lifetime limit of $10,000, and it must be used within 120 days after you receive it.

7.4.2 Non-Qualified Distributions

If you do not meet any of the conditions spelled out in Section 7.4.1 then the distribution is non-qualified. You will have to pay **income taxes** on the earnings (not on the basis, which is your contribution), and you may have to pay a **penalty**. Let us first consider the tax payments that will be due.

Tax Payments for Non-qualified Distributions

A non-qualified distribution does not get tax-free treatment. However, there is a favorable recovery-of-basis rule. Non-qualified distributions are first treated as having been made from **your contributions**. This means you get to first recover your basis amount (amount you converted/contributed). This part will be tax-free. Once the basis is fully recovered (that means once you have withdrawn your basis), further distributions will be taxable.

If the Roth IRA account you hold includes contributions and conversion amounts, the ordering rules (which means the sequence of withdrawals) for distributions are as follows.

1.Contribution basis assets 2. Conversion assets (based on first-tax-year in, first-out and taxable pre-conversion amounts first, followed by non-taxable preconversion amounts); and 3. all earnings.

Note 7.4.2.1   Any amount that is taxable will be taxed at your ordinary income tax rate; not the capital gains tax rate (even if all your asset holdings were in stocks or stock funds).

Note 7.4.2.2   Roth distributions are not subject to Alternative Minimum Taxes. However, State tax deductions for payment of Roth Conversion taxes must be folded back in to the calculation of alternative minimum taxes.

7.4.3 Penalties

If the distribution is non-qualified, then in addition to the income tax payments on the earnings you will also have to pay a 10% **penalty**, unless you meet one of these exceptions:

a)   You have reached age 59 1/2
b)   Death
c)   Disability
d)   Medical expenses
e)   Higher education expenses
f)   First-time home-buyer expenses
g)   A series of substantially equal periodic payments
h)   Distributions made on account of IRS levies
i)   Insurance premiums paid by an unemployed individual

We see that if you have reached 59 1/2, no early-withdrawal penalty is applied. If you die, no penalty is applied. If you are disabled, as defined in Section 7.4.1, no penalty is applied. If you are a first-time home buyer, as defined in Section 7.4.1, no penalty is applied. Thus we see that:

If over 59 1/2, never pay penalties
If over 59 1/2 and qualified no taxes
If over 59 1/2 and not qualified pay taxes
If under 59 1/2 and qualified: no taxes no penalties
If under 59 1/2 not qualified, no exceptions: pay taxes and penalty
If under 59 1/2 not qualified, exceptions apply: pay taxes, no penalties

The following table summarizes the rules for earnings:

	Distributions before 5 yrs		Distributions after 5 yrs	
	Earnings taxable?	10 percent penalty?	Earnings taxable?	10 percent penalty?
After age 59 1/2	Yes	No	No	No
Before age 59 1/2	Yes	Yes unless death disability home-buyer equal payments medical expense insurance by unemployed higher education IRS levies	Yes	Yes unless death disability home-buyer equal payments medical expense insurance by unemployed higher education IRS levies

See Section 7.4.1 for definition of five-year period.

What are higher education expenses?

These include tuition and fees-and such expenses as books, supplies, computers, and equipment-paid for enrolling in or attending an eligible educational institution. These expenses can be for you, your spouse, child, grandchild, or ancestor.

What are qualified medical expenses?

These are medical expenses, exceeding 7.5% of AGI, that qualify as deductible expenses if you were itemizing your deductions. You may also include medical insurance while unemployed (this is not subject to the 7.5% threshold rule).

What are a series of substantially equal payments?

You may elect to take a series of substantially equal payments to avoid the 10% penalty. The payments you receive must be taken at least annually.

If you begin the payments before age 59 1/2, then you must continue taking the payments for five years or until you reach 59 1/2, whichever is later. This five-year rule is waived in case of disability or death.

Payments must be scheduled over your single life expectancy or over the joint life expectancy for you and your beneficiary.

Once the payment schedule is established, the series of payments may not be changed. If you do change the payments, you will be subject to the 10% penalty (with interest).

7.4.4 Minimum Required Distributions

For the Roth IRAs there are no required minimum distributions during your lifetime. There are required minimum distributions after your lifetime. The required withdrawals depend on the selection of beneficiary.

The required minimum distribution rules and items related to selection of beneficiaries are thoroughly covered in Chapters 8 and 9.

7.4.5 Early Withdrawal of a 1998 Conversion: Acceleration Rule

As has been mentioned before, if you convert in 1998, you have the option of spreading the Conversion amount to be included in your taxable income over 4 years; namely, one-fourth in 1998, one-fourth in 1999, one-fourth in 2000, and one-fourth in 2001. This spreads the Conversion tax burden over four years. Further, it allows you more time to come up with the tax dollars if you did not have all the funds available in 1998. This option is called the **4-year-spread.**

However, there is a special "acceleration rule" that applies if you choose to withdraw these 1998 converted amounts before December 31, 2001. Since the withdrawals we are discussing will not be qualified (they take place in less than 5 years), the non-qualified taxes and penalties apply to these withdrawals (see Section 7.4.2). In addition, the following acceleration rule will apply:

If you withdraw any converted amounts prior to the last year of the 4-year spread, you will be required to include in your income [for the year that you withdrew this amount] the amount that was normally includable under the 4-year rule, **plus** an acceleration amount. This acceleration amount is the lesser of a) the taxable amount of the withdrawal and b) the remaining taxable amount of the conversion. The latter amount under b) is the amount of the total conversion that has not been included in income to date. Now what happens in the next year? Assuming there are no other withdrawals, the amount that you will need to include in your income will be the lesser of c) the amount that normally would have been included if there were no withdrawal and d) the remaining taxable amount of the conversion.

7.5 Income Tax Withholdings

There is a 10% **non-mandatory** withholding tax for rollovers: you ware permitted to waive this withholding (by checking the appropriate box in the custodian's form for opening accounts).

7.5.1 Estimated Taxes

You are advised to ensure that sufficient taxes are withheld to avoid penalties for insufficient withholdings. Generally, penalties are not imposed if you have paid at least as much as the previous year's tax.

7.6 Estate and Gift Tax

The total value of the Roth IRA is included in your gross estate for Federal estate-tax purposes. See Chapter 9 for more on this subject.

7.7 Investment Restrictions

7.7.1 Prohibited Transaction

Certain transactions are not permitted with the Roth IRA. For example, you cannot borrow from your account, sell property to it, or buy property from it. The penalty for conducting a non-permitted transaction may be the loss of the tax-free status of the Roth IRA.

There are severe penalties if you lose the tax-free status. You will have to include all the earnings accumulated in your taxable gross income in the year the tax-free status was lost. Those earnings may further be subject to the 10% penalty tax on premature distributions (unless one of the exceptions named above applies).

The Roth IRA cannot be invested in life-insurance contracts or in certain collectibles (e.g., art, rugs, antiques, gems, stamps, coins, and alcoholic beverages. If you do invest in such a collectible, the amount of investment will be treated as a distribution and will be subject to taxes as described in the section on distributions.

Note 7.7.1.1   The Roth IRA may be invested in gold, silver and platinum bullion.

You are not permitted to borrow from the Roth IRA account, nor are you allowed to pledge the Roth IRA account as a security. If you do either, then the amount borrowed or pledged will be treated as a distribution may be subject to taxes and penalties (as described in the section on distribution).

Note 7.7.1.2 After 1998, you may wish to consider self-averaging (spread conversions over a number of years) to reduce taxes. However, note that you will not gain the benefit of tax-free growth on conversions that are deferred.

7.8 Divorce

The transfer to your spouse or former spouse under a qualified domestic relations order is not considered a taxable transfer. After the transfer the Roth IRA will be treated as belonging to the spouse or former spouse.

7.9 State Laws

7.9.1 Taxes

The following states have announced that the State tax treatment will conform with the federal tax treatment for Roth IRAs: AL AZ CA CO CT DE GA HI ID IL IN IA KS KY LA ME MD MA MI MN MT NE NH NJ NM NY NC OH OK OR RI SC TX UT VT VA WA WI . The following states do not have state taxes: AK FL NV SD TN TX WA WY. City, county and local taxes are not addressed here.

7.9.2 Creditor Protection

Some states offer protection against creditors for Traditional IRAs, referencing I.R.C.408. However, the Roth IRA is referenced under I.R.C. 408A not I.R.C. 408. Thus at present the Roth IRA will not be protected against creditors in many states. In other states it will be protected.

7.10   Forms

The following IRS forms are relevant to the Roth Accounts:

7.10.1 Form 5498

The custodian of the Roth account provides form 5498 to the IRS and to the owner (or beneficiary) of the Roth IRA each year. This form provides a valuation of the Roth account at the end of the prior year and a report of your Roth IRA contributions for the prior year made through April 15 of the current year.

7.10.2 Form 5329

The Form 5329 needs to be filed if penalties have been imposed. It is required if:

a)   You owe the 6% excise tax for an excess contribution
b)   You owe the 50% penalty tax for failing to take a minimum distribution
c)   You owe the 10% premature distribution penalty tax
See Appendix B.

7.10.3 Form 5305-Roth

This is the prototype form used to start a Roth IRA contribution or conversion account. See Appendix B.

7.11 Conclusions

This chapter described the rules for the Roth IRA Contributions and Conversions, based on the Taxpayer Relief Act of 1997 and the Technical Corrections Act of 1998.

IRS Regs and Q&As Addendum to Chapter 7

The following addendum to this chapter provides clarifications on the Technical Corrections Act of 1998 as provided by the Internal Revenue Service in the IRS REG-114393-98 and the Question and Answers published in August 1998. See Appendix D for the complete documents.

1. Recharacterization: If you have converted assets to a Roth IRA, you are permitted to convert the assets (some or all) back to a Traditional IRA, prior to the end of the taxable year (including extensions) in which the conversion was made. For example if you converted assets in June 1998, you may convert the assets back or "recharacterize" the assets to a Traditional IRA any time before the end of the taxable year period, including extensions. The recharacterization may be done if you have a failed-conversion due to your Modified Adjusted Gross Income exceeding $100,000, or for any other reason. Thus if the asset value of a converted Roth IRA has decreased, it is possible to convert the Roth IRA to a Traditional IRA, then immediately recharacterize back to a Roth IRA, leading to lower conversion taxes. If the second conversion is done before December 31, 1998, you also retain the benefit of a four-year spread for the converted amounts. Note that transactions must be trustee to trustee transfers. You may recharacterize once in 1998 and once in 1999 (see Appendix F p. 269).

The same procedure may be used for for annual IRA contributions. Thus, individuals who contrinuted $2,000 to a Traditional IRA may change the contribution to a Roth IRA by the due date of the taxable year.

2. MRDs: for 701/2: Any MRD (minimum required distribution) that is due in the year you turn 70 1/2 may not be converted, even if you chose to delay withdrawing this MRD to the following year.

3. Death before 4 years completed: If you convert in 1998 having chosen the 4-year spread, and you die before the four years are completed, all deemed income for the rest of the 4-year period is accelerated into the final return for the decedent. However, a spousal beneficiary may choose to continue paying the remaining taxes over the four years.

4. MRDs and Death before age 70 1/2: If you die before age 70 1/2, a spousal beneficiary may choose to defer withdrawals from the Roth IRA until the year in which you would have reached 70 1/2, or choose to treat the Roth IRA as his or her own (delaying distributions till the the surviving's spouse's death).

5. Education IRA: An Education IRA may not be converted to a Roth IRA.

6. SIMPLE IRA : A Simple IRA may be converted to a Roth IRA. except that an amount distributed from a SIMPLE IRA during the 2-year period which begins on the date that the individual first participated in any SIMPLE IRA Plan maintained by the individual's employer cannot be converted to a Roth IRA. A SEP IRA may be converted to a Roth IRA.

7. **Roth IRAs by Employer**s: An employer or an association of employees can establish a trust to hold contributions of employees or members under a Roth IRA. The employer or association of employees may do acts otherwise required by an individual, for example, establishing and designing a trust as a Roth IRA.

8. **Gifted IRAs:** If a Roth IRA is gifted, the assets are deemed to be distributed to the owner, and are no longer treated as being held in a Roth IRA. However, any gifts made prior to 10/1/1998 can be ignored if the entire Roth IRA was returned to the owner before 1/1/1999.

9 **Home purchases:** Married couples can each take a $10,000 pre-59 1/2 penalty-free distribution from a Roth IRA for a home purchase.

Chapter 8 Minimum Required Distributions

In the last few chapters we saw that the Roth IRA can provide a significant increase in retirement assets. The next two chapters (on minimum required distributions and estate planning) address maximizing benefits from the Roth IRA during your retirement and for your heirs. This will require careful planning for the distribution of assets and for the selection of beneficiaries. You will not be required to withdraw any amount from your Roth IRA during your lifetime. However, your beneficiaries will be **required** to withdraw some amounts from the Roth IRA account after your death, and you will be able to affect the rate of withdrawals.

In the study of required minimum distributions and estate planning we will see that **the Roth IRA provides some additional flexibility that the Traditional IRA does not.** This may provide additional motivation to convert your account to a Roth IRA.

This and the next chapter will help you understand the basic issues related to estate planning, selection of beneficiaries, and the minimum required distribution rules. It will provide guidance in maximizing the benefits from tax-advantaged accounts during your retirement and from assets that you leave to your children. Estate planning and minimum distributions are certainly areas that will require the help of a professional advisor. It is work to go through a chapter of this complexity. However, this is your retirement and your future, so it is most advisable for you to understand the basic considerations, if only to help you ask your advisor the right questions.

This chapter will review the minimum distribution rules applicable to both Traditional IRAs and Roth IRAs. The topics covered in this chapter include:

- Introduction to Minimum Required Distributions (MRD)
- Life Expectancy Tables for MRD
- Differences between Traditional and Roth IRAs
- MRD Rules for Traditional IRAs
- MRD Rules for Roth IRAs
- Conclusion and Summary

8.1 Introduction to Minimum Required Distributions

8.1.1 Why There Are Minimum Distribution Rules

We have seen that the longer you can keep your funds in tax-advantaged accounts, the better these accounts will do (relative to taxable accounts). However, you may not keep the funds in these tax-advantaged accounts indefinitely.

Congress created individual retirement accounts, like other types of tax-advantaged retirement plans, to foster savings during your working years for your future retirement. And, generally, Congress envisioned that during your retirement years you would make distributions from your retirement accounts to aid in paying for your living expenses. In the case of Traditional IRAs, taxes are still owed to the IRS. In the case of the Roth IRAs, no taxes are owed, but the intent is for you to use the money for your retirement needs and to provide for your children after your retirement. Another expectation is that these monies will be infused back into the economy, and thereby strengthen it.

Toward these ends, Congress created a set of rules known as the minimum required distribution (MRD) rules that require you to withdraw a certain minimum amount from the tax-advantaged accounts each year.

8.1.2 The Basic Rules for Traditional and Roth IRA

These minimum distributions are required from all tax-advantaged plans including Traditional IRAs, employee contribution plans (401(k)-type) as well as Roth IRAs. However, there is one major difference in the date when the withdrawals must begin.

With Traditional IRA and 401(k)-type[1] plans, distributions must begin the year after you reach 701/2, while with the new Roth IRA distributions begin only after your death.

> *With the Roth IRA no distributions are required during your life.*

Thus the Roth IRA will let you further stretch the tax-advantaged benefits into the next generation.

There are a variety of methods that may be used to determine rate of withdrawals. These methods include the Term Certain, Recalculation and the Hybrid method. We will describe their relative merits, and the most commonly used methods.

8.1.3 Why You Need to Consider Minimum Withdrawals

You will always need to establish a method of withdrawal even though in some cases you will not be affected by the best choice among the required minimum withdrawal methods: because your retirement plans call for withdrawals that exceed the required minimums anyway.

Consider the Traditional IRAs first. In this case MRDs start the year after you reach 70 1/2. If your non-retirement investable assets are relatively small and are used up before you reach 70, then you will be starting withdrawals from the Traditional IRA at or before age 70. If you plan to use up all of the Traditional IRA by withdrawing an indexed annuity over 20 years, the amounts that you will be withdrawing will always exceed the IRS's required minimum distributions. Thus the calculations of the MRDs (using different complex methods) will not be a concern for you.

> *However, you will need to check that the amount of withdrawal does indeed exceed the MRDs.*

So you will need to establish a method, preferably one that keeps the minimum floor as low as possible so that you are never stuck with drawing more than you need.

---

1 For qualified plans such as the 401(k), if you are not a 5% owner of a business, you may delay the distributions until the date of your retirement.

Next consider the Roth IRA. As we mentioned earlier, there are no withdrawals required during your lifetime. Thus if your planned withdrawals use up all of your assets before your death, the Roth IRA MRD rules will not be triggered for your account. However, death age is unpredictable, so you will need to ensure that you have properly designated your beneficiary to enable a post-death payout for that account.

At the other extreme we have the class of individuals who do not need to withdraw from any of their tax-advantaged accounts since they have adequate funds in their non-retirement accounts. Their main objective is to delay or minimize the amount of the withdrawals. These individuals will benefit most from the Roth IRAs, since no withdrawals are required during their lifetime. If they choose to leave some or all their funds in the Traditional IRAs, for example if a partial conversion is desired, they will want to select the slowest withdrawal method available with the Traditional IRAs. The distribution rules for the Roth IRA accounts will be seen to simpler, with fewer choices.

You need to ensure that you comply with MRD rules and make an informed distribution election upon your required beginning date. Unless you give attention to this matter, you will not know whether the amount you have chosen to withdraw exceeds the amount of your MRDs. Thus you will need to **check** that you are not under the MRD. Note that

> *if you withdraw less than the minimum required, you will be subject to a 50% excise tax on the under-withdrawal (difference between the minimum required withdrawal and the amount actually withdrawn)*

Also, the MRD rules continue to apply after your death to determine the amounts that must be withdrawn by your beneficiaries. Since your death age is not predictable, failure to carefully consider the MRD rules may unnecessarily limit your **beneficiaries**. Thus we can say in closing that

> *All individuals will need to establish their beneficiary designation and determine the amount that must be withdrawn under the MRD rules.*

8.1.4 Life Expectancy Tables

The first step in calculating minimum distributions is to find the correct Life Expectancy (LE) number from tables provided by the IRS. Once you have found this number, determining the exact amount you need to withdraw from your retirement account is straightforward. Divide the value of your account as of December 31 of the **preceding** year by the LE number for the current year based on your age in the current year. That is the amount to be withdrawn.

The life expectancy numbers are called "divisors" or life expectancy factors. The minimum distributions are based on the IRS single and joint life expectancy (LE) tables, which are in Appendix A. These unisex tables are based on mortality data collected in the 1980 census. The IRS is expected to update these tables in the near future to be based on 1990 census data. The life expectancy tables are also published in IRS Publication 590. Note that,

> *The larger the LE, the less money that has to be withdrawn, and the longer you can stretch the tax-advantaged account.*

Different withdrawal methods require different LEs. This will be addressed in Section 8.4

8.2 Differences Between Traditional IRAs and Roth IRAs

There are several important differences between Traditional IRAs and Roth IRAs in the area of the MRD rules. First, an owner of a Traditional IRA must start taking distributions during his or her lifetime, upon the so-called required beginning date (RBD).

> *An owner of a Roth IRA, however, does not have to take any distributions during his or her lifetime.*

Second, the "designated beneficiary" for a Traditional IRA is determined upon the earlier of the owner's RBD or the owner's death.

> *The "designated beneficiary" for a Roth IRA is always determined at the time of the Roth IRA owner's death.*

Third, if the owner of a Traditional IRA survives his or her RBD, the schedule of MRDs that must be taken during the owner's lifetime and after the owner's death is determined at the RBD and may not be subsequently changed to result in smaller distributions. Subject to two exceptions (the spousal rollover and conversion to a Roth IRA), the elections made on the RBD for a Traditional IRA are irrevocable.

> *For Roth IRAs, however, the schedule of MRDs does not become irrevocable until the time of the owner's death. With a spousal rollover, MRDs are delayed till the spouse's death.*

Because the rules and planning techniques are so distinct for Traditional IRAs and Roth IRAs, we are going to review the minimum distribution rules for each type of retirement account separately. Our primary focus in this book, however, is on the rules and planning techniques for Roth IRAs, and for that reason our review of the rules for Traditional IRAs will be abbreviated.

8.3 Traditional IRA Minimum Required Distributions

8.3.1 General Principles

Your goal as the owner of a Traditional IRA will be to properly structure your beneficiary designation and distribution election to minimize the **required distributions** during your lifetime and provide the greatest post-death payout potential possible. The MRD rules are designed to set the minimum that you must withdraw, but you may always withdraw more than the minimum.

> *You may always withdraw as much as you want from your Traditional IRA, but it is not wise to set the minimum floor higher than it otherwise has to be set.*

The MRDs are based either on your single life expectancy (assuming you survive your required beginning date) or the combined life expectancy of you and another person (i.e., a joint life expectancy). Since the joint life expectancy of two persons is greater than the single life expectancy of one person, one of your goals will be to have MRDs for your account determined on the basis of a joint life expectancy. In most cases,

> *The MRD rules are designed to work well when you as the account owner simply name your spouse as primary beneficiary and your children as contingent beneficiaries.*

Even this simple arrangement has its own nuances, but in the majority of cases it will provide favorable results for you and your family.

8.3.2 Required Beginning Date (RBD)

Congress intended that during normal retirement years you would take distributions from your Traditional IRA.

> *You can start taking distributions from your Traditional IRA anytime after age 591/2 without being subject to the 10% early withdrawal penalty tax,*

but you must start distributions on your required beginning date (RBD)[2], which is April 1 of the year following the year in which you reach age 70 1/2.

Upon this most critical date, your interest in your Traditional IRA must be distributed in lump sum **or** you must begin distributions over your life expectancy or over the joint life expectancy of you and your "designated beneficiary." The distribution options are tied to one or two applicable life expectancies (i.e., yours as the Traditional IRA owner, or yours and that of your "designated beneficiary"). The existence of a second life expectancy is dependent upon the nature of your beneficiary as of your RBD. And whether (and to whom) recalculation of life expectancy will apply is also determined as of the RBD.

> *For a Traditional IRA, failure to analyze the overall objectives and make specific choices before the RBD will lock in the default elections in the financial institution's IRA agreement. Remember that the maximum distribution period for a Traditional IRA becomes fixed as of the RBD, as does the actual or default choices concerning recalculation of life expectancy.*

8.3.3 Designated Beneficiary

The term "designated beneficiary" is from the Internal Revenue Code and is to be distinguished from the term "beneficiary" of the retirement account as discussed in Section 9.2 of Chapter 9. Determining the beneficiary is simple. The **beneficiary** is the person who is nominated by the account owner (or the account agreement in default of

---

2 As of January 1997, the RBD is defined differently for those with accounts in qualified plans. If you have not retired by age 70 1/2, you may wait until your retirement from active employment to begin distributions from your qualified plan. However, this special rule does not apply if you are a 5% or greater owner of the employer. Also, if you avail yourself of this rule to delay distributions beyond age 70 1/2, then certain adjustments must be made in determining your required minimum distributions to compensate for the additional delay in making the distributions.

such nomination) to receive the balance of the account upon the death of the account owner. The beneficiary could be an individual person, trust, estate, or charity. **A "designated beneficiary**," however, is always an individual person whose life expectancy can be used to determine the payout period of the retirement account.

A "designated beneficiary" is a person, like a spouse or child or some other individual, entitled to receive at least part of the retirement account following the owner's death (if there is anything remaining in the account), and whose life can be used to determine the allowable payout period of the account. A "person" for these purposes includes only individuals and therefore excludes estates and charities. However, certain trusts named as beneficiary can provide a "designated beneficiary" (and related life expectancy). See Chapter 9 for more on trusts.

It is also helpful to divide "designated beneficiaries" into two types: spouse and non-spouse. The life expectancy of a spouse "designated beneficiary" may be recalculated, whereas the life expectancy of a non-spouse "designated beneficiary" may not be recalculated. The significance of recalculation is discussed in Section 8.4.

For a Traditional IRA the "designated beneficiary" is determined at the earlier of the RBD or the death of the owner. For example, if you are alive on your RBD and your spouse is named as your beneficiary, your spouse will be the "designated beneficiary" and the MRDs will be based on you and your spouse's joint life expectancy. If you die prior to your RBD, your "designated beneficiary" will be determined upon your death and the MRDs will be based on the single life expectancy of the "designated beneficiary."

Remember that if you name your estate or favorite charity as your beneficiary, then upon your RBD or upon your death you will not have a "designated beneficiary."

> *If your goal is to spread out distributions as long as possible, it is critical to have your retirement account beneficiary designation properly structured to provide a "designated beneficiary."*

8.4 Traditional IRA: Rules for Determining LE

Upon the RBD, the owner of a Traditional IRA has an important choice to make regarding the method of determining his or her life expectancy, as well as the method of determining the life expectancy for his or her spouse when the spouse is the "designated beneficiary." This choice in methods will affect both lifetime payments to the owner and payments after the owner's death to the beneficiaries. Too often the effects are not appreciated and the rules apply by default. This choice is irrevocable after the RBD.

8.4.1 Term Certain Method

Under this method, the MRD for the Traditional IRA is calculated on the basis of a fixed term of years. The mortality tables are only consulted once, upon establishing the term.

> **Example:** The life expectancy of a single individual at age 70 is 16 years, according to IRS mortality tables (see Appendix A for age 70). The first year's MRD under the term certain method would be 1/16, the second year's MRD would be 1/15, and so on until after 16 years the account would be fully distributed. The divisor is reduced by one each year. Even if the owner died prior to the expiration of the 16-year term, the same installment payments could continue to the named beneficiary of the IRA.

8.4.2 Recalculation Method

Under this method, the MRDs for the Traditional IRA are calculated on the basis of each year re-determining the life expectancy of the owner (if single) or each year re-determining the joint life expectancy of the owner and spouse, if the spouse is the "designated beneficiary."

> *The life expectancy of a "designated beneficiary" other than a spouse cannot be recalculated (you must use the term certain method).*

> **Example:** The life expectancy of a single individual at age 70 is 16 years according to IRS mortality tables. Assuming there is no "designated beneficiary" for simplicity purposes, the first year's MRD under the recalculation method would be 1/16 (from Appendix A2). So for the first year the distribution is the same under the term certain method and recalculation method. However, under the recalculation method, in the second year (at age 71), the life expectancy is 15.3 years, and in the third year (at age 72), the life expectancy is 14.6 years, and so on.

Under the recalculation method, the life expectancy is reduced by less than one for each year of additional age. This reflects the fact that as you get older, the odds are greater that you will live to an even older age. The life expectancy tables go out to age 115. The minimum withdrawals are smaller, and the account lasts longer.

Appendix A3 needs to be used in the case of a joint recalculation. For instance, if in a particular year the husband's age is 74 and the wife's age is 70, the LE is obtained from Appendix A3 by looking up 74 along the columns and 70 along the rows: these join at (intersect at) 19.1: this is the divisor. This lookup method is repeated in each of the following years.

The Advantages of Recalculation

During the lifetime of the owner and spouse,

> *recalculation of life expectancies makes sense for retirement planning if the account is small and it is intended for the payments to continue for life*

Recalculation reduces the amount of the MRDs and ensures that the owner and spouse cannot outlive the distribution of the account.

The Disadvantages of Recalculation

If recalculation of life expectancy applies, the recalculated life expectancy is reduced to zero in the calendar year following the year of death. When the life expectancy of the owner and spouse are both zero, the IRA must distribute its entire balance prior to the last day of the calendar year following the calendar year in which the survivor dies. Therefore, the beneficiaries are subject to income tax on 100% of the IRA in one taxable year.

For sizable accounts, recalculation of life expectancy for the owner (or the owner and spouse) is not wise for tax and estate planning purposes if the entire balance will be subject to income tax in the year following the death of the survivor, as will often be the case.

8.4.3 The Hybrid Method

If the goal is to extend payments as long as possible, the owner could elect to recalculate life expectancy for one spouse, and use a Term Certain method for the other spouse.

> *Recalculating only the owner's life expectancy will be a good solution when sizable accounts are involved*

In the hybrid method your life expectancy may be recalculated annually, while your spouse's life expectancy may follow a term certain method.

If you (male) die first, the account is rolled over to the spouse, who can elect a child beneficiary. So after her death, the account is distributed using the child's life expectancy. During your life, the single recalculation tables were used, which is only slightly worse then the joint recalculation tables associated with the Joint Recalculation method. After your death, the child (female) benefits from the stretch out of the IRA account with her life expectancy, just as with the Joint Recalculation method. This method is therefore almost as good as the Joint Recalculation method in the case that you die first.

If the spouse dies first, the hybrid method will provide a significant advantage over the Joint Recalculation method, as explained in the following. If the spouse dies first, you can continue taking withdrawals using the spouse's life expectancy because the account was set up using the Term Certain method. Now when you die next the account can continue to be withdrawn using the spouse's term certain method for her life expectancy.

> *So there is no sudden one-year-total-withdrawal as there would have been with the straight Joint Recalculation method. This is the key to the advantage of the hybrid method.*

Let us consider an example to illustrate how the hybrid method works. Suppose you are 70 and your spouse is 68. The following are the steps in the calculation of the LE for the hybrid method:

For the first year use the JRC Table in Appendix A3 with ages 70/68. The LE is 21.5. Keep a record of your spouse's LE from the SLE Table in Appendix A3 at age 68 this is 17.6 (call this SLE-START). We will use this in a later step.

For the second year we will need to determine the two ages to use in looking up the JRC tables. Use your age for age1: this is 71. Your spouse's age is 69. Do not use 69. Instead calculate an **adjusted age** for your spouse. Reduce SLE-START by one, so this year the SLE is 16.6. Look up the age corresponding to 16.6 in the SLE table (round up). This age is 70. Your spouse's adjusted age is 70. Use 71 / 70 from the JLE table to look up the LE for this year: it is 20.2.

For the next year, repeat Step 2. Your age is age1=72. Your spouse's actual age is 70. Reduce the SLE-START by 2: this year it is 15.6. Look up the SLE for 15.6, rounding up: this is 72. This is your spouse's adjusted age. Look up 70 / 72 in the JRC table. This is 19.5: which is the LE to use this year.

Let us compare the LE's for the three methods: joint term certain, joint recalculation (you die first), joint recalculation (your spouse dies first: child is 30 years younger), and the hybrid method with you dying first and your spouse dying first. That makes five cases. The results are shown in Table 8.1.

> *The hybrid method is at least as good as the term certain method (if your spouse dies first) and it is almost as good as the recalculation method (if you die first).*

It is complex, and some institutions do not offer the hybrid method. Many expert financial planners use this method.

8.4.4 MDIB Method for Non-spouse Beneficiaries

If an individual other than a spouse (e.g., a child) is named as beneficiary, the life expectancy of the beneficiary cannot be recalculated (i.e., it is always fixed term). However, the life expectancy of the owner may be recalculated.

Table 8.1

Comparison of Life Expectancy Methods
Case 1:
Spouse Dies First at age 70
Client Dies at Age 74

Client's Age	Spouse's Age	Child's Age	Term Certain LE	Recalculation Both LE's LE	Spouse's Single LE	Hybrid Method* Spouse's Adjusted Age	Hybrid LE	
70	68	38	21.5	21.5	17.6	68	21.5	
71	69	39	20.5	20.7	16.6	70	20.2	
72	70	40	19.5	19.8	15.6	71	19.4	Spouse dies
73	71	41	18.5	13.9	14.6	72	18.5	
74	72	42	17.5	13.2	13.6	74	17.3	Client dies
75	73	43	16.5	1	12.6		12.6	
76	74	44	15.5	1	11.6		11.6	
77	75	45	14.5	1	10.6		10.6	
78	76	46	13.5	1	9.6		9.6	
79	77	47	12.5	1	8.6		8.6	
80	78	48	11.5	1	7.6		7.6	
81	79	49	10.5	1	6.6		6.6	
82	80	50	9.5	1	5.6		5.6	

Case 2:
Client Dies First at age 74   Assume a Spousal Rollover and child as designated beneficiary
Spouse dies next at age 74

Client's Age	Spouse's Age	Child's Age	Term Certain LE	Recalculation (both life expectancies) LE	Spouse's Single LE	Hybrid Method* Spouse's Adjusted Age	Hybrid LE	
70	68	38	21.5	21.5 [JLE]	17.6	68	21.5	
71	69	39	20.5	20.7 [JLE]	16.6	70	20.2	
72	70	40	19.5	19.8 [JLE]	15.6	71	19.4	
73	71	41	18.5	19.0 [JLE]	14.6	72	18.5	
74	72	42	17.5	18.2 [JLE]	13.6	74	17.3	Client dies
75	73	43	16.5	21.8 [MDIB]			21.8[MDIB]	
76	74	44	15.5	20.9 [MDIB]			20.9[MDIB]	Spouse dies
77	75	45	14.5	37.7 [SLE]			37.7 [SLE]	
78	76	46	13.5	36.7			36.7	
79	77	47	12.5	35.7			35.7	
80	78	48	11.5	34.7			34.7	
81	79	49	10.5	33.7			33.7	
82	80	50	9.5	32.7			32.7	

*In the Hybrid Method, we recalculate the life expectancy of the owner, but not the life expectancy of the spouse.

Also, if the beneficiary is more than 10 years younger than the owner of the Traditional IRA, like the owner's child, the tax laws assume that the beneficiary is only 10 years younger than the owner for purposes of determining the MRD from the account to the owner during the owner's lifetime. This is called the minimum distribution incidental benefit (MDIB) rule. However, when the Traditional IRA owner dies, the real age and life expectancy of the named beneficiary are used to determine the required distributions on the balance of the account to the beneficiary.

8.5 Traditional IRA: Post-death Distribution Rules

Following the death of the owner of a Traditional IRA, there are two sets of rules to determine how the beneficiaries will have to distribute the remaining account balance. Which set of rules applies depends on whether the owner dies prior to or after the owner's RBD.

8.5.1 Death Prior to the RBD

Five-Year Rule

The default method is that the account must be distributed by the end of the fifth calendar year following the calendar year of the owner's death. Under the five-year rule if the owner died in 1998 (prior to his RBD), the account must be fully distributed by December 31, 2003. This five-year rule method is always available for accounts when the owner dies prior to his or her RBD. This is the method that is applicable when the life expectancy rule (discussed next) is unavailable because there is no "designated beneficiary" whose life expectancy can be used for purposes of distributing the account.

> *Note that the five-year rule applies only to Traditional IRAs when the owner dies prior to his or her RBD. After the RBD, the at-least-as-rapidly rule (discussed below) applies to a Traditional IRA.*

Life Expectancy Rule

Alternatively, the beneficiary could elect to have the account distributed over the life expectancy of a "designated beneficiary" with payments commencing by December 31 of the year following your death. This is most typical. In order for this method to be available, the account and beneficiary designation must be properly structured to have a "designated beneficiary" (discussed in Section 8.3.3).

> *The owner will always want to ensure that he or she has a*
> *"designated beneficiary" available at the time of his or her death so*
> *that this method is available.*

Special Spouse Methods

The main (and predominantly used) exception to the five-year rule and the life expectancy rule involve spousal beneficiaries. If the owner's spouse is the beneficiary, typically the spouse may elect to treat the account as his or her own Traditional IRA or utilize the life expectancy rule. Under the life expectancy rule, the spouse can wait to start distributions until December 31 of the year the owner would have been age 701/2. If the spouse chooses to treat the IRA as his or her own, the spouse can create a spousal rollover IRA. The spouse can then designate a beneficiary (e.g. a child) of her choice for this rolled over IRA. Upon the spouse's death, the account is distributed following the child's life expectancy. This results in an extension of the withdrawal period. This is a popular method:

> *A common practice is to roll the account over to the spouse upon the*
> *client's death. The spouse then designates a child as the beneficiary*
> *for the new account. Upon the spouse's death, the account is*
> *distributed following the child's life expectancy.*

8.5.2 Death After the RBD

If the owner dies after the RBD, distribution must continue at least as rapidly as during the owner's life. This is known as the "at least as rapidly rule." If the owner was taking payments over the owner and spouse's life expectancies, payments may continue to the surviving spouse under the decedent's distribution election. The spouse could not only take a lump sum payment from a qualified plan and create a rollover Traditional IRA, but also could roll over a Traditional IRA of which the spouse is the beneficiary. Then the spouse would become the owner, and in each case commence distribution as though the new rolled over Traditional IRA was the spouse's own.

The IRA rollover rules for a spouse would suggest that all surviving spouse beneficiaries of Traditional IRAs may roll them over to defer taxation of the distribution and name young beneficiaries to enable the Traditional IRA to act as a tax shelter for a potentially long period of time. Furthermore, the surviving spouse may roll over the account even if the surviving spouse is beyond age 701/2 at the time of the rollover (i.e., beyond the normal RBD for the surviving spouse).

8.6 MRD Rules for Roth IRAs

In the application of the MRD rules, Roth IRAs are very different from Traditional IRAs. These differences, however, increase the attractiveness of Roth IRAs relative to Traditional IRAs.

8.6.1 Pre-death Distributions Rules

No distributions are required during the lifetime of the owner of a Roth IRA. Even if the owner of the Roth IRA lives beyond age 701/2, no distributions are required. Even if the owner of a Traditional IRA converts the account to a Roth IRA after the owner attained age 701/2 (i.e., the RBD for a Traditional IRA), no distributions are required from the Roth IRA. This is one of the major distinctions between Roth IRAs and Traditional IRAs. This feature provides a significant advantage to the Roth IRA.

8.6.2 Post-death Distribution Rules

Following the death of the Roth IRA owner, the beneficiaries of the account will have to distribute the remaining account balance under one of the following methods (which are the same distribution methods applicable to a Traditional IRA when the owner dies prior to the RBD):

Five-Year Rule

The default method is that the account must be distributed by the end of the fifth calendar year following the calendar year of the owner's death. Under the five-year rule, if the owner died in 1998, the account must be fully distributed by December 31,

2003. This five-year rule method is always available. This is the method that is applicable when the life expectancy rule (discussed next) is unavailable because there is no "designated beneficiary" whose life expectancy can be used for purposes of distributing the account.

Life Expectancy Rule

Alternatively, the beneficiary could elect to have the account distributed over the life expectancy of a "designated beneficiary" with payments commencing by December 31 of the year following the owner's death. This life expectancy method is not always available. In order for this method to be available, the account and beneficiary designation must be properly structured to have a "designated beneficiary" (discussed in Section 8.3).

Special Spouse Methods

The main (and predominantly used) exceptions to the five-year rule and the life expectancy rule involve spouse beneficiaries. If the owner's spouse is the beneficiary, typically the spouse may elect to treat the account as his or her own Roth IRA or utilize the life expectancy rule. Under the life expectancy rule, the spouse can wait to start distributions until December 31 of the year the owner would have been age 70 1/2 These special spousal post-death distribution options are discussed further in Chapter 9.

8.6.3 Designated Beneficiaries

The term "designated beneficiary" is defined the same for a Roth IRA as it is for a Traditional IRA. See Section 8.3.3 above. However, since distributions are not required during the lifetime of the Roth IRA owner, the "designated beneficiary" for a Roth IRA is always determined at the death of the owner.

Planning Tip for Trapped Traditional IRAs:

This is one area in which there is an important distinction between Traditional IRAs and Roth IRAs. For a Traditional IRA (or qualified-plan account) the "designated beneficiary" is determined at the earlier of the required beginning date (i.e., April 1 of the year following the year the owner attains age 70 1/2) or death. For a Roth IRA the designated beneficiary is always determined at the owner's death since distributions are not required during the lifetime of the Roth IRA owner.

For example, suppose that recalculation of life expectancy applies to both your and your spouse's life expectancies with respect to a Traditional IRA. Suppose that your spouse predeceases you. The pitfall of recalculation is that your spouse's life expectancy is reduced to zero in the calendar year following the year of her death. Now you are trapped! With a Traditional IRA there is no way to add another life expectancy after the required beginning date. When your and your spouse's life expectancies are both zero, which would be the case upon your subsequent death, the IRA must distribute its entire balance prior to the last day of the year following your death. Therefore, your beneficiaries can be subject to income tax on 100% of the IRA in one taxable year. This can spell disaster and illustrates the danger of recalculation. The Roth IRA provides a solution to this predicament.

Consider converting to a Roth IRA, which allows creation of a new "designated beneficiary" and post-death payout method. Since the "designated beneficiary" is determined at the owner's death for a Roth IRA, what happened prior to the conversion is irrelevant.

> *Conversion to the Roth IRA allows you to create a new designated beneficiary with a more favorable post-death distribution schedule. This alone may often be a good reason to convert to a Roth IRA.*

8.6.4 Determining Life Expectancy

The rules are the same for both Traditional IRAs and Roth IRAs when it comes to the method of determining life expectancy. As discussed in Section 8.4.2 above, the life expectancy of a designated beneficiary other than a spouse may not be recalculated.

In the case of the Roth IRA with a spouse as the beneficiary, and a child as the contingent beneficiary (the most common arrangement), the result is usually relatively simple. When the account owner dies, the account is rolled over by the surviving spouse and he or she establishes a designated beneficiary (typically a child). Upon the surviving spouse's death, distributions would begin to the child under the life expectancy rule, without recalculation of life expectancy (i.e., term certain).

> *With the Roth IRA the mandatory withdrawals start after both spouses die, and follow the term certain method*

The only exception to this is in those rare cases when the surviving spouse is the designated beneficiary, but a spousal rollover is not available (e.g., because the Roth IRA is payable to a bypass trust or QTIP marital trust – see Chapter 9 for a discussion of these trusts). In these cases, the choice of using the recalculation method or term certain method will be available. The advantages and disadvantages of these methods are discussed above in Section 8.4.2. For a detailed discussion on the post-death distribution options for particular beneficiaries see Chapter 9.

8.7 Conclusions on Minimum Required Distributions

In this chapter we have identified some additional benefits of the Roth IRA. In particular, with a Roth IRA:

- There are no mandatory withdrawals during your lifetime
- There are no mandatory withdrawals during your spouse's lifetime (assuming a spousal rollover)
- Conversion to a Roth IRA from a Traditional IRA allows the owner to change the beneficiary and to change the payout method after death
- In general, after the death of both spouses the withdrawals from the Roth IRA will be based on the life expectancy of the contingent beneficiary, usually a child, following a term certain method

The MRD rules provided in this chapter are intended to provide a broad overview of this technical area of tax law. It is a complex subject and you would be well served to seek the advice of a skilled professional advisor. In the next chapter, we provide further background on the MRD rules in the estate-planning context.

Chapter 9 Roth IRA in Estate Planning

"The American Dream ... and if you work hard, you will have a comfortable retirement and be able to leave something for your children." Senator Roth

This chapter is for those of you who wish to provide an inheritance for your children and loved ones. As we will show, the Roth IRA is suited very well to meet these objectives. We assume you have reached the conclusion (or will after reading this chapter on post-death benefits) that the Roth Conversion is right for you. What do you do to ensure that the Roth IRA you set up meets your objectives? This is certainly a technical topic, worthy of a good financial advisor. But again, even more so than the topic of minimum distributions, discussed in Chapter 8, this is one that you should familiarize yourself with; you will be well advised to understand the basics, so that you can help your advisor provide you what you truly want. This chapter will teach you the basics.

In particular, the chapter will discuss who will be legally entitled to your Roth IRA following your death, the tax implications for your account following your death, and what steps you should take to obtain the most favorable result for your beneficiaries. Beneficiary designation planning, post-death distribution planning and estate tax planning will be explained. As you review this chapter, remember that your Roth IRA can be a valuable asset, and requires good planning for tax and property law purposes. Use an advisor, for sure. But read this chapter first. The topics in this chapter are:

- Importance of Reviewing Your Roth IRA Plan Documents
- Beneficiaries for Property Law Purposes
- Post-Death Distribution Planning
- Estate Tax Planning
- Post-Death Distribution and Estate Tax Planning for Particular Beneficiaries
- Funding a Generation-Skipping Trust with a Roth IRA
- IRS prototype Roth IRA Agreements

9.1 Review Your Roth IRA Plan Documents

At the outset you should be aware of the provisions of your financial institution's prototype Roth IRA agreement. You will need to verify that the Roth prototype agreement used by the institution provides all of the options allowable under the minimum distribution rules for distribution of the account following your death. In particular you should check that the agreement allows your beneficiary to change custodians or trustees and to accelerate distributions from the account at any time. The agreement should provide for a beneficiary of the account in the event your named beneficiary survives your death, but dies prior to the account being fully depleted. For estate planning purposes, all of these issues are important. It is important for you to recognize that Roth IRA agreements (like Traditional IRAs) vary by institution. An estate lawyer should be consulted.

9.2 Beneficiaries for Property Law Purposes

From the time you establish your Roth IRA, you will need to affirmatively state who is to receive the balance of your Roth IRA upon your death. That person or persons will be your "beneficiary" and for property law purposes will be entitled to the benefits of your account after your death. The beneficiary of a Roth IRA can be one or more individuals, such as your spouse or children, a trust (whether revocable or irrevocable), an estate, a charity, or any combination these, unless your institution's prototype Roth IRA agreement limits your options. However, the consequences of your selection will vary greatly and the decision should be made only after careful analysis.

> *You should name your own beneficiaries and consult your lawyer for the ramifications.*

9.2.1 Primary and Contingent Beneficiaries

You should carefully select the primary beneficiary that you wish to receive the balance of the account following your death. The post-death distribution options and tax related issues that are discussed below will impact that decision. It is also necessary for you to select a contingent beneficiary in the event the primary beneficiary fails to survive your death.

Typically, your primary beneficiary may be your spouse, but if your spouse fails to survive you, your contingent beneficiary may be your child (or children).

9.2.2 Disclaimer and Simultaneous Death

In many cases you will also want to plan for the possibility of a tax motivated disclaimer by a beneficiary. Suppose that no other assets were available to fund your estate tax exemption trust (bypass trust). Your beneficiary designation could be planned such that in the event of disclaimer by your spouse, the disclaimed assets would pass to your bypass trust created under your will or revocable trust for the benefit of your spouse. Most attorneys will consider a tax motivated disclaimer, which can prove very useful in the appropriate circumstances.

> *Question for attorney: Does your beneficiary designation and will (or revocable trust) need to consider disclaimers?*

In your beneficiary designation planning it is also important to consider the possibility of a **simultaneous death.** Most states' laws provide that if two people die simultaneously, the property of each person shall be disposed of as if that person had survived the other. Therefore if you and your primary beneficiary die as a result of a common accident, your Roth IRA will be distributed as if your primary beneficiary predeceased you (i.e., it will pass to the contingent beneficiary). However, you have the right to change this presumption so that in the event of a simultaneous death your beneficiary will be considered to have survived you. In certain cases this may be beneficial for estate tax planning purposes.

> *Question for attorney: Does beneficiary designation and will (or revocable trust) need to consider the possibility of a simultaneous death?*

9.2.3 Post-Death Distribution Planning

The post-death benefits of the Roth IRA are:

First, distributions to your beneficiaries following your death are income tax free.

Second, with proper planning, your beneficiaries may continue your Roth IRA long after your death as an inherited account and continue taking advantage of the tax-free growth inside your Roth IRA.

As discussed in Chapter 8, minimum distributions are not required during the lifetime of a Roth IRA owner. However, the minimum distribution rules are applicable to a Roth IRA after the owner's death. Therefore, it is important to understand these rules so that you can structure your Roth IRA and beneficiary designation in a manner that maximizes this potential tax free growth period following your death.

Following your death, your Roth IRA is an investment vehicle outside the present Federal income tax system.

> *Therefore, with Roth IRAs it is more important than ever to properly plan the post-death distribution and, when appropriate, to take advantage of what is often called the "stretch-out" Roth IRA.*

9.3 Estate Tax Planning

A basic question that many people ask is whether the Roth IRA is subject to estate tax. It is.

> *Roth IRAs are fully subject to Federal estate taxes.*

So in addition to ensuring that you have properly planned the beneficiary designation and planned the post-death distribution of your Roth IRA, if your estate (i.e., all of your property, including cash, stocks, bonds, real estate, retirement accounts like Roth IRAs, insurance and annuities) is worth more than $625,000 in 1998, you will need to address the Federal estate tax. Although a detailed discussion of the Federal estate tax is beyond the scope of this book, a brief summary is provided below.

9.3.1 Background on Estate Taxes

Congress first created the estate tax back in the early part of the century to help finance World War I. This tax has changed significantly over the years. In recent times, the estate tax has been coordinated with the gift taxation system. Estate and gift taxes now work in a coordinated way to impose a tax upon the value of your wealth (as opposed to a tax on income) that is transferred either by gifts during your lifetime or at your death. For this purpose, the tax is generally imposed upon the fair market value of the property at the time of transfer. Like the income tax system, Congress has provided certain exemptions, deductions, and credits in the estate and gift tax area. Planning in advance is often necessary to fully utilize these tax advantages.

In planning for your Roth IRA you will be principally concerned with the unlimited marital deduction and the "exemption amount."

The Marital Deduction

The marital deduction is a deduction from your gross estate for property passing to your spouse.

Whatever property one spouse leaves the surviving spouse will pass free of estate tax in the estate of the first spouse to die, regardless of the amount. Thus, a married couple will rarely have to pay estate tax on the death of the first spouse.

The "Exemption Amount"

In addition to the unlimited marital deduction, you may transfer a certain amount, the "exemption amount," of property to a non-spousal beneficiary free of federal estate and gift taxes. The exemption amounts will be increased between now and 2006, as shown in Table 9.1.

Table 9.1

Decedents Dying and Gifts made during:	The Exemption Amount is:
1998	$ 625,000
1999	$ 650,000
2000 and 2001	$ 675,000
2002 and 2003	$ 700,000
2004	$ 850,000
2005	$ 950,000
2006 and thereafter	$1,000,000

In effect this allows any person, married or not, to pass property equal in value to the applicable exemption amount free of estate or gift tax.

Careful planning for a married couple is critical to ensure that each spouse's exemption amount is used. [1]

Tax Rates

The estate tax begins at an effective rate of 37%. As the size of the taxable estate increases, the tax rate increases until it reaches a top marginal rate of 55% when the taxable estate is $3,000,000 in value. The benefits afforded by the exemption amount and the lower marginal brackets on large estates are phased out when the taxable estate is above $10,000,000. This is accomplished by assessing an additional 5% tax.

---

[1] Note that exemption amount is referred to by many names, including unified credit amount, exempt amount, and applicable credit amount. Technically, the exemption amount operates as a tax credit, but is commonly referred to an exemption.

Coordination of Marital Deduction and Exemption Amount for Maximum Benefit

The marital deduction and exemption amount must be coordinated properly to obtain the maximum tax benefit. Upon the death of the first spouse, that spouse's exemption amount must be set aside in such a way as to not cause its inclusion in the estate of the surviving spouse. Generally, this is accomplished by the use of a bypass trust (i.e., bypass taxation in the surviving spouse's estate). The bypass trust is sometimes called a family trust, credit shelter trust, or the "B" trust in an "A/B" trust plan. The surviving spouse may be given certain interests in the bypass trust: for example, mandatory distributions of all net income and principal distributions for the spouse's health, maintenance, and support to maintain the surviving spouse in his or her accustomed standard of living. When properly designed, these rights in the surviving spouse to the income and principal of the bypass trust will not cause the assets of the bypass trust to be included in the surviving spouse's estate. By sheltering $625,000 (or the applicable exemption amount) in the bypass trust at the death of the first spouse to die, and structuring the bypass trust in a manner that does not cause the trust to be taxed at the surviving spouse's death, the $625,000 bypass trust passes at the surviving spouse's death free of estate tax. In addition, the surviving spouse is able to apply his or her exemption amount to his or her own estate.

> *The result of effective planning is that $1,250,000 is sheltered from tax because each spouse fully utilized the $625,000 exemption amount. In the year 2006 and thereafter, a married couple will be able to shelter $2,000,000 from estate taxes as a result of the exemption amount increasing.*

9.3.2 An Example: Estate taxes with Roth vs Traditional IRA

When you convert to a Roth IRA, the conversion taxes are removed from your estate for estate tax purposes, which reduces the overall income and estate tax burden. This is illustrated by the following example. Marie who is age 74 in 1998 has been recently diagnosed with a terminal disease and is not expected to survive 6 months. Marie has a $1 million Traditional IRA and non-IRA assets of $4 million. Marie has no "designated beneficiary" for the Traditional IRA, and according to the terms of the default election under the controlling IRA agreement, she unknowingly elected at her required beginning date to **recalculate** her life expectancy (see Section 8.4.2 for definition of recalculation method). Consequently, prior to the end of the calendar year following Marie's death, the entire Traditional IRA must be distributed, accelerating all of the income.

Should Marie convert her Traditional IRA to a Roth IRA before her death? Yes she should, to minimize estate and income taxes (and to enable a new "designated beneficiary"). Table 9.2 illustrates the effect of removing the conversion taxes from her estate for estate tax purposes. In this example, we are assuming a 40% income tax rate applicable in both cases.

Table 9.2

691(c) Deduction Example	Traditional IRA	Roth IRA
Estate Taxes		
Balance of retirement account at death 1,000,000	1,000,000	1,000,000
Amount of NonIRA assets at death (net value of 40% conversion taxes in the case of the Roth IRA)	4,000,000	3,600,000
Total gross estate	5,000,000	4,600,000
Less estate tax	(2,188,750)	(1,968,750)
IRA subject to income tax after death	1,000,000	-
Less 691(c) deduction	(438,800)	-
Tax base	561,200	-
Less 40% income tax on IRA after death	(224,480)	-
Total to Family after Estate and Income Taxes		
Total gross estate	5,000,000	4,600,000
Less estate tax	(2,188,750)	(1,968,750)
Less 40% income tax on IRA after death	(224,480)	-
Total to family after estate and income taxes	2,586,770	2,631,250

If Marie converts her Traditional IRA during her lifetime, the funds used to pay the income taxes are removed from her estate for estate tax purposes. If Marie dies with the Traditional IRA, estate taxes are paid on the entire Traditional IRA, including the funds that eventually will be used by her beneficiaries to pay the income taxes on the Traditional IRA following her death. The beneficiaries are, however, entitled to an income tax deduction under IRC §691(c) for the Federal estate taxes attributable to the Traditional IRA. Even though the 691(c) deduction is designed to mitigate the illustrated duplicative taxation, it will not produce a wash because the 691(c) deduction is calculated without regard to the state death tax credit. Converting prior to death in this example results in an almost immediate $44,480 saving.

9.3.3 Deathbed Conversions

This above example illustrates that simply converting to a Roth IRA has an estate tax advantage. It also illustrates an additional advantage i.e. someone on her deathbed who has a taxable estate for estate tax purposes and has a Traditional IRA may want to consider converting to a Roth IRA to obtain the estate tax advantage discussed above. Moreover, the new Roth IRA would be completely tax-free after the death of the owner and could be paid out over the life expectancy of the "designated beneficiary." Therefore, in Marie's case,

> *A deathbed conversion of $1,000,000 to the Roth IRA saves $44,480 immediately and provides her beneficiaries with $1,000,000 in Roth IRA assets that can be continued after her death with tax free growth over the life expectancy of her "designated beneficiary."*

The benefits of the deathbed Roth IRA Conversion therefore are:

* An immediate benefit of ~3 to 5% from savings in income taxes
* Ability to obtain a new designated a beneficiary of choice (as opposed to no designated beneficiary)
* Extends tax-free growth of the Roth IRA account over the life expectancy of the beneficiary [as opposed to an immediate withdrawal]. This represents a major financial advantage.

9.3.4 Post-death distributions for Particular Beneficiaries

Post-death distributions depend on the class of beneficiary. Let us consider each of these classes.

Spouse as Outright Beneficiary

Flexibility and simplicity generally suggest that you name your spouse as the outright beneficiary of your Roth IRA.

> *Your spouse is a favored beneficiary under the tax laws, having certain options not provided to other beneficiaries.*

When the spouse is the outright beneficiary of a Roth IRA, the spouse can in most cases elect to treat the Roth IRA as the spouse's own, and postpone distributions until following the spouse's death, as well as postpone estate taxes until the spouse's death.

Occasionally, however, naming your spouse as the outright beneficiary of your Roth IRA may be inconsistent with your estate planning objectives. You may wish to name a trust as the beneficiary of your Roth IRA, which provides benefits to your spouse as the trust beneficiary.

> *For example, naming a marital trust as beneficiary of your Roth IRA may be appropriate if you are in a second marriage. You may want the Roth IRA balance to eventually pass to children of your first marriage*

or you may have concerns about your spouse's possible remarriage and diversion or loss of control of the Roth IRA funds to a new spouse, new beneficiaries, or new investment advisor. Additionally, effective planning to use your estate tax exemption amount may indicate naming a trust as beneficiary of your Roth IRA.

9.3.5 Minimum Distribution Options

A spouse named as the outright beneficiary qualifies as a "designated beneficiary" under the minimum distribution rules. Distributions are not restricted to the Five-Year rule, which would force a total distribution over five years. The surviving spouse is the favored beneficiary under the minimum distribution rules. Typically the spouse may choose among the following payout options, but timely action may be necessary.

Spousal Rollover

Generally, the spouse could elect to treat the inherited Roth IRA as the spouse's own, and postpone distributions until the spouse's death. Actually, in the recently issued IRS prototype Roth IRA agreements the spousal rollover is always available and is actually automatic. See Article V, 1. of the IRS Form 5305-R in Appendix B.

> *You should check that the automatic spousal rollover is provided in the agreement provided by your financial institution.*

Life Expectancy Rule: Wait Until Owner's Age 70 1/2

In those rare cases where a spousal rollover is not wanted, the spouse, as the outright beneficiary, will qualify as a "designated beneficiary." As a result, the account may be distributed over the life expectancy of the surviving spouse, with payments commencing by December 31 of the year following the decedent spouse's death. Either the Term Certain or Recalculation withdrawal method is permitted. If the decedent spouse dies prior to age 701/2, then under a special rule available only when a spouse is the "designated beneficiary," the time for starting distributions may be delayed until December 31 of the year the decedent spouse would have been age 70 1/2.

Estate Tax Consequences

If a U.S. citizen spouse is the outright beneficiary, the Roth IRA may qualify for the marital deduction in the owner's estate if the spouse can choose the form of benefit, including a lump sum distribution, and accelerate payment of the account balance to her at any time.

With a retirement account like a Roth IRA, this is the preferred method since the surviving spouse could also rollover the account under the minimum distribution rules and obtain a longer distribution period.

Funding a Bypass Trust with a Roth IRA

You should consider the disclaimer approach if you want to provide benefits from your Roth IRA to your surviving spouse as well as utilize the value in your Roth IRA to fund your estate tax exemption amount. If you name your spouse as primary beneficiary of your Roth IRA, the spouse may be able to disclaim all or a portion of your Roth IRA and allow the disclaimed part to pass to your bypass trust to enable full utilization of your estate tax exemption amount. To do this, your bypass trust needs to be designated as the contingent beneficiary for disclaimed assets.

For example, suppose that our husband and wife have an estate of approximately $1,300,000. The estate consists of their residence worth $600,000, which is owned in the wife's sole name, and the husband's Roth IRA, worth $700,000. If the husband names the wife as beneficiary of his Roth IRA, and she treats the account as her own at the husband's death (assuming she survives), then all of his estate (i.e., the Roth IRA) would pass to the wife under the marital deduction for estate tax purposes. The husband's estate tax exemption amount would be wasted, as there are no assets to fund his bypass trust.

The husband and wife could avoid this unnecessary result by planning for the wife to disclaim the portion of the husband's Roth IRA needed at the time of the husband's death to fully fund his bypass trust. After the disclaimer, the wife could receive the benefits of the portion of the account disclaimed by virtue of her being the beneficiary of the bypass trust. The bypass trust would take distributions from the disclaimed portion of the Roth IRA over the life expectancy of the oldest beneficiary of the trust (i.e., over the life expectancy of the wife).

Before the surviving spouse actually effects a disclaimer following the owner's death, the spouse would have the opportunity to ensure that the value of fully using the deceased spouse's estate tax exemption amount exceeds the value of the additional tax free growth that would normally be available from having the surviving spouse rollover the Roth IRA (and defer distributions until the surviving spouse's death) and name the children as beneficiaries.

> *The disclaimer method is a popular technique used by attorneys to fund a bypass trust with retirement assets at the first spouse's death.*

There are, however, other alternatives to consider, such as naming the bypass trust as the primary beneficiary of the Roth IRA. which may be appropriate if , for example, you are in a second marriage.

> *Roth IRAs are better for funding a bypass trust than Traditional IRAs, since Roth IRAs are free of income taxes. This is another reason why Roth IRAs are superior to Traditional IRAs for estate planning.*

> *If your choice is between making your Roth IRA the beneficiary of a bypass trust or a QTIP marital trust (as discussed below), having the Roth IRA payable first to the bypass trust is the better approach.*

This is because the Roth IRA will likely have a higher rate of return than the other assets. Garnering that higher rate of return in the bypass trust is wise since it is not subject to estate taxes at the surviving spouse's death. This is in contrast with the conventional planning for Traditional IRAs, where funding the bypass trust with the IRA is typically unfavorable (when you have the choice) since a Traditional IRA will be depleted by income taxes as distributions are made. This is complex tax planning and it would be imprudent to proceed upon this course without the assistance of an attorney who specializes in this area of law.

9.3.6 Providing Benefits to a Surviving Spouse in Trust

Occasionally, naming your spouse as the outright beneficiary of your Roth IRA may be inconsistent with your estate planning objectives. You may wish to name a trust as the beneficiary of your Roth IRA, which provides benefits to your spouse as the trust beneficiary. For example, naming a marital trust as beneficiary of your Roth IRA may be appropriate if you are in a second marriage.and you want the Roth IRA balance to eventually pass to children of your first marriage; or if you have concerns about your spouse's possible remarriage and diversion or loss of control of the Roth IRA funds to a new spouse, new beneficiaries, or new investment advisor.

> *The QTIP (qualified terminable interest property) marital trust is typically used when the owner of the Roth IRA would like to provide some benefits to the surviving spouse, like the income generated by the account, but ensure that upon the spouse's subsequent death that the trust property will pass to the beneficiaries selected by the owner.*

In its simplest terms a QTIP trust is one in which the surviving spouse is entitled to all of the income from the trust, payable at annual or more frequent intervals, for life. The following example will give you an idea of how these trusts work.

Suppose that the husband and wife are both age 68 in 1998 and have a $2,500,000 estate. The husband has children by a prior marriage. He would like for his current spouse to have the income from his property, including his new Roth IRA, following his death, but he wants to ensure that upon his spouse's death the balance of the property will pass to his children by the prior marriage. The husband can accomplish this by utilizing a QTIP marital trust under his will or revocable trust and making sure that his assets pass to this trust. The Roth IRA would become an asset of the QTIP marital trust by the husband making it the primary beneficiary of the account. The QTIP marital trust can be qualified for the estate tax deduction in husband's estate. A similar type of marital trust called a QDOT (qualified domestic trust) is used when the surviving spouse is not a U.S. citizen.

When the Roth IRA is made payable to the QTIP marital trust, the surviving spouse will not be able to rollover the account and treat it as her own. However, assuming the QTIP marital trust is properly structured for the surviving spouse to qualify as a "designated beneficiary," the Roth IRA could be paid out over the life expectancy of the surviving spouse under the Life Expectancy rule.

9.3.7 Children (and other non-spouse individuals) Beneficiaries

Often you will want to name your children or grandchildren or some other non-spouse individual as beneficiaries of your Roth IRA account.

Naming a much younger individual as beneficiary of a Roth IRA is especially appealing for purposes of ensuring a long post-death distribution period.

Children and other non-spouse beneficiaries may be treated as "designated beneficiaries." Distributions are subject to the Five-Year rule, unless they are made over the life expectancy of the "designated beneficiary" and payments commence by December 31 of the year following the owner's death.

> **Example**: Owner dies at age 50 on January 31, 1995. Owner's "designated beneficiary" is Child A, and Child A will receive Owner's interest over Child A's life expectancy. The date on which distributions are required to commence to Child A is December 31, 1996. Child A's life expectancy is calculated based on Child A's attained age as of Child A's birthday in calendar year 1996.

Unless separate accounts are established, the child who has the shortest life expectancy (i.e., the oldest child) is treated as the "designated beneficiary" for purposes of calculating the minimum required distribution.

> *If you want to enable each child to use his or her life expectancy to determine the payout period of his or her separate share, then you need to establish separate Roth IRA accounts for each of your children prior to your death.*

Estate Tax Consequences

Roth IRAs payable to children (and other non-spouse individuals) are fully subject to estate taxes. It is important to plan how estate taxes on the Roth IRA are to be paid, and if possible to have estate taxes paid from sources other than the Roth IRA. This is wise since the Roth IRA will generally provide a higher rate of return than non-tax advantaged assets.

9.3.8 Trust as the Beneficiary

When you name a trust as beneficiary (revocable or irrevocable trust or a trust arising under your will at the time of your death), you have to comply with some special rules in order for you to have a "designated beneficiary." These rules will determine the life expectancy that can be used following your death in determining the payout of your Roth IRA. With a little planning, the life expectancy of the oldest trust beneficiary following your death will qualify as the "designated beneficiary."

When naming a trust as beneficiary, complicated trust drafting issues must also be considered, such as the trustee's power to make elections regarding Roth IRA distributions and the allocation of the Roth IRA installments between principal and income for trust accounting purposes. These need to be discussed with your lawyer.

Minimum Distribution Options

Distributions are subject to the Five-Year rule, which requires distribution to be fully made by December 31 of the fifth anniversary of the owner's death, unless they are made over the life or life expectancy of the "designated beneficiary" and payments commence by December 31 of the year following your death.

The five-year rule can generally be avoided

After the owner's death, the trustee of the revocable trust (or QTIP trust or bypass trust) would usually effect an election to have the account distributed to the trust over the life expectancy of the oldest trust beneficiary and commence payments by December 31 of the year following the owner's death. According to the Roth IRA agreement or beneficiary designation, the trustee should have the power to fully accelerate distributions from the Roth IRA to the trust. Having that power and specifically providing it as part of any beneficiary designation is important for flexibility, as well as for marital deduction qualification purposes when payable to a QTIP marital trust.

Multiple Beneficiaries

If the trust has more than one beneficiary, the trust beneficiary who has the shortest life expectancy (i.e., the oldest beneficiary) is treated as the "designated beneficiary" for purposes of calculating the minimum required distributions to that trust.

> *If a person other than an individual (i.e., a charity) is named as a trust beneficiary, the owner will be treated as not having a "designated beneficiary", and the Five-year rule will apply.*

9.3.8 Estate as the Beneficiary

> *This generally occurs by application of the default provisions of your Roth IRA account agreement when you fail to designate a beneficiary (or contingent beneficiary). It can be avoided.*

Minimum Distribution Options

A person who is not an individual, such as the owner's estate, may not be a "designated beneficiary."

Since there is no "designated beneficiary", distribution must be made in accordance with the Five-Year rule.

Spousal Rollover

A surviving spouse has been allowed to rollover an IRA of her deceased spouse when there was no IRA beneficiary designated and when the spouse was sole beneficiary and executor of the estate.

Estate Tax Consequences

> *Roth IRAs payable to the estate of the owner are fully subject to estate taxes (unless they pass through the estate to the surviving spouse or a charity).*

9.3.9 Creditor Protection

Many states protect all or a portion of a Traditional IRA from creditors. At this early stage in the development of Roth IRAs, it is unclear under the law of some of these states whether similar creditor protection will be provided to Roth IRAs.

> *Whatever creditor protection is provided to Roth IRAs under your state's laws, however, would likely be lost if the beneficiary were the owner's estate.*

9.3.10 Charity as Beneficiary

The costs of giving Traditional IRAs to charities may be low in estates subject to the Federal estate tax, since the combined income and estate taxes that would otherwise be applicable to the account can easily approach 70%. This is a strong motivation for owners of Traditional IRAs to give these assets to charity. However, this motivation is reduced with Roth IRAs, since distributions from these new tax favored accounts are exempt from income taxes after the owner's death. The recommended sequence of giving funds to charities is :

> *If you are giving money to charity at the time of your death, give your Traditional IRAs first, your non-tax-advantaged accounts next, and your Roth IRAs last.*

Income Tax Distribution Options

Like an estate, a charity may not be a "designated beneficiary." Essentially, this means there would be no "designated beneficiary" upon the Roth IRA owner's death and that distribution must be made in accordance with the Five-Year rule.

> *For a charity this will matter little since the charity is exempt from income tax anyway and will want the money as soon as possible.*

Estate Tax Consequences

> *Roth IRAs payable to a charity are deductible from the Federal estate tax.*

9.4 Funding a Generation-Skipping Trust with a Roth IRA

There are tax and non-tax benefits of leaving your Roth IRA payable to a trust for the benefit of your grandchildren (or lower descendants). Giving your Roth IRA at your death to your grandchildren has a special appeal because the relative young age of your grandchildren will help maximize the post-death distribution potential of your Roth IRA. Remember that the longer your Roth IRA can stay in existence (with its more

TABLE 9.3

Grandchild's Age	Life Expectancy
10	65
15	60
20	55
25	51
30	46
35	41
40	37

favorable rate of return), the greater the benefits it will provide. For example, Table 9.3 shows the life expectancy for various aged grandchildren.

Actually, many grandparents prefer to protect what they give to their grandchildren from unintended beneficiaries of family wealth. Your legacy, including your Roth IRA, for your beneficiaries can be an exposed outright legacy, a protected legacy in trust, or some combination.

> *If you are going to fund a GST (Generation Skipping Trust) at your death, there will usually not be a better asset than a Roth IRA to fund the trust. As we have already seen, the Roth IRA provides a higher rate of return compared to taxable investments or even other tax favored investments, such as a Traditional IRA.*

An outright legacy is immediately exposed to claims of outsiders, including a grandchild's creditors or potentially a divorcing spouse. A protected inheritance is largely shielded from these claims, as well as estate taxes at your grandchild's death (in some cases this may not be possible). You can protect your grandchild's inheritance in a manner she cannot do for herself, while leaving your grandchild in control of his inheritance as discussed below.

The same planning technique may also be appropriate for your children. The primary advantage to having a Roth IRA payable to a trust for a grandchild versus a trust for a child is that the grandchild will be younger and have a longer life expectancy. The generation of the children will have a marginally shorter life expectancy compared to the grandchildren. However, the same planning technique works well for children, if you do not want to skip providing benefits from your Roth IRA to the generation of your children.

You should consider the impact your estate plan will have on each child and grandchild's estate plan. For example, there are opportunities for tax savings if your child's estate would be subject to estate tax. In such an event, it may be wise to transfer a child's inheritance in trust to avoid having your legacy to the child taxed again at your child's death. When weighing the protection and potential tax savings, however, be mindful that although a trust arrangement can come close, it is not the equivalent of outright ownership. A trust has certain restrictions. The **trustee** is obligated to make prudent investments and may not simply distribute all the trust assets for just any reason. On the other hand, the trust may be very flexibly written and provide your child or grandchild with the right to all the trust income for life and liberal rights to the trust principal. The child or grandchild may even be allowed to become a co-trustee or sole trustee of his separate trust.

The selection of the trustee is a critical decision

9.5 Life Insurance versus the Roth IRA

In considering your estate planning for your retirement accounts, you may want to take a special look at life insurance. In some cases, investing a portion of your retirement assets in life insurance may result in greater economic benefit to your family. Determining the amount, if any, to invest in life insurance requires careful analysis by qualified advisors. Note that life insurance cannot be purchased with a Traditional or a Roth IRA.

Life insurance has some appeal in estate planning. First, the ownership of the policy can be structured outside your taxable estate for estate tax purposes. Second, the internal build-up of cash value is income tax deferred. Third, if the policy is kept until maturity, the proceeds are received by the beneficiaries tax free in most cases. Fourth, life insurance can be used to target specific amounts, as well as cover the risk of premature death. The combination of these factors enable life insurance to play an important role in many estate plans. However, life insurance is not for everyone. Age and health status determines the economic viability of life insurance. If the primary objective is to maximize inheritance for a beneficiary, and if you need to choose between paying for a life insurance policy or Roth Conversion taxes (assuming you cannot afford both), in some cases life insurance will be the preferred choice.

In some cases, life insurance will provide a larger inheritance than a Roth Conversion.

The comparative analysis will depend on life insurance rates. This is a specialty area that should be discussed with your advisor.

9.6 IRS Prototype Roth IRA Agreements

Early in December 1997, the IRS issued two forms that set forth model Roth IRA documents for banks and financial institutions to use in establishing Roth IRAs for their customers. These forms can be found in Appendix B. Article V.1 of Form 5305R provides that upon the death of the account owner the Life Expectancy rule is available as long as distributions begin within the required time frame. There is no indication that such treatment is limited to certain cases. That is, according to this form the Life Expectancy rule is available even if the Roth IRA was created as a result of a conversion of a Traditional IRA after the owner's RBD. Moreover, the IRS document indicates that in those cases where the owner's spouse is the sole beneficiary, the spousal rollover is always available and is actually automatic.

> *Some brokerage firms may not have incorporated the automatic rollover in their documents, so this is a question to ask your financial institution.*

Titling Requirements

A Roth IRA beneficiary should be able to identify the source of each Roth IRA he holds. This is necessary because under various sections of the IRC the rules that apply in the case of a Roth IRA held by a non-spouse beneficiary are different from the rules that apply to the original Roth IRA owner.[3] Also, different treatment may be required with respect to Roth IRAs received due to the deaths of different original Roth IRA owners. A Roth IRA received by a non-spouse beneficiary upon the death of a given Roth IRA owner must be kept separate from any Roth IRA established by the non-spouse as an original owner, and also separate from any Roth IRA received upon the death of any other original Roth IRA owner. The beneficiary's taxpayer identification number is to be used in completing the Form 5498 reporting the portion of the Roth IRA belonging to that beneficiary.

9.7 Conclusions on Estate Planning

In this chapter we have provided some guidelines that will help ensure that you maximize the benefits from the Roth IRA. We showed that it is important that you properly designate your beneficiaries; ensure that your beneficiaries can avail themselves of the tax-free growth potential of the Roth IRA following your death; and coordinate your Roth IRA with your estate plan to minimize the imposition of estate and death taxes.

In most cases having the spouse as primary beneficiary with child as contingent beneficiary works well. We also showed the impact of using a trust or a charity as the beneficiary. Naming younger children and grandchildren as the beneficiaries is an effective way of stretching out the benefits from the Roth IRA. We also demonstrated the benefits of a deathbed conversion from a Traditional IRA to the Roth IRA.

The following is a summary of the main points in the chapter:

- Select a beneficiary
- Whenever possible, plan for a spousal rollover
- Establish a bypass trust to save estate taxes
- Consider a disclaimer plan to fund the bypass trust if insufficient non-retirement account assets are available to fund the trust
- Consider a deathbed conversion
- Consider a QTIP trust if you want to ensure that the benefits will get to your children after the death of your spouse
- Consider funding a generation-skipping trust with a Roth IRA
- Consider a life insurance policy as an alternate to or in addition to a Roth Conversion

While this chapter provides you with the basics, estate planning definitely requires the help of a professional. This chapter prepares you to select the right professional and to help you ask the right questions. Again, it is your retirement, so you need to educate yourself in these important life and death matters.

Chapter 10 The Education IRA

"... the best thing you can give your children is a good education ... it is quite tragic that so many young people have to start their careers being significantly in debt because of the high cost of education... we want to expand the $500 limit..." Senator Roth

The vision of the Roth project is to help people realize the American Dream: buying a home, retiring comfortably, and providing for their children, by saving and investing.

Another initiative in concert with this vision is the Education IRA. Its focus is to provide **attractive returns on investments on funds that will be used for education**. The investments provide tax-free growth and tax-free withdrawals, much as the Roth Contribution IRA does. As we have seen in previous chapters, such tax-free investments provide significantly greater yields than taxable accounts.

The amount of investment permitted is $500 per child. This is a relatively small beginning. However, this is one of the areas that the Roth project hopes to expand in the future.

This chapter will describe the rules for Education IRAs. It will compare the investment with taxable investments. It will also provide a what-if analysis showing how much the present $500 will provide and what the results would be if the law were expanded in the future to allow a flat $2,000-per-year investment and an inflation-indexed $2,000-per-year investment. Our conclusion is that:

> *To be meaningful, the Education IRA needs to provide a significant portion of higher education costs. Only then will it be effectively marketed by the securities industry. We propose that the bill should be expanded to provide an inflation-indexed $2,000-per-year investment, or something close to this, for the Education IRA.*

10.1 The Rules for the Education IRA

The rules for the Education IRA are very close to those for the Roth contribution IRA. These are reviewed here.

Contributions can be made for the benefit of an individual under 18 years of age for qualified higher education programs (higher education). We will need to define each of these terms.

Who can contribute

Anyone can set up an Education IRA. "Anyone" means anyone: relative or friend or the student.

The eligibility criteria for the individual or couple setting it up are exactly the same as for the Roth Contribution IRA discussed in Chapter 7. Specifically, to make a full contribution, an individual's modified adjusted gross income (MAGI) will need to be less than $95,000 and a married couple's MAGI will need to be less than $150,000. Partial contributions are phased out at $110,000 for the individual and at $160,000 for the couple.

For whom can the Education IRA be set up

The person (referred to as the student) for whom the Education IRA is being set up must be under 18 years of age.

How much can be contributed

Up to $500 can be contributed annually. Anyone can contribute for the child (the friend, relative, or the student himself or herself who contributes is referred to as **the contributor**); however, the maximum contribution any one child can receive (from all contributors) in a year is limited to $500.

Partial Contributions:

If the contributor is single with a MAGI between $95,000 and $110,000 a partial contribution may be made. The amount permitted is $500 reduced by $10 for every $300 in excess of $95,000. If the MAGI is greater than $110,000 no contribution is permitted.

If the contributor is married filing jointly and the MAGI is between $150,000 and $160,000, a partial contribution is permitted. The permitted amount is $500 reduced by $10 for every $100 in excess of $150,000. If the MAGI is greater than $160,000, no contribution is permitted.

What is considered higher education

Eligible institutions include accredited post-secondary educational institutions offering credits toward the following:

- Graduate level or post-graduate degree
- Professional degree
- Bachelor's degree
- Associate degree

Certain proprietary schools and post-secondary institutions are eligible if they are eligible to participate in U.S. Department of Education student-aid programs.

Who administers the account

The person who administers the account is called the guardian. He or she may be a contributor, the student, a parent, or another specified individual.

Uses of the education IRA

The Education IRA funds will need to be used before the child reaches age 30, and they may be used for any of the following qualified expenses:

- tuition
- fees
- books
- supplies
- equipment required for enrollment
- attend an eligible education program
- room and board (if enrolled on at least a half-time basis)
- contribution to an account under a qualified state tuition program

The qualified expenses in any one year are computed by adding all of the above expenses. The following items are then subtracted from the total: qualified scholarships, education assistance to military veterans, payments for education expenses that are excludable from the student's gross income. This is the reference **difference.**

Distributions may not exceed this **difference** if they are to be tax-free.

Withdrawals and Taxes

Tax-free withdrawals are allowed as long as the distributions are qualified, as defined above. There is no tax on the growth and there is no tax upon withdrawal.

Deductibility

The amounts contributed are not deductible from Federal income taxes.

Penalty and taxes on over-withdrawals

If the amounts withdrawn exceed the qualified amounts as defined above, the excess will be subject to taxation, and there will be a penalty imposed. The taxable amount and penalties are computed as follows.

Calculate the amount that is qualified. Call this $Q

Call the amount withdrawn $W

If W is less than or equal to Q, then there is no penalty or tax

If W is greater than Q, the excess is E=W-Q

Call the amount that has been distributed from the account in the past years $PAST

Call the present-year value of the account, before distributions, $PRESENT

Calculate the ratio of PAST / PRESENT = R

The taxable amount is R*E

For example, say the account balance in 2015 is $20,000, of which $4,000 was drawn in previous years, the qualified educational expense in 2010 is $5,000, and the amount actually withdrawn in 2010 is $7,000. What is the taxable amount? In this example: E = W - Q = 7,000-5,000 = 2,000; and R = PAST / PRESENT = 4,000 / 20,000 = .2. So the taxable amount is R*E = .2*2,000 = $400.

There is a 10% penalty on the taxable amount. So the penalty in this example is $40.

Transferability

Unused balances may be rolled over to another member of the family. Alternatively, the balance may be distributed to the student, but then taxes will need to be paid.

Limitations

Contributions may not be made for State Tuition Plan and contributors may not also claim Hope or Lifetime Learning tax credits in the same year that the child has a distribution from the Education IRA. However, tax-free status can be waived in order to benefit from tax credits.

Deadlines

The contribution must be made in a particular year by the end of the year (December 31).

Required distributions

A distribution of assets to the designated beneficiary is required before age 30, or death. Any balance at the death of the student will need to be distributed to his estate within 30 days of his or her death.

10.2 Comparison of Education IRA with a Taxable Investment

This section compares investments in an Education IRA with an alternate $500 investment in a taxable account.

Consider a contribution of $500 for 15 years, assuming a 10% growth rate, a 25% tax bracket, and an inflation rate of 3.5%. What is the value of such an investment in today's dollars after taxes. The results are shown in Table 10.1.

We see that with a taxable account, the 15-year annual $500 contribution will provide $8,609 in today's dollars, while the Education IRA will provide $10,678—an advantage of over 24%.

It is also clear that, in most cases, this alone will not cover a significant portion of education expenses.

Let us next consider the impact of expanding the maximum Education IRA contribution to $2,000 per year (this is being considered by Congress). We will consider a flat yearly $2,000 contribution as well as a contribution that starts at $2,000 and is indexed—i.e., is allowed to increase each year to keep up with inflation (we will assume a 3.5% inflation rate). If the contribution limit were expanded to $2,000, the same 15-year annual $2,000 contributions would provide 4*10,678 = $42,713 (today's dollars after taxes), which typically could pay for a reasonable portion of college expenses. What if the $2,000 were indexed to increase each year keeping up with inflation?

> *If the $2,000 were indexed at a 3.5% inflation rate, the contributions would provide $69,140 (today's dollars after taxes), which is much closer to a desirable goal for college savings.*

Table 10.1 Education IRA

Contribution	$500
Current Tax rate	25%
Rate of Return	10%
Inflation	3.50%

		Education IRA	Taxable Account	ED IRA PV	Txbl PV
1998	1	500	500	500	500
1999	2	1,100	1,075	1,063	1,039
2000	3	1,760	1,693	1,643	1,581
2001	4	2,486	2,358	2,242	2,126
2002	5	3,285	3,072	2,862	2,677
2003	6	4,163	3,840	3,505	3,233
2004	7	5,129	4,665	4,173	3,795
2005	8	6,192	5,553	4,867	4,364
2006	9	7,362	6,507	5,590	4,941
2007	10	8,648	7,532	6,345	5,527
2008	11	10,062	8,635	7,133	6,121
2009	12	11,619	9,820	7,958	6,726
2010	13	13,331	11,094	8,822	7,342
2011	14	15,214	12,463	9,728	7,969
2012	15	17,285	13,935	10,678	8,609
2013	16	19,563	15,518	11,677	9,263
2014	17	22,070	17,219	12,728	9,931
2015	18	24,827	19,048	13,834	10,614
2016	19	27,860	21,014	14,998	11,313
2017	20	31,195	23,128	16,226	12,030
2018	21	34,865	25,400	17,522	12,765
2019	22	38,901	27,843	18,889	13,520
2020	23	43,342	30,468	20,334	14,294
2021	24	48,226	33,291	21,860	15,090
2022	25	53,598	36,325	23,474	15,909

10.3 Conclusions

We show that the Education IRA annual $500 contribution over 15 years provides $10,678, which is 24% more than a taxable investment (assuming a 25% tax bracket and 10% growth). If the Education IRA were expanded to allow contributions of $2,000 indexed for 3.5% inflation, the contributions would grow to about $70,000 in 15 years. These figures are expressed in today's dollars after taxes.

Appendices

Appendix A1 Single Life Expectancy

Age	Divisor	Age	Divisor	Age	Divisor
5	76.6	42	40.6	79	10.0
6	75.6	43	39.6	80	9.5
7	74.7	44	38.7	81	8.9
8	73.7	45	37.7	82	8.4
9	72.7	46	36.8	83	7.9
10	71.7	47	35.9	84	7.4
11	70.7	48	34.9	85	6.9
12	69.7	49	34.0	86	6.5
13	68.8	50	33.1	87	6.1
14	67.8	51	32.2	88	5.7
15	66.8	52	31.3	89	5.3
16	65.8	53	30.4	90	5.0
17	64.8	54	29.5	91	4.7
18	63.9	55	28.6	92	4.4
19	62.9	56	27.7	93	4.1
20	61.9	57	26.8	94	3.9
21	60.9	58	25.9	95	3.7
22	59.9	59	25.0	96	3.4
23	59.0	60	24.2	97	3.2
24	58.0	61	23.3	98	3.0
25	57.0	62	22.5	99	2.8
26	56.0	63	21.6	100	2.7
27	55.1	64	20.8	101	2.5
28	54.1	65	20.0	102	2.3
29	53.1	66	19.2	103	2.1
30	52.2	67	18.4	104	1.9
31	51.2	68	17.6	105	1.8
32	50.2	69	16.8	106	1.6
33	49.3	70	16.0	107	1.4
34	48.3	71	15.3	108	1.3
35	47.3	72	14.6	109	1.1
36	46.4	73	13.9	110	1.0
37	45.4	74	13.2	111	0.9
38	44.4	75	12.5	112	0.8
39	43.5	76	11.9	113	0.7
40	42.5	77	11.2	114	0.6
41	41.5	78	10.6	115	0.5

Appendix A2 Minimum Distribution Applicable Divisor (MDIB)

Age	Divisor	Age	Divisor
70	26.2	93	8.8
71	25.3	94	8.3
72	24.4	95	7.8
73	23.5	96	7.3
74	22.7	97	6.9
75	21.8	98	6.5
76	20.9	99	6.1
77	20.1	100	5.7
78	19.2	101	5.3
79	18.4	102	5.0
80	17.6	103	4.7
81	16.8	104	4.4
82	16.0	105	4.1
83	15.3	106	3.8
84	14.5	107	3.6
85	13.8	108	3.3
86	13.1	109	3.1
87	12.4	110	2.8
88	11.8	111	2.6
89	11.1	112	2.4
90	10.5	113	2.2
91	9.9	114	2.0
92	9.4	115 and older	1.8

Appendix A3 Joint Life and Survivor Expectancy (JLE)

Age	5	6	7	8	9	10	11	12	13	14	15	16	17	18	19	20	21	22	23	24	25	26	27	28	29	30	31	32
5	83.8	83.3	82.8	82.4	82.0	81.6	81.2	80.9	80.6	80.3	80.0	79.8	79.5	79.3	79.1	78.9	78.7	78.6	78.4	78.3	78.2	78.0	77.9	77.8	77.7	77.7	77.6	77.5
6	83.3	82.8	82.3	81.8	81.4	81.0	80.6	80.3	79.9	79.6	79.3	79.0	78.8	78.6	78.3	78.1	77.9	77.7	77.6	77.4	77.3	77.2	77.1	76.9	76.8	76.8	76.7	76.6
7	82.8	82.3	81.8	81.3	80.9	80.4	80.0	79.6	79.3	79.0	78.6	78.3	78.0	77.8	77.5	77.3	77.1	76.9	76.7	76.6	76.4	76.3	76.2	76.1	76.0	75.9	75.8	75.7
8	82.4	81.8	81.3	80.8	80.3	79.9	79.4	78.9	78.6	78.3	77.9	77.6	77.3	77.0	76.8	76.5	76.3	76.1	75.9	75.7	75.6	75.4	75.3	75.2	75.1	75.0	74.9	74.8
9	82.0	81.4	80.9	80.3	79.8	79.3	78.9	78.4	78.0	77.6	77.3	76.9	76.6	76.3	76.0	75.8	75.5	75.3	75.1	74.9	74.8	74.6	74.4	74.3	74.2	74.1	74.0	73.9
10	81.6	81.0	80.4	79.9	79.3	78.8	78.3	77.9	77.4	77.0	76.6	76.3	75.9	75.6	75.3	75.0	74.8	74.5	74.3	74.1	73.9	73.8	73.6	73.5	73.4	73.3	73.2	73.0
11	81.2	80.6	80.0	79.4	78.9	78.3	77.8	77.3	76.9	76.4	76.0	75.6	75.3	74.9	74.6	74.3	74.0	73.8	73.5	73.3	73.1	72.9	72.8	72.6	72.5	72.3	72.2	72.1
12	80.9	80.3	79.6	79.0	78.4	77.9	77.3	76.8	76.3	75.9	75.4	75.0	74.6	74.3	73.9	73.6	73.3	73.0	72.8	72.6	72.3	72.1	71.9	71.8	71.6	71.5	71.3	71.2
13	80.6	79.9	79.3	78.6	78.0	77.4	76.9	76.3	75.8	75.3	74.9	74.4	74.0	73.6	73.3	72.9	72.6	72.3	72.1	71.8	71.6	71.3	71.1	70.9	70.8	70.6	70.5	70.3
14	80.3	79.6	78.9	78.3	77.6	77.0	76.4	75.9	75.3	74.8	74.3	73.9	73.4	73.0	72.6	72.3	71.9	71.6	71.3	71.1	70.8	70.6	70.3	70.1	70.0	69.8	69.6	69.5
15	80.0	79.3	78.6	77.9	77.3	76.6	76.0	75.4	74.9	74.3	73.8	73.3	72.9	72.4	72.0	71.6	71.3	70.9	70.6	70.3	70.1	69.8	69.6	69.3	69.1	69.0	68.8	68.6
16	79.8	79.0	78.3	77.6	76.9	76.3	75.6	75.0	74.4	73.9	73.3	72.8	72.3	71.9	71.4	71.0	70.7	70.3	70.0	69.6	69.3	69.1	68.8	68.6	68.4	68.2	68.0	67.8
17	79.5	78.8	78.0	77.3	76.6	75.9	75.3	74.6	74.0	73.4	72.9	72.3	71.8	71.3	70.9	70.5	70.0	69.6	69.3	69.0	68.6	68.3	68.1	67.8	67.6	67.4	67.2	67.0
18	79.3	78.5	77.8	77.0	76.3	75.6	74.9	74.3	73.6	73.0	72.4	71.9	71.3	70.9	70.4	69.9	69.6	69.0	68.7	68.3	68.0	67.7	67.4	67.1	66.8	66.6	66.4	66.2
19	79.1	78.3	77.5	76.8	76.0	75.3	74.6	73.9	73.3	72.6	72.0	71.4	70.9	70.4	69.8	69.4	68.9	68.5	68.1	67.7	67.3	67.0	66.7	66.4	66.1	65.8	65.6	65.4
20	78.9	78.1	77.3	76.5	75.8	75.0	74.4	73.6	72.9	72.3	71.6	71.0	70.5	69.9	69.4	68.8	68.4	67.9	67.5	67.1	66.7	66.3	66.0	65.7	65.4	65.1	64.8	64.6
21	78.7	77.9	77.1	76.3	75.5	74.8	74.0	73.3	72.6	71.9	71.3	70.7	70.0	69.5	68.9	68.4	67.9	67.4	66.9	66.5	66.1	65.7	65.3	65.0	64.7	64.4	64.1	63.8
22	78.6	77.7	76.9	76.1	75.3	74.5	73.8	73.0	72.3	71.6	70.9	70.3	69.7	69.1	68.5	67.9	67.4	66.9	66.4	65.9	65.5	65.1	64.7	64.3	64.0	63.7	63.4	63.1
23	78.4	77.6	76.7	75.9	75.1	74.3	73.5	72.8	72.1	71.3	70.6	70.0	69.3	68.7	68.1	67.5	66.9	66.4	65.9	65.4	64.9	64.5	64.1	63.7	63.3	63.0	62.7	62.4
24	78.3	77.4	76.6	75.7	74.9	74.1	73.3	72.6	71.8	71.1	70.3	69.6	69.0	68.3	67.7	67.1	66.5	65.9	65.4	64.9	64.4	63.9	63.5	63.1	62.7	62.3	62.0	61.7
25	78.2	77.3	76.4	75.6	74.8	73.9	73.1	72.5	71.6	70.8	70.1	69.3	68.6	68.0	67.4	66.7	66.1	65.5	64.9	64.4	63.9	63.4	62.9	62.5	62.1	61.7	61.3	61.0
26	78.0	77.2	76.3	75.4	74.6	73.8	73.1	72.3	71.5	70.7	69.9	69.3	68.6	68.0	67.3	66.7	66.1	65.5	65.0	64.5	64.0	63.4	62.9	62.4	61.9	61.5	61.1	61.0
27	77.9	77.0	76.2	75.3	74.4	73.6	72.8	71.9	71.1	70.3	69.5	68.8	68.1	67.4	66.7	66.0	65.3	64.7	64.1	63.5	62.9	62.4	61.9	61.4	60.9	60.5	60.1	59.7
28	77.8	76.9	76.1	75.2	74.3	73.5	72.6	71.8	70.9	70.1	69.4	68.6	67.8	67.1	66.4	65.7	65.0	64.3	63.7	63.1	62.5	61.9	61.4	60.9	60.4	60.0	59.5	59.1
29	77.7	76.9	76.0	75.1	74.2	73.3	72.5	71.6	70.8	70.0	69.2	68.4	67.6	66.9	66.1	65.4	64.7	64.0	63.3	62.7	62.1	61.5	60.9	60.4	59.9	59.4	59.0	58.5
30	77.7	76.8	75.9	75.0	74.1	73.2	72.3	71.5	70.6	69.8	69.0	68.2	67.4	66.6	65.8	65.1	64.4	63.7	63.0	62.3	61.7	61.1	60.5	60.0	59.4	58.9	58.4	58.0
31	77.6	76.7	75.8	74.9	74.0	73.1	72.2	71.3	70.5	69.6	68.8	68.0	67.2	66.4	65.6	64.8	64.1	63.4	62.7	62.0	61.3	60.7	60.1	59.5	59.0	58.4	57.9	57.4
32	77.5	76.6	75.7	74.8	73.9	73.0	72.1	71.2	70.3	69.5	68.6	67.8	67.0	66.2	65.4	64.6	63.8	63.1	62.4	61.7	61.0	60.4	59.7	59.1	58.5	58.0	57.4	56.9
33	77.5	76.5	75.6	74.7	73.8	72.9	72.0	71.1	70.2	69.3	68.5	67.6	66.8	66.0	65.2	64.4	63.6	62.9	62.1	61.4	60.7	60.0	59.4	58.7	58.1	57.5	57.0	56.4
34	77.4	76.5	75.5	74.6	73.7	72.8	71.9	71.0	70.1	69.2	68.3	67.5	66.6	65.8	65.0	64.2	63.4	62.6	61.9	61.1	60.4	59.7	59.0	58.4	57.7	57.1	56.5	56.0
35	77.3	76.4	75.5	74.5	73.6	72.7	71.8	70.9	70.0	69.1	68.2	67.4	66.5	65.7	64.8	64.0	63.2	62.4	61.6	60.9	60.1	59.4	58.7	58.0	57.4	56.7	56.1	55.6
36	77.3	76.3	75.4	74.5	73.5	72.6	71.7	70.8	69.9	69.0	68.1	67.2	66.4	65.5	64.7	63.8	63.0	62.3	61.4	60.6	59.9	59.1	58.4	57.7	57.0	56.4	55.8	55.1
37	77.2	76.3	75.4	74.4	73.5	72.6	71.6	70.7	69.8	68.9	68.0	67.2	66.2	65.4	64.5	63.7	62.9	62.1	61.2	60.5	59.6	58.9	58.1	57.4	56.7	56.0	55.4	54.8
38	77.2	76.2	75.3	74.4	73.4	72.5	71.6	70.6	69.7	68.8	67.9	67.0	66.1	65.3	64.4	63.5	62.7	61.8	61.0	60.2	59.4	58.6	57.9	57.1	56.4	55.8	55.1	54.4
39	77.2	76.2	75.3	74.3	73.3	72.4	71.5	70.6	69.6	68.7	67.8	66.9	66.0	65.1	64.2	63.4	62.5	61.7	60.8	60.0	59.2	58.4	57.6	56.9	56.1	55.4	54.7	54.1
40	77.1	76.2	75.2	74.3	73.3	72.4	71.4	70.5	69.6	68.6	67.7	66.8	65.9	65.0	64.1	63.3	62.4	61.5	60.7	59.9	59.0	58.2	57.4	56.7	55.9	55.2	54.5	53.8
41	77.1	76.1	75.2	74.2	73.3	72.3	71.4	70.4	69.5	68.6	67.7	66.7	65.8	64.9	64.0	63.1	62.3	61.4	60.5	59.7	58.9	58.0	57.2	56.4	55.7	54.9	54.2	53.5

Joint Life and Survivor Expectancy (JLE) (continued)

Age	33	34	35	36	37	38	39	40	41	42	43	44	45	46	47	48	49	50	51	52	53	54	55	56	57	58	59	60
5	77.5	77.4	77.3	77.3	77.2	77.2	77.2	77.1	77.1	77.0	77.0	77.0	77.0	76.9	76.9	76.9	76.9	76.9	76.8	76.8	76.8	76.8	76.8	76.8	76.8	76.8	76.7	76.7
6	76.5	76.5	76.4	76.3	76.3	76.2	76.2	76.1	76.1	76.1	76.1	76.0	76.0	76.0	75.9	75.9	75.9	75.9	75.9	75.9	75.8	75.8	75.8	75.8	75.8	75.8	75.8	75.8
7	75.6	75.5	75.5	75.4	75.4	75.3	75.3	75.2	75.2	75.1	75.1	75.0	75.0	75.0	75.0	75.0	74.9	74.9	74.9	74.9	74.9	74.9	74.8	74.8	74.8	74.8	74.8	74.8
8	74.7	74.6	74.6	74.5	74.4	74.4	74.3	74.3	74.2	74.2	74.1	74.1	74.1	74.0	74.0	74.0	74.0	73.9	73.9	73.9	73.9	73.9	73.9	73.8	73.8	73.8	73.8	73.8
9	73.8	73.7	73.6	73.5	73.5	73.4	73.4	73.3	73.3	73.2	73.2	73.1	73.1	73.1	73.1	73.0	73.0	73.0	73.0	72.9	72.9	72.9	72.9	72.9	72.9	72.8	72.8	72.8
10	72.9	72.8	72.7	72.6	72.6	72.5	72.4	72.4	72.4	72.3	72.3	72.2	72.2	72.1	72.1	72.1	72.0	72.0	72.0	72.0	71.9	71.9	71.9	71.9	71.9	71.9	71.8	71.8
11	72.0	71.9	71.8	71.7	71.6	71.6	71.5	71.4	71.4	71.3	71.3	71.2	71.2	71.2	71.1	71.1	71.1	71.1	71.0	71.0	71.0	71.0	71.0	71.0	70.9	70.9	70.9	70.9
12	71.1	71.0	70.9	70.8	70.7	70.6	70.6	70.5	70.4	70.4	70.3	70.3	70.2	70.2	70.2	70.1	70.1	70.1	70.1	70.0	70.0	70.0	70.0	70.0	70.0	69.9	69.9	69.9
13	70.2	70.1	70.0	69.9	69.8	69.7	69.6	69.6	69.5	69.4	69.4	69.3	69.3	69.3	69.2	69.2	69.1	69.1	69.1	69.1	69.0	69.0	69.0	69.0	69.0	69.0	68.9	68.9
14	69.3	69.2	69.1	69.0	68.9	68.8	68.7	68.6	68.6	68.5	68.5	68.4	68.4	68.3	68.3	68.2	68.2	68.2	68.1	68.1	68.1	68.1	68.0	68.0	68.0	68.0	68.0	67.9
15	68.5	68.3	68.2	68.1	68.0	67.9	67.8	67.7	67.7	67.6	67.5	67.4	67.4	67.4	67.3	67.3	67.2	67.2	67.2	67.2	67.1	67.1	67.1	67.1	67.1	67.0	67.0	67.0
16	67.6	67.5	67.4	67.2	67.1	67.0	66.9	66.8	66.7	66.7	66.6	66.6	66.5	66.5	66.4	66.4	66.3	66.3	66.2	66.2	66.2	66.2	66.1	66.1	66.1	66.1	66.0	66.0
17	66.8	66.6	66.5	66.4	66.2	66.1	66.0	66.0	65.9	65.8	65.7	65.6	65.6	65.5	65.4	65.4	65.3	65.3	65.3	65.2	65.2	65.1	65.1	65.1	65.1	65.0	65.0	65.0
18	66.0	65.8	65.7	65.5	65.4	65.3	65.1	65.0	65.0	64.9	64.8	64.7	64.6	64.6	64.5	64.5	64.4	64.4	64.4	64.3	64.3	64.2	64.2	64.2	64.1	64.1	64.1	64.1
19	65.2	65.0	64.8	64.7	64.5	64.4	64.2	64.1	64.0	63.9	63.8	63.8	63.7	63.6	63.6	63.5	63.5	63.4	63.4	63.3	63.3	63.2	63.2	63.2	63.1	63.1	63.1	63.1
20	64.4	64.2	64.0	63.8	63.7	63.5	63.4	63.3	63.1	63.0	62.9	62.9	62.8	62.7	62.6	62.6	62.5	62.5	62.4	62.4	62.3	62.3	62.3	62.2	62.2	62.2	62.1	62.1
21	63.6	63.4	63.2	63.0	62.8	62.7	62.5	62.4	62.3	62.2	62.1	61.9	61.9	61.8	61.7	61.6	61.6	61.5	61.5	61.4	61.4	61.4	61.3	61.3	61.2	61.2	61.2	61.2
22	62.8	62.6	62.4	62.2	62.0	61.8	61.7	61.5	61.4	61.3	61.2	61.0	61.0	60.9	60.8	60.7	60.7	60.6	60.5	60.5	60.4	60.4	60.3	60.3	60.3	60.2	60.2	60.2
23	62.1	61.9	61.6	61.4	61.2	61.0	60.8	60.7	60.5	60.4	60.3	60.2	60.1	60.0	59.9	59.8	59.7	59.7	59.6	59.6	59.5	59.5	59.4	59.4	59.3	59.3	59.3	59.2
24	61.4	61.1	60.9	60.6	60.4	60.2	60.0	59.9	59.7	59.6	59.4	59.3	59.2	59.1	59.0	58.9	58.8	58.8	58.7	58.6	58.6	58.5	58.5	58.4	58.4	58.4	58.3	58.3
25	60.7	60.4	60.1	59.9	59.6	59.4	59.2	59.0	58.9	58.7	58.6	58.4	58.3	58.2	58.1	58.0	57.9	57.8	57.8	57.7	57.6	57.6	57.5	57.5	57.4	57.4	57.4	57.3
26	60.0	59.7	59.4	59.1	58.9	58.6	58.4	58.2	58.0	57.9	57.7	57.6	57.4	57.3	57.2	57.1	57.0	56.9	56.8	56.8	56.7	56.7	56.6	56.5	56.5	56.5	56.4	56.4
27	59.4	59.0	58.7	58.4	58.1	57.9	57.7	57.4	57.2	57.1	56.9	56.7	56.6	56.5	56.3	56.2	56.1	56.0	55.9	55.8	55.8	55.7	55.6	55.6	55.6	55.5	55.5	55.4
28	58.7	58.4	58.0	57.7	57.4	57.1	56.9	56.7	56.4	56.2	56.1	55.9	55.7	55.6	55.5	55.3	55.2	55.1	55.0	54.9	54.9	54.8	54.7	54.7	54.6	54.6	54.5	54.5
29	58.1	57.7	57.4	57.0	56.7	56.4	56.2	55.9	55.7	55.5	55.3	55.1	54.9	54.8	54.6	54.5	54.4	54.2	54.1	54.1	54.0	53.9	53.9	53.8	53.7	53.6	53.6	53.6
30	57.5	57.1	56.7	56.4	56.0	55.7	55.4	55.2	54.9	54.7	54.5	54.3	54.1	53.9	53.8	53.6	53.5	53.4	53.3	53.2	53.1	53.0	53.0	52.9	52.8	52.7	52.7	52.6
31	57.0	56.5	56.1	55.8	55.4	55.1	54.7	54.4	54.2	53.9	53.7	53.5	53.3	53.1	52.9	52.8	52.6	52.5	52.4	52.3	52.2	52.1	52.0	51.9	51.9	51.8	51.7	51.7
32	56.4	56.0	55.5	55.1	54.8	54.4	54.1	53.8	53.5	53.2	53.0	52.7	52.5	52.3	52.1	51.9	51.8	51.6	51.5	51.4	51.3	51.2	51.1	51.0	50.9	50.9	50.8	50.8
33	55.9	55.5	55.0	54.6	54.2	53.8	53.4	53.1	52.8	52.5	52.2	52.0	51.7	51.5	51.3	51.1	51.0	50.8	50.7	50.5	50.4	50.3	50.2	50.1	50.0	50.0	49.9	49.8
34	55.5	54.9	54.5	54.0	53.6	53.2	52.8	52.4	52.1	51.8	51.5	51.2	51.0	50.7	50.5	50.3	50.1	50.0	49.8	49.7	49.6	49.4	49.3	49.2	49.1	49.1	49.0	48.9
35	55.0	54.5	54.0	53.5	53.0	52.6	52.2	51.8	51.5	51.1	50.8	50.5	50.2	50.0	49.7	49.5	49.3	49.2	49.0	48.8	48.7	48.6	48.5	48.3	48.3	48.2	48.1	48.0
36	54.6	54.0	53.5	53.0	52.5	52.0	51.6	51.2	50.8	50.4	50.1	49.8	49.5	49.2	49.0	48.8	48.5	48.4	48.2	48.0	47.9	47.7	47.6	47.5	47.4	47.3	47.2	47.1
37	54.2	53.6	53.2	52.5	52.0	51.5	51.0	50.6	50.2	49.8	49.5	49.1	48.8	48.5	48.3	48.0	47.8	47.6	47.4	47.2	47.0	46.9	46.7	46.6	46.5	46.4	46.3	46.2
38	53.8	53.2	52.6	52.0	51.5	51.0	50.5	50.0	49.6	49.2	48.8	48.5	48.1	47.8	47.5	47.3	47.0	46.8	46.6	46.4	46.2	46.0	45.8	45.6	45.6	45.5	45.4	45.3
39	53.4	52.8	52.2	51.6	51.0	50.5	50.0	49.5	49.1	48.6	48.2	47.8	47.5	47.2	46.8	46.6	46.3	46.0	45.8	45.6	45.4	45.2	44.9	44.8	44.7	44.5	44.5	44.4
40	53.1	52.4	51.8	51.2	50.6	50.0	49.5	49.0	48.5	48.1	47.6	47.2	46.9	46.5	46.2	45.9	45.6	45.3	45.1	44.8	44.6	44.4	44.2	44.1	43.9	43.8	43.7	43.6
41	52.8	52.1	51.4	50.8	50.2	49.6	49.1	48.5	48.0	47.5	47.1	46.6	46.3	45.9	45.5	45.2	44.9	44.6	44.3	44.1	43.9	43.6	43.4	43.3	43.1	43.0	42.8	42.7

Joint Life and Survivor Expectancy (JLE) (continued)

Age	61	62	63	64	65	66	67	68	69	70	71	72	73	74	75	76	77	78	79	80	81	82	83	84	85	86	87	88
5	76.7	76.7	76.7	76.7	76.7	76.7	76.7	76.7	76.7	76.7	76.7	76.7	76.7	76.7	76.7	76.6	76.6	76.6	76.6	76.6	76.6	76.6	76.6	76.6	76.6	76.6	76.6	76.6
6	75.7	75.7	75.7	75.7	75.7	75.7	75.7	75.7	75.7	75.7	75.7	75.7	75.7	75.7	75.7	75.7	75.7	75.7	75.7	75.7	75.7	75.7	75.7	75.7	75.7	75.7	75.7	75.7
7	74.8	74.8	74.8	74.7	74.7	74.7	74.7	74.7	74.7	74.7	74.7	74.7	74.7	74.7	74.7	74.7	74.7	74.7	74.7	74.7	74.7	74.7	74.7	74.7	74.7	74.7	74.7	74.7
8	73.8	73.8	73.8	73.8	73.8	73.7	73.7	73.7	73.7	73.7	73.7	73.7	73.7	73.7	73.7	73.7	73.7	73.7	73.7	73.7	73.7	73.7	73.7	73.7	73.7	73.7	73.7	73.7
9	72.8	72.8	72.8	72.8	72.8	72.8	72.8	72.8	72.7	72.7	72.7	72.7	72.7	72.7	72.7	72.7	72.7	72.7	72.7	72.7	72.7	72.7	72.7	72.7	72.7	72.7	72.7	72.7
10	71.8	71.8	71.8	71.8	71.8	71.8	71.8	71.8	71.8	71.8	71.8	71.8	71.7	71.7	71.7	71.7	71.7	71.7	71.7	71.7	71.7	71.7	71.7	71.7	71.7	71.7	71.7	71.7
11	70.9	70.8	70.8	70.8	70.8	70.8	70.8	70.8	70.8	70.8	70.8	70.8	70.8	70.8	70.8	70.8	70.8	70.7	70.7	70.7	70.7	70.7	70.7	70.7	70.7	70.7	70.7	70.7
12	69.9	69.9	69.9	69.8	69.8	69.8	69.8	69.8	69.8	69.8	69.8	69.8	69.8	69.8	69.8	69.8	69.8	69.8	69.8	69.8	69.8	69.8	69.8	69.8	69.8	69.8	69.8	69.7
13	68.9	68.9	68.9	68.9	68.9	68.8	68.8	68.8	68.8	68.8	68.8	68.8	68.8	68.8	68.8	68.8	68.8	68.8	68.8	68.8	68.8	68.8	68.8	68.8	68.8	68.8	68.8	68.8
14	67.9	67.9	67.9	67.9	67.9	67.9	67.9	67.9	67.8	67.8	67.8	67.8	67.8	67.8	67.8	67.8	67.8	67.8	67.8	67.8	67.8	67.8	67.8	67.8	67.8	67.8	67.8	67.8
15	67.0	66.9	66.9	66.9	66.9	66.9	66.9	66.9	66.9	66.9	66.9	66.9	66.8	66.8	66.8	66.8	66.8	66.8	66.8	66.8	66.8	66.8	66.8	66.8	66.8	66.8	66.8	66.8
16	66.0	66.0	66.0	65.9	65.9	65.9	65.9	65.9	65.9	65.9	65.9	65.9	65.9	65.9	65.9	65.9	65.9	65.8	65.8	65.8	65.8	65.8	65.8	65.8	65.8	65.8	65.8	65.8
17	65.0	65.0	65.0	65.0	65.0	64.9	64.9	64.9	64.9	64.9	64.9	64.9	64.9	64.9	64.9	64.9	64.9	64.9	64.9	64.9	64.9	64.9	64.9	64.8	64.8	64.8	64.8	64.8
18	64.1	64.0	64.0	64.0	64.0	64.0	64.0	64.0	64.0	64.0	64.0	63.9	63.9	63.9	63.9	63.9	63.9	63.9	63.9	63.9	63.9	63.9	63.9	63.9	63.9	63.9	63.9	63.9
19	63.1	63.1	63.0	63.0	63.0	63.0	63.0	63.0	63.0	63.0	62.9	62.9	62.9	62.9	62.9	62.9	62.9	62.9	62.9	62.9	62.9	62.9	62.9	62.9	62.9	62.9	62.9	62.9
20	62.1	62.1	62.1	62.1	62.0	62.0	62.0	62.0	62.0	62.0	62.0	62.0	62.0	61.9	61.9	61.9	61.9	61.9	61.9	61.9	61.9	61.9	61.9	61.9	61.9	61.9	61.9	61.9
21	61.1	61.1	61.1	61.1	61.1	61.1	61.0	61.0	61.0	61.0	61.0	61.0	61.0	61.0	61.0	61.0	61.0	61.0	61.0	60.9	61.0	60.9	60.9	60.9	60.9	60.9	60.9	60.9
22	60.2	60.2	60.1	60.1	60.1	60.1	60.1	60.1	60.0	60.0	60.0	60.0	60.0	60.0	60.0	60.0	60.0	60.0	60.0	60.0	60.0	60.0	60.0	60.0	60.0	60.0	60.0	60.0
23	59.2	59.2	59.2	59.2	59.1	59.1	59.1	59.1	59.1	59.1	59.1	59.1	59.0	59.0	59.0	59.0	59.0	59.0	59.0	59.0	59.0	59.0	59.0	59.0	59.0	59.0	59.0	59.0
24	58.3	58.2	58.2	58.2	58.2	58.2	58.1	58.1	58.1	58.1	58.1	58.1	58.1	58.1	58.1	58.1	58.1	58.0	58.0	58.0	58.0	58.0	58.0	58.0	58.0	58.0	58.0	58.0
25	57.3	57.3	57.3	57.2	57.2	57.2	57.2	57.2	57.1	57.1	57.1	57.1	57.1	57.1	57.1	57.1	57.1	57.1	57.1	57.1	57.0	57.0	57.0	57.0	57.0	57.0	57.0	57.0
26	56.4	56.3	56.3	56.3	56.3	56.2	56.2	56.2	56.2	56.2	56.2	56.1	56.1	56.1	56.1	56.1	56.1	56.1	56.1	56.1	56.1	56.1	56.1	56.1	56.1	56.1	56.1	56.1
27	55.4	55.4	55.3	55.3	55.3	55.3	55.3	55.2	55.2	55.2	55.2	55.2	55.2	55.2	55.1	55.1	55.1	55.1	55.1	55.1	55.1	55.1	55.1	55.1	55.1	55.1	55.1	55.1
28	54.5	54.4	54.4	54.4	54.3	54.3	54.3	54.3	54.3	54.2	54.2	54.2	54.2	54.2	54.2	54.2	54.2	54.2	54.1	54.1	54.1	54.1	54.1	54.1	54.1	54.1	54.1	54.1
29	53.5	53.5	53.4	53.4	53.4	53.4	53.3	53.3	53.3	53.3	53.3	53.2	53.2	53.2	53.2	53.2	53.2	53.2	53.2	53.2	53.2	53.2	53.2	53.2	53.2	53.2	53.1	53.1
30	52.6	52.5	52.5	52.5	52.4	52.4	52.4	52.4	52.4	52.3	52.3	52.3	52.3	52.3	52.2	52.2	52.2	52.2	52.2	52.2	52.2	52.2	52.2	52.2	52.2	52.2	52.2	52.2
31	51.6	51.6	51.6	51.5	51.5	51.5	51.4	51.4	51.4	51.4	51.3	51.3	51.3	51.3	51.3	51.3	51.3	51.3	51.2	51.2	51.2	51.2	51.2	51.2	51.2	51.2	51.2	51.2
32	50.7	50.7	50.6	50.6	50.5	50.5	50.5	50.4	50.4	50.4	50.4	50.4	50.3	50.3	50.3	50.3	50.3	50.3	50.3	50.3	50.3	50.3	50.3	50.3	50.2	50.2	50.2	50.2
33	49.8	49.7	49.7	49.6	49.6	49.6	49.5	49.5	49.5	49.4	49.4	49.4	49.4	49.4	49.4	49.3	49.3	49.3	49.3	49.3	49.3	49.3	49.3	49.3	49.3	49.3	49.3	49.3
34	48.8	48.8	48.7	48.7	48.7	48.6	48.6	48.6	48.5	48.5	48.5	48.5	48.4	48.4	48.4	48.4	48.4	48.4	48.4	48.3	48.3	48.3	48.3	48.3	48.3	48.3	48.3	48.3
35	47.9	47.9	47.8	47.8	47.7	47.7	47.6	47.6	47.6	47.5	47.5	47.5	47.5	47.5	47.4	47.4	47.4	47.4	47.4	47.4	47.4	47.4	47.4	47.4	47.4	47.3	47.3	47.3
36	47.0	47.0	46.9	46.8	46.8	46.7	46.7	46.7	46.6	46.6	46.6	46.6	46.5	46.5	46.5	46.5	46.5	46.4	46.4	46.4	46.4	46.4	46.4	46.4	46.4	46.4	46.4	46.4
37	46.1	46.0	46.0	45.9	45.9	45.8	45.8	45.7	45.7	45.7	45.6	45.6	45.6	45.6	45.5	45.5	45.5	45.5	45.5	45.5	45.4	45.4	45.4	45.4	45.4	45.4	45.4	45.4
38	45.2	45.1	45.1	45.0	44.9	44.9	44.8	44.8	44.8	44.7	44.7	44.7	44.6	44.6	44.6	44.6	44.6	44.5	44.5	44.5	44.5	44.5	44.5	44.5	44.5	44.5	44.5	44.5
39	44.3	44.2	44.2	44.1	44.0	44.0	43.9	43.9	43.8	43.8	43.8	43.7	43.7	43.7	43.6	43.6	43.6	43.6	43.6	43.6	43.5	43.5	43.5	43.5	43.5	43.5	43.5	43.5
40	43.5	43.4	43.3	43.2	43.1	43.1	43.0	42.9	42.9	42.9	42.8	42.8	42.8	42.7	42.7	42.7	42.7	42.6	42.6	42.6	42.6	42.6	42.6	42.6	42.6	42.5	42.5	42.5
41	42.6	42.5	42.4	42.3	42.2	42.2	42.1	42.0	42.0	41.9	41.9	41.9	41.8	41.8	41.8	41.7	41.7	41.7	41.7	41.7	41.6	41.6	41.6	41.6	41.6	41.6	41.6	41.6

Joint Life and Survivor Expectancy (JLE) (continued)

Age	89	90	91	92	93	94	95	96	97	98	99	100	101	102	103	104	105	106	107	108	109	110	111	112	113	114	115
5	76.6	76.6	76.6	76.6	76.6	76.6	76.6	76.6	76.6	76.6	76.6	76.6	76.6	76.6	76.6	76.6	76.6	76.6	76.6	76.6	76.6	76.6	76.6	76.6	76.6	76.6	76.6
6	75.7	75.6	75.6	75.6	75.6	75.6	75.6	75.6	75.6	75.6	75.6	75.6	75.6	75.6	75.6	75.6	75.6	75.6	75.6	75.6	75.6	75.6	75.6	75.6	75.6	75.6	75.6
7	74.7	74.7	74.7	74.7	74.7	74.7	74.7	74.7	74.7	74.7	74.7	74.7	74.7	74.7	74.7	74.7	74.7	74.7	74.7	74.7	74.7	74.7	74.7	74.7	74.7	74.7	74.7
8	73.7	73.7	73.7	73.7	73.7	73.7	73.7	73.7	73.7	73.7	73.7	73.7	73.7	73.7	73.7	73.7	73.7	73.7	73.7	73.7	73.7	73.7	73.7	73.7	73.7	73.7	73.7
9	72.7	72.7	72.7	72.7	72.7	72.7	72.7	72.7	72.7	72.7	72.7	72.7	72.7	72.7	72.7	72.7	72.7	72.7	72.7	72.7	72.7	72.7	72.7	72.7	72.7	72.7	72.7
10	71.7	71.7	71.7	71.7	71.7	71.7	71.7	71.7	71.7	71.7	71.7	71.7	71.7	71.7	71.7	71.7	71.7	71.7	71.7	71.7	71.7	71.7	71.7	71.7	71.7	71.7	71.7
11	70.7	70.7	70.7	70.7	70.7	70.7	70.7	70.7	70.7	70.7	70.7	70.7	70.7	70.7	70.7	70.7	70.7	70.7	70.7	70.7	70.7	70.7	70.7	70.7	70.7	70.7	70.7
12	69.7	69.7	69.7	69.7	69.7	69.7	69.7	69.7	69.7	69.7	69.7	69.7	69.7	69.7	69.7	69.7	69.7	69.7	69.7	69.7	69.7	69.7	69.7	69.7	69.7	69.7	69.7
13	68.8	68.8	68.8	68.8	68.8	68.8	68.8	68.8	68.8	68.8	68.8	68.8	68.8	68.8	68.8	68.8	68.8	68.8	68.8	68.8	68.8	68.8	68.8	68.8	68.8	68.8	68.8
14	67.8	67.8	67.8	67.8	67.8	67.8	67.8	67.8	67.8	67.8	67.8	67.8	67.8	67.8	67.8	67.8	67.8	67.8	67.8	67.8	67.8	67.8	67.8	67.8	67.8	67.8	67.8
15	66.8	66.8	66.8	66.8	66.8	66.8	66.8	66.8	66.8	66.8	66.8	66.8	66.8	66.8	66.8	66.8	66.8	66.8	66.8	66.8	66.8	66.8	66.8	66.8	66.8	66.8	66.8
16	65.8	65.8	65.8	65.8	65.8	65.8	65.8	65.8	65.8	65.8	65.8	65.8	65.8	65.8	65.8	65.8	65.8	65.8	65.8	65.8	65.8	65.8	65.8	65.8	65.8	65.8	65.8
17	64.8	64.8	64.8	64.8	64.8	64.8	64.8	64.8	64.8	64.8	64.8	64.8	64.8	64.8	64.8	64.8	64.8	64.8	64.8	64.8	64.8	64.8	64.8	64.8	64.8	64.8	64.8
18	63.9	63.9	63.9	63.9	63.9	63.9	63.9	63.9	63.9	63.9	63.9	63.9	63.9	63.9	63.9	63.9	63.9	63.9	63.9	63.9	63.9	63.9	63.9	63.9	63.9	63.9	63.9
19	62.9	62.9	62.9	62.9	62.9	62.9	62.9	62.9	62.9	62.9	62.9	62.9	62.9	62.9	62.9	62.9	62.9	62.9	62.9	62.9	62.9	62.9	62.9	62.9	62.9	62.9	62.9
20	61.9	61.9	61.9	61.9	61.9	61.9	61.9	61.9	61.9	61.9	61.9	61.9	61.9	61.9	61.9	61.9	61.9	61.9	61.9	61.9	61.9	61.9	61.9	61.9	61.9	61.9	61.9
21	60.9	60.9	60.9	60.9	60.9	60.9	60.9	60.9	60.9	60.9	60.9	60.9	60.9	60.9	60.9	60.9	60.9	60.9	60.9	60.9	60.9	60.9	60.9	60.9	60.9	60.9	60.9
22	60.0	60.0	60.0	59.9	59.9	59.9	59.9	59.9	59.9	59.9	59.9	59.9	59.9	59.9	59.9	59.9	59.9	59.9	59.9	59.9	59.9	59.9	59.9	59.9	59.9	59.9	59.9
23	59.0	59.0	59.0	59.0	59.0	59.0	59.0	59.0	59.0	59.0	59.0	59.0	59.0	59.0	59.0	59.0	59.0	59.0	59.0	59.0	59.0	59.0	59.0	59.0	59.0	59.0	59.0
24	58.0	58.0	58.0	58.0	58.0	58.0	58.0	58.0	58.0	58.0	58.0	58.0	58.0	58.0	58.0	58.0	58.0	58.0	58.0	58.0	58.0	58.0	58.0	58.0	58.0	58.0	58.0
25	57.0	57.0	57.0	57.0	57.0	57.0	57.0	57.0	57.0	57.0	57.0	57.0	57.0	57.0	57.0	57.0	57.0	57.0	57.0	57.0	57.0	57.0	57.0	57.0	57.0	57.0	57.0
26	56.1	56.1	56.1	56.1	56.1	56.0	56.0	56.0	56.0	56.0	56.0	56.0	56.0	56.0	56.0	56.0	56.0	56.0	56.0	56.0	56.0	56.0	56.0	56.0	56.0	56.0	56.0
27	55.1	55.1	55.1	55.1	55.1	55.1	55.1	55.1	55.1	55.1	55.1	55.1	55.1	55.1	55.1	55.1	55.1	55.1	55.1	55.1	55.1	55.1	55.1	55.1	55.1	55.1	55.1
28	54.1	54.1	54.1	54.1	54.1	54.1	54.1	54.1	54.1	54.1	54.1	54.1	54.1	54.1	54.1	54.1	54.1	54.1	54.1	54.1	54.1	54.1	54.1	54.1	54.1	54.1	54.1
29	53.1	53.1	53.1	53.1	53.1	53.1	53.1	53.1	53.1	53.1	53.1	53.1	53.1	53.1	53.1	53.1	53.1	53.1	53.1	53.1	53.1	53.1	53.1	53.1	53.1	53.1	53.1
30	52.2	52.2	52.2	52.2	52.2	52.2	52.2	52.2	52.2	52.2	52.2	52.2	52.2	52.2	52.2	52.2	52.2	52.2	52.2	52.2	52.2	52.2	52.2	52.2	52.2	52.2	52.2
31	51.2	51.2	51.2	51.2	51.2	51.2	51.2	51.2	51.2	51.2	51.2	51.2	51.2	51.2	51.2	51.2	51.2	51.2	51.2	51.2	51.2	51.2	51.2	51.2	51.2	51.2	51.2
32	50.2	50.2	50.2	50.2	50.2	50.2	50.2	50.2	50.2	50.2	50.2	50.2	50.2	50.2	50.2	50.2	50.2	50.2	50.2	50.2	50.2	50.2	50.2	50.2	50.2	50.2	50.2
33	49.3	49.3	49.3	49.3	49.3	49.3	49.3	49.3	49.3	49.3	49.3	49.3	49.3	49.3	49.3	49.3	49.3	49.3	49.3	49.3	49.3	49.3	49.3	49.3	49.3	49.3	49.3
34	48.3	48.3	48.3	48.3	48.3	48.3	48.3	48.3	48.3	48.3	48.3	48.3	48.3	48.3	48.3	48.3	48.3	48.3	48.3	48.3	48.3	48.3	48.3	48.3	48.3	48.3	48.3
35	47.3	47.3	47.3	47.3	47.3	47.3	47.3	47.3	47.3	47.3	47.3	47.3	47.3	47.3	47.3	47.3	47.3	47.3	47.3	47.3	47.3	47.3	47.3	47.3	47.3	47.3	47.3
36	46.4	46.4	46.4	46.4	46.4	46.4	46.4	46.4	46.4	46.4	46.4	46.4	46.4	46.4	46.4	46.4	46.4	46.4	46.4	46.4	46.4	46.4	46.4	46.4	46.4	46.4	46.4
37	45.4	45.4	45.4	45.4	45.4	45.4	45.4	45.4	45.4	45.4	45.4	45.4	45.4	45.4	45.4	45.4	45.4	45.4	45.4	45.4	45.4	45.4	45.4	45.4	45.4	45.4	45.4
38	44.4	44.4	44.4	44.4	44.4	44.4	44.4	44.4	44.4	44.4	44.4	44.4	44.4	44.4	44.4	44.4	44.4	44.4	44.4	44.4	44.4	44.4	44.4	44.4	44.4	44.4	44.4
39	43.5	43.5	43.5	43.5	43.5	43.5	43.5	43.5	43.5	43.5	43.5	43.5	43.5	43.5	43.5	43.5	43.5	43.5	43.5	43.5	43.5	43.5	43.5	43.5	43.5	43.5	43.5
40	42.5	42.5	42.5	42.5	42.5	42.5	42.5	42.5	42.5	42.5	42.5	42.5	42.5	42.5	42.5	42.5	42.5	42.5	42.5	42.5	42.5	42.5	42.5	42.5	42.5	42.5	42.5
41	41.6	41.6	41.6	41.6	41.6	41.6	41.6	41.6	41.6	41.6	41.5	41.5	41.5	41.5	41.5	41.5	41.5	41.5	41.5	41.5	41.5	41.5	41.5	41.5	41.5	41.5	41.5

Joint Life and Survivor Expectancy (JLE) (continued)

Age	5	6	7	8	9	10	11	12	13	14	15	16	17	18	19	20	21	22	23	24	25	26	27	28	29	30	31	32
42	77.0	76.1	75.1	74.2	73.2	72.3	71.3	70.4	69.4	68.5	67.6	66.7	65.7	64.9	63.9	63.0	62.2	61.3	60.4	59.6	58.7	57.9	57.1	56.2	55.5	54.7	53.9	53.2
43	77.0	76.1	75.1	74.1	73.2	72.2	71.3	70.3	69.4	68.5	67.5	66.6	65.7	64.8	63.8	62.9	62.1	61.2	60.3	59.4	58.6	57.7	56.9	56.1	55.3	54.5	53.7	52.9
44	77.0	76.0	75.0	74.1	73.1	72.2	71.2	70.3	69.3	68.4	67.4	66.5	65.6	64.7	63.8	62.8	61.9	61.0	60.2	59.3	58.4	57.6	56.7	55.9	55.1	54.3	53.5	52.7
45	77.0	76.0	75.0	74.1	73.1	72.2	71.2	70.2	69.3	68.4	67.4	66.5	65.5	64.6	63.7	62.8	61.9	61.0	60.1	59.2	58.3	57.4	56.6	55.7	54.9	54.1	53.3	52.5
46	76.9	76.0	75.0	74.0	73.1	72.1	71.2	70.2	69.3	68.3	67.4	66.4	65.5	64.6	63.6	62.7	61.8	60.9	60.0	59.1	58.2	57.3	56.5	55.6	54.8	53.9	53.1	52.3
47	76.9	75.9	75.0	74.0	73.1	72.1	71.1	70.2	69.2	68.3	67.3	66.4	65.4	64.5	63.6	62.6	61.7	60.8	59.9	59.0	58.1	57.2	56.3	55.5	54.6	53.8	52.9	52.1
48	76.9	75.9	74.9	74.0	73.0	72.1	71.1	70.1	69.2	68.2	67.3	66.3	65.4	64.5	63.5	62.6	61.6	60.7	59.8	58.9	58.0	57.1	56.2	55.3	54.5	53.6	52.8	51.9
49	76.9	75.9	74.9	74.0	73.0	72.0	71.1	70.1	69.1	68.2	67.2	66.3	65.3	64.4	63.5	62.5	61.6	60.7	59.7	58.8	57.9	57.0	56.1	55.2	54.4	53.5	52.6	51.8
50	76.9	75.9	74.9	73.9	73.0	72.0	71.0	70.1	69.1	68.2	67.2	66.2	65.3	64.4	63.4	62.5	61.5	60.6	59.7	58.8	57.8	56.9	56.0	55.1	54.2	53.4	52.5	51.7
51	76.8	75.9	74.9	73.9	73.0	72.0	71.0	70.1	69.1	68.1	67.2	66.2	65.3	64.3	63.4	62.4	61.5	60.5	59.6	58.7	57.8	56.9	56.0	55.0	54.1	53.3	52.4	51.5
52	76.8	75.9	74.9	73.9	72.9	72.0	71.0	70.0	69.1	68.1	67.1	66.2	65.2	64.3	63.3	62.4	61.4	60.5	59.6	58.6	57.7	56.8	55.9	55.0	54.1	53.2	52.3	51.4
53	76.8	75.8	74.8	73.9	72.9	72.0	71.0	70.0	69.0	68.1	67.1	66.2	65.2	64.3	63.3	62.3	61.4	60.4	59.5	58.6	57.6	56.7	55.8	54.9	54.0	53.1	52.2	51.3
54	76.8	75.8	74.8	73.9	72.9	71.9	71.0	70.0	69.0	68.1	67.1	66.1	65.2	64.2	63.2	62.3	61.3	60.4	59.5	58.5	57.6	56.7	55.7	54.8	53.9	53.0	52.1	51.2
55	76.8	75.8	74.8	73.8	72.9	71.9	70.9	70.0	69.0	68.0	67.1	66.1	65.1	64.2	63.2	62.3	61.3	60.4	59.4	58.5	57.5	56.6	55.7	54.7	53.8	52.9	52.0	51.1
56	76.8	75.8	74.8	73.8	72.9	71.9	70.9	69.9	69.0	68.0	67.0	66.1	65.1	64.1	63.2	62.2	61.3	60.3	59.4	58.4	57.5	56.6	55.6	54.7	53.8	52.8	51.9	51.0
57	76.8	75.8	74.8	73.8	72.9	71.9	70.9	69.9	68.9	68.0	67.0	66.1	65.1	64.1	63.2	62.2	61.2	60.3	59.3	58.4	57.4	56.5	55.6	54.6	53.7	52.8	51.9	50.9
58	76.8	75.8	74.8	73.8	72.8	71.9	70.9	69.9	68.9	68.0	67.0	66.0	65.1	64.1	63.1	62.2	61.2	60.3	59.3	58.4	57.4	56.5	55.5	54.6	53.6	52.7	51.8	50.9
59	76.7	75.8	74.8	73.8	72.8	71.9	70.9	69.9	68.9	67.9	67.0	66.0	65.0	64.1	63.1	62.1	61.2	60.2	59.3	58.3	57.4	56.4	55.5	54.5	53.6	52.7	51.7	50.8
60	76.7	75.8	74.8	73.8	72.8	71.8	70.9	69.9	68.9	67.9	67.0	66.0	65.0	64.1	63.1	62.1	61.2	60.2	59.2	58.3	57.3	56.4	55.4	54.5	53.6	52.6	51.7	50.8
61	76.7	75.7	74.8	73.8	72.8	71.8	70.9	69.9	68.9	67.9	66.9	66.0	65.0	64.0	63.1	62.1	61.1	60.2	59.2	58.3	57.3	56.4	55.4	54.5	53.5	52.6	51.6	50.7
62	76.7	75.7	74.8	73.8	72.8	71.8	70.8	69.9	68.9	67.9	66.9	66.0	65.0	64.0	63.1	62.1	61.1	60.2	59.2	58.2	57.3	56.3	55.4	54.4	53.5	52.5	51.6	50.7
63	76.7	75.7	74.8	73.8	72.7	71.8	70.8	69.9	68.9	67.9	66.9	65.9	65.0	64.0	63.0	62.1	61.1	60.1	59.2	58.2	57.3	56.3	55.3	54.4	53.4	52.5	51.6	50.6
64	76.7	75.7	74.7	73.8	72.7	71.8	70.8	69.8	68.9	67.9	66.9	65.9	65.0	64.0	63.0	62.1	61.1	60.1	59.2	58.2	57.2	56.3	55.3	54.4	53.4	52.5	51.5	50.6
65	76.7	75.7	74.7	73.7	72.7	71.8	70.8	69.8	68.8	67.9	66.9	65.9	64.9	64.0	63.0	62.0	61.1	60.1	59.1	58.2	57.2	56.3	55.3	54.3	53.4	52.4	51.5	50.5
66	76.7	75.7	74.7	73.7	72.7	71.8	70.8	69.8	68.8	67.9	66.9	65.9	64.9	64.0	63.0	62.0	61.1	60.1	59.1	58.2	57.2	56.2	55.3	54.3	53.4	52.4	51.5	50.5
67	76.7	75.7	74.7	73.7	72.7	71.8	70.8	69.8	68.8	67.9	66.8	65.9	64.9	63.9	63.0	62.0	61.0	60.1	59.1	58.1	57.2	56.2	55.3	54.3	53.3	52.4	51.4	50.5
68	76.7	75.7	74.7	73.7	72.7	71.8	70.8	69.8	68.8	67.8	66.8	65.9	64.9	63.9	62.9	62.0	61.0	60.1	59.1	58.1	57.2	56.2	55.2	54.3	53.3	52.4	51.4	50.4
69	76.7	75.7	74.7	73.7	72.7	71.8	70.8	69.8	68.8	67.8	66.8	65.9	64.9	63.9	62.9	62.0	61.0	60.0	59.1	58.1	57.2	56.2	55.2	54.3	53.3	52.3	51.4	50.4
70	76.7	75.7	74.7	73.7	72.7	71.8	70.8	69.8	68.8	67.8	66.8	65.9	64.9	63.9	62.9	62.0	61.0	60.0	59.1	58.1	57.1	56.2	55.2	54.2	53.3	52.3	51.4	50.4
71	76.7	75.7	74.7	73.7	72.7	71.8	70.8	69.8	68.8	67.8	66.8	65.9	64.9	63.9	62.9	62.0	61.0	60.0	59.1	58.1	57.1	56.2	55.2	54.2	53.2	52.3	51.3	50.4
72	76.7	75.7	74.7	73.7	72.7	71.7	70.8	69.8	68.8	67.8	66.8	65.9	64.9	63.9	62.9	62.0	61.0	60.0	59.1	58.1	57.1	56.1	55.2	54.2	53.2	52.3	51.3	50.4
73	76.7	75.7	74.7	73.7	72.7	71.7	70.8	69.8	68.8	67.8	66.8	65.8	64.9	63.9	62.9	62.0	61.0	60.0	59.0	58.1	57.1	56.1	55.2	54.2	53.2	52.3	51.3	50.3
74	76.6	75.7	74.7	73.7	72.7	71.7	70.8	69.8	68.8	67.8	66.8	65.8	64.9	63.9	62.9	61.9	61.0	60.0	59.0	58.1	57.1	56.1	55.2	54.2	53.2	52.3	51.3	50.3
75	76.7	75.7	74.7	73.7	72.7	71.7	70.8	69.8	68.8	67.8	66.8	65.8	64.9	63.9	62.9	61.9	61.0	60.0	59.0	58.1	57.1	56.1	55.1	54.2	53.2	52.3	51.3	50.3
76	76.6	75.7	74.7	73.7	72.7	71.7	70.8	69.8	68.8	67.8	66.8	65.8	64.9	63.9	62.9	61.9	61.0	60.0	59.0	58.0	57.1	56.1	55.1	54.2	53.2	52.2	51.3	50.3
77	76.6	75.7	74.7	73.7	72.7	71.7	70.8	69.8	68.8	67.8	66.8	65.8	64.9	63.9	62.9	61.9	61.0	60.0	59.0	58.0	57.1	56.1	55.1	54.2	53.2	52.2	51.3	50.3
78	76.6	75.7	74.7	73.7	72.7	71.7	70.7	69.8	68.8	67.8	66.8	65.8	64.9	63.9	62.9	61.9	61.0	60.0	59.0	58.0	57.1	56.1	55.1	54.2	53.2	52.2	51.3	50.3

Joint Life and Survivor Expectancy (JLE) (continued)

Age	33	34	35	36	37	38	39	40	41	42	43	44	45	46	47	48	49	50	51	52	53	54	55	56	57	58	59	60
42	52.5	51.8	51.1	50.4	49.8	49.2	48.6	48.1	47.5	47.0	46.6	46.1	45.7	45.3	44.9	44.5	44.2	43.9	43.6	43.3	43.1	42.9	42.7	42.5	42.3	42.1	42.0	41.9
43	52.2	51.5	50.8	50.1	49.5	48.8	48.2	47.6	47.1	46.6	46.0	45.6	45.1	44.7	44.3	43.9	43.6	43.2	42.9	42.6	42.4	42.1	41.9	41.7	41.5	41.3	41.2	41.0
44	51.9	51.2	50.5	49.8	49.1	48.5	47.8	47.2	46.6	46.1	45.6	45.0	44.6	44.1	43.7	43.3	42.9	42.6	42.2	41.9	41.6	41.4	41.1	40.9	40.7	40.5	40.3	40.2
45	51.7	51.0	50.2	49.5	48.8	48.1	47.5	46.9	46.3	45.7	45.1	44.6	44.1	43.6	43.2	42.7	42.3	42.0	41.6	41.3	41.0	40.7	40.4	40.2	40.0	39.7	39.6	39.4
46	51.5	50.7	50.0	49.2	48.5	47.8	47.2	46.5	45.9	45.3	44.7	44.1	43.6	43.1	42.6	42.2	41.8	41.4	41.0	40.6	40.3	40.0	39.7	39.5	39.2	39.0	38.8	38.6
47	51.3	50.5	49.7	49.0	48.3	47.5	46.8	46.2	45.5	44.9	44.3	43.7	43.2	42.6	42.1	41.7	41.2	40.8	40.4	40.0	39.7	39.3	39.0	38.7	38.5	38.2	38.0	37.8
48	51.1	50.3	49.5	48.8	48.0	47.3	46.6	45.9	45.2	44.5	43.9	43.3	42.7	42.2	41.7	41.2	40.7	40.2	39.8	39.4	39.0	38.7	38.4	38.1	37.8	37.5	37.3	37.1
49	51.0	50.1	49.3	48.5	47.6	47.0	46.3	45.6	44.9	44.2	43.6	42.9	42.3	41.8	41.2	40.7	40.2	39.7	39.3	38.8	38.4	38.1	37.7	37.4	37.1	36.8	36.6	36.3
50	50.8	50.0	49.2	48.4	47.6	46.8	46.0	45.3	44.6	43.9	43.2	42.6	42.0	41.4	40.8	40.2	39.7	39.2	38.7	38.3	37.9	37.5	37.1	36.8	36.4	36.1	35.9	35.6
51	50.7	49.8	49.0	48.2	47.4	46.6	45.8	45.1	44.3	43.6	42.9	42.2	41.6	41.0	40.4	39.8	39.3	38.7	38.2	37.8	37.3	36.9	36.5	36.1	35.8	35.5	35.2	34.9
52	50.5	49.7	48.8	48.0	47.2	46.4	45.6	44.8	44.1	43.3	42.6	41.9	41.3	40.6	40.0	39.4	38.8	38.3	37.8	37.3	36.8	36.4	35.9	35.6	35.2	34.8	34.5	34.2
53	50.4	49.6	48.7	47.9	47.0	46.2	45.4	44.6	43.9	43.1	42.4	41.6	41.0	40.3	39.7	39.0	38.4	37.9	37.3	36.8	36.3	35.8	35.4	35.0	34.6	34.2	33.9	33.6
54	50.3	49.4	48.6	47.7	46.9	46.0	45.2	44.4	43.6	42.9	42.1	41.4	40.7	40.0	39.3	38.7	38.1	37.5	36.9	36.4	35.8	35.3	34.9	34.4	34.0	33.6	33.3	32.9
55	50.2	49.3	48.5	47.6	46.7	45.9	45.1	44.2	43.4	42.7	41.9	41.1	40.4	39.7	39.0	38.4	37.7	37.1	36.5	35.9	35.4	34.9	34.4	33.9	33.5	33.1	32.7	32.3
56	50.1	49.2	48.3	47.5	46.6	45.8	44.9	44.1	43.3	42.5	41.7	41.0	40.2	39.5	38.7	38.1	37.4	36.8	36.1	35.6	35.0	34.4	33.9	33.4	33.0	32.5	32.1	31.7
57	50.0	49.1	48.3	47.4	46.5	45.6	44.8	43.9	43.1	42.3	41.5	40.7	40.0	39.2	38.5	37.8	37.1	36.4	35.8	35.2	34.6	34.0	33.5	33.0	32.5	32.0	31.6	31.2
58	50.0	49.1	48.2	47.3	46.4	45.5	44.7	43.8	43.0	42.1	41.3	40.5	39.7	39.0	38.2	37.5	36.8	36.1	35.5	34.8	34.2	33.6	33.1	32.5	32.0	31.5	31.1	30.6
59	49.9	49.0	48.1	47.2	46.3	45.4	44.5	43.7	42.8	42.0	41.2	40.3	39.6	38.8	38.0	37.3	36.6	35.9	35.2	34.5	33.9	33.3	32.7	32.1	31.6	31.1	30.6	30.1
60	49.8	48.9	48.0	47.1	46.2	45.3	44.4	43.6	42.7	41.9	41.0	40.2	39.4	38.6	37.8	37.1	36.3	35.6	34.9	34.2	33.6	32.9	32.3	31.7	31.2	30.6	30.1	29.7
61	49.8	48.9	47.9	47.0	46.1	45.2	44.3	43.5	42.6	41.7	40.9	40.0	39.2	38.4	37.6	36.9	36.1	35.4	34.6	33.9	33.3	32.6	32.0	31.4	30.8	30.2	29.7	29.2
62	49.7	48.8	47.9	47.0	46.0	45.1	44.2	43.4	42.5	41.6	40.8	39.9	39.1	38.3	37.5	36.7	35.9	35.1	34.4	33.7	33.0	32.3	31.7	31.0	30.4	29.9	29.3	28.8
63	49.7	48.7	47.8	46.9	46.0	45.1	44.2	43.3	42.4	41.5	40.6	39.8	38.9	38.1	37.3	36.5	35.7	34.9	34.2	33.5	32.7	32.0	31.4	30.7	30.1	29.5	28.9	28.4
64	49.6	48.7	47.8	46.8	45.9	45.0	44.1	43.2	42.3	41.4	40.5	39.7	38.8	38.0	37.2	36.3	35.5	34.8	34.0	33.2	32.5	31.8	31.1	30.4	29.8	29.2	28.6	28.0
65	49.6	48.7	47.7	46.8	45.9	44.9	44.0	43.1	42.2	41.3	40.4	39.6	38.7	37.9	37.0	36.2	35.4	34.6	33.8	33.0	32.3	31.6	30.9	30.2	29.5	28.9	28.2	27.6
66	49.6	48.6	47.7	46.7	45.8	44.9	44.0	43.1	42.2	41.3	40.4	39.5	38.6	37.8	36.9	36.1	35.2	34.4	33.6	32.9	32.1	31.4	30.6	29.9	29.2	28.6	27.9	27.3
67	49.5	48.6	47.6	46.7	45.8	44.8	43.9	43.0	42.1	41.2	40.3	39.4	38.5	37.7	36.8	36.0	35.1	34.3	33.5	32.7	31.9	31.2	30.4	29.7	29.0	28.3	27.6	27.0
68	49.5	48.6	47.6	46.7	45.7	44.8	43.9	43.0	42.1	41.1	40.2	39.3	38.4	37.6	36.7	35.8	35.0	34.2	33.4	32.5	31.8	31.0	30.2	29.5	28.8	28.1	27.4	26.7
69	49.5	48.5	47.6	46.6	45.7	44.8	43.8	42.9	42.0	41.1	40.2	39.2	38.4	37.5	36.6	35.7	34.9	34.1	33.2	32.4	31.6	30.8	30.1	29.3	28.6	27.8	27.1	26.5
70	49.4	48.5	47.5	46.6	45.7	44.7	43.8	42.9	41.9	41.0	40.1	39.2	38.3	37.4	36.5	35.7	34.8	34.0	33.1	32.3	31.5	30.7	29.9	29.1	28.4	27.6	26.9	26.2
71	49.4	48.5	47.5	46.6	45.6	44.7	43.8	42.8	41.9	41.0	40.0	39.1	38.2	37.3	36.5	35.6	34.7	33.9	33.0	32.2	31.4	30.5	29.7	29.0	28.2	27.5	26.7	26.0
72	49.4	48.5	47.5	46.6	45.6	44.7	43.7	42.8	41.9	40.9	40.0	39.1	38.2	37.3	36.4	35.5	34.6	33.8	32.9	32.1	31.2	30.4	29.6	28.8	28.1	27.3	26.5	25.8
73	49.4	48.4	47.5	46.5	45.6	44.6	43.7	42.8	41.8	40.9	40.0	39.0	38.1	37.2	36.3	35.4	34.6	33.7	32.8	32.0	31.1	30.3	29.5	28.7	27.9	27.1	26.4	25.6
74	49.4	48.4	47.5	46.5	45.6	44.6	43.7	42.7	41.8	40.9	39.9	39.0	38.1	37.2	36.3	35.4	34.5	33.6	32.8	31.9	31.1	30.2	29.4	28.6	27.8	27.0	26.2	25.5
75	49.4	48.4	47.5	46.5	45.5	44.6	43.6	42.7	41.8	40.8	39.9	39.0	38.1	37.1	36.2	35.3	34.5	33.6	32.7	31.8	31.0	30.1	29.3	28.5	27.7	26.9	26.1	25.3
76	49.3	48.4	47.4	46.5	45.5	44.6	43.6	42.7	41.7	40.8	39.8	38.9	38.0	37.1	36.2	35.3	34.4	33.5	32.6	31.8	30.9	30.1	29.2	28.4	27.6	26.8	26.0	25.2
77	49.3	48.4	47.4	46.5	45.5	44.6	43.6	42.7	41.7	40.8	39.8	38.9	38.0	37.1	36.2	35.3	34.4	33.5	32.6	31.7	30.8	30.0	29.1	28.3	27.5	26.7	25.9	25.1
78	49.3	48.3	47.4	46.4	45.5	44.5	43.6	42.6	41.7	40.7	39.8	38.9	37.9	37.0	36.1	35.2	34.3	33.4	32.5	31.7	30.8	29.9	29.1	28.2	27.4	26.6	25.8	25.0

Joint Life and Survivor Expectancy (JLE) (continued)

Age	88	87	86	85	84	83	82	81	80	79	78	77	76	75	74	73	72	71	70	69	68	67	66	65	64	63	62	61
42	40.6	40.6	40.6	40.7	40.7	40.7	40.7	40.7	40.7	40.7	40.7	40.8	40.8	40.8	40.9	40.9	40.9	41.0	41.0	41.1	41.1	41.2	41.3	41.3	41.4	41.5	41.6	41.7
43	39.7	39.7	39.7	39.7	39.7	39.7	39.7	39.8	39.8	39.8	39.8	39.8	39.9	39.9	39.9	40.0	40.0	40.0	40.1	40.2	40.2	40.3	40.4	40.4	40.5	40.6	40.8	40.9
44	38.7	38.7	38.7	38.7	38.8	38.8	38.8	38.8	38.8	38.8	38.9	38.9	38.9	39.0	39.0	39.0	39.1	39.1	39.2	39.2	39.3	39.4	39.5	39.6	39.7	39.8	39.9	40.0
45	37.8	37.8	37.8	37.8	37.8	37.9	37.9	37.9	37.9	37.9	38.0	38.0	38.0	38.1	38.1	38.1	38.2	38.2	38.3	38.4	38.4	38.5	38.6	38.7	38.8	38.9	39.1	39.2
46	36.9	36.9	36.9	36.9	36.9	36.9	36.9	37.0	37.0	37.0	37.0	37.1	37.1	37.1	37.2	37.2	37.3	37.3	37.4	37.5	37.6	37.7	37.8	37.9	38.0	38.1	38.3	38.4
47	35.9	35.9	36.0	36.0	36.0	36.0	36.0	36.0	36.1	36.1	36.1	36.2	36.2	36.2	36.3	36.3	36.4	36.5	36.5	36.6	36.7	36.8	36.9	37.0	37.2	37.3	37.5	37.6
48	35.0	35.0	35.0	35.1	35.1	35.1	35.1	35.1	35.2	35.2	35.2	35.3	35.3	35.3	35.4	35.4	35.5	35.6	35.7	35.7	35.8	36.0	36.1	36.2	36.3	36.5	36.7	36.9
49	34.1	34.1	34.1	34.1	34.2	34.2	34.2	34.2	34.2	34.3	34.3	34.4	34.4	34.5	34.5	34.6	34.6	34.7	34.8	34.9	35.0	35.1	35.2	35.4	35.5	35.7	35.9	36.1
50	33.2	33.2	33.2	33.2	33.2	33.3	33.3	33.3	33.4	33.4	33.4	33.5	33.5	33.6	33.6	33.7	33.8	33.9	34.0	34.1	34.2	34.3	34.4	34.6	34.8	34.9	35.1	35.4
51	32.3	32.3	32.3	32.3	32.3	32.4	32.4	32.4	32.5	32.5	32.5	32.6	32.6	32.7	32.8	32.8	32.9	33.0	33.1	33.2	33.4	33.5	33.6	33.8	34.0	34.2	34.4	34.6
52	31.4	31.4	31.4	31.4	31.4	31.5	31.5	31.5	31.6	31.6	31.7	31.7	31.8	31.8	31.9	32.0	32.1	32.2	32.3	32.4	32.5	32.7	32.9	33.0	33.2	33.5	33.7	33.9
53	30.5	30.5	30.5	30.5	30.6	30.6	30.6	30.7	30.7	30.7	30.8	30.8	30.9	31.0	31.1	31.1	31.2	31.4	31.5	31.6	31.8	31.9	32.1	32.3	32.5	32.7	33.0	33.3
54	29.6	29.6	29.6	29.6	29.7	29.7	29.7	29.8	29.8	29.9	29.9	30.0	30.1	30.1	30.2	30.3	30.4	30.5	30.7	30.8	31.0	31.2	31.4	31.6	31.8	32.0	32.3	32.6
55	28.7	28.7	28.7	28.8	28.8	28.8	28.9	28.9	29.0	29.0	29.1	29.1	29.2	29.3	29.4	29.5	29.6	29.7	29.9	30.1	30.2	30.4	30.6	30.9	31.1	31.4	31.7	32.0
56	27.8	27.8	27.9	27.9	27.9	28.0	28.0	28.1	28.1	28.2	28.2	28.3	28.4	28.5	28.6	28.7	28.8	29.0	29.1	29.3	29.5	29.7	29.9	30.2	30.4	30.7	31.0	31.4
57	27.0	27.0	27.0	27.0	27.1	27.1	27.2	27.2	27.3	27.3	27.4	27.5	27.6	27.7	27.8	27.9	28.1	28.2	28.4	28.6	28.8	29.0	29.2	29.5	29.8	30.1	30.4	30.8
58	26.1	26.1	26.1	26.2	26.2	26.3	26.3	26.4	26.4	26.5	26.6	26.7	26.8	26.9	27.0	27.1	27.3	27.5	27.6	27.8	28.1	28.3	28.6	28.9	29.2	29.5	29.9	30.2
59	25.2	25.3	25.3	25.3	25.4	25.4	25.5	25.5	25.6	25.7	25.8	25.9	26.0	26.1	26.2	26.4	26.5	26.7	26.9	27.1	27.4	27.6	27.9	28.2	28.6	28.9	29.3	29.7
60	24.4	24.4	24.5	24.5	24.5	24.6	24.6	24.7	24.8	24.9	25.0	25.1	25.2	25.3	25.5	25.6	25.8	26.0	26.2	26.5	26.7	27.0	27.3	27.6	28.0	28.4	28.8	29.2
61	23.5	23.5	23.6	23.6	23.7	23.8	23.8	23.9	24.0	24.1	24.2	24.3	24.4	24.6	24.7	24.9	25.1	25.3	25.6	25.8	26.1	26.4	26.7	27.1	27.4	27.8	28.3	28.7
62	22.7	22.8	22.8	22.8	22.9	23.0	23.1	23.1	23.2	23.3	23.5	23.6	23.7	23.8	24.0	24.2	24.4	24.7	24.9	25.2	25.5	25.8	26.1	26.5	26.9	27.3	27.8	28.3
63	21.9	21.9	22.0	22.0	22.1	22.2	22.3	22.3	22.4	22.6	22.7	22.8	23.0	23.1	23.3	23.5	23.7	24.0	24.3	24.6	24.9	25.2	25.6	26.0	26.4	26.9	27.3	27.8
64	21.1	21.1	21.2	21.3	21.3	21.4	21.5	21.6	21.7	21.8	21.9	22.1	22.2	22.4	22.6	22.9	23.1	23.4	23.7	24.0	24.3	24.7	25.1	25.5	25.9	26.4	26.9	27.4
65	20.3	20.3	20.4	20.5	20.5	20.6	20.7	20.8	21.0	21.1	21.2	21.4	21.6	21.8	22.0	22.2	22.5	22.8	23.1	23.4	23.8	24.2	24.6	25.0	25.5	26.0	26.5	27.1
66	19.5	19.6	19.6	19.7	19.8	19.9	20.0	20.1	20.2	20.4	20.5	20.7	20.9	21.1	21.4	21.6	21.9	22.2	22.5	22.9	23.3	23.7	24.1	24.6	25.0	25.6	26.1	26.7
67	18.8	18.8	18.9	19.0	19.1	19.2	19.3	19.4	19.5	19.7	19.9	20.1	20.3	20.5	20.8	21.0	21.3	21.7	22.0	22.4	22.8	23.2	23.7	24.2	24.7	25.2	25.8	26.4
68	18.0	18.1	18.2	18.3	18.4	18.5	18.6	18.7	18.9	19.0	19.2	19.4	19.7	19.9	20.2	20.5	20.8	21.2	21.5	21.9	22.3	22.8	23.3	23.8	24.3	24.9	25.5	26.1
69	17.3	17.4	17.5	17.6	17.7	17.8	17.9	18.1	18.2	18.4	18.5	18.8	19.1	19.3	19.6	19.9	20.3	20.7	21.1	21.5	21.9	22.4	22.9	23.4	24.0	24.6	25.2	25.8
70	16.6	16.7	16.8	16.9	17.0	17.1	17.3	17.4	17.6	17.8	18.0	18.3	18.5	18.8	19.1	19.4	19.8	20.2	20.6	21.1	21.5	22.0	22.5	23.1	23.7	24.3	24.9	25.6
71	15.9	16.0	16.1	16.2	16.3	16.5	16.6	16.8	17.0	17.2	17.4	17.7	18.0	18.3	18.6	19.0	19.4	19.8	20.2	20.7	21.2	21.7	22.2	22.8	23.4	24.0	24.7	25.3
72	15.3	15.4	15.5	15.6	15.7	15.9	16.0	16.2	16.4	16.7	16.9	17.2	17.5	17.8	18.2	18.5	18.9	19.4	19.8	20.3	20.8	21.3	21.9	22.5	23.1	23.8	24.4	25.1
73	14.6	14.7	14.8	15.0	15.1	15.3	15.5	15.7	15.9	16.1	16.4	16.7	17.0	17.3	17.7	18.1	18.5	19.0	19.4	20.0	20.5	21.0	21.6	22.2	22.9	23.5	24.2	24.9
74	14.0	14.1	14.2	14.4	14.5	14.7	14.9	15.1	15.4	15.6	15.9	16.2	16.5	16.9	17.3	17.7	18.2	18.6	19.1	19.6	20.2	20.7	21.4	22.0	22.7	23.3	24.0	24.7
75	13.4	13.5	13.7	13.8	14.0	14.2	14.4	14.6	14.9	15.1	15.4	15.8	16.1	16.5	16.9	17.3	17.8	18.3	18.8	19.3	19.9	20.5	21.1	21.8	22.4	23.1	23.8	24.6
76	12.8	13.0	13.1	13.3	13.5	13.7	13.9	14.1	14.4	14.7	15.0	15.4	15.7	16.1	16.5	17.0	17.5	18.0	18.5	19.1	19.7	20.3	20.9	21.6	22.3	23.0	23.7	24.4
77	12.3	12.4	12.6	12.8	13.0	13.2	13.4	13.7	14.0	14.3	14.6	15.0	15.4	15.8	16.2	16.7	17.2	17.7	18.3	18.8	19.4	20.1	20.7	21.4	22.1	22.8	23.6	24.3
78	11.8	11.9	12.1	12.3	12.5	12.7	13.0	13.2	13.5	13.9	14.2	14.6	15.0	15.4	15.9	16.4	16.9	17.4	18.0	18.6	19.2	19.9	20.5	21.2	21.9	22.7	23.4	24.2

Joint Life and Survivor Expectancy (JLE) (continued)

Age	89	90	91	92	93	94	95	96	97	98	99	100	101	102	103	104	105	106	107	108	109	110	111	112	113	114	115
42	40.6	40.6	40.6	40.6	40.6	40.6	40.6	40.6	40.6	40.6	40.6	40.6	40.6	40.6	40.6	40.6	40.6	40.6	40.6	40.6	40.6	40.6	40.6	40.6	40.6	40.6	40.6
43	39.7	39.7	39.7	39.7	39.7	39.7	39.7	39.6	39.6	39.6	39.6	39.6	39.6	39.6	39.6	39.6	39.6	39.6	39.6	39.6	39.6	39.6	39.6	39.6	39.6	39.6	39.6
44	38.7	38.7	38.7	38.7	38.7	38.7	38.7	38.7	38.7	38.7	38.7	38.7	38.7	38.7	38.7	38.7	38.7	38.7	38.7	38.7	38.7	38.7	38.7	38.7	38.7	38.7	38.7
45	37.8	37.8	37.8	37.8	37.8	37.8	37.8	37.8	37.8	37.8	37.8	37.8	37.8	37.8	37.7	37.7	37.7	37.7	37.7	37.7	37.7	37.7	37.7	37.7	37.7	37.7	37.7
46	36.9	36.9	36.8	36.8	36.8	36.8	36.8	36.8	36.8	36.8	36.8	36.8	36.8	36.8	36.8	36.8	36.8	36.8	36.8	36.8	36.8	36.8	36.8	36.8	36.8	36.8	36.8
47	35.9	35.9	35.9	35.9	35.9	35.9	35.9	35.9	35.9	35.9	35.9	35.9	35.9	35.9	35.9	35.9	35.9	35.9	35.9	35.9	35.9	35.9	35.9	35.9	35.9	35.9	35.9
48	35.0	35.0	35.0	35.0	35.0	35.0	35.0	35.0	35.0	35.0	35.0	35.0	35.0	35.0	34.9	34.9	34.9	34.9	34.9	34.9	34.9	34.9	34.9	34.9	34.9	34.9	34.9
49	34.1	34.1	34.1	34.1	34.1	34.1	34.0	34.0	34.0	34.0	34.0	34.0	34.0	34.0	34.0	34.0	34.0	34.0	34.0	34.0	34.0	34.0	34.0	34.0	34.0	34.0	34.0
50	33.2	33.2	33.2	33.2	33.1	33.1	33.1	33.1	33.1	33.1	33.1	33.1	33.1	33.1	33.1	33.1	33.1	33.1	33.1	33.1	33.1	33.1	33.1	33.1	33.1	33.1	33.1
51	32.3	32.3	32.2	32.2	32.2	32.2	32.2	32.2	32.2	32.2	32.2	32.2	32.2	32.2	32.2	32.2	32.2	32.2	32.2	32.2	32.2	32.2	32.2	32.2	32.2	32.2	32.2
52	31.4	31.3	31.3	31.3	31.3	31.3	31.3	31.3	31.3	31.3	31.3	31.3	31.3	31.3	31.3	31.3	31.3	31.3	31.3	31.3	31.3	31.3	31.3	31.3	31.3	31.3	31.3
53	30.5	30.5	30.4	30.4	30.4	30.4	30.4	30.4	30.4	30.4	30.4	30.4	30.4	30.4	30.4	30.4	30.4	30.4	30.4	30.4	30.4	30.4	30.4	30.4	30.4	30.4	30.4
54	29.6	29.6	29.5	29.5	29.5	29.5	29.5	29.5	29.5	29.5	29.5	29.5	29.5	29.5	29.5	29.5	29.5	29.5	29.5	29.5	29.5	29.5	29.5	29.5	29.5	29.5	29.5
55	28.7	28.7	28.7	28.6	28.6	28.6	28.6	28.6	28.6	28.6	28.6	28.6	28.6	28.6	28.6	28.6	28.6	28.6	28.6	28.6	28.6	28.6	28.6	28.6	28.6	28.6	28.6
56	27.8	27.8	27.8	27.8	27.8	27.7	27.7	27.7	27.7	27.7	27.7	27.7	27.7	27.7	27.7	27.7	27.7	27.7	27.7	27.7	27.7	27.7	27.7	27.7	27.7	27.7	27.7
57	26.9	26.9	26.9	26.9	26.9	26.9	26.9	26.9	26.8	26.8	26.8	26.8	26.8	26.8	26.8	26.8	26.8	26.8	26.8	26.8	26.8	26.8	26.8	26.8	26.8	26.8	26.8
58	26.1	26.1	26.0	26.0	26.0	26.0	26.0	26.0	26.0	26.0	26.0	26.0	25.9	25.9	25.9	25.9	25.9	25.9	25.9	25.9	25.9	25.9	25.9	25.9	25.9	25.9	25.9
59	25.2	25.2	25.2	25.2	25.1	25.1	25.1	25.1	25.1	25.1	25.1	25.1	25.1	25.1	25.1	25.1	25.1	25.1	25.0	25.0	25.0	25.0	25.0	25.0	25.0	25.0	25.0
60	24.4	24.3	24.3	24.3	24.3	24.3	24.3	24.2	24.2	24.2	24.2	24.2	24.2	24.2	24.2	24.2	24.2	24.2	24.2	24.2	24.2	24.2	24.2	24.2	24.2	24.2	24.2
61	23.5	23.5	23.5	23.5	23.4	23.4	23.4	23.4	23.4	23.4	23.4	23.4	23.4	23.3	23.3	23.3	23.3	23.3	23.3	23.3	23.3	23.3	23.3	23.3	23.3	23.3	23.3
62	22.7	22.7	22.6	22.6	22.6	22.6	22.6	22.6	22.5	22.5	22.5	22.5	22.5	22.5	22.5	22.5	22.5	22.5	22.5	22.5	22.5	22.5	22.5	22.5	22.5	22.5	22.5
63	21.9	21.8	21.8	21.8	21.8	21.7	21.7	21.7	21.7	21.7	21.7	21.7	21.7	21.7	21.7	21.6	21.6	21.6	21.8	21.8	21.8	21.8	21.8	21.8	21.8	21.8	21.8
64	21.1	21.0	21.0	21.0	20.9	20.9	20.9	20.9	20.9	20.9	20.9	20.8	20.8	20.8	20.8	20.8	20.8	20.8	20.8	20.8	20.8	20.8	20.8	20.8	20.8	20.8	20.8
65	20.3	20.2	20.2	20.2	20.1	20.1	20.1	20.1	20.1	20.1	20.0	20.0	20.0	20.0	20.0	20.0	20.0	20.0	20.0	20.0	20.0	20.0	20.0	20.0	20.0	20.0	20.0
66	19.5	19.4	19.4	19.4	19.3	19.3	19.3	19.3	19.3	19.3	19.2	19.2	19.2	19.2	19.2	19.2	19.2	19.2	19.2	19.2	19.2	19.2	19.2	19.2	19.2	19.2	19.2
67	18.7	18.7	18.6	18.6	18.6	18.5	18.5	18.5	18.5	18.5	18.5	18.4	18.4	18.4	18.4	18.4	18.4	18.4	18.4	18.4	18.4	18.4	18.4	18.4	18.4	18.4	18.4
68	18.0	17.9	17.9	17.8	17.8	17.8	17.8	17.7	17.7	17.7	17.7	17.7	17.7	17.6	17.6	17.6	17.6	17.6	17.6	17.6	17.6	17.6	17.6	17.6	17.6	17.6	17.6
69	17.2	17.2	17.1	17.1	17.1	17.0	17.0	17.0	17.0	16.9	16.9	16.9	16.9	16.9	16.9	16.9	16.8	16.8	16.8	16.8	16.8	16.8	16.8	16.8	16.8	16.8	16.8
70	16.5	16.5	16.4	16.4	16.3	16.3	16.3	16.2	16.2	16.2	16.2	16.2	16.1	16.1	16.1	16.1	16.1	16.1	16.1	16.1	16.1	16.1	16.0	16.0	16.0	16.0	16.0
71	15.8	15.8	15.7	15.7	15.6	15.6	15.6	15.5	15.5	15.5	15.5	15.4	15.4	15.4	15.4	15.4	15.4	15.3	15.3	15.3	15.3	15.3	15.3	15.3	15.3	15.3	15.3
72	15.2	15.1	15.0	15.0	14.9	14.9	14.9	14.8	14.8	14.8	14.7	14.7	14.7	14.7	14.7	14.7	14.6	14.6	14.6	14.6	14.6	14.6	14.6	14.6	14.6	14.6	14.6
73	14.5	14.5	14.4	14.3	14.3	14.2	14.2	14.2	14.1	14.1	14.1	14.0	14.0	14.0	14.0	14.0	13.9	13.9	13.9	13.9	13.9	13.9	13.9	13.9	13.9	13.9	13.9
74	13.9	13.8	13.7	13.7	13.6	13.6	13.5	13.5	13.5	13.4	13.4	13.4	13.3	13.3	13.3	13.3	13.3	13.3	13.2	13.2	13.2	13.2	13.2	13.2	13.2	13.2	13.2
75	13.3	13.2	13.1	13.1	13.0	12.9	12.9	12.9	12.8	12.8	12.7	12.7	12.7	12.7	12.6	12.6	12.6	12.6	12.6	12.6	12.6	12.6	12.6	12.6	12.6	12.6	12.6
76	12.7	12.6	12.5	12.5	12.4	12.3	12.3	12.2	12.2	12.2	12.1	12.1	12.1	12.0	12.0	12.0	12.0	11.9	11.9	11.9	11.9	11.9	11.9	11.9	11.9	11.9	11.9
77	12.2	12.1	12.0	11.9	11.8	11.7	11.7	11.6	11.6	11.5	11.5	11.5	11.4	11.4	11.4	11.4	11.3	11.3	11.3	11.3	11.3	11.3	11.3	11.3	11.3	11.3	11.3
78	11.6	11.5	11.4	11.3	11.3	11.2	11.1	11.1	11.0	11.0	10.9	10.9	10.8	10.8	10.8	10.8	10.7	10.7	10.7	10.7	10.7	10.7	10.7	10.7	10.7	10.7	10.7

Joint Life and Survivor Expectancy (JLE) (continued)

Age	5	6	7	8	9	10	11	12	13	14	15	16	17	18	19	20	21	22	23	24	25	26	27	28	29	30	31	32
79	76.6	75.7	74.7	73.7	72.7	71.7	70.7	69.8	68.8	67.8	66.8	65.8	64.9	63.9	62.9	61.9	61.0	60.0	59.0	58.0	57.1	56.1	55.1	54.1	53.2	52.2	51.2	50.3
80	76.6	75.7	74.7	73.7	72.7	71.7	70.7	69.8	68.8	67.8	66.8	65.8	64.9	63.9	62.9	61.9	60.9	60.0	59.0	58.0	57.1	56.1	55.1	54.1	53.2	52.2	51.2	50.3
81	76.6	75.7	74.7	73.7	72.7	71.7	70.7	69.8	68.8	67.8	66.8	65.8	64.9	63.9	62.9	61.9	60.9	60.0	59.0	58.0	57.0	56.1	55.1	54.1	53.2	52.2	51.2	50.3
82	76.6	75.7	74.7	73.7	72.7	71.7	70.7	69.8	68.8	67.8	66.8	65.8	64.9	63.9	62.9	61.9	60.9	60.0	59.0	58.0	57.0	56.1	55.1	54.1	53.2	52.2	51.2	50.3
83	76.6	75.7	74.7	73.7	72.7	71.7	70.7	69.8	68.8	67.8	66.8	65.8	64.9	63.9	62.9	61.9	60.9	60.0	59.0	58.0	57.0	56.1	55.1	54.1	53.2	52.2	51.2	50.3
84	76.6	75.7	74.7	73.7	72.7	71.7	70.7	69.8	68.8	67.8	66.8	65.8	64.8	63.9	62.9	61.9	60.9	60.0	59.0	58.0	57.0	56.1	55.1	54.1	53.2	52.2	51.2	50.3
85	76.6	75.7	74.7	73.7	72.7	71.7	70.7	69.8	68.8	67.8	66.8	65.8	64.8	63.9	62.9	61.9	60.9	60.0	59.0	58.0	57.0	56.1	55.1	54.1	53.2	52.2	51.2	50.2
86	76.6	75.7	74.7	73.7	72.7	71.7	70.7	69.8	68.8	67.8	66.8	65.8	64.8	63.9	62.9	61.9	60.9	60.0	59.0	58.0	57.0	56.1	55.1	54.1	53.2	52.2	51.2	50.2
87	76.6	75.7	74.7	73.7	72.7	71.7	70.7	69.8	68.8	67.8	66.8	65.8	64.8	63.9	62.9	61.9	60.9	60.0	59.0	58.0	57.0	56.1	55.1	54.1	53.1	52.2	51.2	50.2
88	76.6	75.6	74.7	73.7	72.7	71.7	70.7	69.8	68.8	67.8	66.8	65.8	64.8	63.9	62.9	61.9	60.9	60.0	59.0	58.0	57.0	56.1	55.1	54.1	53.1	52.2	51.2	50.2
89	76.6	75.6	74.7	73.7	72.7	71.7	70.7	69.7	68.8	67.8	66.8	65.8	64.8	63.9	62.9	61.9	60.9	60.0	59.0	58.0	57.0	56.1	55.1	54.1	53.1	52.2	51.2	50.2
90	76.6	75.6	74.7	73.7	72.7	71.7	70.7	69.7	68.8	67.8	66.8	65.8	64.8	63.9	62.9	61.9	60.9	60.0	59.0	58.0	57.0	56.1	55.1	54.1	53.1	52.2	51.2	50.2
91	76.6	75.6	74.7	73.7	72.7	71.7	70.7	69.7	68.8	67.8	66.8	65.8	64.8	63.9	62.9	61.9	60.9	60.0	59.0	58.0	57.0	56.1	55.1	54.1	53.1	52.2	51.2	50.2
92	76.6	75.6	74.7	73.7	72.7	71.7	70.7	69.7	68.8	67.8	66.8	65.8	64.8	63.9	62.9	61.9	60.9	60.0	59.0	58.0	57.0	56.1	55.1	54.1	53.1	52.2	51.2	50.2
93	76.6	75.6	74.7	73.7	72.7	71.7	70.7	69.7	68.8	67.8	66.8	65.8	64.8	63.9	62.9	61.9	60.9	60.0	59.0	58.0	57.0	56.1	55.1	54.1	53.1	52.2	51.2	50.2
94	76.6	75.6	74.7	73.7	72.7	71.7	70.7	69.7	68.8	67.8	66.8	65.8	64.8	63.9	62.9	61.9	60.9	59.9	59.0	58.0	57.0	56.1	55.1	54.1	53.1	52.2	51.2	50.2
95	76.6	75.6	74.7	73.7	72.7	71.7	70.7	69.7	68.8	67.8	66.8	65.8	64.8	63.9	62.9	61.9	60.9	59.9	59.0	58.0	57.0	56.1	55.1	54.1	53.1	52.2	51.2	50.2
96	76.6	75.6	74.7	73.7	72.7	71.7	70.7	69.7	68.8	67.8	66.8	65.8	64.8	63.9	62.9	61.9	60.9	59.9	59.0	58.0	57.0	56.1	55.1	54.1	53.1	52.2	51.2	50.2
97	76.6	75.6	74.7	73.7	72.7	71.7	70.7	69.7	68.8	67.8	66.8	65.8	64.8	63.9	62.9	61.9	60.9	59.9	59.0	58.0	57.0	56.0	55.1	54.1	53.1	52.2	51.2	50.2
98	76.6	75.6	74.7	73.7	72.7	71.7	70.7	69.7	68.8	67.8	66.8	65.8	64.8	63.9	62.9	61.9	60.9	59.9	59.0	58.0	57.0	56.0	55.1	54.1	53.1	52.2	51.2	50.2
99	76.6	75.6	74.7	73.7	72.7	71.7	70.7	69.7	68.8	67.8	66.8	65.8	64.8	63.9	62.9	61.9	60.9	59.9	59.0	58.0	57.0	56.0	55.1	54.1	53.1	52.2	51.2	50.2
100	76.6	75.6	74.7	73.7	72.7	71.7	70.7	69.7	68.7	67.8	66.8	65.8	64.8	63.9	62.9	61.9	60.9	59.9	59.0	58.0	57.0	56.0	55.1	54.1	53.1	52.2	51.2	50.2
101	76.6	75.6	74.7	73.7	72.7	71.7	70.7	69.7	68.7	67.8	66.8	65.8	64.8	63.9	62.9	61.9	60.9	59.9	59.0	58.0	57.0	56.0	55.1	54.1	53.1	52.1	51.2	50.2
102	76.6	75.6	74.7	73.7	72.7	71.7	70.7	69.7	68.7	67.7	66.8	65.8	64.8	63.9	62.9	61.9	60.9	59.9	59.0	58.0	57.0	56.0	55.1	54.1	53.1	52.1	51.2	50.2
103	76.6	75.6	74.7	73.7	72.7	71.7	70.7	69.7	68.7	67.7	66.8	65.8	64.8	63.9	62.8	61.9	60.9	59.9	59.0	58.0	57.0	56.0	55.1	54.1	53.1	52.1	51.2	50.2
104	76.6	75.6	74.6	73.6	72.7	71.7	70.7	69.7	68.7	67.7	66.8	65.8	64.8	63.9	62.8	61.9	60.9	59.9	59.0	58.0	57.0	56.0	55.1	54.1	53.1	52.1	51.2	50.2
105	76.6	75.6	74.6	73.6	72.7	71.7	70.7	69.7	68.7	67.7	66.8	65.8	64.8	63.9	62.8	61.9	60.9	59.9	59.0	58.0	57.0	56.0	55.1	54.1	53.1	52.1	51.2	50.2
106	76.6	75.6	74.6	73.6	72.7	71.7	70.7	69.7	68.7	67.7	66.8	65.8	64.8	63.9	62.8	61.9	60.9	59.9	59.0	58.0	57.0	56.0	55.1	54.1	53.1	52.1	51.2	50.2
107	76.6	75.6	74.6	73.6	72.7	71.7	70.7	69.7	68.7	67.7	66.8	65.8	64.8	63.9	62.8	61.9	60.9	59.9	59.0	58.0	57.0	56.0	55.1	54.1	53.1	52.1	51.2	50.2
108	76.6	75.6	74.6	73.6	72.7	71.7	70.7	69.7	68.7	67.7	66.8	65.8	64.8	63.9	62.8	61.9	60.9	59.9	59.0	58.0	57.0	56.0	55.1	54.1	53.1	52.1	51.2	50.2
109	76.6	75.6	74.6	73.6	72.7	71.7	70.7	69.7	68.7	67.7	66.8	65.8	64.8	63.9	62.8	61.9	60.9	59.9	59.0	58.0	57.0	56.0	55.1	54.1	53.1	52.1	51.2	50.2
110	76.6	75.6	74.6	73.6	72.7	71.7	70.7	69.7	68.7	67.7	66.8	65.8	64.8	63.9	62.8	61.9	60.9	59.9	59.0	58.0	57.0	56.0	55.1	54.1	53.1	52.1	51.2	50.2
111	76.6	75.6	74.6	73.6	72.7	71.7	70.7	69.7	68.7	67.7	66.8	65.8	64.8	63.9	62.8	61.9	60.9	59.9	59.0	58.0	57.0	56.0	55.1	54.1	53.1	52.1	51.2	50.2
112	76.6	75.6	74.6	73.6	72.7	71.7	70.7	69.7	68.7	67.7	66.8	65.8	64.8	63.9	62.8	61.9	60.9	59.9	59.0	58.0	57.0	56.0	55.1	54.1	53.1	52.1	51.2	50.2
113	76.6	75.6	74.6	73.6	72.7	71.7	70.7	69.7	68.7	67.7	66.8	65.8	64.8	63.9	62.8	61.9	60.9	59.9	59.0	58.0	57.0	56.0	55.1	54.1	53.1	52.1	51.2	50.2
114	76.6	75.6	74.6	73.6	72.7	71.7	70.7	69.7	68.7	67.7	66.8	65.8	64.8	63.9	62.8	61.9	60.9	59.9	59.0	58.0	57.0	56.0	55.1	54.1	53.1	52.1	51.2	50.2
115	76.6	75.6	74.6	73.6	72.7	71.7	70.7	69.7	68.7	67.7	66.8	65.8	64.8	63.9	62.8	61.9	60.9	59.9	59.0	58.0	57.0	56.0	55.1	54.1	53.1	52.1	51.2	50.2

Joint Life and Survivor Expectancy (JLE) (continued)

Age	33	34	35	36	37	38	39	40	41	42	43	44	45	46	47	48	49	50	51	52	53	54	55	56	57	58	59	60
79	49.3	48.4	47.4	46.4	45.5	44.5	43.6	42.6	41.7	40.7	39.8	38.8	37.9	37.0	36.1	35.2	34.3	33.4	32.5	31.6	30.7	29.9	29.0	28.2	27.3	26.5	25.7	24.9
80	49.3	48.3	47.4	46.4	45.5	44.5	43.6	42.6	41.7	40.7	39.8	38.8	37.9	37.0	36.1	35.2	34.2	33.4	32.5	31.6	30.7	29.8	29.0	28.1	27.3	26.4	25.6	24.8
81	49.3	48.3	47.4	46.4	45.5	44.5	43.5	42.6	41.6	40.7	39.8	38.8	37.9	37.0	36.0	35.1	34.2	33.3	32.4	31.5	30.7	29.8	28.9	28.1	27.2	26.4	25.5	24.7
82	49.3	48.3	47.4	46.4	45.4	44.5	43.5	42.6	41.6	40.7	39.7	38.8	37.9	36.9	36.0	35.1	34.2	33.3	32.4	31.5	30.6	29.7	28.9	28.0	27.2	26.3	25.5	24.6
83	49.3	48.3	47.4	46.4	45.4	44.5	43.5	42.6	41.6	40.7	39.7	38.8	37.9	36.9	36.0	35.1	34.2	33.3	32.4	31.5	30.6	29.7	28.8	28.0	27.1	26.3	25.4	24.6
84	49.3	48.3	47.4	46.4	45.4	44.5	43.5	42.6	41.6	40.7	39.7	38.8	37.8	36.9	36.0	35.1	34.2	33.2	32.3	31.4	30.6	29.7	28.8	27.9	27.1	26.2	25.4	24.5
85	49.3	48.3	47.4	46.4	45.4	44.5	43.5	42.6	41.6	40.7	39.7	38.7	37.8	36.9	36.0	35.1	34.1	33.2	32.3	31.4	30.5	29.6	28.8	27.9	27.0	26.2	25.3	24.5
86	49.3	48.3	47.3	46.4	45.4	44.5	43.5	42.5	41.6	40.6	39.7	38.7	37.8	36.9	35.9	35.0	34.1	33.2	32.3	31.4	30.5	29.6	28.7	27.9	27.0	26.1	25.3	24.4
87	49.3	48.3	47.3	46.4	45.4	44.5	43.5	42.5	41.6	40.6	39.7	38.7	37.8	36.9	35.9	35.0	34.1	33.2	32.3	31.4	30.5	29.6	28.7	27.8	27.0	26.1	25.3	24.4
88	49.3	48.3	47.3	46.4	45.4	44.4	43.5	42.5	41.6	40.6	39.7	38.7	37.8	36.9	35.9	35.0	34.1	33.2	32.3	31.4	30.5	29.6	28.7	27.8	27.0	26.1	25.2	24.4
89	49.3	48.3	47.3	46.4	45.4	44.4	43.5	42.5	41.6	40.6	39.7	38.7	37.8	36.9	35.9	35.0	34.1	33.2	32.3	31.4	30.5	29.6	28.7	27.8	26.9	26.1	25.2	24.3
90	49.3	48.3	47.3	46.4	45.4	44.4	43.5	42.5	41.6	40.6	39.7	38.7	37.8	36.9	35.9	35.0	34.1	33.2	32.3	31.4	30.5	29.6	28.7	27.8	26.9	26.1	25.2	24.3
91	49.3	48.3	47.3	46.4	45.4	44.4	43.5	42.5	41.6	40.6	39.7	38.7	37.8	36.8	35.9	35.0	34.1	33.2	32.2	31.3	30.4	29.5	28.7	27.8	26.9	26.0	25.2	24.3
92	49.3	48.3	47.3	46.4	45.4	44.4	43.5	42.5	41.6	40.6	39.7	38.7	37.8	36.8	35.9	35.0	34.1	33.2	32.2	31.3	30.4	29.5	28.6	27.8	26.9	26.0	25.2	24.3
93	49.3	48.3	47.3	46.4	45.4	44.4	43.5	42.5	41.6	40.6	39.7	38.7	37.8	36.8	35.9	35.0	34.1	33.1	32.2	31.3	30.4	29.5	28.6	27.8	26.9	26.0	25.1	24.3
94	49.3	48.3	47.3	46.4	45.4	44.4	43.5	42.5	41.6	40.6	39.7	38.7	37.8	36.8	35.9	35.0	34.1	33.1	32.2	31.3	30.4	29.5	28.6	27.7	26.9	26.0	25.1	24.3
95	49.3	48.3	47.3	46.4	45.4	44.4	43.5	42.5	41.6	40.6	39.7	38.7	37.8	36.8	35.9	35.0	34.0	33.1	32.2	31.3	30.4	29.5	28.6	27.7	26.9	26.0	25.1	24.2
96	49.3	48.3	47.3	46.4	45.4	44.4	43.5	42.5	41.6	40.6	39.7	38.7	37.8	36.8	35.9	35.0	34.0	33.1	32.2	31.3	30.4	29.5	28.6	27.7	26.9	26.0	25.1	24.2
97	49.3	48.3	47.3	46.4	45.4	44.4	43.5	42.5	41.6	40.6	39.7	38.7	37.8	36.8	35.9	35.0	34.0	33.1	32.2	31.3	30.4	29.5	28.6	27.7	26.8	26.0	25.1	24.2
98	49.3	48.3	47.3	46.4	45.4	44.4	43.5	42.5	41.6	40.6	39.6	38.7	37.8	36.8	35.9	35.0	34.0	33.1	32.2	31.3	30.4	29.5	28.6	27.7	26.8	26.0	25.1	24.2
99	49.3	48.3	47.3	46.4	45.4	44.4	43.5	42.5	41.6	40.6	39.6	38.7	37.7	36.8	35.9	34.9	34.0	33.1	32.2	31.3	30.4	29.5	28.6	27.7	26.8	26.0	25.1	24.2
100	49.3	48.3	47.3	46.4	45.4	44.4	43.5	42.5	41.6	40.6	39.6	38.7	37.7	36.8	35.9	34.9	34.0	33.1	32.2	31.3	30.4	29.5	28.6	27.7	26.8	26.0	25.1	24.2
101	49.3	48.3	47.3	46.4	45.4	44.4	43.5	42.5	41.6	40.6	39.6	38.7	37.7	36.8	35.9	34.9	34.0	33.1	32.2	31.3	30.4	29.5	28.6	27.7	26.8	25.9	25.1	24.2
102	49.3	48.3	47.3	46.4	45.4	44.4	43.5	42.5	41.5	40.6	39.6	38.7	37.7	36.8	35.9	34.9	34.0	33.1	32.2	31.3	30.4	29.5	28.6	27.7	26.8	25.9	25.1	24.2
103	49.3	48.3	47.3	46.4	45.4	44.4	43.5	42.5	41.5	40.6	39.6	38.7	37.7	36.8	35.9	34.9	34.0	33.1	32.2	31.3	30.4	29.5	28.6	27.7	26.8	25.9	25.1	24.2
104	49.3	48.3	47.3	46.4	45.4	44.4	43.5	42.5	41.5	40.6	39.6	38.7	37.7	36.8	35.9	34.9	34.0	33.1	32.2	31.3	30.4	29.5	28.6	27.7	26.8	25.9	25.1	24.2
105	49.3	48.3	47.3	46.4	45.4	44.4	43.5	42.5	41.5	40.6	39.6	38.7	37.7	36.8	35.9	34.9	34.0	33.1	32.2	31.3	30.4	29.5	28.6	27.7	26.8	25.9	25.1	24.2
106	49.3	48.3	47.3	46.3	45.4	44.4	43.5	42.5	41.5	40.6	39.6	38.7	37.7	36.8	35.9	34.9	34.0	33.1	32.2	31.3	30.4	29.5	28.6	27.7	26.8	25.9	25.1	24.2
107	49.2	48.3	47.3	46.3	45.4	44.4	43.5	42.5	41.5	40.6	39.6	38.7	37.7	36.8	35.9	34.9	34.0	33.1	32.2	31.3	30.4	29.5	28.6	27.7	26.8	25.9	25.1	24.2
108	49.2	48.3	47.3	46.3	45.4	44.4	43.5	42.5	41.5	40.6	39.6	38.7	37.7	36.8	35.9	34.9	34.0	33.1	32.2	31.3	30.4	29.5	28.6	27.7	26.8	25.9	25.1	24.2
109	49.2	48.3	47.3	46.3	45.4	44.4	43.5	42.5	41.5	40.6	39.6	38.7	37.7	36.8	35.9	34.9	34.0	33.1	32.2	31.3	30.4	29.5	28.6	27.7	26.8	25.9	25.0	24.2
110	49.2	48.3	47.3	46.3	45.4	44.4	43.5	42.5	41.5	40.6	39.6	38.7	37.7	36.8	35.9	34.9	34.0	33.1	32.2	31.3	30.4	29.5	28.6	27.7	26.8	25.9	25.0	24.2
111	49.2	48.3	47.3	46.3	45.4	44.4	43.5	42.5	41.5	40.6	39.6	38.7	37.7	36.8	35.9	34.9	34.0	33.1	32.2	31.3	30.4	29.5	28.6	27.7	26.8	25.9	25.0	24.2
112	49.2	48.3	47.3	46.3	45.4	44.4	43.5	42.5	41.5	40.6	39.6	38.7	37.7	36.8	35.9	34.9	34.0	33.1	32.2	31.3	30.4	29.5	28.6	27.7	26.8	25.9	25.0	24.2
113	49.2	48.3	47.3	46.3	45.4	44.4	43.5	42.5	41.5	40.6	39.6	38.7	37.7	36.8	35.9	34.9	34.0	33.1	32.2	31.3	30.4	29.5	28.6	27.7	26.8	25.9	25.0	24.2
114	49.2	48.3	47.3	46.3	45.4	44.4	43.5	42.5	41.5	40.6	39.6	38.7	37.7	36.8	35.9	34.9	34.0	33.1	32.2	31.3	30.4	29.5	28.6	27.7	26.8	25.9	25.0	24.2
115	49.2	48.3	47.3	46.3	45.4	44.4	43.5	42.5	41.5	40.6	39.6	38.7	37.7	36.8	35.9	34.9	34.0	33.1	32.2	31.3	30.4	29.5	28.6	27.7	26.8	25.9	25.0	24.2

Joint Life and Survivor Expectancy (JLE) (continued)

Age	61	62	63	64	65	66	67	68	69	70	71	72	73	74	75	76	77	78	79	80	81	82	83	84	85	86	87	88
79	24.1	23.3	22.6	21.8	21.1	20.4	19.7	19.0	18.4	17.8	17.2	16.7	16.1	15.6	15.1	14.7	14.3	13.9	13.5	13.2	12.8	12.5	12.3	12.0	11.8	11.6	11.4	11.3
80	24.0	23.2	22.4	21.7	21.0	20.2	19.5	18.9	18.2	17.6	17.0	16.4	15.9	15.4	14.9	14.4	14.0	13.5	13.2	12.8	12.5	12.2	11.9	11.6	11.4	11.2	11.0	10.8
81	23.9	23.1	22.3	21.6	20.8	20.1	19.4	18.7	18.1	17.4	16.8	16.2	15.7	15.1	14.6	14.1	13.7	13.2	12.8	12.5	12.1	11.8	11.5	11.2	11.0	10.8	10.6	10.4
82	23.8	23.0	22.3	21.5	20.7	20.0	19.3	18.6	17.9	17.3	16.6	16.0	15.5	14.9	14.4	13.9	13.4	13.0	12.5	12.2	11.8	11.5	11.1	10.9	10.6	10.4	10.1	10.0
83	23.8	23.0	22.2	21.4	20.6	19.9	19.2	18.5	17.8	17.1	16.5	15.9	15.3	14.7	14.2	13.7	13.2	12.7	12.3	11.9	11.6	11.1	10.8	10.5	10.2	10.0	9.8	9.6
84	23.7	22.9	22.1	21.3	20.5	19.8	19.1	18.4	17.7	17.0	16.3	15.7	15.1	14.5	14.0	13.5	13.0	12.5	12.0	11.6	11.4	10.9	10.5	10.2	9.9	9.7	9.4	9.2
85	23.7	22.8	22.0	21.3	20.5	19.7	19.0	18.3	17.6	16.9	16.2	15.6	15.0	14.4	13.8	13.3	12.8	12.3	11.8	11.4	11.0	10.6	10.2	9.9	9.6	9.3	9.1	8.9
86	23.6	22.8	22.0	21.2	20.4	19.6	18.9	18.2	17.5	16.8	16.1	15.5	14.8	14.2	13.7	13.1	12.6	12.1	11.6	11.2	10.8	10.4	10.0	9.7	9.3	9.1	8.8	8.6
87	23.6	22.8	21.9	21.2	20.4	19.6	18.8	18.1	17.4	16.7	16.0	15.4	14.7	14.1	13.5	13.0	12.4	11.9	11.4	11.0	10.6	10.2	9.8	9.4	9.1	8.8	8.5	8.3
88	23.5	22.7	21.9	21.1	20.3	19.5	18.8	18.0	17.3	16.6	15.9	15.3	14.6	14.0	13.4	12.8	12.3	11.8	11.3	10.8	10.4	10.0	9.6	9.2	8.9	8.6	8.3	8.0
89	23.5	22.7	21.9	21.1	20.3	19.5	18.7	18.0	17.2	16.5	15.8	15.2	14.5	13.9	13.3	12.7	12.2	11.6	11.1	10.7	10.2	9.8	9.4	9.0	8.7	8.3	8.1	7.8
90	23.5	22.6	21.8	21.0	20.2	19.4	18.7	17.9	17.2	16.4	15.8	15.1	14.4	13.8	13.2	12.6	12.1	11.5	11.0	10.5	10.1	9.6	9.2	8.8	8.5	8.2	8.0	7.6
91	23.5	22.6	21.8	21.0	20.2	19.4	18.6	17.8	17.1	16.4	15.7	15.0	14.4	13.7	13.1	12.5	12.0	11.4	10.8	10.4	9.9	9.5	9.1	8.7	8.3	8.0	7.7	7.4
92	23.5	22.6	21.8	21.0	20.2	19.4	18.6	17.8	17.1	16.3	15.7	15.0	14.3	13.7	13.1	12.5	11.9	11.3	10.7	10.3	9.8	9.4	8.9	8.5	8.2	8.0	7.7	7.2
93	23.4	22.6	21.7	20.9	20.1	19.3	18.6	17.8	17.0	16.3	15.6	14.9	14.3	13.5	13.0	12.4	11.8	11.3	10.7	10.2	9.7	9.3	8.8	8.4	8.0	7.8	7.5	7.1
94	23.4	22.6	21.7	20.9	20.1	19.3	18.5	17.8	17.0	16.3	15.6	14.9	14.2	13.5	12.9	12.3	11.7	11.2	10.6	10.1	9.6	9.2	8.7	8.3	7.9	7.7	7.4	6.9
95	23.4	22.6	21.7	20.9	20.1	19.3	18.5	17.7	17.0	16.3	15.6	14.9	14.2	13.5	12.9	12.3	11.7	11.1	10.6	10.1	9.6	9.1	8.6	8.2	7.8	7.6	7.2	6.8
96	23.4	22.6	21.7	20.9	20.1	19.3	18.5	17.7	17.0	16.2	15.6	14.8	14.2	13.5	12.9	12.3	11.6	11.1	10.5	10.0	9.5	9.0	8.5	8.1	7.7	7.5	7.1	6.7
97	23.4	22.5	21.7	20.9	20.1	19.3	18.5	17.7	17.0	16.2	15.5	14.8	14.1	13.5	12.8	12.2	11.6	11.1	10.5	9.9	9.4	9.0	8.5	8.1	7.7	7.3	7.1	6.6
98	23.4	22.5	21.6	20.8	20.0	19.2	18.5	17.7	16.9	16.2	15.5	14.8	14.1	13.4	12.8	12.2	11.6	11.0	10.5	9.9	9.4	8.9	8.4	8.0	7.6	7.3	7.0	6.5
99	23.4	22.5	21.6	20.8	20.0	19.2	18.4	17.6	16.9	16.2	15.5	14.7	14.1	13.4	12.7	12.2	11.5	10.9	10.4	9.8	9.3	8.9	8.4	8.0	7.5	7.2	6.9	6.4
100	23.4	22.5	21.6	20.8	20.0	19.2	18.4	17.6	16.9	16.2	15.4	14.7	14.0	13.4	12.7	12.1	11.5	10.8	10.4	9.8	9.2	8.8	8.3	7.9	7.4	7.1	6.8	6.3
101	23.4	22.5	21.6	20.8	20.0	19.2	18.4	17.6	16.9	16.1	15.4	14.7	14.0	13.4	12.7	12.1	11.4	10.8	10.3	9.7	9.2	8.7	8.2	7.8	7.3	7.0	6.7	6.2
102	23.3	22.5	21.6	20.8	20.0	19.2	18.4	17.6	16.9	16.1	15.4	14.7	14.0	13.3	12.7	12.0	11.4	10.8	10.3	9.7	9.2	8.7	8.2	7.8	7.3	7.0	6.6	6.2
103	23.3	22.5	21.6	20.8	20.0	19.2	18.4	17.6	16.9	16.1	15.4	14.7	14.0	13.3	12.6	12.0	11.4	10.7	10.2	9.7	9.1	8.6	8.1	7.7	7.2	6.9	6.6	6.1
104	23.3	22.5	21.6	20.8	20.0	19.2	18.4	17.6	16.9	16.1	15.4	14.7	14.0	13.3	12.6	12.0	11.4	10.7	10.2	9.6	9.1	8.6	8.1	7.7	7.2	6.9	6.5	6.1
105	23.3	22.5	21.6	20.8	20.0	19.2	18.4	17.6	16.8	16.1	15.3	14.6	13.9	13.2	12.6	11.9	11.3	10.7	10.2	9.6	9.0	8.5	8.0	7.6	7.1	6.7	6.3	6.0
106	23.3	22.5	21.6	20.8	20.0	19.2	18.4	17.6	16.8	16.1	15.3	14.6	13.9	13.2	12.6	11.9	11.3	10.7	10.1	9.6	9.0	8.5	8.0	7.6	7.1	6.7	6.3	6.0
107	23.3	22.5	21.6	20.8	20.0	19.2	18.4	17.6	16.8	16.1	15.3	14.6	13.9	13.2	12.6	11.9	11.3	10.7	10.1	9.6	9.0	8.5	8.0	7.5	7.1	6.7	6.3	5.9
108	23.3	22.5	21.6	20.8	20.0	19.2	18.4	17.6	16.8	16.1	15.3	14.6	13.9	13.2	12.6	11.9	11.3	10.7	10.1	9.5	9.0	8.4	7.9	7.5	7.0	6.6	6.2	5.9
109	23.3	22.5	21.6	20.8	20.0	19.2	18.4	17.6	16.8	16.1	15.3	14.6	13.9	13.2	12.6	11.9	11.3	10.6	10.1	9.5	9.0	8.4	7.9	7.5	7.0	6.6	6.2	5.8
110	23.3	22.5	21.6	20.8	20.0	19.2	18.4	17.6	16.8	16.1	15.3	14.6	13.9	13.2	12.6	11.9	11.3	10.6	10.1	9.5	9.0	8.4	7.9	7.4	7.0	6.6	6.2	5.8
111	23.3	22.5	21.6	20.8	20.0	19.2	18.4	17.6	16.8	16.1	15.3	14.6	13.9	13.2	12.6	11.9	11.3	10.6	10.1	9.5	8.9	8.4	7.9	7.4	7.0	6.6	6.2	5.8
112	23.3	22.5	21.6	20.8	20.0	19.2	18.4	17.6	16.8	16.1	15.3	14.6	13.9	13.2	12.6	11.9	11.3	10.6	10.0	9.5	8.9	8.4	7.9	7.4	7.0	6.5	6.1	5.7
113	23.3	22.5	21.6	20.8	20.0	19.2	18.4	17.6	16.8	16.1	15.3	14.6	13.9	13.2	12.6	11.9	11.2	10.6	10.0	9.5	8.9	8.4	7.9	7.4	6.9	6.5	6.1	5.7
114	23.3	22.5	21.6	20.8	20.0	19.2	18.4	17.6	16.8	16.1	15.3	14.6	13.9	13.2	12.6	11.9	11.2	10.6	10.0	9.5	8.9	8.4	7.9	7.4	6.9	6.5	6.1	5.7
115	23.3	22.5	21.6	20.8	20.0	19.2	18.4	17.6	16.8	16.1	15.3	14.6	13.9	13.2	12.6	11.9	11.2	10.5	10.0	9.5	8.9	8.4	7.9	7.4	6.9	6.5	6.1	5.7

Joint Life and Survivor Expectancy (JLE) (continued)

Age	89	90	91	92	93	94	95	96	97	98	99	100	101	102	103	104	105	106	107	108	109	110	111	112	113	114	115
79	11.1	11.0	10.9	10.8	10.7	10.6	10.6	10.5	10.5	10.4	10.4	10.3	10.3	10.2	10.2	10.2	10.2	10.1	10.1	10.1	10.1	10.1	10.1	10.1	10.0	10.0	10.0
80	10.7	10.5	10.4	10.3	10.2	10.1	10.1	10.0	9.9	9.9	9.8	9.8	9.7	9.7	9.7	9.6	9.6	9.6	9.6	9.5	9.5	9.5	9.5	9.5	9.5	9.5	9.5
81	10.2	10.1	9.9	9.8	9.7	9.6	9.6	9.5	9.4	9.4	9.3	9.2	9.2	9.2	9.1	9.1	9.1	9.0	9.0	9.0	8.9	8.9	8.9	8.9	8.9	8.9	8.9
82	9.8	9.6	9.5	9.4	9.3	9.2	9.1	9.0	8.9	8.9	8.8	8.7	8.7	8.7	8.6	8.6	8.5	8.5	8.5	8.4	8.4	8.4	8.4	8.4	8.4	8.4	8.4
83	9.4	9.2	9.1	8.9	8.8	8.7	8.6	8.5	8.5	8.4	8.3	8.2	8.2	8.1	8.1	8.1	8.0	8.0	8.0	7.9	7.9	7.9	7.9	7.9	7.9	7.9	7.9
84	9.0	8.8	8.7	8.5	8.4	8.3	8.2	8.1	8.0	7.9	7.9	7.8	7.7	7.7	7.7	7.6	7.6	7.5	7.5	7.5	7.5	7.4	7.4	7.4	7.4	7.4	7.4
85	8.7	8.5	8.3	8.2	8.0	7.9	7.8	7.7	7.6	7.6	7.5	7.4	7.3	7.3	7.2	7.2	7.1	7.1	7.1	7.0	7.0	7.0	7.0	7.0	6.9	6.9	6.9
86	8.3	8.2	8.0	7.8	7.7	7.6	7.5	7.3	7.3	7.2	7.1	7.0	6.9	6.9	6.8	6.8	6.7	6.7	6.6	6.6	6.6	6.6	6.5	6.5	6.5	6.5	6.5
87	8.1	7.9	7.7	7.5	7.4	7.2	7.1	7.0	6.9	6.8	6.7	6.6	6.6	6.5	6.4	6.4	6.3	6.3	6.2	6.2	6.2	6.2	6.1	6.1	6.1	6.1	6.1
88	7.8	7.6	7.4	7.2	7.1	6.9	6.8	6.7	6.6	6.5	6.4	6.3	6.2	6.2	6.1	6.0	6.0	5.9	5.9	5.9	5.9	5.9	5.7	5.7	5.7	5.7	5.7
89	7.5	7.3	7.1	6.9	6.8	6.6	6.5	6.4	6.3	6.2	6.1	6.0	5.9	5.8	5.8	5.7	5.6	5.6	5.5	5.5	5.5	5.4	5.4	5.4	5.4	5.3	5.3
90	7.3	7.1	6.9	6.7	6.5	6.4	6.3	6.1	6.0	5.9	5.8	5.7	5.6	5.5	5.5	5.4	5.3	5.3	5.2	5.2	5.1	5.1	5.1	5.0	5.0	5.0	5.0
91	7.1	6.9	6.7	6.5	6.3	6.1	6.0	5.9	5.7	5.6	5.5	5.4	5.3	5.3	5.2	5.1	5.0	5.0	4.9	4.9	4.8	4.8	4.8	4.7	4.7	4.7	4.7
92	6.9	6.7	6.5	6.3	6.1	5.9	5.8	5.7	5.5	5.4	5.3	5.2	5.1	5.0	4.9	4.8	4.8	4.7	4.6	4.6	4.5	4.5	4.4	4.4	4.4	4.4	4.4
93	6.8	6.5	6.3	6.1	5.9	5.8	5.6	5.5	5.4	5.2	5.2	5.1	5.0	4.9	4.8	4.8	4.7	4.6	4.5	4.5	4.4	4.3	4.3	4.3	4.2	4.1	4.1
94	6.6	6.4	6.1	5.9	5.8	5.6	5.4	5.3	5.2	5.0	5.0	4.9	4.8	4.7	4.6	4.5	4.4	4.4	4.3	4.2	4.1	4.1	4.0	4.0	3.9	3.9	3.9
95	6.5	6.3	6.0	5.8	5.6	5.4	5.3	5.1	5.0	4.8	4.7	4.6	4.5	4.4	4.3	4.2	4.1	4.0	4.0	3.9	3.8	3.8	3.7	3.7	3.7	3.7	3.7
96	6.4	6.1	5.9	5.7	5.5	5.3	5.1	5.0	4.8	4.7	4.6	4.5	4.4	4.3	4.2	4.1	4.0	3.9	3.8	3.8	3.7	3.6	3.6	3.5	3.5	3.5	3.4
97	6.3	6.0	5.7	5.5	5.3	5.1	5.0	4.8	4.7	4.5	4.4	4.3	4.2	4.1	4.0	3.9	3.8	3.7	3.7	3.6	3.5	3.4	3.4	3.4	3.3	3.3	3.2
98	6.2	5.9	5.6	5.4	5.2	5.0	4.8	4.7	4.6	4.4	4.3	4.2	4.1	4.0	3.9	3.8	3.7	3.6	3.5	3.5	3.4	3.3	3.2	3.2	3.1	3.1	3.0
99	6.1	5.8	5.5	5.3	5.1	4.9	4.7	4.6	4.4	4.3	4.2	4.0	3.9	3.8	3.7	3.6	3.5	3.4	3.3	3.3	3.2	3.1	3.1	3.0	2.9	2.9	2.8
100	6.0	5.7	5.4	5.2	5.0	4.8	4.6	4.4	4.3	4.1	4.0	3.8	3.7	3.6	3.5	3.3	3.3	3.2	3.1	3.0	2.9	2.8	2.8	2.7	2.7	2.7	2.7
101	5.9	5.6	5.3	5.1	4.9	4.7	4.5	4.3	4.1	4.0	3.8	3.7	3.6	3.4	3.3	3.2	3.1	3.0	2.9	2.8	2.7	2.7	2.6	2.6	2.5	2.5	2.5
102	5.8	5.5	5.2	5.0	4.8	4.6	4.4	4.2	4.0	3.9	3.7	3.6	3.4	3.3	3.2	3.1	3.0	2.9	2.8	2.7	2.6	2.5	2.4	2.4	2.3	2.3	2.3
103	5.8	5.5	5.1	4.9	4.7	4.5	4.3	4.1	3.9	3.8	3.6	3.5	3.3	3.2	3.0	2.9	2.8	2.7	2.6	2.5	2.4	2.3	2.3	2.2	2.2	2.2	2.1
104	5.7	5.4	5.0	4.8	4.6	4.4	4.2	4.0	3.8	3.7	3.5	3.4	3.2	3.1	2.9	2.8	2.7	2.5	2.4	2.3	2.3	2.2	2.1	2.1	2.0	2.0	1.9
105	5.6	5.3	5.0	4.8	4.5	4.3	4.1	3.9	3.7	3.6	3.4	3.3	3.1	2.9	2.8	2.7	2.5	2.4	2.3	2.3	2.1	2.0	2.0	1.9	1.8	1.8	1.8
106	5.6	5.3	4.9	4.7	4.5	4.2	4.0	3.8	3.6	3.5	3.3	3.1	3.0	2.8	2.7	2.5	2.4	2.3	2.2	2.1	2.0	1.9	1.8	1.7	1.7	1.6	1.6
107	5.5	5.2	4.9	4.6	4.4	4.2	4.0	3.8	3.6	3.4	3.2	3.1	2.9	2.7	2.6	2.4	2.3	2.2	2.1	1.9	1.8	1.7	1.7	1.6	1.5	1.5	1.4
108	5.5	5.2	4.8	4.6	4.3	4.1	3.9	3.7	3.5	3.3	3.1	3.0	2.8	2.7	2.5	2.3	2.2	2.1	1.9	1.8	1.7	1.6	1.5	1.5	1.3	1.3	1.3
109	5.5	5.1	4.8	4.5	4.3	4.1	3.8	3.6	3.4	3.2	3.0	2.9	2.7	2.6	2.4	2.3	2.2	2.0	1.8	1.7	1.6	1.5	1.5	1.3	1.3	1.3	1.3
110	5.4	5.1	4.8	4.5	4.3	4.0	3.8	3.6	3.4	3.2	3.0	2.8	2.7	2.5	2.3	2.2	2.0	1.9	1.7	1.6	1.5	1.4	1.3	1.3	1.2	1.1	1.0
111	5.4	5.1	4.8	4.5	4.3	4.1	3.8	3.6	3.3	3.2	3.0	2.8	2.6	2.4	2.3	2.2	2.0	1.8	1.7	1.6	1.5	1.4	1.3	1.2	1.1	1.1	1.0
112	5.4	5.0	4.7	4.5	4.2	4.0	3.7	3.5	3.3	3.1	2.9	2.7	2.5	2.4	2.3	2.1	1.9	1.7	1.6	1.5	1.3	1.3	1.2	1.0	0.9	0.8	0.8
113	5.4	5.0	4.7	4.4	4.2	3.9	3.7	3.5	3.3	3.1	2.9	2.7	2.5	2.3	2.2	2.1	1.9	1.7	1.5	1.4	1.3	1.2	1.1	1.0	0.9	0.8	0.7
114	5.3	5.0	4.7	4.4	4.1	3.9	3.7	3.5	3.3	3.1	2.9	2.7	2.5	2.4	2.2	2.0	1.8	1.6	1.5	1.3	1.2	1.1	1.1	0.9	0.8	0.7	0.6
115	5.3	5.0	4.7	4.4	4.1	3.9	3.7	3.4	3.2	3.0	2.8	2.7	2.5	2.3	2.1	1.9	1.8	1.6	1.4	1.3	1.1	1.0	1.0	0.8	0.7	0.6	0.5

Form **5305-R**
(January 1998)
Department of the Treasury
Internal Revenue Service

Roth Individual Retirement Trust Account

(Under Section 408A of the Internal Revenue Code)

**DO NOT File
with the Internal
Revenue Service**

Name of grantor	Date of birth of grantor	Social security number

Address of grantor		Check if Roth Conversion IRA . . . . ▶ ☐
		Check if Amendment . . ▶ ☐

Name of trustee	Address or principal place of business of trustee

The grantor whose name appears above is establishing a Roth individual retirement account (Roth IRA) under section 408A to provide for his or her retirement and for the support of his or her beneficiaries after death.

The trustee named above has given the grantor the disclosure statement required under Regulations section 1.408-6.

The grantor has assigned the trust $ ....

The grantor and the trustee make the following agreement:

Article I

1. If this Roth IRA is not designated as a Roth Conversion IRA, then, except in the case of a rollover contribution described in section 408A(e), the trustee will accept only cash contributions and only up to a maximum amount of $2,000 for any tax year of the grantor.

2. If this Roth IRA is designated as a Roth Conversion IRA, no contributions other than IRA Conversion Contributions made during the same tax year will be accepted.

Article II

The $2,000 limit described in Article I is gradually reduced to $0 between certain levels of adjusted gross income (AGI). For a single grantor, the $2,000 annual contribution is phased out between AGI of $95,000 and $110,000; for a married grantor who files jointly, between AGI of $150,000 and $160,000; and for a married grantor who files separately, between $0 and $10,000. In the case of a conversion, the trustee will not accept IRA Conversion Contributions in a tax year if the grantor's AGI for that tax year exceeds $100,000 or if the grantor is married and files a separate return. Adjusted gross income is defined in section 408A(c)(3) and does not include IRA Conversion Contributions.

Article III

The grantor's interest in the balance in the trust account is nonforfeitable.

Article IV

1. No part of the trust funds may be invested in life insurance contracts, nor may the assets of the trust account be commingled with other property except in a common trust fund or common investment fund (within the meaning of section 408(a)(5)).

2. No part of the trust funds may be invested in collectibles (within the meaning of section 408(m)) except as otherwise permitted by section 408(m)(3), which provides an exception for certain gold, silver, and platinum coins, coins issued under the laws of any state, and certain bullion.

Article V

1. If the grantor dies before his or her entire interest is distributed to him or her and the grantor's surviving spouse is not the sole beneficiary, the entire remaining interest will, at the election of the grantor or, if the grantor has not so elected, at the election of the beneficiary or beneficiaries, either:

(a) Be distributed by December 31 of the year containing the fifth anniversary of the grantor's death, or

(b) Be distributed over the life expectancy of the designated beneficiary starting no later than December 31 of the year following the year of the grantor's death.

If distributions do not begin by the date described in **(b)**, distribution method **(a)** will apply.

2. In the case of distribution method **1.(b)** above, to determine the minimum annual payment for each year, divide the grantor's entire interest in the trust as of the close of business on December 31 of the preceding year by the life expectancy of the designated beneficiary using the attained age of the designated beneficiary as of the beneficiary's birthday in the year distributions are required to commence and subtract 1 for each subsequent year.

3. If the grantor's spouse is the sole beneficiary on the grantor's date of death, such spouse will then be treated as the grantor.

Article VI

1. The grantor agrees to provide the trustee with information necessary for the trustee to prepare any reports required under sections 408(i) and 408A(d)(3)(E), and Regulations section 1.408-5 and 1.408-6, and under guidance published by the Internal Revenue Service.

2. The trustee agrees to submit reports to the Internal Revenue Service and the grantor as prescribed by the Internal Revenue Service.

Cat. No. 25093N

Form **5305-R** (1-98)

Article VII

Notwithstanding any other articles which may be added or incorporated, the provisions of Articles I through IV and this sentence will be controlling. Any additional articles that are not consistent with section 408A, the related regulations, and other published guidance will be invalid.

Article VIII

This agreement will be amended from time to time to comply with the provisions of the Code, related regulations, and other published guidance. Other amendments may be made with the consent of the persons whose signatures appear below.

Note: *The following space (Article IX) may be used for any other provisions you want to add. If you do not want to add any other provisions, draw a line through this space. If you do add provisions, they must comply with applicable requirements of state law and the Internal Revenue Code.*

Article IX

Grantor's signature .... Date ....

Trustee's signature .... Date ....

Witness' signature .... Date ....
(Use only if signature of the grantor or the trustee is required to be witnessed.)

General Instructions

(Section references are to the Internal Revenue Code unless otherwise noted.)

Purpose of Form

Form 5305-R is a model trust account agreement that meets the requirements of section 408A and has been automatically approved by the IRS. A Roth individual retirement account (Roth IRA) is established after the form is fully executed by both the individual (grantor) and the trustee. This account must be created in the United States for the exclusive benefit of the grantor or his or her beneficiaries.

Do not file Form 5305-R with the IRS. Instead, keep it for your records.

Unlike contributions to traditional individual retirement arrangements, contributions to a Roth IRA are not deductible from the grantor's gross income; and distributions after 5 years that are made when the grantor is 59½ years of age or older or on account of death, disability, or the purchase of a home by a first-time homebuyer (limited to $10,000), are not includible in gross income. For more information on Roth IRAs, including the required disclosure the grantor can get from the trustee, get **Pub. 590,** Individual Retirement Arrangements (IRAs).

This Roth IRA can be used by a grantor to hold: (1) IRA Conversion Contributions, amounts rolled over or transferred from another Roth IRA, and annual cash contributions of up to $2,000 from the grantor; or (2) if designated as a Roth Conversion IRA (by checking the box on page 1), only IRA Conversion Contributions for the same tax year.

To simplify the identification of funds distributed from Roth IRAs, grantors are encouraged to maintain IRA Conversion Contributions for each tax year in a separate Roth IRA.

Definitions

Roth Conversion IRA. A Roth Conversion IRA is a Roth IRA that accepts only IRA Conversion Contributions made during the same tax year.

IRA Conversion Contributions. IRA Conversion Contributions are amounts rolled over, transferred, or considered transferred from a nonRoth IRA to a Roth IRA. A nonRoth IRA is an individual retirement account or annuity described in section 408(a) or 408(b), other than a Roth IRA.

Trustee. The trustee must be a bank or savings and loan asociation, as defined in section 408(n), or any person who has the approval of the IRS to act as trustee.

Grantor. The grantor is the person who establishes the trust account.

Specific Instructions

Article I. The grantor may be subject to a 6 percent tax on excess contributions if **(1)** contributions to other individual retirement arrangements of the grantor have been made for the same tax year, **(2)** the grantor's adjusted gross income exceeds the applicable limits in Article II for the tax year, or **(3)** the grantor's and spouse's compensation does not exceed the amount contributed for them for the tax year. The grantor should see the disclosure statement or Pub. 590 for more information.

Article IX. Article IX and any that follow it may incorporate additional provisions that are agreed to by the grantor and trustee to complete the agreement. They may include, for example, definitions, investment powers, voting rights, exculpatory provisions, amendment and termination, removal of the trustee, trustee's fees, state law requirements, beginning date of distributions, accepting only cash, treatment of excess contributions, prohibited transactions with the grantor, etc. Use additional pages if necessary and attach them to this form.

Note: *Form 5305-R may be reproduced and reduced in size for adaption to passbook purposes.*

Form **5305-RA**
(January 1998)
Department of the Treasury
Internal Revenue Service

Roth Individual Retirement Custodial Account

(Under section 408A of the Internal Revenue Code)

**DO NOT File
With the
Internal
Revenue Service**

Name of depositor	Date of birth of depositor	Social security number

Address of depositor	Check if Roth Conversion IRA ▶ ☐
	Check if Amendment . . . ▶ ☐

Name of custodian	Address or principal place of business of custodian

The depositor whose name appears above is establishing a Roth individual retirement account (Roth IRA) under section 408A to provide for his or her retirement and for the support of his or her beneficiaries after death.

The custodian named above has given the depositor the disclosure statement required under Regulations section 1.408-6.

The depositor assigned the custodial account $ ....

The depositor and the custodian make the following agreement:

Article I

1. If this Roth IRA is not designated as a Roth Conversion IRA, then, except in the case of a rollover contribution described in section 408A(e), the custodian will accept only cash contributions and only up to a maximum amount of $2,000 for any tax year of the depositor.

2. If this Roth IRA is designated as a Roth Conversion IRA, no contributions other than IRA Conversion Contributions made during the same tax year will be accepted.

Article II

The $2,000 limit described in Article I is gradually reduced to $0 between certain levels of adjusted gross income (AGI). For a single depositor, the $2,000 annual contribution is phased out between AGI of $95,000 and $110,000; for a married depositor who files jointly, between AGI of $150,000 and $160,000; and for a married depositor who files separately, between $0 and $10,000. In the case of a conversion, the custodian will not accept IRA Conversion Contributions in a tax year if the depositor's AGI for that tax year exceeds $100,000 or if the depositor is married and files a separate return. Adjusted gross income is defined in section 408A(c)(3) and does not include IRA Conversion Contributions.

Article III

The depositor's interest in the balance in the custodial account is nonforfeitable.

Article IV

1. No part of the custodial funds may be invested in life insurance contracts, nor may the assets of the custodial account be commingled with other property except in a common trust fund or common investment fund (within the meaning of section 408(a)(5)).

2. No part of the custodial funds may be invested in collectibles (within the meaning of section 408(m)) except as otherwise permitted by section 408(m)(3), which provides an exception for certain gold, silver, and platinum coins, coins issued under the laws of any state, and certain bullion.

Article V

1. If the depositor dies before his or her entire interest is distributed to him or her and the depositor's surviving spouse is not the sole beneficiary, the entire remaining interest will, at the election of the depositor or, if the depositor has not so elected, at the election of the beneficiary or beneficiaries, either:

(a) Be distributed by December 31 of the year containing the fifth anniversary of the depositor's death, or

(b) Be distributed over the life expectancy of the designated beneficiary starting no later than December 31 of the year following the year of the depositor's death.

If distributions do not begin by the date described in **(b)**, distribution method **(a)** will apply.

2. In the case of distribution method **1(b)** above, to determine the minimum annual payment for each year, divide the depositor's entire interest in the custodial account as of the close of business on December 31 of the preceding year by the life expectancy of the designated beneficiary using the attained age of the designated beneficiary as of the beneficiary's birthday in the year distributions are required to commence and subtract 1 for each subsequent year.

3. If the depositor's spouse is the sole beneficiary on the depositor's date of death, such spouse will then be treated as the depositor.

Article VI

1. The depositor agrees to provide the custodian with information necessary for the custodian to prepare any reports required under sections 408(i) and 408A(d)(3)(E), Regulations sections 1.408-5 and 1.408-6, and under guidance published by the Internal Revenue Service.

2. The custodian agrees to submit reports to the Internal Revenue Service and the depositor prescribed by the Internal Revenue Service.

Article VII

Notwithstanding any other articles which may be added or incorporated, the provisions of Articles I through IV and this sentence will be controlling. Any additional articles that are not consistent with section 408A, the related regulations, and other published guidance will be invalid.

Article VIII

This agreement will be amended from time to time to comply with the provisions of the Code, related regulations, and other published guidance. Other amendments may be made with the consent of the persons whose signatures appear below.

Note: *The following space (Article IX) may be used for any other provisions you want to add. If you do not want to add any other provisions, draw a line through this space. If you do add provisions, they must comply with applicable requirements of state law and the Internal Revenue Code.*

Article IX

Depositor's signature .... Date ....

Custodian's signature .... Date ....

Witness' signature .... Date ....

(Use only if signature of the depositor or the custodian is required to be witnessed.)

General Instructions

Section references are to the Internal Revenue Code unless otherwise noted.

Purpose of Form

Form 5305-RA is a model custodial account agreement that meets the requirements of section 408A and has been automatically approved by the IRS. A Roth individual retirement account (Roth IRA) is established after the form is fully executed by both the individual (depositor) and the custodian. This account must be created in the United States for the exclusive benefit of the depositor or his or her beneficiaries.

Do not file Form 5305-RA with the IRS. Instead, keep it for your records.

Unlike contributions to traditional individual retirement arrangements, contributions to a Roth IRA are not deductible from the depositor's gross income; and distributions after 5 years that are made when the depositor is 59½ years of age or older or on account of death, disability, or the purchase of a home by a first-time homebuyer (limited to $10,000), are not includible in gross income. For more information on Roth IRAs, including the required disclosure the depositor can get from the custodian, see **Pub. 590,** Individual Retirement Arrangements (IRAs).

This Roth IRA can be used by a despositor to hold: **(1)** IRA Conversion Contributions, amounts rolled over or transferred from another Roth IRA, and annual cash contributions of up to $2,000 from the depositor; or **(2)** if designated as a Roth Conversion IRA (by checking the box on page 1), only IRA Conversion Contributions for the same tax year.

To simplify the identification of funds distributed from Roth IRAs, depositors are encouraged to maintain IRA Conversion Contributions for each tax year in a separate Roth IRA.

Definitions

Roth Conversion IRA. A Roth Conversion IRA is a Roth IRA that accepts only IRA Conversion Contributions made during the same tax year.

IRA Conversion Contributions. IRA Conversion Contributions are amounts rolled over, transferred, or considered transferred from a nonRoth IRA to a Roth IRA. A nonRoth IRA is an individual retirement account or annuity described in section 408(a) or 408(b), other than a Roth IRA.

Custodian. The custodian must be a bank or savings and loan association, as defined in section 408(n), or any person who has the approval of the IRS to act as custodian.

Depositor. The depositor is the person who establishes the custodial account.

Specific Instructions

Article I. The depositor may be subject to a 6 percent tax on excess contributions if **(1)** contributions to other individual retirement arrangements of the depositor have been made for the same tax year, **(2)** the depositor's adjusted gross income exceeds the applicable limits in Article II for the tax year, or **(3)** the depositor's and spouse's compensation does not exceed the amount contributed for them for the tax year. The depositor should see the disclosure statement or Pub. 590 for more information.

Article IX.—Article IX and any that follow it may incorporate additional provisions that are agreed to by the depositor and custodian to complete the agreement. They may include, for example, definitions, investment powers, voting rights, exculpatory provisions, amendment and termination, removal of the custodian, custodian's fees, state law requirements, beginning date of distributions, accepting only cash, treatment of excess contributions, prohibited transactions with the depositor, etc. Use additional pages if necessary and attach them to this form.

Note: *Form 5305-RA may be reproduced and reduced in size for adaption to passbook purposes.*

Form **5305-RB**	**Roth Individual Retirement Annuity Endorsement**	**DO NOT File**
(May 1998) Department of the Treasury Internal Revenue Service	(Under section 408A of the Internal Revenue Code)	**with the Internal Revenue Service**

Name of issuer	Check if this endorsement supersedes a prior Roth IRA endorsement . . . . ▶ ☐
	Check if Roth Conversion IRA . . . . ▶ ☐

This endorsement is made a part of the annuity contract to which it is attached, and the following provisions apply in lieu of any provisions in the contract to the contrary.

The annuitant is establishing a Roth individual retirement annuity (Roth IRA) under section 408A to provide for his or her retirement and for the support of his or her beneficiaries after death.

Article I

1. If this Roth IRA is not designated as a Roth Conversion IRA, then, except in the case of a rollover contribution described in section 408A(e), the issuer will accept only cash contributions and only up to a maximum amount of $2,000 for any tax year of the annuitant.

2. If this Roth IRA is designated as a Roth Conversion IRA, no contributions other than IRA Conversion Contributions made during the same tax year will be accepted.

Article II

The $2,000 limit described in Article I is gradually reduced to $0 between certain levels of adjusted gross income (AGI). For a single annuitant, the $2,000 annual contribution is phased out between AGI of $95,000 and $110,000; for a married annuitant who files jointly, between AGI of $150,000 and $160,000; and for a married annuitant who files separately, between $0 and $10,000. In the case of a conversion, the issuer will not accept IRA Conversion Contributions in a tax year if the annuitant's AGI for that tax year exceeds $100,000 or if the annuitant is married and files a separate return. Adjusted gross income is defined in section 408A(c)(3) and does not include IRA Conversion Contributions.

Article III

The annuitant's interest in the contract is nonforfeitable and nontransferable.

Article IV

1. The contract does not require fixed contributions.

2. Any dividends (refund of contributions other than those attributable to excess contributions) arising under the contract will be applied before the close of the calendar year following the year of the dividend as contributions toward the contract.

Article V

1. If the annuitant dies before his or her entire interest in the contract is distributed to him or her and the annuitant's surviving spouse is not the sole beneficiary, the entire remaining interest will, at the election of the annuitant or, if the annuitant has not so elected, at the election of the beneficiary, either:

(a) Be distributed by December 31 of the calendar year containing the fifth anniversary of the annuitant's death, or

(b) Be distributed over the life, or a period not longer than the life expectancy, of the designated beneficiary starting no later than December 31 of the calendar year following the calendar year of the annuitant's death. Life expectancy is computed using the expected return multiples in Table V of section 1.72-9 of the Income Tax Regulations.

If distributions do not begin by the date described in **(b)**, distribution method **(a)** will apply.

2. If the annuitant's spouse is the sole beneficiary on the annuitant's date of death, such spouse will then be treated as the annuitant.

Article VI

1. The annuitant agrees to provide the issuer with information necessary for the issuer to prepare any reports required under sections 408(i) and 408A(d)(3)(E), and Regulations section 1.408-5 and 1.408-6, and under guidance published by the Internal Revenue Service.

2. The issuer agrees to submit reports to the Internal Revenue Service and the annuitant as prescribed by the Internal Revenue Service.

Article VII

Notwithstanding any other articles which may be added or incorporated, the provisions of Articles I through IV and this sentence will be controlling. Any additional articles that are not consistent with section 408A, the related regulations, and other published guidance will be invalid.

Article VIII

This endorsement will be amended from time to time to comply with the provisions of the Code, related regulations, and other published guidance. Other amendments may be made with the consent of the persons whose signatures appear on the contract.

Cat. No. 25871H   Form **5305-RB** (5-98)

Note: *The following space (Article IX) may be used for any other provisions the annuitant and the issuer want to add. If no other provisions will be added, draw a line through this space. If provisions are added, they must comply with applicable requirements of state law and the Internal Revenue Code.*

Article IX

General Instructions

(Section references are to the Internal Revenue Code unless otherwise noted.)

Purpose of Form

Form 5305-RB is a model annuity endorsement that meets the requirements of section 408A and has been automatically approved by the IRS. A Roth individual retirement annuity (Roth IRA) is established after the contract, which includes this endorsement, is fully executed by both the individual (annuitant) and the issuer. The contract must be for the exclusive benefit of the annuitant or his or her beneficiaries.

Do not file Form 5305-RB with the IRS. Instead, keep it for records purposes.

Unlike contributions to traditional individual retirement arrangements, contributions to a Roth IRA are not deductible from the annuitant's gross income; and distributions after 5 years that are made when the annuitant is 59½ years of age or older or on account of death, disability, or the purchase of a home by a first-time homebuyer (limited to $10,000), are not includible in gross income. For more information on Roth IRAs, including the required disclosure the annuitant can get from the issuer, get **Pub. 590,** Individual Retirement Arrangements (IRAs).

This Roth IRA can be used by an annuitant to hold: (1) IRA Conversion Contributions, amounts rolled over or transferred from another Roth IRA, and annual cash contributions of up to $2,000 from the annuitant; or (2) if designated as a Roth Conversion IRA (by checking the box on page 1), only IRA Conversion Contributions for the same tax year.

To simplify the identification of funds distributed from Roth IRAs, annuitants are encouraged to maintain IRA Conversion Contributions for each tax year in a separate Roth IRA.

Definitions

Roth Conversion IRA. A Roth Conversion IRA is a Roth IRA that accepts only IRA Conversion Contributions made during the same tax year.

IRA Conversion Contributions. IRA Conversion Contributions are amounts rolled over, transferred, or considered transferred from a nonRoth IRA to a Roth IRA. A nonRoth IRA is an individual retirement account or annuity described in section 408(a) or 408(b), other than a Roth IRA.

Issuer. The issuer is the insurance company providing the annuity contract. The insurance company may use other terms besides "issuer" to refer to itself, such as, "company," "insurer," or "us."

Annuitant. The annuitant is the person who establishes the annuity contract. The insurance company may use other terms besides "annuitant" to refer to the person who establishes the annuity contract, such as, "owner," "applicant," "insured," or "you."

Specific Instructions

Article I. The annuitant may be subject to a 6-percent tax on excess contributions if **(1)** contributions to other individual retirement arrangements of the annuitant have been made for the same tax year, **(2)** the annuitant's adjusted gross income exceeds the applicable limits in Article II for the tax year, or **(3)** the annuitant's and spouse's compensation does not exceed the amount contributed for them for the tax year. The annuitant should see the disclosure statement or Pub. 590 for more information.

Article IX. Article IX and any that follow it may incorporate additional provisions that are agreed to by the annuitant and issuer to complete the contract. They may include, for example, definitions, investment powers, voting rights, exculpatory provisions, amendment and termination, removal of the issuer, issuer's fees, state law requirements, beginning date of distributions, accepting only cash, treatment of excess contributions, prohibited transactions with the annuitant, etc. Use additional pages if necessary and attach them to this form.

Note: *Form 5305-RB may be reproduced and reduced in size for adaption to passbook purposes.*

Form 5329

Additional Taxes Attributable to Qualified Retirement Plans (Including IRAs), Annuities, Modified Endowment Contracts, and MSAs

Department of the Treasury
Internal Revenue Service

(Under Sections 72, 4973, and 4974 of the Internal Revenue Code)
▶ Attach to Form 1040. See separate instructions.

OMB No. 1545-0203

1997

Attachment
Sequence No. **29**

Name of individual subject to additional tax. (If married filing jointly, see page 2 of the instructions.)

Your social security number

Fill in Your Address Only If You Are Filing This Form by Itself and Not With Your Tax Return

Home address (number and street), or P.O. box if mail is not delivered to your home

Apt. no.

City, town or post office, state, and ZIP code

If this is an amended return, check here ▶

If you are subject to the 10% tax on early distributions **only,** see **Who Must File** in the instructions before continuing. You may be able to report this tax directly on Form 1040 without filing Form 5329.

Part I   Tax on Early Distributions

Complete this part if a taxable distribution was made from your qualified retirement plan (including an IRA), annuity contract, or modified endowment contract before you reached age 59½ (or was incorrectly indicated as such on your Form 1099-R—see instructions). **Note:** *You must include the amount of the distribution on line 15b or 16b of Form 1040.*

1	Early distributions included in gross income (see page 2 of the instructions)	**1**	
2	Distributions excepted from additional tax (see page 2 of the instructions). Enter appropriate exception number from instructions ▶ _____	**2**	
3	Amount subject to additional tax. Subtract line 2 from line 1	**3**	
4	**Tax due.** Multiply line 3 by 10% (.10). Enter here and on Form 1040, line 50	**4**	

Caution: *If any amount on line 0 was a distribution from a SIMPLE retirement plan, you must multiply that distribution by 25% (.25) instead of 10%. See instructions for more information.*

Part II   Tax on Excess Contributions to Individual Retirement Arrangements

Complete this part if, either in this year or in earlier years, you contributed more to your IRA than is or was allowable and you have an excess contribution subject to tax.

5	Excess contributions for 1997 (see page 3 of the instructions). Do not include this amount on Form 1040, line 23		**5**	
6	Earlier year excess contributions not previously eliminated (see page 3 of the instructions)	**6**		
7	Contribution credit. If your actual contribution for 1997 is less than your maximum allowable contribution, see page 3 of the instructions; otherwise, enter -0-	**7**		
8	1997 distributions from your IRA account that are includible in taxable income	**8**		
9	1996 tax year excess contributions (if any) withdrawn after the due date (including extensions) of your 1996 income tax return, and 1995 and earlier tax year excess contributions withdrawn in 1997 . . .	**9**		
10	Add lines 7, 8, and 9	**10**		
11	Adjusted earlier year excess contributions. Subtract line 10 from line 6. Enter the result, but not less than zero		**11**	
12	Total excess contributions. Add lines 5 and 11		**12**	
13	**Tax due.** Enter the **smaller** of 6% (.06) of line 12 or 6% (.06) of the value of your IRA on the last day of 1997. Also enter this amount on Form 1040, line 50		**13**	

For Paperwork Reduction Act Notice, see page 4 of separate instructions.

Cat. No. 13329Q

Form **5329** (1997)

Part III   Tax on Excess Contributions to Medical Savings Accounts

14   Excess contributions for 1997 (see page 4 of the instructions). Do not include this amount on Form 1040, line 24 . . . . **14**

15   **Tax due.** Enter the **smaller** of 6% (.06) of line 14 or 6% (.06) of the value of your MSA on the last day of 1997. Also enter this amount on Form 1040, line 50 . . . . **15**

Part IV   Tax on Excess Accumulation in Qualified Retirement Plans (Including IRAs)

16   Minimum required distribution (see page 4 of the instructions) **16**

17   Amount actually distributed to you **17**

18   Subtract line 17 from line 16. If line 17 is more than line 16, enter -0- **18**

19   **Tax due.** Multiply line 18 by 50% (.50). Enter here and on Form 1040, line 50 . . . . . . **19**

Signature. *Complete **ONLY** if you are filing this form by itself and not with your tax return.*

Please Sign Here	Under penalties of perjury, I declare that I have examined this form, including accompanying schedules and statements, and to the best of my knowledge and belief, it is true, correct, and complete. Declaration of preparer (other than taxpayer) is based on all information of which preparer has any knowledge.		
	▶ _____ Your signature		▶ _____ Date
Paid Preparer's Use Only	Preparer's signature ▶ _____	Date	Check if self-employed ▶ ☐	Preparer's social security no. ⋮ ⋮
	Firm's name (or yours, if self-employed) and address ▶ _____		EIN ▶ ZIP code ▶

SEC. 408A. Roth IRA per Technical Corrections Act of 1998

408A(a)   GENERAL RULE- Except as provided in this section, a Roth IRA shall be treated for purpose of this title in the same manner as an individual retirement plan.

408A(b)   ROTH IRA- For purposes of this title, the term "Roth IRA" means an individual retirement plan (as defined in section 7701(a)(37)) which is designated (in such manner as the Secretary may prescribe) at the time of establishment of the plan as a Roth IRA. Such designation shall be made in such manner as the Secretary may prescribe.

408A(c)   TREATMENT OF CONTRIBUTIONS

408A(c)(1)   **NO DEDUCTION ALLOWED-** No deduction shall be allowed under section 219 for a contribution to a Roth IRA.

408A(c)(2)   **CONTRIBUTION LIMIT-** The aggregate amount of contributions for any taxable year to all Roth IRAs maintained for the benefit of an individual shall not exceed the excess (if any) of—

408A(c)(2)(A)   the maximum amount allowable as a deduction under section 219 with respect to such individual for such taxable year (computed without regard to subsection (d)(1) or (g) of such section), over

408A(c)(2)(B)   the aggregate amount of contributions for such taxable year to all other individual retirement plans (other than Roth IRAs) maintained for the benefit of the individual.

408A(c)(3)   LIMITS BASED ON MODIFIED ADJUSTED GROSS INCOME-

408A(c)(3)(A)   DOLLAR LIMIT- The amount determined under paragraph (2) for any taxable year shall not exceed an amount equal to the amount determined under paragraph (2)(A) for such taxable year, reduced (but not below zero) by the amount which bears the same ratio to such amount as—

408A(c)(3)(A)(i)   the excess of—

408A(c)(3)(A)(i)(I)   the taxpayer's adjusted gross income for such taxable year, over

408A(c)(3)(A)(i)(II)   the applicable dollar amount, bears to

408A(c)(3)(A)(ii) $15,000 ($10,000 in the case of a joint return or a married individual filing a separate return).

     The rules of subparagraphs (B) and (C) of section 219(g)(2) shall apply to any reduction under this sub-paragraph.

408A(c)(3)(B)   **ROLLOVER FROM IRA-** A taxpayer shall not be allowed to make a qualified rollover contribution to a Roth IRA from an individual retirement plan other than a Roth IRA during any taxable year if, for the taxable year of the distribution to which such contribution relates—

408A(c)(3)(B)(i)   the taxpayer's adjusted gross income exceeds $100,000, or

408A (c)(3)(B)(ii)   the taxpayer is a married individual filing a separate return.

408A(c)(3)(C)   **DEFINITIONS-** For purposes of this paragraph—

408A(c)(3)(C)(i)   adjusted gross income shall be determined in the same manner as under section 219(g)(3), except that

408A(c)(3)(C)(i)(I)   any amount included in gross income under subsection (d)(3) shall not be taken into account, and

Topic is mentioned in this column. See index for reference page in book

deduction

contribution limit

MAGI

partial contribution

conversion limit

married filing separately

408A(c)(3)(C)(i)(II)   any amount included in gross income by reason of a required distribution under a provision described in paragraph (5) shall not be taken into account for purposes of subparagraph (B)(i).

> **EFFECTIVE DATE** — The amendment made by this section shall apply to taxable years beginning after December 31, 2004.

MRD after 70 1/2 2004-r rule

408A(c)(3)(C)(ii)   the applicable dollar amount is—

408A(c)(3)(C)(ii)(I)   in the case of a taxpayer filing a joint return, $150,000,

contribution maximum MAGI

408A(c)(3)(C)(ii)(II)   in the case of any other taxpayer (other than married individual filing a separate return), $95,0000 and

408A(c)(3)(C)(ii)(III) in the case of a married individual filing a separate return, zero.

married filing separately living apart

408A(c)(3)(D) MARITAL STATUS- Section 219(g)(4) shall apply for purposes of this paragraph.

408A(c)(4)   **CONTRIBUTIONS PERMITTED AFTER AGE** 70 1/2 - Contributions to a Roth IRA may be made even after the individual for whom the account is maintained has attained age 70 1/2.

contribution after age 70 1/2

408A(c)(5)   **MANDATORY DISTRIBUTION RULES NOT TO APPLY BEFORE DEATH-**

Notwithstanding subsections (a)(6) and (b)(3) of section 408 (relating to required distributions), the following provisions shall not apply to any Roth IRA:

MRD after death

408A(c)(5)(A) Section 401(a)(9)(A).

408A(c)(5)(B) The incidental death benefit requirements of section 401(a).

408A(c)(6)   **ROLLOVER CONTRIBUTIONS-**

408A(c)(6)(A)   **IN GENERAL-** No rollover contribution may be made to a Roth IRA unless it is a qualified rollover contribution.

408A(c)(6)(B)   **COORDINATION WITH LIMIT-** A qualified rollover contribution shall not be taken into account for purposes of paragraph (2).

408A(c)(7)   **TIME WHEN CONTRIBUTIONS MADE-** For purposes of this section, the rule of section 219(f)(3) shall apply.

deadlines

408A(d)   **DISTRIBUTION RULES-** For purposes of this title—

408A(d)(1)   **EXCLUSION.** —Any qualified distribution from a Roth IRA shall not be includable in gross income.

408A(d)(2)   **QUALIFIED DISTRIBUTION-** For purposes of this subsection—

qualified distributions

408A(d)(2)(A)   **IN GENERAL-** The term "qualified distribution" means any payment or distribution—

408A(d)(2)(A)(i)   made on or after the date on which the individual attains 1/2,

408A(d)(2)(A)(ii)   made to a beneficiary (or to the estate of the individual) on or after the death of the individual

408A(d)(2)(A)(iii) attributable to the individual's being disabled (within meaning of section 72(m)(7)), or

408A(d)(2)(A)(iv) which is a qualified special purpose distribution

408A(d)(2)(B) DISTRIBUTIONS WITHIN NONEXCLUSION PERIOD. —

five-year clock

A payment or distribution from a Roth IRA shall not be treated as a qualified distribution under subparagraph (A) if such payment or distribution is made within the 5-taxable year period beginning with the 1st taxable year for which the individual made a contribution to a Roth IRA (or such individual's spouse made a contribution to a Roth IRA) established for such individual

408A(d)(2)(C) DISTRIBUTIONS OF EXCESS CONTRIBUTIONS AND EARNINGS.— The term 'qualified distribution' shall not include any distribution of any contribution describe in section 408(d)(4) and any net income allocable to the contribution.

excess contributions

408A(d)(3) ROLLOVERS FROM AN IRA OTHER THAN A ROTH IRA-

408A(d)(3)(A) IN GENERAL- Notwithstanding section 408(d)(3), in the case of any distribution to which this paragraph applies—

408A(d)(3)(A) (i) there shall be included in gross income any amount which would be includible were it not part of a qualified rollover contribution,

408A(d)(3)(A)(ii) section 72(t) shall not apply, and

408A(d)(3)(A) (iii) unless the taxpayer elects not to have this clause apply for any taxable year any amount required to be included in gross income for such taxable year by reason of this paragraph for any distribution before January 1, 1999, shall be so included ratably over the 4-taxable year period beginning with such taxable year. Any election under clause (iii) for any distributions during a taxable year may not be changed after the due date for such taxable year.

four-year spread choice 1998

408A(d)(3)(B) DISTRIBUTIONS TO WHICH PARAGRAPH APPLIES- This paragraph shall apply to a distribution from an individual retirement plan (other than a Roth IRA) maintained for the benefit of an individual which is contributed to a Roth IRA maintained for the benefit of such individual in a qualified rollover contribution.

408A(d)(3)(C) CONVERSIONS- The conversion of an individual retirement plan (other than a Roth IRA) to a Roth IRA shall be treated for purposes of this paragraph as a distribution to which this paragraph applies.

408A(d)(3)(D) ADDITIONAL REPORTING REQUIREMENTS- Trustees of Roth IRAs, trustees of individual or both, whichever is appropriate, shall include such additional information in reports required under section 408(i) as the Secretary may require to ensure that amounts required to be included in gross income under subparagraph (A) are so included.

408A(d)(3)(E) SPECIAL RULES FOR CONTRIBUTIONS TO WHICH 4 YEAR AVERAGING APPLIES. — In the case of a qualified rollover contribution to a Roth IRA of a distribution to which subparagraph (A)(iii) applied, the following rules shall apply:

408A(d)(3)(E)(i) ACCELERATION OF INCLUSION

408A(d)(3)(E)(i)(I) IN GENERAL. — The amount required to be included in gross income for each of the first 3 taxable years in the 4-year period under subparagraph (a)(iii) shall be increased by the aggregate distributions from Roth IRAs for such taxable year which are allocable under paragraph (4) to the portion of such qualified rollover contribution required to be included in gross income under subparagraph (A)(i).

acceleration rule for 4-year spread

408A(d)(3)(E)(i)(II) LIMITATION ON AGGREGATE AMOUNT INCLUDED. The amount required to be included in gross income for any taxable year under subparagraph (A)(iii) shall not exceed the aggregate amount required to be included in gross income under subparagraph (a)(iii) for all taxable years in the 4-year period (without regard to sub-clause (I)) reduced by amounts included for all preceding taxable years.

408A(d)(3)(F)(ii) **DEATH OF DISTRIBUTEE.**

408A(d)(3)(E)(ii)(I) **IN GENERAL.** — If the individual required to include amounts in gross income under such subparagraph dies before all of such amounts are included, all remaining amounts shall be included in gross income for the taxable year which includes the date of death.

408A(d)(3)(E)(ii)(II) **SPECIAL RULE FOR SURVIVING SPOUSE.** — If the spouse of the individual described in sub clause (I) acquires the individual's entire interest in any Roth IRA to which such qualified rollover contribution is properly allocable, the spouse may elect to treat the remaining amounts described in sub clause (I) as includible in the spouse's gross income in the taxable years of the spouse ending with or within the taxable years of such individual in which such amounts would otherwise have been includible. Any such election may not be made or changed after the due date for the spouse's taxable year which includes the date of death.

408A(d)(3)(F) **SPECIAL RULE FOR APPLYING SECTION** 72

408A(d)(3)(F)(i) In **GENERAL** if

408A(d)(3)(G)(i)(I) any portion of a distribution from a Roth IRA is properly allocable to a qualified rollover contribution described in this paragraph, and

408A(d)(3)(F)(i)(II) such distribution is made within the 5-taxable year period beginning with the taxable year in which such contribution was made,

then section 72(t) shall be applied as if such portion were includible in gross income.

408A(d)(3)(F)(ii) **LIMITATION.** — Clause (i) shall apply only to the extent of the amount of the qualified rollover contribution includible in gross income under subparagraph (a)(i)

408A(d)(4) **AGGREGATION AND ORDERING RULES.**

408A(d)(4)(A) **AGGREGATION RULES.** — Section 408(d)(2) shall be applied separately with respect to Roth IRAs and other individual retirement plans.

408A(d)(4)(B) **ORDERING RULES.** — For purposes of applying this section and section 72 to any distribution from a Roth IRA, such distribution shall be treated as made

408A(d)(4)(B)(i) from contributions to the extent that the amount of such distribution, when added to all previous distributions from the Roth IRA, does not exceed the aggregate contributions to the Roth IRA, and

408A(d)(4)(B)(ii) from such contributions in the following order:

408A(d)(4)(B)(ii)(I) Contributions other than qualified rollover contributions to which paragraph (3) applies.

408A(d)(4)(B)(ii)(II) Qualified rollover contributions to which paragraph 3) applies on a first-in, first-out basis. Any distribution allocated to a qualified rollover contribution under clause (ii)(II) shall be allocated first to the portion of such contribution required to be included in gross income.

408A(d)(5) **QUALIFIED SPECIAL PURPOSE DISTRIBUTION**- For purposes of this section, the term "qualified special purpose distribution" means any distribution to which subparagraph (F) of section 72(t)(2) applies.

death

spousal rollover

ordering rules

408A(d)(6) **TAXPAYER MAY MAKE ADJUSTMENTS BEFORE DUE DATE.**

408A(d)(6)(A) **IN GENERAL**. — Except as provided by the Secretary, if, on or before the due date for any taxable year, a taxpayer transfers in a trustee-to-trustee transfer any contribution to an individual retirement plan made during such taxable year from such plan to any other individual retirement plan, then, for purposes of this chapter, such contribution shall be treated as having been made to the transferee plan (and not the transferor plan).

transfer back to IRA

408A(d)(6)(B) **SPECIAL RULES**

408A(d)(6)(B)(i) **TRANSFER OF EARNINGS**. — Subparagraph (A) shall not apply o the transfer of any contribution unless such transfer is accompanied by any net income allocable to such contribution.

408A(d(6)(B)(ii) **NO DEDUCTION**. — Subparagraph (A) shall apply to the transfer of any contribution only to the extent no deduction was allowed with respect to the contribution to the transferor plan

408A(d)(7) **DUE DATE**. — For purposes of this subsection, the due date for any taxable year is the date prescribed by law (including extensions of time) for filing the taxpayer's return for such taxable year.

due date extensions

408A(e) **QUALIFIED ROLLOVER CONTRIBUTION**- For purposes of this section, the term "qualified rollover contribution" means a rollover contribution to a Roth IRA from another such account, or from an individual retirement plan, but only if such rollover contribution meets the requirements of section 408(d)(3). For purposes of section 408(d)(3)(B), there shall be disregarded any qualified rollover contribution from an individual retirement plan (other than a Roth IRA) to a Roth IRA.

408A(f) **INDIVIDUAL RETIREMENT PLAN.** For purposes of this section

see SIMPLE IRA

408A(f)(1) a simplified employee pension or a simple retirement account may not be designated as a Roth IRA, and

408A(f)(2) contributions to any such pension or account shall not be taken into account for purposes of subsection (c)(2)(B)

(End of Sec. 408A)

Explanations provided by the Conferees

1. SAVINGS INCENTIVES OF THE 1997 ACT

Conversion of IRAs into Roth IRAs: Under the Senate amendment, in the case of conversions of IRAs into Roth IRAs, the taxpayer is able to elect to have the amount converted includible in income in the year of the conversion (or the year of withdrawal if the conversion is accomplished through a rollover) rather than ratably over 4 years. The Senate amendment does not include the additional 10-percent recapture tax applicable to premature withdrawals of amounts to which the 4-year spread applies. Instead, under the Senate amendment, if an individual elects application of the 4-year spread and withdraws amounts before the entire amount of the conversion has been included in income, the amount withdrawn is includible in income (in addition to any amount required to be included under the 4-year spread). In no case will the amount includible under this provision exceed the amount converted. The Senate amendment does not include the rules in the House bill regarding separate accounts for converted amounts and instead includes ordering rules for determining the character of withdrawals from Roth IRAs.

Four-year spread

Under the Senate amendment, a new 5-year holding period for determining whether distributions from a Roth IRA are qualified distributions does not apply to converted amounts. Thus, the 5-year holding period begins with the year for which a contribution (including a rollover contribution) was made.

five year clock

The Senate amendment also clarifies calculation of adjusted gross income for purposes of applying the $100,000 adjusted gross income ('AGI') limit on individuals eligible to convert IRAs to Roth IRAs. Under the Senate amendment, the applicable AGI is AGI for the year of the distribution to which the conversion relates. In addition, under the Senate amendment, it is intended that in determining AGI, the conversion amount (to the extent otherwise includible in AGI) is subtracted from AGI for the year of the distribution.

Conversion MAGI $100,000

2. SAVINGS AND INVESTMENT INCENTIVES OF THE 1997 ACT

Conversion of IRAs into Roth IRAs: The conferees wish to clarify that for purposes of determining the $100,000 adjusted gross income ('AGI') limit on IRA conversions to Roth IRAs, the conversion amount is not taken into account. Thus, for this purpose, AGI (and all AGI-based phaseouts) are to be determined without taking into account the conversion amount. For purposes of computing taxable income, the conversion amount (to the extent otherwise includible in AGI) is to be taken into account in computing the AGI-based phaseout amounts. The conferees wish to clarify that the language of the Senate Finance committee report (appearing in connection with section 6005(b) of the Senate amendment) relating to calculation of AGI limit for conversions is superceded.

H. EXCLUSION OF MINIMUM REQUIRED DISTRIBUTIONS FROM AGI FOR ROTH IRA

CONVERSIONS (SEC. 5008 OF THE SENATE AMENDMENT)

Under present law, uniform minimum distribution rules generally apply to all types of tax-favored retirement vehicles, including qualified retirement plans and annuities, individual retirement arrangements ('IRAs') other than Roth IRAs, and tax-sheltered annuities (sec 403(b)).

Under present law, distributions are required to begin no later than the individual's required beginning date (sec. 401(a)(9)). In the case of an IRA, the required beginning date, means the April 1 of the calendar year following the calendar year in which the IRA owner attains age 70 1/2. The Internal Revenue Service has issued extensive Regulations for purposes of calculating minimum distributions. In general, minimum distributions are includible in gross income in the year of distribution. An excise tax equal to 50 percent of the required distribution applies to the extent a required distribution is not made.

Under present law, all or any part of amounts in a deductible or nondeductible IRA may be converted into a Roth IRA. Only taxpayers with adjusted gross income ('AGI') of $100,000 or less are eligible to convert an IRA into a Roth IRA. In the case of a married taxpayer, AGI is the combined AGI of the couple. Married taxpayers filing a separate return are not eligible to make a conversion. The Senate amendment excludes minimum required distributions from IRAs from the definition of AGI solely for purposes of determining eligibility to convert from an IRA to a Roth IRA. As under present law, the required minimum distribution would not be eligible for conversion and would be includible in gross income.

conversion MAGI $100,000

Effective date: The provision is effective for taxable years beginning after December 31, 2004.

MRD rule over 70 1/2 after 2004

Sec. 219. Retirement Savings

219(a)   Allowance Of Deduction

In the case of an individual, there shall be allowed as a deduction an amount equal to the qualified retirement contributions of the individual for the taxable year.

219(b)   Maximum Amount Of Deduction

219(b)(1)   In General

The amount allowable as a deduction under subsection (a) to any individual for any taxable year shall not exceed the lesser of—

219(b)(1)(A) $2,000, or

219(b)(1)(B)   an amount equal to the compensation includible in the individual's gross income for such taxable year.

219(d)   Other Limitations And Restrictions

219(d)(1)   Beneficiary Must Be Under Age 70-1/2

No deduction shall be allowed under this section with respect to any qualified retirement contribution for the benefit of an individual if such individual has attained age 70-1/2 before the close of such individual's taxable year for which the contribution was made.

219(f)(3)   Time When Contributions Deemed Made

For purposes of this section, a taxpayer shall be deemed to have made a contribution to an individual retirement plan on the last day of the preceding taxable year if the contribution is made on account of such taxable year and is made not later than the time prescribed by law for filing the return for such taxable year (not including extensions thereof).

219(g) Limitation On Deduction For Active Participants In Certain Pension Plans

219(g)(1) In General

If (for any part of any plan year ending with or within a taxable year) an individual is an active participant, each of the dollar limitations contained in subsections (b)(1)(A) and (c)(1)(A) for such taxable year shall be reduced (but not below zero) by the amount determined under paragraph (2).

219(g)(2)   Amount Of Reduction

219(g)(2)(A)   In General

The amount determined under this paragraph with respect to any dollar limitation shall be the amount which bears the same ratio to such limitation as—

219(g)(2)(A)(i)   the excess of—

219(g)(2)(A)(i)(I)   the taxpayer's adjusted gross income for such taxable year, over

219(g)(2)(A)(i)(II)   the applicable dollar amount, bears to

219(g)(2)(A)(ii) $10,000 ($20,000 in the case of a joint return for a taxable year beginning after December 31, 2006).

219(g)(2)(B)   No Reduction Below $200 Until Complete Phase-out

No dollar limitation shall be reduced below $200 under paragraph (1) unless (without regard to this subparagraph) such limitation is reduced to zero.

contribution limits

contribution to IRA after age 70 1/2

contribution dates

219(g)(2)(C)   Rounding

Any amount determined under this paragraph which is not a multiple of $10 shall be rounded to the next lowest $10.

partial contributions

219(g)(3)   Adjusted Gross Income; Applicable Dollar Amount

For purposes of this subsection—

219(g)(3)(A)   Adjusted Gross Income

Adjusted gross income of any taxpayer shall be determined—

219(g)(3)(A)(i)   after application of sections 86 and 469, and

219(g)(3)(A)(ii)   without regard to sections 135 , 137, and 911 or the deduction allowable under this section.

219(g)(3)(B)   Applicable Dollar Amount—

The term 'applicable dollar amount' means the following:

219(g)(3)(B)(i) In the case of a taxpayer filing a joint return:

For taxable years beginning in:	The applicable dollar amount is:
1998	$50,000
1999	$51,000
2000	$52,000
2001	$53,000
2002	$54,000
2003	$60,000
2004	$65,000
2005	$70,000
2006	$75,000
2007 and thereafter	$80,000.

AGI Traditional IRA

219(g)(3)(B)(ii)   In the case of any other taxpayer (other than a married individual filing a separate return):

For taxable years beginning in:	The applicable dollar amount is:
1998	$30,000
1999	$31,000
2000	$32,000
2001	$33,000
2002	$34,000
2003	$40,000
2004	$45,000
2005 and thereafter	$50,000.

219(g)(3)(B)(iii)   In the case of a married individual filing a separate return, zero.

219(g)(4)   Special Rule For Married Individuals Filing Separately And Living Apart

A husband and wife who—

219(g)(4)(A)   file separate returns for any taxable year, and

219(g)(4)(B)   live apart at all times during such taxable year, shall not be treated as married individuals for purposes of this subsection.

married filing separate live apart

219(g)(5)   Active Participant

For purposes of this subsection, the term "active participant" means, with respect to any plan year, an individual—

219(g)(5)(A)   who is an active participant in—

219(g)(5)(A)(i)   a plan described in section 401(a) which includes a trust exempt from tax under section 501(a),

219(g)(5)(A)(ii)   an annuity plan described in section 403(a),

219(g)(5)(A)(iii)   a plan established for its employees by the United States, by a State or political subdivision thereof, or by an agency or instrumentality of any of the foregoing,

219(g)(5)(A)(iv)   an annuity contract described in section 403(b),

219(g)(5)(A)(v)   a simplified employee pension (within the meaning of section 408(k)), or

219(g)(5)(A)(vi)   any simple retirement account (within the meaning of section 408(p)), or

219(g)(5)(B)   who makes deductible contributions to a trust described in section 501(c)(18). The determination of whether an individual is an active participant shall be made without regard to whether or not such individual's rights under a plan, trust, or contract are nonforfeitable. An eligible deferred compensation plan (within the meaning of section 457(b)) shall not be treated as a plan described in subparagraph (A)(iii).

219(g)(6)   Certain Individuals Not Treated As Active Participants

For purposes of this subsection, any individual described in any of the following subparagraphs shall not be treated as an active participant for any taxable year solely because of any participation so described:

219(g)(6)(A)   Members Of Reserve Components

Participation in a plan described in subparagraph (A)(iii) of paragraph (5) by reason of service as a member of a reserve component of the Armed Forces (as defined in section 10101 of title 10), unless such individual has served in excess of 90 days on active duty (other than active duty for training) during the year.

219(g)(6)(B)   Volunteer Firefighters

A volunteer firefighter—

219(g)(6)(B)(i)   who is a participant in a plan described in subparagraph (A)(iii) of paragraph (5) based on his activity as a volunteer firefighter, and

219(g)(6)(B)(ii)   whose accrued benefit as of the beginning of the taxable year is not more than an annual benefit of $1,800 (when expressed as a single life annuity commencing at age 65).

219(g)(7)   Special Rule For Certain Spouses.—

In the case of an individual who is an active participant at no time during any plan year ending with or within the taxable year but whose spouse is an active participant for any part of any such plan year—

219(g)(7)(A)   the applicable dollar amount under paragraph (3)(B)(i) with respect to the taxpayer shall be $150,000, and

219(g)(7)(B)   the amount applicable under paragraph (2)(A)(ii) shall be $10,000.

219(h)   Cross Reference

For failure to provide required reports, see section 6652(g).

Sec. 408. Individual Retirement Accounts

408(a)   Individual Retirement Account

For purposes of this section, the term "individual retirement account" means a trust created or organized in the United States for the exclusive benefit of an individual or his beneficiaries, but only if the written governing instrument creating the trust meets the following requirements:

408(a)(1)   Except In The Case Of A Rollover Contribution Described In Subsection (d)(3) In Section 402(c), 403(a)(4), or 403(b)(8), no contribution will be accepted unless it is in cash, and contributions will not be accepted for the taxable year in excess of $2,000 on behalf of any individual. 1

trustee

408(a)(2)   The trustee is a bank (as defined in subsection (n)) or such other person who demonstrates to the satisfaction of the Secretary that the manner in which such other person will administer the trust will be consistent with the requirements of this section.

life insurance

408(a)(3)   No part of the trust funds will be invested in life insurance contracts.

408(a)(4)   The interest of an individual in the balance in his account is nonforfeitable.

408(a)(5)   The assets of the trust will not be commingled with other property except in a common trust fund or common investment fund.

408(a)(6)   Under regulations prescribed by the Secretary, rules similar to the rules of section

401(a)(9)   and the incidental death benefit requirements of section 401(a) shall apply to the distribution of the entire interest of an individual for whose benefit the trust is maintained.

408(b)(3)   Under regulations prescribed by the Secretary, rules similar to the rules of section 401(a)(9) and the incidental death benefit requirements of section 401(a) shall apply to the distribution of the entire interest of the owner.

4408(d)(3) Rollover Contribution

An amount is described in this paragraph as a rollover contribution if it meets the requirements of subparagraphs (A) and (B).

contribution rules

408(d)(3)(A)   In General

Paragraph (1) does not apply to any amount paid or distributed out of an individual retirement account or individual retirement annuity to the individual for whose benefit the account or annuity is maintained if—

408(d)(3)(A)(i)   the entire amount received (including money and any other property) is paid into an individual retirement account or individual retirement annuity (other than an endowment contract) for the benefit of such individual not later than the 60th day after the day on which he receives the payment or distribution;

408(d)(3)(A) (ii) no amount in the account and no part of the value of the annuity is attributable to any source other than a rollover contribution (as defined in section 402) from an employee's trust described in section 401(a) which is exempt from tax under section 501(a) or from an annuity plan described in section 403(a) (and any earnings on such contribution), and the entire amount received (including property and other money) is paid (for the benefit of such individual) into another such trust or annuity plan not later than the 60th day on which the individual receives the payment or the distribution; or 2

408(d)(3)(A)(iii)

408(d)(3)(A)(iii)(I)   the entire amount received (including money and other property) represents the entire interest in the account or the entire value of the annuity,

408(d)(3)(A)(iii)(II)   no amount in the account and no part of the value of the annuity is attributable to any source other than a rollover contribution from an annuity contract described in section 403(b) and any earnings on such rollover, and

408(d)(3)(A)(iii)(III)   the entire amount thereof is paid into another annuity contract described in section 403(b) (for the benefit of such individual) not later than the 60th day after he receives the payment or distribution.

408(d)(3)(B)   Limitation 3

This paragraph does not apply to any amount described in subparagraph (A)(i) received by an individual from an individual retirement account or individual retirement annuity if at any time during the 1-year period ending on the day of such receipt such individual received any other amount described in that subparagraph from an individual retirement account or an individual retirement annuity which was not includible in his gross income because of the application of this paragraph.

408(d)(3)(C)   Denial Of Rollover Treatment For Inherited Accounts, Etc.

408(d)(3)(C)(i)   In General

In the case of an inherited individual retirement account or individual retirement annuity—

408(d)(3)(C)(i)(I)   this paragraph shall not apply to any amount received by an individual from such an account or annuity (and no amount transferred from such account or annuity to another individual retirement account or annuity shall be excluded from gross income by reason of such transfer), and

408(d)(3)(C)(i)(II)   such inherited account or annuity shall not be treated as an individual retirement account or annuity for purposes of determining whether any other amount is a rollover contribution.

408(d)(3)(C)(ii)   Inherited Individual Retirement Account Or Annuity

An individual retirement account or individual retirement annuity shall be treated as inherited if—

408(d)(3)(C)(ii)(I)   the individual for whose benefit the account or annuity is maintained acquired such account by reason of the death of another individual, and

408(d)(3)(C)(ii)(II)   such individual was not the surviving spouse of such other individual.

408(d)(3)(D)   Partial Rollovers Permitted

408(d)(3)(D)(i)   In General

If any amount paid or distributed out of an individual retirement account or individual retirement annuity would meet the requirements of subparagraph (A) but for the fact that the entire amount was not paid into an eligible plan as required by clause (i), (ii), or (iii) of subparagraph (A), such amount shall be treated as meeting the requirements of subparagraph (A) to the extent it is paid into an eligible plan referred to in such clause not later than the 60th day referred to in such clause.

*inherited
IRA*

*partial
rollover*

408(d)(3)(D)(ii)   Eligible Plan

> For purposes of clause (i), the term "eligible plan" means any account, annuity, contract, or plan referred to in subparagraph (A).

408(d)(3)(E)   Denial Of Rollover Treatment For Required Distributions

> This paragraph shall not apply to any amount to the extent such amount is required to be distributed under subsection (a)(6) or (b)(3).

408(d)(3)(F)   Frozen Deposits

> For purposes of this paragraph, rules similar to the rules of section 402(c)(7) (relating to frozen deposits) shall apply. 4

408(d)(3)(G)   Simple Retirement Accounts

> This paragraph shall not apply to any amount paid or distributed out of a simple retirement account (as defined in subsection (p)) unless—

408(d)(3)(G)(i)   it is paid into another simple retirement account, or

408(d)(3)(G)(ii)   in the case of any payment or distribution to which section 72(t)(6) does not apply, it is paid into an individual retirement plan.

408(d)(4)   Contributions Returned Before Due Date Of Return

> Paragraph (1) does not apply to the distribution of any contribution paid during a taxable year to an individual retirement account or for an individual retirement annuity if—

408(d)(4)(A)   such distribution is received on or before the day prescribed by law (including extensions of time) for filing such individual's return for such taxable year,

408(d)(4)(B)   no deduction is allowed under section 219 with respect to such contribution, and

408(d)(4)(C)   such distribution is accomplished by the amount of the net income attributable to such contribution. In the case of such a contribution, for purposes of section 61, any net income described in subparagraph (C) shall be deemed to have been earned and receivable in the taxable year in which such contribution is made.

408(i) Reports

> The trustee of an individual retirement account and the issuer of an endowment contract described in subsection (b) or an individual retirement annuity shall make such reports regarding such account, contract, or annuity to the Secretary and to the individuals for whom the account, contract, or annuity is, or is to be, maintained with respect to contributions (and the years to which they relate), distributions aggregating $10 or more in any calendar year, and such other matters as the Secretary may require. The reports required by this subsection—

trustee reports

408(i)(1)   shall be filed at such time and in such manner as the Secretary prescribes, and

408(i)(2)   shall be furnished to individuals—

408(i)(2)(A)   not later than January 31 of the calendar year following the calendar year to which such reports relate, and

408(i)(2)(B)   in such manner as the Secretary prescribes.

APPENDIX D IRS REGS

INTERNAL REVENUE SERVICE REGS

REG-115393-98

DEPARTMENT OF THE TREASURY

Internal Revenue Service 26 CFR Part 1 RIN 1545-AW62

[1] AGENCY: Internal Revenue Service (IRS), Treasury.

[2] ACTION: Notice of proposed rulemaking and notice of public hearing.

[3] SUMMARY: This document contains proposed regulations relating to Roth IRAs. Roth IRAs were created by the Taxpayer Relief Act of 1997 as a new type of IRA that individuals can use beginning in 1998. The proposed regulations reflect changes relating to Roth IRAs contained in the Internal Revenue Service Restructuring and Reform Act of 1998. The proposed regulations affect individuals establishing Roth IRAs, beneficiaries under Roth IRAs, and trustees, custodians or issuers of Roth IRAs. This document also provides notice of a public hearing on these proposed regulations.

BACKGROUND

[19] Section 408A of the Internal Revenue Code (Code), which was added by section 302 of the Taxpayer Relief Act of 1997, Public Law 105-34 (111 Stat. 788), establishes the Roth IRA as a new type of individual retirement plan, effective for taxable years beginning on or after January 1, 1998. The provisions of section 408A were amended by the Internal Revenue Service Restructuring and Reform Act of 1998, Public Law 105-206 (112 Stat. 685).

[20] A Roth IRA generally is treated under the Code like a traditional IRA with several significant exceptions. Similar to traditional IRAs, income on undistributed amounts accumulated under a Roth IRA is exempt from Federal income tax, and contributions to Roth IRAs are subject to specific limitations. Unlike traditional IRAs, contributions to Roth IRAs cannot be deducted from gross income, but qualified distributions from Roth IRAs are excludable from gross income. These proposed regulations set forth specific rules for Roth IRAs in accordance with the provisions of section 408A.

EXPLANATION OF PROVISIONS

GENERAL PROVISIONS AND ESTABLISHMENT OF ROTH IRAS

[21] Proposed section 1.408A-1 contains general provisions regarding Roth IRAs, and proposed section 1.408A-1 con

tains provisions regarding the establishment of Roth IRAs. As described in proposed section 1.408A-1, a Roth IRA is treated for Federal tax purposes in the same manner as an individual retirement plan except as otherwise provided in section 408A and the proposed regulations. Thus, all the rules of section 408 and the regulations under section 408 apply to Roth IRAs to the extent they are not inconsistent with section 408A or these proposed regulations.

[22] Section 408A(b) defines a Roth IRA as an individual retirement plan which is designated at the time of its establishment as a Roth IRA. That section also grants the Secretary of the Treasury authority to prescribe the manner for designating an individual retirement plan as a Roth IRA. Proposed section 1.408A-2 provides that a Roth IRA instrument must clearly designate the IRA as a Roth IRA, and that designation cannot later be changed. Thus, a taxpayer may not designate an IRA as a Roth IRA and later redesignate the Roth IRA as a traditional IRA or otherwise treat the Roth IRA as though it were a traditional IRA.

REGULAR CONTRIBUTIONS

[23] Proposed section 1.408A-3 sets forth rules regarding regular (i.e., non-conversion) contributions to a Roth IRA. Unlike contributions to traditional IRAs, contributions to Roth IRAs are not deductible under any circumstances. A taxpayer's regular contributions to all his or her Roth IRAs for a year are limited to the lesser of $2,000 or the taxpayer's compensation for that year. As with traditional IRAs, a special rule for married taxpayers permits one spouse to treat the other spouse's compensation as his or her own for purposes of the limit on regular contributions. The limit is reduced by any amounts that the taxpayer contributes for that year to an individual retirement plan other than a Roth IRA (although employer contributions, including elective contributions, to a SEP or SIMPLE IRA Plan do not reduce the contribution limit). Additionally, the contribution limit (determined without regard to any reduction for traditional IRA contributions) is phased out for modified adjusted gross income between $95,000 and $110,000 for single taxpayers, between $150,000 and $160,000 for married taxpayers filing joint returns, and between $0 and $10,000 for married taxpayers filing separate returns. Any contribution in excess of the contribution limit is subject to the 6-percent excise tax under section 4973 unless it is distributed to the taxpayer (with allocable net income) under section 408(d)(4) by the Federal income tax return due date (with extensions) for the year of the contribution.

[24] The proposed regulations define the terms compensation and modified adjusted gross income. The definition of compensation is the same as that applicable under section 219(f)(1) for determining the amount, if any, that a taxpayer may contribute to a traditional IRA. This definition does not include amounts transferred from one individual to another by gift (for example, a gift from a parent to a child). The definition of modified adjusted gross income is based on the definition of adjusted gross income applicable under section 219(g)(3)(A) for determining the amount, if any, that a taxpayer may deduct for a contribution to a traditional IRA where the taxpayer is an active participant in an employee plan. However, the definition of modified adjusted gross income applicable to Roth IRAs provides that any amount includible in gross income because of a Roth IRA conversion is disregarded in determining modified adjusted gross income. Additionally, for taxable years beginning after December 31, 2004, modified adjusted gross income does not include the amount of any required minimum distribution from an IRA for purposes of determining conversion eligibility.

[25] As with traditional IRAs, regular contributions to a Roth IRA may be made as late as the Roth IRA owner's Federal income tax return due date (not including extensions) for the taxable year to which they relate. Thus, Roth IRA contributions may be made by most taxpayers for taxable year 1998 at any time until April 15, 1999. Unlike traditional IRAs, contributions to a Roth IRA may be made after the Roth IRA owner has reached age 70-1/2.

Conversions

[26] Proposed section 1.408A-4 provides rules regarding Roth IRA conversions. In general, a taxpayer whose modified adjusted gross income does not exceed $100,000 may "convert" an amount held in a non-Roth IRA (i.e., a traditional IRA or SIMPLE IRA) to a Roth IRA. The conversion may be made in one of three ways: (1) a distribution from a non-Roth IRA may be rolled over to a Roth IRA within 60 days; (2) an amount in a non-Roth IRA of one financial institution may be transferred in a trustee-to-trustee transfer to a Roth IRA of a different financial institution; or (3) an amount in a non-Roth IRA may be transferred to a Roth IRA of the same financial institution. (In the third case, no physical transfer of assets is necessary, but the instrument governing the non-Roth IRA must, of course, be replaced by a Roth IRA instrument.) The conversion amount must be a qualified rollover contribution under section 408A(e) and, therefore, must satisfy section 408(d)(3) (other than the one-rollover-per-year rule of that section). Any amount distributed from a non-Roth IRA prior to the 1998 taxable year may not be contributed to a Roth IRA as a conversion contribution.

[27] In the case of a conversion made by means of a distribution and rollover contribution, the $100,000 limit applies to the year in which the distribution from the non-Roth IRA is made. For married taxpayers, the $100,000 limit applies to the joint modified adjusted gross income of the couple, and a married taxpayer filing a separate return is not allowed to convert regardless of modified adjusted gross income (although a taxpayer who has lived apart from his or her spouse for the entire taxable year is treated as not married for these purposes).

[28] The proposed regulations provide that amounts held in a SEP IRA or a SIMPLE IRA may be converted to a Roth IRA. In the case of a SIMPLE IRA, a conversion may be done only after the expiration of the 2-year period described in section 72(t)(6). See Q&A I-2 of Notice 98-4 (1998-2 I.R.B. 25). Once a SEP IRA or SIMPLE IRA has been converted to a Roth IRA, the SEP IRA or the SIMPLE IRA becomes a Roth IRA and ceases to be part of a SEP or a SIMPLE IRA Plan thus, no SEP or SIMPLE IRA Plan contributions may be made to the Roth IRA. Amounts held in retirement plans other than IRAs — such as section 401(a) qualified plans and section 403(b) annuity contracts — cannot be directly converted to a Roth IRA.

[29] Any amount converted from a non-Roth IRA to a Roth IRA is treated as distributed from the non-Roth IRA and rolled over to the Roth IRA regardless of the actual means by which the conversion is effected. The conversion amount is generally includible in gross income for the year of the conversion under sections 408(d)(1) and 408(d)(2). For this purpose, in the case of a conversion effected by an actual distribution and rollover contribution (rather than a trustee-to-trustee transfer or a transfer between IRAs of the same financial institution), the year of the distribution from the non- Roth IRA is the year that the conversion amount is includible in gross income.

[30] The conversion amount generally is not subject to the 10- percent additional tax under section 72(t). However, section 408A(d)(3)(F) provides that the 10-percent tax applies to a distribution of a conversion amount made within the 5-taxable-year period beginning with the taxable year in which the conversion to which it is attributable was made. Additionally, the proposed regulations provide that a taxpayer's conversion of an amount from a non-Roth IRA from which the taxpayer was receiving a series of substantially equal periodic payments under section 72(t)(2)(A)(iv) will not be treated as a modification of that series under section 72(t)(4) and thus will not trigger recapture of the section 72(t) tax on previous distributions from the non-Roth IRA as long as the series of substantially equal periodic payments is continued under the Roth IRA (or if section 72(t)(4) would otherwise not apply).

[31] Taxpayers making conversions during 1998 are eligible for a 4-year spread under which a conversion amount can be included in income ratably over taxable years 1998 through 2001 rather than solely in 1998. Special rules apply to this 4-year spread if a taxpayer dies before inclusion of the full conversion amount. In such a case, any remaining includible portion of the conversion amount generally must be included in the taxpayer's gross income for the taxable year that includes the date of his or her death. However, if the taxpayer's surviving spouse is the sole beneficiary of all the taxpayer's Roth IRAs (as determined under the aggregation rule of section 408A(d)(4)(A)), the spouse may elect to continue application of the 4-year spread. Finally, the distribution of any amount attributable to a 1998 conversion to which the 4-year spread applies will accelerate the inclusion of any amount otherwise deferred to a later taxable year.

[32] A required minimum distribution may not be converted to a Roth IRA because section 408(d)(3)(E) prohibits the rollover of any such distribution. Under the proposed regulations, if a non-Roth IRA owner has reached age 70-1/2, any amount distributed (or treated as distributed because of a conversion) from the IRA for that year consists of the required minimum distribution to the extent that an amount equal to the required minimum distribution for that year has not yet been distributed (or treated as distributed). Thus, if a taxpayer who is required to receive a minimum distribution of $10,000 from his or her non-Roth IRA for a taxable year attempts to convert $11,000 to a Roth IRA prior to receiving the required minimum distribution, $10,000 of the conversion amount would be treated as the required minimum distribution and would be ineligible for conversion. This result is not affected by the means through which the taxpayer effects the conversion or by whether an amount greater than or equal to $10,000 remains in the taxpayer's non-Roth IRA after the conversion.

RECHARACTERIZATIONS OF IRA CONTRIBUTIONS

[33] Proposed section 1.408A-5 provides special rules for the recharacterization of IRA contributions (including Roth IRA regular and conversion contributions). Section 408A(d)(6) provides that, except as otherwise provided by the Secretary of the Treasury, an IRA contribution that is transferred to another IRA in a trustee-to- trustee transfer on or before the Federal income tax return due date (with extensions) for the taxable year of the contribution is treated as made to the transferee IRA and not the transferor IRA. Section 408A(d)(6) requires that the transfer include allocable net income on the contribution and that no deduction be allowed for the contribution to the transferor IRA. This statutory provision was intended to permit a taxpayer who had converted an amount held in a non-Roth IRA to a Roth IRA and later discovered that his or her modified adjusted gross income for the year of the conversion exceeded $100,000 to correct the conversion by retransferring the converted amount to a non-Roth IRA. The proposed regulations interpret section 408A(d)(6) liberally to provide broad relief to taxpayers who wish to change the nature of an IRA contribution (and not only to allow taxpayers to correct Roth IRA conversions for which they were ineligible). Moreover, the proposed regulations make application of section 408A(d)(6) elective by the taxpayer and permit the taxpayer to recharacterize all or any portion of an IRA contribution.

[34] Under the proposed regulations, a taxpayer may elect whether to recharacterize a contribution made to one type of IRA by having it transferred in a trustee-to-trustee transfer to a different type of IRA. As with a conversion, a recharacterization can be effected simply by transferring IRA assets between two IRAs of a single financial institution. Regardless of how effected, a recharacterization transfer is not considered a rollover for purposes of the one-rollover-per-year rule of section 408(d)(3). The mtaxpayer makes the election to recharacterize by notifying both the transferor IRA trustee and the transferee IRA trustee and by providing certain information to these trustees (including a direction to make the transfer). Notification to the trustees constitutes the taxpayer's election to apply section 408A(d)(6), and the taxpayer cannot revoke or modify that election after the recharacterization transfer has been made. A recharacterized contribution will be treated for Federal income tax purposes as having been contributed to

the transferee IRA (rather than the transferor IRA) on the same date and for the same taxable year that the contribution was initially made to the transferor IRA. In effect, the transferee IRA "steps into the shoes" of the transferor IRA with respect to the taxpayer's original contribution.

[35] The recharacterization transfer must include allocable earnings on the original contribution, and the proposed regulations provide that the rules of Treasury Regulations section 1.408- 4(c)(2)(ii) apply for determining such allocable earnings. If the original contribution has experienced net losses as of the time of the recharacterization, the transfer of the entire original contribution less such losses will generally constitute a transfer of the entire contribution. The taxpayer must treat the contribution as made to the transferee IRA on his or her Federal income tax return for the year to which the original contribution (to the transferor IRA) relates.

[36] Amounts that cannot be recharacterized include amounts paid into an IRA by tax-free rollover or transfer (other than a rollover or transfer from a traditional IRA to a SIMPLE IRA) and employer contributions under a SIMPLE IRA Plan or a SEP. The proposed regulations also provide that, once an amount has been contributed to an IRA, any tax-free rollover or transfer of that amount to another IRA may be disregarded in applying the recharacterization rules. Thus, for example, if a taxpayer contributes $2,000 to a Roth IRA during a taxable year and rolls that contribution over to another Roth IRA during the following taxable year, the rollover between Roth IRAs is disregarded, and the taxpayer may recharacterize the $2,000 Roth IRA contribution by having it transferred from the second Roth IRA to a traditional IRA in accordance with section 408A(d)(6) and the proposed regulations.

DISTRIBUTIONS

[37] Proposed section 1.408A-6 provides rules for the treatment of Roth IRA distributions. Under section 408A(d), qualified distributions from a Roth IRA are not includible in gross income. A qualified distribution is a distribution that is both (1) made after the end of the 5-taxable-year period that begins with the first taxable year for which an individual first makes any regular or conversion contribution to a Roth IRA and (2) made at any time after the Roth IRA owner has reached age 59-1/2, made to a beneficiary (or to the Roth IRA owner's estate) after the Roth IRA owner's death, attributable to the Roth IRA owner's being disabled within the meaning of section 72(m)(7), or made for a first-time home purchase to which section 72(t)(2)(F) applies. The proposed regulations provide that any distribution from a Roth IRA made to the surviving spouse of a Roth IRA owner who has elected to treat the Roth IRA as his or her own in accordance with the terms of the trust instrument o under Q&A-4 of Proposed Treasury Regulations section 1.408-8 is not treated as made after the Roth IRA owner's death.

[38] The proposed regulations provide that the 5-taxable-year period for determining whether a distribution is a qualified distribution is not recalculated when a Roth IRA owner dies. Thus, if a Roth IRA owner contributes an amount to a Roth IRA in 1998 and dies in 2004, a distribution made to a beneficiary in 2004 will be a qualified distribution. Generally, the 5-taxable- year period with respect to a beneficiary's inherited Roth IRA is determined independently of the 5-taxable-year period for any Roth IRA of which the beneficiary is the owner. However, if the beneficiary of a Roth IRA is the surviving spouse of the Roth IRA owner and if the surviving spouse owns his or her own Roth IRA, the 5-taxable-year period for both the Roth IRA of which the surviving spouse is the beneficiary and the Roth IRA of which the surviving spouse is the owner ends with the earlier of the 5-taxable-year periods for the two Roth IRAs.

[39] A Roth IRA distribution other than a qualified distribution is generally includible in the taxpayer's gross income to the extent that the distribution, when added to all prior distributions from the taxpayer's Roth IRAs (whether or not those distributions were qualified distributions) exceeds the taxpayer's total contributions to all his or her Roth IRAs. To the extent includible in gross income, such a distribution will also be subject to the 10-percent additional tax of section 72(t) unless there is an applicable exception under that section. Such a distribution, however, will not be includible in gross income if it is rolled over to is not includible in gross income (although the allocable net income that must be distributed with the excess contribution is includible in gross income for the taxable year of the excess contribution).

[40] The proposed regulations provide aggregation and ordering rules for Roth IRAs in accordance with section 408A(d)(4). Under these rules, a Roth IRA is not aggregated with a non-Roth IRA, but all a taxpayer's Roth IRAs are aggregated with each other. Roth IRA distributions are treated as made first from Roth IRA contributions and second from earnings. Distributions that are treated as made from contributions are treated as made first from regular contributions and then from conversion contributions on a first-in, first-out basis. A distribution allocable to a particular conversion contribution is treated as consisting first of the portion (if any) of the conversion contribution that was includible in gross income by reason of the conversion.

[41] The proposed regulations provide that, in applying these aggregation and ordering rules: all distributions from all of a taxpayer's Roth IRAs during a taxable year are aggregated; all regular contributions made for the same taxable year to all the individual's Roth IRAs are aggregated and added to the undistributed total regular contributions for prior taxable years; all conversion contributions received during the same taxable year by all the individual's Roth IRAs are aggregated (with a special rule for a conversion contribu-

tion made by distribution during 1998 and rollover during 1999 to which the 4-year spread applies); and rollovers between Roth IRAs are disregarded. The proposed regulations also provide special rules for applying the aggregation and ordering rules in the case of recharacterizations under section 408A(d)(6). Distributions of excess contributions and allocable net income pursuant to section 408(d)(4) are treated differently under the ordering rules. Specifically, an excess contribution that is distributed under section 408(d)(4) is treated as though it was never contributed, and any allocable net income thereon is includible in gross income for the taxable year of the contribution without regard to whether the taxpayer still has undistributed basis in his or her Roth IRAs. The proposed regulations provide that, for purposes of these ordering rules, different types of contributions are allocated pro rata among multiple Roth IRA beneficiaries after the Roth IRA owner's death.

[42] Unlike traditional IRAs, the pre-death minimum distribution rules of sections 408(a)(6) and 408(b)(3) (which incorporate the rules of section 401(a)(9)) do not apply to Roth IRAs. Under the proposed regulations, on the death of a Roth IRA owner, the rules in Proposed Treasury Regulations section 1.408-8 apply as though the Roth IRA owner died before his or her required beginning date. Thus, the entire amount of the Roth IRA must generally be distributed within five years of the Roth IRA owner's death unless it is distributed over the life expectancy of a designated beneficiary beginning prior to the end of the calendar year following the year of the owner's death. The proposed regulations also provide that, where the sole beneficiary of a Roth IRA is the Roth IRA owner's surviving spouse, the spouse may delay distributions until the Roth IRA owner would have reached age 70-1/2 or may treat the Roth IRA as his or her own. Under the proposed regulations, section 401(a)(9) applies separately to Roth IRAs and other retirement plans; it also applies separately to Roth IRAs inherited by a beneficiary from one decedent and any other Roth IRAs of which the beneficiary is either the beneficiary of another decedent or the owner.

[43] The proposed regulations provide that section 3405 withholding applies to distributions from Roth IRAs and to Roth IRA conversions (although transition relief is provided for 1998 conversions effected by means of direct transfers of funds between IRAs). The proposed regulations provide that the basis of property distributed from a Roth IRA is its fair market value as of the date of the distribution and that any amount distributed from a Roth IRA and contributed to a retirement plan other than a Roth IRA is not a rollover contribution under section 408(d)(3) or a qualified rollover contribution under section 408A(e). The proposed regulations also provide that a transfer of a Roth IRA by gift would constitute an assignment of the Roth IRA, with the effect that the assets of the Roth IRA would be deemed to be distributed to the Roth IRA owner and, accordingly, treated as no longer held in a Roth IRA.

REPORTING REQUIREMENTS

[44] Proposed 1.408A-7 sets out the reporting requirements applicable to Roth IRAs. In general, Roth IRA trustees (including custodians and issuers) are subject to the same reporting requirements that apply to trustees of traditional IRAs. However, the instructions to applicable Federal tax forms modify the information generally required from Roth IRA trustees (as well as Roth IRA owners) in certain circumstances. For example, conversions require the filing of a Form 1099-R and a Form 8606. The proposed regulations include special rules for reporting of recharacterization transactions. Trustees are permitted to rely on reasonable representations of a Roth IRA owner or distributee in discharging their reporting obligations.

[45] The IRS is issuing additional guidance on the reporting requirements applicable to Roth IRAs and on other changes in the laws relating to IRAs. This guidance will be in the form of a notice published in the Internal Revenue Bulletin.

RELIANCE

[46] Taxpayers may rely on these proposed regulations for guidance pending the issuance of final regulations. If, and to the extent, future guidance is more restrictive than the guidance in these proposed regulations, the future guidance will b applied without retroactive effect.

PROPOSED EFFECTIVE DATE

[47] These regulations are applicable to taxable years beginning on or after January 1, 1998, the effective date for section 408A.

APPENDIX E IRS Q & A's

INTERNAL REVENUE SERVICE

QUESTIONS AND ANSWERS

SECTION 1.408A-0 TABLE OF CONTENTS.

This table of contents lists the regulations relating to Roth IRAs under section 408A of the Internal Revenue Code as follows:

SECTION 1.408A-1 ROTH IRAS IN GENERAL.

Q-1 What is a Roth IRA?

A-1. (a) A Roth IRA is a new type of individual retirement plan that individuals can use, beginning in 1998. Roth IRAs are described in section 408A, which was added by the Taxpayer Relief Act of 1997 (TRA 97), Public Law 105-34 (111 Stat. 788).

(b) Roth IRAs are treated like traditional IRAs except where the Internal Revenue Code specifies different treatment. For example, aggregate contributions (other than by a conversion or other rollover) to all an individual's Roth IRAs are not permitted to exceed $2,000 for a taxable year. Further, income earned on funds held in a Roth IRA is generally not taxable. Similarly, the rules of section 408(e), such as the loss of exemption of the account where the owner engages in a prohibited transaction, apply to Roth IRAs in the same manner as to traditional IRAs.

Q-2. What are the significant differences between traditional IRAs and Roth IRAs?

A-2. There are several significant differences between traditional IRAs and Roth IRAs under the Internal Revenue Code. For example, eligibility to contribute to a Roth IRA is subject to special modified AGI (adjusted gross income) limits; contributions to a Roth IRA are never deductible; qualified distributions from a Roth IRA are not includible in gross income; the required 401(a)(9) do not apply to a Roth IRA during the lifetime of the owner; and contributions to a Roth IRA can be made after the owner has attained age 70-1/2.

SECTION 1.408A-2 ESTABLISHING A ROTH IRA.

Q-1. Who can establish a Roth IRA?

A-1. Except as provided in A-3 of this section, only an individual can establish a Roth IRA. In addition, in order to be eligible to contribute to a Roth IRA for a particular year, an individual must satisfy certain compensation requirements and adjusted gross income limits (see section 1.408A-3 A-3).

Q-2. How is a Roth IRA established?

A-2. A Roth IRA can be established with any bank, insurance company, or other person authorized in accordance with section 1.408- 2(e) to serve as a trustee with respect to IRAs. The document establishing the Roth IRA must clearly designate the IRA as a Roth IRA, and this designation cannot be changed at a later date. Thus, an IRA that is designated as a Roth IRA cannot later be treated as a traditional IRA. However, see section 1.408A-5 for rules for recharacterizing certain IRA contributions.

Q-3. Can an employer or an association of employees establish a Roth IRA to hold contributions of employees or members?

A-3. Yes. Pursuant to section 408(c), an employer or an association of employees can establish a trust to hold contributions of employees or members made under a Roth IRA. Each employee's or member's account in the trust is treated as a separate Roth IRA that is subject to the generally applicable Roth IRA rules. The employer or association of employees may do certain acts otherwise required by an individual, for example, establishing and designating a trust as a Roth IRA.

Q-4. What is the effect of a surviving spouse of a Roth IRA owner treating an IRA as his or her own?

A-4. If the surviving spouse of a Roth IRA owner treats a Roth IRA as his or her own as of a date, from that date forward, the Roth IRA is treated as though it were established for the benefit of the surviving spouse and not the original Roth IRA owner. Thus, for example, the surviving spouse is treated as the Roth IRA owner for purposes of applying the minimum distribution requirements under section 408(a)(6) and (b)(3). Similarly, the surviving spouse is treated as the Roth IRA owner rather than a beneficiary for purposes of determining the amount of any distribution from the Roth IRA that is includible in gross income and whether the distribution is subject to the 10-percent additional tax under section 72(t).

SECTION 1.408A-3 CONTRIBUTIONS TO ROTH IRAS.

Q-1. What types of contributions are permitted to be made to a Roth IRA?

A-1. There are two types of contributions that are permitted to be made to a Roth IRA: regular contributions and qualified rollover contributions (including conversion contributions). The term regular contributions means contributions other than qualified rollover contributions.

Q-2. When are contributions permitted to be made to a Roth IRA?

A-2. (a) The provisions of section 408A are effective for taxable years beginning on or after January 1, 1998. Thus, the first taxable year for which contributions are permitted to be made to a Roth IRA by an individual is the individual's taxable year beginning in 1998.

(b) Regular contributions for a particular taxable year must generally be contributed by the due date (not including extensions) for filing a Federal income tax return for that taxable year. (See section 1.408A-5 regarding recharacterization of certain contributions.)

Q-3. What is the maximum aggregate amount of regular contributions an individual is eligible to contribute to a Roth IRA for a taxable year?

A-3. (a) The maximum aggregate amount that an individual is eligible to contribute to all his or her Roth IRAs as a regular contribution for a taxable year is the same as the maximum for traditional IRAs: $2,000 or, if less, that individual's compensation for the year.

(b) For Roth IRAs, the maximum amount described in paragraph (a) of this A-3 is phased out between certain levels of modified AGI. For an individual who is not married, the dollar amount is phased out ratably between modified AGI of $95,000 and $110,000; for a married individual filing a joint return, between modified AGI of $150,000 and $160,000; and for a married individual filing separately, between modified AGI of $0 and $10,000. For this purpose, a married individual who has lived apart from his or her spouse for the entire taxable year and who files separately is treated as not married. Under section 408A(c)(3)(A), in applying the phase-out, the maximum amount is rounded up to the next higher multiple of $10 and is not reduced below $200 until completely phased out.

(c) If an individual makes regular contributions to both traditional IRAs and Roth IRAs for a taxable year, the maximum limit for the Roth IRA is the lesser of —

(1) The amount described in paragraph (a) of this A-3 reduced by the amount contributed to traditional IRAs for the taxable year; and
(2) The amount described in paragraph (b) of this A-3. Employer contributions, including elective deferrals, made under a SEP or SIMPLE IRA Plan on behalf of an individual (including a self-employed individual) do not reduce the amount of the individual's maximum regular contribution.
(d) The rules in this A-3 are illustrated by the following examples:

> Example 1. In 1998, unmarried, calendar-year taxpayer B, age 60, has modified AGI of $40,000 and compensation of $5,000. For 1998, B can contribute a maximum of $2,000 to a traditional IRA, a Roth IRA or a combination of traditional and Roth IRAs.

Example 2. The facts are the same as in Example 1. However, assume that B violates the maximum regular contribution limit by contributing $2,000 to a traditional IRA and $2,000 to a Roth IRA for 1998. The $2,000 to B's Roth IRA would be an excess contribution to B's Roth IRA for 1998 because an individual's contributions are applied first to a traditional IRA then to a Roth IRA.

Example 3. The facts are the same as in Example 1, except that B's compensation is $900. The maximum amount B can contribute to either a traditional IRA or a Roth (or a combination of the two) for 1998 is $900.

Example 4. In 1998, unmarried, calendar-year taxpayer C, age 60, has modified AGI of $100,000 and compensation of $5,000. For 1998, C contributes $800 to a traditional IRA and $1,200 to a Roth IRA. Because C's $1,200 Roth IRA contribution does not exceed the phased-out maximum Roth IRA contribution of $1,340 and because C's total IRA contributions do not exceed $2,000, C's Roth IRA contribution does not exceed the maximum permissible contribution.

Q-4. How is compensation defined for purposes of the Roth IRA contribution limit?

A-4. For purposes of the contribution limit described in A-3 of this section, an individual's compensation is the same as that used to determine the maximum contribution an individual can make to a traditional IRA. This amount is defined in section 219(f)(1) to include wages, commissions, professional fees, tips, and other amounts received for personal services, as well as taxable alimony and separate maintenance payments received under a decree of divorce or separate maintenance. Compensation also includes earned income as defined in section 401(c)(2), but does not include any amount received as a pension or annuity or as deferred compensation. In addition, under section 219(c), a married individual filing a joint return is permitted to make an IRA contribution by treating his or her spouse's higher compensation as his or her own, but only to the extent that the spouse's compensation is not being used for purpose of the spouse making a contribution to a Roth IRA or a deductible contribution to a traditional IRA.

Q-5. What is the significance of modified AGI and how is it determined?

A-5. Modified AGI is used for purposes of the phase-out rules described in A-3 of this section and for purposes of the $100,000 modified AGI limitation described in section 1.408A-4 A-2(a) (relating to eligibility for conversion). As defined in section 408A(c)(3)(C)(i), modified AGI is the same as adjusted gross income under section 219(g)(3)(A) (used to determine the amount of deductible contributions that can be made to a traditional IRA by an individual who is an active participant in an employer-sponsored retirement plan), except that any conversion is disregarded in determining modified AGI. For example, the deduction for contributions to an IRA is not taken into account for purposes of determining adjusted gross income under section 219 and thus does not apply in determining modified AGI for Roth IRA purposes.

Q-6. Is a required minimum distribution from an IRA for a year included in income for purposes of determining modified AGI?

A-6. (a) Yes. For taxable years beginning before January 1, 2005, any required minimum distribution from an IRA under section 408(a)(6) and (b)(3) (which generally incorporate the provisions of section 401(a)(9)) is included in income for purposes of determining modified AGI.

(b) For taxable years beginning after December 31, 2004, and solely for purposes of the $100,000 limitation applicable to conversions, modified AGI does not include any required minimum distributions from an IRA under section 408(a)(6) and (b)(3).

Q-7. Does an excise tax apply if an individual exceeds the aggregate regular contribution limits for Roth IRAs?

A-7. Yes. Section 4973 imposes an annual 6-percent excise tax on aggregate amounts contributed to Roth IRAs that exceed the maximum contribution limits described in A-3 of this section. Any contribution that is distributed, together with net income, from a Roth IRA on or before the tax return due date (plus extensions) for the taxable year of the contribution is treated as not contributed. Net income described in the previous sentence is includible in gross income for the taxable year in which the contribution is made. Section 4973 applies separately to an individual's Roth IRAs and other IRAs.

SECTION 1.408A-4 CONVERTING AMOUNTS TO ROTH IRAS.

Q-1. Can an individual convert an amount in his or her traditional IRA to a Roth IRA?

A-1. (a) Yes. An amount in a traditional IRA may be converted to an amount in a Roth IRA if two requirements are satisfied. First, the IRA owner must satisfy the modified AGI limitation described in A-2(a) of this section and, if married, the joint filing requirement described in A-2(b) of this section. Second, the amount contributed to the Roth IRA must satisfy the definition of a qualified rollover contribution in section 408A(e) (i.e., it must satisfy the requirements for a rollover contribution as defined in section

408(d)(3), except that the one-rollover-per-year limitation in section 408(d)(3)(B) does not apply).

(b) An amount can be converted by any of three methods —

(1) An amount distributed from a traditional IRA is contributed (rolled over) to a Roth IRA within 60 days after the distribution;

(2) An amount in a traditional IRA is transferred in a trustee- to-trustee transfer from the trustee of the traditional IRA to the trustee of the Roth IRA; or
(3) An amount in a traditional IRA is transferred to a Roth IRA maintained by the same trustee.

(c) Any converted amount is treated as a distribution from the traditional IRA and a qualified rollover contribution to the Roth IRA for purposes of section 408 and section 408A, even if the conversion is accomplished by means of a trustee-to-trustee transfer or a transfer between IRAs of the same trustee.

Q-2. What are the modified AGI limitation and joint filing requirements for conversions?

A-2. (a) An individual with modified AGI in excess of $100,000 for a taxable year is not permitted to convert an amount to a Roth IRA during that taxable year. This $100,000 limitation applies to the taxable year that the funds are paid from the traditional IRA, rather than the year they are contributed to the Roth IRA.

(b) If the individual is married, he or she is permitted to convert an amount to a Roth IRA during a taxable year only if the individual and the individual's spouse file a joint return for the taxable year that the funds are paid from the traditional IRA. In this case, the modified AGI subject to the $100,000 limit is the modified AGI derived from the joint return using the couple's combined income. The only exception to this joint filing requirement is for an individual who has lived apart from his or her spouse for the entire taxable year. If the married individual has lived apart from his or her spouse for the entire taxable year, then such individual can treat himself or herself as not married for purposes of this paragraph, file a separate return and be subject to the $100,000 limit on his or her separate modified AGI. In all other cases, a married individual filing a separate return is not permitted to convert an amount to a Roth IRA, regardless of the individual's modified AGI.

Q-3. Is a remedy available to an individual who, intending to make a conversion, contributes amounts from a traditional IRA to a Roth IRA, but who is ineligible to make a conversion (a failed conversion)?

A-3. (a) Yes. See section 1.408A-5 for rules permitting a failed conversion amount to be recharacterized as a contribution to a traditional IRA. If the requirements in section 1.408A-5 are satisfied, the failed conversion amount will be treated as having been contributed to the traditional IRA and not to the Roth IRA.

(b) If the contribution is not recharacterized in accordance with section 1.408A-5, the contribution will be treated as a regular contribution to the Roth IRA and, thus, an excess contribution subject to the excise tax under section 4973 to the extent that it exceeds the individual's regular contribution limit. Additionally, the distribution from the traditional IRA will not be eligible for the 4-year spread and will be subject to the additional tax under section 72(t) (unless an exception under that section applies).

Q-4. Do any special rules apply to a conversion of an amount in an individual's SEP IRA or SIMPLE IRA to a Roth IRA?

A-4. (a) An amount in an individual's SEP IRA can be converted to a Roth IRA on the same terms as an amount in any other traditional IRA.

(b) An amount in an individual's SIMPLE IRA can be converted to a Roth IRA on the same terms as a conversion from a traditional IRA, except that an amount distributed from a SIMPLE IRA during the 2-year period described in section 72(t)(6), which begins on the date that the individual first participated in any SIMPLE IRA Plan maintained by the individual's employer, cannot be converted to a Roth IRA. Pursuant to section 408(d)(3)(G), a distribution of an amount from an individual's SIMPLE IRA during this 2-year period is not eligible to be rolled over into an IRA that is not a SIMPLE IRA and thus cannot be a qualified rollover contribution. This 2-year period of section 408(d)(3)(G) applies separately to the contributions of each of an individual's employers maintaining a SIMPLE IRA Plan.

(c) Once an amount in a SEP IRA or SIMPLE IRA has been converted to a Roth IRA, it is treated as a contribution to a Roth IRA for all purposes. Future contributions under the SEP or under the SIMPLE IRA Plan may not be made to the Roth IRA.

Q-5. Can amounts in other kinds of retirement plans be converted to a Roth IRA?

A-5. No. Only amounts in another IRA can be converted to a Roth IRA. For example, amounts in a qualified plan or annuity plan described in section 401(a) or 403(a) cannot be converted directly to a Roth IRA. Also, amounts held in an annuity contract or account described in section 403(b) cannot be converted directly to a Roth IRA.

Q-6. Can an individual who has attained at least age 70-1/2 by the end of a calendar year convert an amount distributed from a traditional IRA during that year to a Roth IRA before receiving his or her required minimum distribution with respect to the traditional IRA for the year of the conversion?

A-6. (a) No. In order to be eligible for a conversion, an amount first must be eligible to be rolled over. Section 408(d)(3) prohibits the rollover of a required minimum distribution. If a minimum distribution is required for a year with respect to an IRA, the first dollars distributed during that year are treated as consisting of the required minimum distribution until an amount equal to the required minimum distribution for that year has been distributed.

(b) As provided in A-1(c) of this section, any amount converted is treated as a distribution from a traditional IRA and a rollover contribution to a Roth IRA and not as a trustee-to-trustee transfer for purposes of section 408 and section 408A. Thus, in a year for which a minimum distribution is required (including the calendar year in which the individual attains age 70-1/2), an individual may not convert the assets of an IRA (or any portion of those assets) to a Roth IRA to the extent that the required minimum distribution for the traditional IRA for the year has not been distributed.

(c) If a required minimum distribution is contributed to a Roth IRA, it is treated as having been distributed, subject to the normal rules under section 408(d)(1) and (2), and then contributed as a regular contribution to a Roth IRA. The amount of the required minimum distribution is not a conversion contribution.

Q-7. What are the tax consequences when an amount is converted to a Roth IRA?

A-7. (a) Any amount that is converted to a Roth IRA is includible in gross income as a distribution according to the rules of section 408(d)(1) and (2) for the taxable year in which the amount is distributed or transferred from the traditional IRA. Thus, any portion of the distribution or transfer that is treated as a return of basis under section 408(d)(1) and (2) is not includible in gross income as a result of the conversion.

(b) The 10-percent additional tax under section 72(t) generally does not apply to the taxable conversion amount. But see section 1.408A-6 A-5 for circumstances under which the taxable conversion amount would be subject to the additional tax under section 72(t).

(c) Pursuant to section 408A(e), a conversion is not treated as a rollover for purposes of the one-rollover-per-year

Q-8. Is there an exception to the income-inclusion rule described in A-7 of this section for 1998 conversions?

A-8. Yes. In the case of a distribution (including a trustee- to-trustee transfer) from a traditional IRA on or before December 31, 1998, that is converted to a Roth IRA, instead of having the entire taxable conversion amount includible in income in 1998, an individual includes in gross income for 1998 only one quarter of that amount and one quarter of that amount for each of the next 3 years. This 4-year spread also applies if the conversion amount was distributed in 1998 and contributed to the Roth IRA within 60 days, but after December 31, 1998. However, see section 1.408A-6 A-6 for special rules requiring acceleration of inclusion if an amount subject to the 4- year spread is distributed from the Roth IRA before 2001.

Q-9. Is the taxable conversion amount included in income for all purposes?

A-9. Except as provided below, any taxable conversion amount includible in gross income for a year as a result of the conversion (regardless of whether the individual is using a 4-year spread) is included in income for all purposes. Thus, for example, it is counted for purposes of determining the taxable portion of social security payments under section 86 and for purposes of determining the phase-out of the $25,000 exemption under section 469(i) relating to the disallowance of passive activity losses from rental real estate activities. However, as provided in section 1.408A-3 A-5, the taxable conversion amount (and any resulting change in other elements of adjusted gross income) is disregarded for purposes of determining modified AGI for section 408A.

Q-10. Can an individual who makes a 1998 conversion elect not to have the 4-year spread apply and instead have the full taxable conversion amount includible in gross income for 1998?

A-10. Yes. Instead of having the taxable conversion amount for a 1998 conversion included over 4 years as provided under A-8 of this section, an individual can elect to include the full taxable conversion amount in income for 1998. The election is made on Form 8606 and cannot be made or changed after the due date (including extensions) for filing the 1998 Federal income tax return.

Q-11. What happens when an individual who is using the 4-year spread dies before the full taxable conversion amount has been included in gross income?

A-11. (a) If an individual who is using the 4-year spread described in A-8 of this section dies before the full taxable conversion amount has been included in gross income, then the remainder must be included in the individual's gross income for the taxable year that includes the date of death.

(b) However, if the sole beneficiary of all the decedent's Roth IRAs is the decedent's spouse, then the spouse can elect to continue the 4-year spread. Thus, the spouse can elect to include in gross income the same amount that the decedent would have included in each of the remaining years of the 4-year period. Where the spouse makes such an election, the amount includible under the 4-year spread for the taxable year that includes the date of the decedent's death remains includible in the decedent's gross income and is reported on the decedent's final Federal income tax return. The election is made on either Form 8606 or Form 1040, in accordance with the instructions to the applicable form, for the taxable year that includes the decedent's date of death and cannot be changed after the due date (including extensions) for filing the Federal income tax return for the spouse's taxable year that includes the decedent's date of death.

Q-12. Can an individual convert a traditional IRA to a Roth IRA if he or she is receiving substantially equal periodic payments within the meaning of section 72(t)(2)(A)(iv) from that traditional IRA?

A. Yes. Not only is the conversion amount itself not subject to the early distribution tax under section 72(t), but the conversion amount is also not treated as a distribution for purposes of determining whether a modification within the meaning of section 72(t)(4)(A) has occurred. However, if the original series of substantially equal periodic payments does not continue to be distributed in substantially equal periodic payments from the Roth IRA after the conversion, the series of payments will have been modified and, if this modification occurs within 5 years of the first payment or prior to the individual becoming disabled or attaining age 59-1/2, the taxpayer will be subject to the recapture tax of section 72(t)(4)(A).

Q-13. Can a 1997 distribution from a traditional IRA be converted to a Roth IRA in 1998?

A-13. No. An amount distributed from a traditional IRA in 1997 that is contributed to a Roth IRA in 1998 would not be a conversion contribution. See A-2 of this section regarding the remedy for a failed conversion.

SECTION 1.408A-5 RECHARACTERIZED CONTRIBUTIONS.

Q-1. Can an IRA owner recharacterize certain contributions (i.e., treat a contribution made to one type of IRA as made to a different type of IRA) for a taxable year?

A-1. (a) Yes. In accordance with section 408A(d)(6), except as otherwise provided in this section, if an individual makes a contribution to an IRA (the FIRST IRA) for a taxable year and then transfers the contribution (or a portion of the contribution) in a trustee-to-trustee transfer from the trustee of the FIRST IRA to the trustee of another IRA (the SECOND IRA), the individual can elect to treat the contribution as having been made to the SECOND IRA, instead of to the FIRST IRA, for Federal tax purposes. A transfer between the FIRST IRA and the SECOND IRA will not fail to be a trustee-to- trustee transfer merely because both IRAs are maintained by the same trustee.

(b) This recharacterization election can be made only if the trustee-to-trustee transfer from the FIRST IRA to the SECOND IRA is made on or before the due date (including extensions) for filing the individual's Federal income tax return for the taxable year for which the contribution was made to the FIRST IRA. For purposes of this section, a conversion that is accomplished through a rollover of a distribution from a traditional IRA in a taxable year that, within 60 days after the distribution, is contributed to a Roth IRA in the next taxable year is treated as a contribution for the earlier taxable year.

Q-2. What is the proper treatment of the net income attributable to the contribution that is being recharacterized?

A-2. (a) The net income attributable to the contribution that is being recharacterized must be transferred to the SECOND IRA along with the contribution.

(b) If the amount of the contribution being recharacterized was contributed to a separate IRA and no distributions or additional contributions have been made from or to that IRA at any time, then the contribution is recharacterized by the trustee of the FIRST IRA transferring the entire account balance of the FIRST IRA to the trustee of the SECOND IRA. In this case, the net income (or loss) attributable to the contribution being recharacterized is the difference between the amount of the original contribution and the amount transferred.

(c) If paragraph (b) of this A-2 does not apply, then the net income attributable to the contribution is calculated in the manner prescribed by section 1.408-4(c)(2)(ii).

Q-3. What is the effect of recharacterizing a contribution made to the FIRST IRA as a contribution made to the SECOND IRA?

A-3. The contribution that is being recharacterized as a contribution to the SECOND IRA is treated as having been originally contributed to the SECOND IRA on the same date and (in the case of a regular contribution) for the same taxable year that the contribution was made to the FIRST IRA. Thus, for example, no deduction would be allowe fo contribution to the FIRST IRA, and any net income transferred with the recharacterized contribution is treated as earned in the SECOND IRA, and not the FIRST IRA.

Q-4. Can an amount contributed to an IRA in a tax-free transfer be recharacterized under A-1 of this section?

A-4. No. If an amount is contributed to the FIRST IRA in a tax-free transfer, the amount cannot be recharacterized as a contribution to the SECOND IRA under A-1 of this section. However, if an amount is erroneously rolled over or transferred from a traditional IRA to a SIMPLE IRA, the contribution can subsequently be recharacterized as a contribution to another traditional IRA.

Q-5. Can an amount contributed by an employer under a SIMPLE IRA Plan or a SEP be recharacterized under A-1 of this section?

A-5. No. Employer contributions (including elective deferrals) under a SIMPLE IRA Plan or a SEP cannot be recharacterized as contributions to another IRA under A-1 of this section.

Q-6. How does a taxpayer make the election to recharacterize a contribution to an IRA for a taxable year?

A-6. (a) An individual makes the election described in this section by notifying, on or before the date of the transfer, both the trustee of the FIRST IRA and the trustee of the SECOND IRA, that the individual has elected to treat the contribution as having been made to the SECOND IRA, instead of the FIRST IRA, for Federal tax purposes. The notification of the election must include the following information: the type and amount of the contribution to the FIRST IRA that is to be recharacterized; the date on which the contribution was made to the FIRST IRA and the year for which it was made; a direction to the trustee of the FIRST IRA to transfer, in a trustee-to-trustee transfer, the amount of the contribution and net income allocable to the contribution to the trustee of the SECOND IRA; and the name of the trustee of the FIRST IRA and the trustee of the SECOND IRA and any additional information needed to make the transfer.

(b) The election and the trustee-to-trustee transfer must occur on or before the due date (including extensions) for filing the individual's Federal income tax return for the taxable year for which the recharacterized contribution was made to the FIRST IRA, and the election cannot be revoked after the transfer. An individual who makes this election must report the recharacterization, and must treat the contribution as having been made to the SECOND IRA, instead of the FIRST IRA, on the individual's Federal income tax return for the taxable year described in the preceding sentence in accordance with the applicable Federal tax forms and instructions.

Q-7. If an amount is initially contributed to an IRA for a taxable year, then is moved (with net income attributable to the contribution) in a tax-free transfer to another IRA (the FIRST IRA for purposes of A-1 of this section), can the tax-free transfer be disregarded, so that the initial contribution that is transferred from the FIRST IRA to the SECOND IRA is treated as a recharacterization of that initial contribution?

A-7. Yes. In applying section 408A(d)(6), tax-free transfers between IRAs are disregarded. Thus, if a contribution to an IRA for a year is followed by one or more tax-free transfers between IRAs prior to the recharacterization, then for purposes of section 408A(d)(6), the contribution is treated as if it remained in the initial IRA. Consequently, an individual may elect to recharacterize an initial contribution made to the initial IRA that was involved in a series of tax-free transfers by making a trustee-to-trustee transfer from the last IRA in the series to the SECOND IRA. In this case the contribution to the SECOND IRA is treated as made on the same date (and for the same taxable year) as the date the contribution being recharacterized was made to the initial IRA.

Q-8. If a contribution is recharacterized, is the recharacterization treated as a rollover for purposes of the one-rollover-per-year limitation of section 408(d)(3)(B)?

A-8. No, recharacterizing a contribution under A-1 of this section is never treated as a rollover for purpose of the one-rollover-per-year limitation of section 408(d)(3)(B), even if the contribution would have been treated as a rollover contribution by the SECOND IRA if it had been made directly to the SECOND IRA, rather than as a result of a recharacterization of a contribution to the FIRST IRA.

Q-9. Are there examples to illustrate the rules in this section?

A-9. The rules in this section are illustrated by the following examples:

260

Example 1. In 1998, Individual C converts the entire amount in his traditional IRA to a Roth IRA. Individual C thereafter determines that his modified AGI for 1998 exceeded $100,000 so that he was ineligible to have made a conversion in that year. Accordingly, prior to the due date (plus extensions) for filing the individual's Federal income tax return for 1998, he decides to recharacterize the conversion contribution. He instructs the trustee of the Roth IRA (FIRST IRA) to transfer in a trustee-to-trustee transfer the amount of the contribution, plus net income, to the trustee of a new traditional IRA (SECOND IRA). The individual notifies the trustee of the FIRST IRA and the trustee of the SECOND IRA that he is recharacterizing his IRA contribution (and provides the other information described in A-6 of this section). On the individual's Federal income tax return for 1998, he treats the original amount of the conversion as having been contributed to the SECOND IRA and not the Roth IRA. As a result, for Federal tax purposes, the contribution is treated as having been made to the SECOND IRA and not to the Roth IRA. The result would be the same if the conversion amount had been transferred in a tax-free transfer to another Roth IRA prior to the recharacterization.

Example 2. In 1998, an individual makes a $2,000 regular contribution for 1998 to his traditional IRA (FIRST IRA). Prior to the due date (plus extensions) for filing the individual's Federal income tax return for 1998, he decides that he would prefer to contribute to a Roth IRA instead. The individual instructs the trustee of the FIRST IRA to transfer in a trustee-to-trustee transfer the amount of the contribution, plus attributable net income, to the trustee of a Roth IRA (SECOND IRA). The individual notifies the trustee of the FIRST IRA and the trustee of the SECOND IRA that he is recharacterizing his $2,000 contribution for 1998 (and provides the other information described in A-6 of this section). On the individual's Federal income tax return for 1998, he treats the $2,000 as having been contributed to the Roth IRA for 1998 and not to the traditional IRA. As a result, for Federal tax purposes, the contribution is treated as having been made to the Roth IRA for 1998 and not to the traditional IRA. The result would be the same if the conversion amount had been transferred in a tax-free transfer to another traditional IRA prior to the recharacterization.

Example 3. The facts are the same as in Example 2, except that the $2,000 regular contribution is initially made to a Roth IRA and the recharacterizing transfer is made to a traditional IRA. On the individual's Federal income tax return for 1998, he treats

the $2,000 as having been contributed to the traditional IRA for 1998 and not the Roth IRA. As a result, for Federal tax purposes, the contribution is treated as having been made to the traditional IRA for 1998 and not the Roth IRA. The result would be the same if the contribution had been transferred in a tax-free transfer to another Roth IRA prior to the recharacterization, except that the only Roth IRA trustee the individual must notify is the one actually making the recharacterization transfer.

Example 4. In 1998, an individual receives a distribution from traditional IRA 1 and contributes the entire amount to traditional IRA 2 in a rollover contribution described in section 408(d)(3). In this case, the individual cannot elect to recharacterize the contribution by transferring the contribution amount, plus net income, to a Roth IRA, because an amount contributed to an IRA in a tax-free transfer cannot be recharacterized. However, the individual may convert (other than by recharacterization) the amount in traditional IRA 2 to a Roth IRA at any time, provided the requirements of section 1.408A-4 A-1 are satisfied.

SECTION 1.408A-6 DISTRIBUTIONS.

Q-1. How are distributions from Roth IRAs taxed?

A-1. (a) The taxability of a distribution from a Roth IRA generally depends on whether or not the distribution is a qualified distribution. This A-1 provides rules for qualified distributions and certain other nontaxable distributions. A-4 of this section provides rules for the taxability of distributions that are not qualified distributions.

(b) A distribution from a Roth IRA is not includible in the owner's gross income if it is a qualified distribution or to the extent that it is a return of the owner's contributions to the Roth IRA (determined in accordance with A-8 of this section). A qualified distribution is one that is both —

(1) Made after a 5-taxable-year period (defined in A-2 of this section); and

(2) Made on or after the date on which the owner attains age 59 section, made to a beneficiary or the estate of the owner on or after the date of the owner's death, attributable to the owner's being disabled within the meaning of section 72(m)(7), or to which section

72(t)(2)(F) applies (exception for first-time home purchase).

(c) An amount distributed from a Roth IRA will not be included in gross income to the extent it is rolled over to another Roth IRA on a tax-free basis under the rules of sections 408(d)(3) and 408A(e).

(d) Excess contributions that are returned to the Roth IRA owner in accordance with section 408(d)(4) (corrective distributions) are not includible in gross income, but any net income required to be distributed under section 408(d)(4) together with the excess contribution is includible in gross income for the taxable year in which the excess contribution was made.

Q-2. When does the 5-taxable-year period described in A-1 of this section (relating to qualified distributions) begin and end?

A-2. The 5-taxable-year period described in A-1 of this section begins on the first day of the individual's taxable year for which the first regular contribution is made to any Roth IRA of the individual or, if earlier, the first day of the individual's taxable year in which the first conversion contribution is made to any Roth IRA of the individual. The 5-taxable-year period ends on the last day of the individual's fifth consecutive taxable year beginning with the taxable year described in the preceding sentence. For example, if an individual whose taxable year is the calendar year makes a first-time regular Roth IRA contribution any time between January 1, 1998, and April 15, 1999, for 1998, the 5-taxable-year period begins on January 1, 1998. Thus, each Roth IRA owner has only one 5-taxable- year period described in A-1 of this section for all the Roth IRAs of which he or she is the owner. Further, because of the requirement of the 5-taxable-year period, no qualified distributions can occur before taxable years beginning in 2003.

Q-3. If a distribution is made to an individual who is the sole beneficiary of his or her deceased spouse's Roth IRA and the individual is treating the Roth IRA as his or her own, can the distribution be a qualified distribution based on being made to a beneficiary on or after the owner's death?

A-3. No. If a distribution is made to an individual who is the sole beneficiary of his or her deceased spouse's Roth IRA and the individual is treating the Roth IRA as his or her own, then, in accordance with section 1.408A-2 A-4, the distribution is treated as coming from the individual's own Roth IRA and not the deceased spouse's Roth IRA. Therefore, for purposes of determining whether the distribution is a qualified distribution, it is not treated as made to a beneficiary on or after the owner's death.

Q-4. How is a distribution from a Roth IRA taxed if it is not a qualified distribution?

A-4. A distribution that is not a qualified distribution, and is neither contributed to another Roth IRA in a qualified rollover contribution nor constitutes a corrective distribution, is includible in the owner's gross income to the extent that the amount of the distribution, when added to the amount of all previous distributions from the owner's Roth IRAs (whether or not they were qualified distributions), exceeds the owner's contributions to all his or her Roth IRAs. For purposes of this A-4, any amount distributed as a corrective distribution is treated as if it was never contributed.

Q-5. Will the additional tax under 72(t) apply to the amount of a distribution that is not a qualified distribution?

A-5. (a) The 10-percent additional tax under section 72(t) will apply (unless the distribution is excepted under section 72(t)) to any distribution from a Roth IRA includible in gross income.

(b) The 10-percent additional tax under section 72(t) also applies to a nonqualified distribution, even if it is not then includible in gross income, to the extent it is allocable to a conversion contribution, if the distribution is made within the 5- taxable-year period beginning with the first day of the individual's taxable year in which the conversion contribution was made. The 5- taxable-year period ends on the last day of the individual's fifth consecutive taxable year beginning with the taxable year described in the preceding sentence. For purposes of applying the tax, only the amount of the conversion includible in gross income as a result of the conversion is taken into account. The exceptions under section 72(t) also apply to such a distribution.

(c) The 5-taxable-year period described in this A-5 for purposes of determining whether section 72(t) applies to a distribution allocable to a conversion contribution is separately determined for each conversion contribution, and need not be the same as the 5- taxable-year period used for purposes of determining whether a distribution is a qualified distribution under A-1(b) of this section. For example, if a calendar-year taxpayer who received a distribution from a traditional IRA on December 31, 1998, makes a conversion contribution by contributing the distributed amount to a Roth IRA on February 25, 1999 in a qualifying rollover contribution and makes a regular contribution for 1998 on the same date, the 5- taxable-year period for purposes of this A-5 begins on January 1, 1999, while the 5-taxable-year period for purposes of A-1(b) of this section begins on January 1, 1998.

Q-6. Is there a special rule for taxing distributions allocable to a 1998 conversion?

A-6. Yes. In the case of a distribution from a Roth IRA in 1998, 1999 or 2000 of amounts allocable to a 1998 conversion with respect to which the 4-year spread for the resultant income inclusion applies (see section 1.408A-4 A-8), any income deferred as a result of the election to years after the year of the distribution is accelerated so that it is includible in gross income in the year of the distribution up to the amount of the distribution allocable to the 1998 conversion (determined under A-8 of this section). This amount is in addition to the amount otherwise includible in the owner's gross income for that taxable year as a result of the conversion. However, this rule will not require the inclusion of any amount to the extent it exceeds the total amount of income required to be included over the 4-year period. The acceleration of income inclusion described in this A-6 applies in the case of a surviving spouse who elects to continue the 4-year spread in accordance with section 1.408A-4 A-11(b).

Q-7. Is the 5-taxable-year period described in A-1 of this section redetermined when a Roth IRA owner dies?

A-7. (a) No. The beginning of the 5-taxable-year period described in A-1 of this section is not redetermined when the Roth IRA owner dies. Thus, in determining the 5-taxable-year period, the period the Roth IRA is held in the name of a beneficiary, or in the name of a surviving spouse who treats the decedent's Roth IRA as his or her own, includes the period it was held by the decedent.

(b) The 5-taxable-year period for a Roth IRA held by an individual as a beneficiary of a deceased Roth IRA owner is

determined independently of the 5-taxable-year period for the beneficiary's own Roth IRA. However, if a surviving spouse treats the Roth IRA as his or her own, the 5-taxable-year period with respect to any of the surviving spouse's Roth IRAs (including the one that the surviving spouse treats as his or her own) ends at the earlier of the end of either the 5-taxable-year period for the decedent or the 5-taxable-year period applicable to the spouse's own Roth IRAs.

Q-8. How is it determined whether an amount distributed from a Roth IRA is allocated to regular contributions, conversion contributions, or earnings?

A-8. (a) Any amount distributed from an individual's Roth IRA is treated as made in the following order (determined as of the end of a taxable year and exhausting each category before moving to the following category) —

(1) From regular contributions;

(2) From conversion contributions, on a first-in-first-out basis; and

(3) from earnings

(b) To the extent a distribution is treated as made from a particular conversion contribution, it is treated as made first from the portion, if any, that was includible in gross income as a result of the conversion.

Q-9. Are there special rules for determining the source of distributions under A-8 of this section?

A-9. Yes. For purposes of determining the source of distributions, the following rules apply:

(a) All distributions from all an individual's Roth IRAs made during a taxable year are aggregated.

(b) All regular contributions made for the same taxable year to all the individual's Roth IRAs are aggregated and added to the undistributed total regular contributions for prior taxable years. Regular contributions for a year include contributions made in the following taxable year that are identified as made for the taxable year. For example, a regular contribution made in 1999 for 1998 is aggregated with the contributions made in 1998 for 1998.

(c) All conversion contributions received during the same taxable year by all the individual's Roth IRAs are aggregated. Notwithstanding the preceding sentence, all conversion contributions made by an individual during 1999 that were distributed from a traditional IRA in 1998 and with respect to which the 4-year spread applies are treated for purposes of A-8(b) of this section as contributed to the individual's Roth IRAs prior to any other conversion contributions made by the individual during 1999.

(d) A distribution from an individual's Roth IRA that is rolled over to another Roth IRA of the individual is disregarded for purposes of determining the amount of both contributions and distributions.

(e) Any amount distributed as a corrective distribution (including net income), as described in A-1(d) of this section, is disregarded in determining the amount of contributions, earnings, and distributions.

(f) If an individual recharacterizes a contribution made to a traditional IRA (FIRST IRA) by transferring the contribution to a Roth IRA (SECOND IRA) in accordance with section 1.408A-5, then, pursuant to section 1.408A-5 A-3, the contribution to the Roth IRA is taken into account for the same taxable year for which it would have been taken into account if the contribution had originally been made to the Roth IRA and had never been contributed to the traditional IRA. Thus, the contribution to the Roth IRA is treated as contributed to the Roth IRA on the same date and for the same taxable year that the contribution was made to the traditional IRA.

(g) If an individual recharacterizes a regular or conversion contribution made to a Roth IRA (FIRST IRA) by transferring the contribution to a traditional IRA (SECOND IRA) in accordance with section 1.408A-5, then pursuant to section 1.408A-5 A-3, the contribution to the Roth IRA and the recharacterizing transfer are disregarded in determining the amount of both contributions and distributions for the taxable year with respect to which the original contribution was made to the Roth IRA.

(h) Pursuant to section 1.408A-5 A-3, the effect of income or loss (determined in accordance with section 1.408A-5 A-2) occurring after the contribution to the FIRST IRA is disregarded in determining the amounts described in paragraphs (f) and (g) of this A-9. Thus, for purposes of paragraphs (f) and (g) of this A-9, the amount of the contribution is determined based on the original contribution.

Q-10. Are there examples to illustrate the ordering rules described in A-8 and A-9 of this section?

A-10. Yes. The following examples illustrate the ordering rules in A-8 and A-9 of this section:

Example 1. In 1998, individual B converts $80,000 in his traditional IRA to a Roth IRA. B has a basis of $20,000 in the conversion amount and so must include the remaining $60,000 in gross income. He decides to spread the $60,000 income by including $15,000 in each of the 4 years 1998-2001, under the rules of section 1.408A-4 A-8. B also makes a regular contribution of $2,000 in 1998. If a distribution of $2,000 is made to B anytime in 1998, it will be treated as made entirely from the regular contributions, so there will be no Federal income tax consequences as a result of the distribution.

Example 2. The facts are the same as in Example 1, except that the distribution made in 1998 is $5,000. The distribution is treated as made from $2,000 of regular contributions and $3,000 of conversion contributions that were includible in gross income. As a result, B must include $18,000 in gross income for 1998: $3,000 as a result of the acceleration of amounts that otherwise would have been included in later years under the 4-year-spread rule and $15,000 includible under the regular 4-year-spread rule. In addition, because the $3,000 is allocable to a conversion made within the previous 5 taxable years, the 10-percent additional tax under section 72(t) would apply to this $3,000 distribution as if it were includible in gross income for 1998, unless an exception applies. Under the 4- year-spread rule, B would now include in gross income $15,000 for 1999 and 2000, but only $12,000 for 2001, because of the accelerated inclusion of the $3,000 distribution.

Example 3. The facts are the same as in Example 1, except that B makes an additional $2,000 regular contribution in 1999 and he does not take a distribution in 1998. In 1999, the entire balance in the account, $90,000 ($84,000 of contributions and $6,000 of earnings), is distributed to B. The distribution is treated as made from $4,000 of regular contributions, $60,000 of conversion contributions that were includible in gross income, $20,000 of conversion contributions that were not includible in gross income, and $6,000 of earnings. Because a distribution has been made within the 4-year-spread period, B must accelerate the income inclusion under the 4-year-spread rule and must include in gross income the $45,000 remaining under the 4- year-spread rule in addition to the $6,000 of earnings. Because $60,000 of the distribution is allocable to a conversion made within the previous 5 taxable years, it is subject to the 10-percent additional tax under section 72(t) as if it were includible in gross income for 1999, unless an exception applies. The $6,000 allocable to earnings would be subject to the tax under section 72(t), unless an exception applies. Under the 4-year-spread rule, no amount would be includible in gross income for 2000 or 2001 because the entire amount of the conversion that was includible in gross income has already been included.

Example 4. The facts are the same as in Example 1, except that B also makes a $2,000 regular contribution in each year 1999 through 2002 and he does not take a distribution in 1998. A distribution of $85,000 is made to B in 2002. The distribution is treated as made from the $10,000 of regular contributions (the total regular contributions made in the years 1998-2002), $60,000 of conversion contributions that were includible in gross income, and $15,000 of conversion contributions that were not includible in gross income. As a result, no amount of the distribution is includible in gross income; however, because the distribution is allocable to a conversion made within the previous 5 years, the $60,000 is subject to the 10-percent additional tax under section 72(t) as if it were includible in gross income for 2002, unless an exception applies.

Example 5. The facts are the same as in Example 4, except no distribution occurs in 2002. In 2003, the entire balance in the account, $170,000 ($90,000 of contributions and $80,000 of earnings), is distributed to B. The distribution is treated as made from $10,000 of regular contributions, $60,000 of conversion contributions that were includible I gross income, $20,000 of conversion contributions that were not includible in gross income, and $80,000 of earnings. As a result, for 2003, B must include in gross income the $80,000 allocable to earnings, unless the distribution is a qualified distribution; and if it is not a qualified distribution, the $80,000 would be subject to the 10-percent additional tax under section 72(t), unless an exception applies.

Example 6. Individual C converts $20,000 to a Roth IRA in 1998 and $15,000 (in which amount C had a basis of $2,000) to another Roth IRA in 1999. No other contributions are made. In 2003, a $30,000 distribution, that is not a qualified distribution, is made to C. The distribution is treated as made from $20,000 of the 1998 conversion contribution and $10,000 of the 1999 conversion contribution that was includible in gross income. As a result, for 2003, no amount is includible in gross income; however, because $10,000 is allocable to a conversion contribution made within the previous 5 taxable years, that amount issubject to the 10-percent additional tax under section 72(t) as if the amount were includible in gross income for 2003, unless an exception applies. The result would be the same whichever of C's Roth IRAs made the distribution.

Example 7. The facts are the same as in Example 6, except that the distribution is a qualified distribution. The result is the same as in Example 6, except that no amount would be subject to the 10- percent additional tax under section 72(t), because, to be aqualified distribution, the distribution must be made on or after the date on which the owner attains age 59-1/2, made to a beneficiary or the estate of the owner on or after the date of the owner's death, attributable to the owner's being disabled within the meaning of section 72(m)(7), or to which section 72(t)(2)(F) applies (exception for a first-time home purchase). Under section 72(t)(2), each of these conditions is also an exception to the tax under section 72(t).

Example 8. Individual D makes a $2,000 regular contribution to a traditional IRA on January 1, 1999, for 1998. On April 15,1999, when the $2,000 has increased to $2,500, D recharacterizes the contribution by transferring the $2,500 to a Roth IRA (pursuant to section 1.408A-5 A-1). In this case, D's regular contribution to the Roth IRA for 1998 is $2,000. The $500 of earnings is not treated as a contribution to the Roth IRA. The results would be the same if the $2,000 had decreased to $1,500 prior to the recharacterization.

Example 9. In December 1998, individual E receives a distribution from his traditional IRA of $300,000 and in January 1999 he contributes the $300,000 to a Roth IRA as a conversion contribution. In April 1999, when the $300,000 has increased to $350,000, E recharacterizes the conversion contribution by transferring the $350,000 to a traditional IRA. In this case, E's conversion contribution for 1998 is $0, because the $300,000 conversion contribution and the earnings of $50,000 are disregarded. The results would be the same if the $300,000 had decreased to $250,000 prior to the recharacterization. Further, since the conversion is disregarded, the $300,000 is not includible in gross income in 1998.

Q-11. If the owner of a Roth IRA dies prior to the end of the 5-taxable-year period described in A-1 of this section (relating to qualified distributions) or prior to the end of the 5-taxable-year period described in A-5 of this section (relating to conversions), how are different types of contributions in the Roth IRA allocated to multiple beneficiaries?

A-11. Each type of contribution is allocated to each beneficiary on a pro-rata basis. Thus, for example, if a Roth IRA owner dies in 1999, when the Roth IRA contains a regular contribution of $2,000, a conversion contribution of $6,000 and earnings of $1,000, and the owner leaves his Roth IRA equally to four children, each child will receive one quarter of each type of contribution. Pursuant to the ordering rules in A-8 of this section, an immediate distribution of $2,000 to one of the children will be deemed to consist of $500 of regular contributions and $1,500 of conversion contributions.

Q-12. How do the withholding rules under section 3405 apply to Roth IRAs?

A-12. Distributions from a Roth IRA are distributions from an individual retirement plan for purposes of section 3405 and thus are designated distributions unless one of the exceptions in section 3405(e)(1) applies. Pursuant to section 3405 (a) and (b), nonperiodic distributions from a Roth IRA are subject to 10-percent withholding by the payor and periodic payments are subject to withholding as if the payments were wages. However, an individual can elect to have no amount withheld in accordance with section 3405(a)(2) and (b)(2).

Q-13. Do the withholding rules under section 3405 apply to conversions?

A-13. Yes. A conversion by any method described in section 1.408A-4 A-1 is considered a designated distribution subject to section 3405. However, a conversion occurring in 1998 by means of a trustee-to-trustee transfer of an amount from a traditional IRA to a

Roth IRA established with the same or a different trustee is not required to be treated as a designated distribution for purposes of section 3405. Consequently, no withholding is required with respect to such a conversion (without regard to whether or not the individual elected to have no withholding).

Q-14. What minimum distribution rules apply to a Roth IRA?

A-14. (a) No minimum distributions are required to be made from a Roth IRA under section 408(a)(6) and (b)(3) (which generally incorporate the provisions of section 401(a)(9)) while the owner is alive. The post-death minimum distribution rules under section 401(a)(9)(B) that apply to traditional IRAs, with the exception of the at-least-as-rapidly rule described in section 401(a)(9)(B)(i), also apply to Roth IRAs.

(b) The minimum distribution rules apply to the Roth IRA as though the Roth IRA owner died before his or her required beginning date. Thus, generally, the entire interest in the Roth IRA must be distributed by the end of the fifth calendar year after the year of the owner's death unless the interest is payable to a designated beneficiary over a period not greater than that beneficiary's life expectancy and distribution commences before the end of the calendar year following the year of death. If the sole beneficiary is the decedent's spouse, such spouse may delay distributions until the decedent would have attained age 70section or may treat the Roth IRA as his or her own.

(c) Distributions to a beneficiary that are not qualified distributions will be includible in the beneficiary's gross income according to the rules in A-4 of this section.

Q-15. Does section 401(a)(9) apply separately to Roth IRAs and individual retirement plans that are not Roth IRAs?

A-15. Yes. An individual required to receive minimum distributions from his or her own traditional or SIMPLE IRA cannot choose to take the amount of the minimum distributions from any Roth IRA. Similarly, an individual required to receive minimum distributions from a Roth IRA cannot choose to take the amount of the minimum distributions from a traditional or SIMPLE IRA. In addition, an individual required to receive minimum distributions as a beneficiary under a Roth IRA can only satisfy the minimum distributions for one Roth IRA by distributing from another Roth IRA if the Roth IRAs were inherited from the same decedent.

Q-16. How is the basis of property distributed from a Roth IRA determined for purposes of a subsequent disposition?

A-16. The basis of property distributed from a Roth IRA is its fair market value (FMV) on the date of distribution, whether or not the distribution is a qualified distribution. Thus, for example, if a distribution consists of a share of stock in XYZ Corp. with an FMV of $40.00 on the date of distribution, for purposes of determining gain or loss on the subsequent sale of the share of XYZ Corp. stock, it has a basis of $40.00.

Q-17. What is the effect of distributing an amount from a Roth IRA and contributing it to another type of retirement plan other than a Roth IRA?

A-17. Any amount distributed from a Roth IRA and contributed to another type of retirement plan (other than a Roth IRA) is treated as a distribution from the Roth IRA that is neither a rollover contribution for purposes of section 408(d)(3) nor a qualified rollover contribution within the meaning of section 408A(e) to the other type of retirement plan. This treatment also applies to any amount transferred from a Roth IRA to any other type of retirement plan unless the transfer is a recharacterization described in section 1.408A-5.

Q-18. Can an amount be transferred directly from an education IRA to a Roth IRA (or distributed from an education IRA and rolled over to a Roth IRA)?

A-18. No amount may be transferred directly from an education IRA to a Roth IRA. A transfer of funds (or distribution and rollover) from an education IRA to a Roth IRA constitutes a distribution from the education IRA and a regular contribution to the Roth IRA (rather than a qualified rollover contribution to the Roth IRA).

Q-19. What are the Federal income tax consequences of a Roth IRA owner transferring his or her Roth IRA to another individual by gift?

A-19. A Roth IRA owner's transfer of his or her Roth IRA to another individual by gift constitutes an assignment of the owner's rights under the Roth IRA. At the time of the gift, the assets of the Roth IRA are deemed to be distributed to the owner and, accordingly, are treated as no longer held in a Roth IRA. In the case of any such gift of a Roth IRA made prior to October 1, 1998, if the entire interest in the Roth IRA is reconveyed to the Roth IRA owner prior to January 1, 1999, the Internal Revenue Service will treat the gift and reconveyance as never having occurred for estate tax, gift tax, and generation-skipping tax purposes and for purposes of this A- 19.

SECTION 1.408A-7 REPORTING.

Q-1. What reporting requirements apply to Roth IRAs?

A-1. Generally, the reporting requirements applicable to IRAs other than Roth IRAs also apply to Roth IRAs, except that, pursuant to section 408A(d)(3)(D), the trustee of a Roth IRA must include on Forms 1099-R and 5498 additional information as described in the instructions thereto. Any conversion of amounts from an IRA other than a Roth IRA to a Roth IRA is treated as a distribution for which a Form 1099-R must be filed by the trustee maintaining the non-Roth IRA. In addition, the owner of such IRAs must report the conversion by completing Form 8606. In the case of a recharacterization described in section 1.408A-5 A-1, IRA owners must report such transactions in the manner prescribed in the instructions to the applicable Federal tax forms.

Q-2. Can a trustee rely on reasonable representations of a Roth IRA contributor or distributee for purposes of fulfilling reporting obligations?

A-2. A trustee maintaining a Roth IRA is permitted to rely on reasonable representations of a Roth IRA contributor or distributee for purposes of fulfilling reporting obligations.

SECTION 1.408A-8 DEFINITIONS.

Q-1. Are there any special definitions that govern in applying the provisions of sections 1.408A-1 through 1.408A-7 and this section?

A-1. Yes, the following definitions govern in applying the provisions of section section 1.408A-1 through 1.408A-7 and this section. Unless the context indicates otherwise, the use of a particular term excludes the use of the other terms. The definitions are as follows:

(a) DIFFERENT TYPES OF IRAS — (1) IRA. Sections 408(a) and (b), respectively, describe an individual retirement account and an individual retirement annuity. The term IRA means an IRA described in either section 408(a) or (b), including each IRA described in paragraphs (a)(2) through (5) of this A-1. However, the term IRA does not include an education IRA described in section 530.

(2) TRADITIONAL IRA. The term traditional IRA means an individual retirement account or individual retirement annuity described in section 408(a) or (b), respectively. This term includes a SEP IRA but does not include a SIMPLE IRA or a Roth IRA.

(3) SEP IRA. Section 408(k) describes a simplified employee pension (SEP) as an employer-sponsored plan under which an employer can make contributions to IRAs established for its employees. The term SEP IRA means an IRA that receives contributions made under a SEP. The term SEP includes a salary reduction SEP (SARSEP) described in section 408(k)(6).

(4) SIMPLE IRA. Section 408(p) describes a SIMPLE IRA Plan as an employer-sponsored plan under which an employer can make contributions to SIMPLE IRAs established for its employees. The term SIMPLE IRA means an IRA to which the only contributions that can be made are contributions under a SIMPLE IRA Plan or rollovers or transfers from another SIMPLE IRA.

(5) ROTH IRA. The term Roth IRA means an IRA that meets the requirements of section 408A.

(b) OTHER DEFINED TERMS OR PHRASES — (1) 4-YEAR SPREAD. The term 4-year spread is described in section 1.408A-4 A-8.

(2) CONVERSION. The term conversion means a transaction satisfying the requirements of section 1.408A-4 A-1.

(3) CONVERSION AMOUNT OR CONVERSION CONTRIBUTION. The term conversion amount or conversion contribution is the amount of a distribution and contribution with respect to which a conversion described in section 1.408A-4 A-1 is made.

(4) MODIFIED AGI. The term modified AGI is defined in section 1.408A-3 A-5.

(5) RECHARACTERIZATION. The term recharacterization means a transaction described in section 1.408A-5 A-1.

(6) RECHARACTERIZED AMOUNT OR RECHARACTERIZED CONTRIBUTION. The term recharacterized amount or recharacterized contribution means an amount or contribution treated as contributed to an IRA other than the one to which it was originally contributed pursuant to a recharacterization described in section 1.408A-5 A-1.

(7) TAXABLE CONVERSION AMOUNT. The term taxable conversion amount means the portion of a conversion amount includible in income on account of a conversion, determined under the rules of section 408(d)(1) and (2).

(8) TAX-FREE TRANSFER. The term tax-free transfer means a tax-free rollover described in section 402(c), 402(e)(6), 403(a)(4), 403(a)(5), 403(b)(8), 403(b)(10) or 408(d)(3), or a tax-free trustee-to-trustee transfer.

(9) TREAT AN IRA AS HIS OR HER OWN. The phrase treat an IRA as his or her own means to treat an IRA of a surviving spouse for which one is the beneficiary as his or her own IRA after the death of the IRA owner in accordance with the terms of the IRA instrument or in the manner provided in the regulations under section 408(a)(6) or (b)(3).

(10) TRUSTEE. The term trustee includes a custodian or issuer (in the case of an annuity) of an IRA (except where the context clearly indicates otherwise).

SECTION 1.408A-9 EFFECTIVE DATE.

Q-1. To what taxable years do section section 1.408A-1 through 1.408A-8 apply?
A-1 Sections 1.408A-1 through 1.408A-8 apply to taxable years beginning on or after January 1, 1998.

A. These regulations are effective for taxable years beginning on or after January 1, 1998.

Excessive Recharacterizations: IRS Notice 98-50

PURPOSE

This notice responds to questions that have arisen regarding whether a taxpayer who has converted an amount from a traditional IRA to a Roth IRA may not only transfer the amount back to a traditional IRA in a recharacterization but also subsequently "reconvert" that amount from the traditional IRA to a Roth IRA.

BACKGROUND

Section 408A of the Internal Revenue Code (the "Code"), which was added by section 302 of the Taxpayer Relief Act of 1997, Pub. L. 105-34, establishes the Roth IRA as a new type of individual retirement plan, effective for taxable years beginning on or after January 1, 1998. The provisions of section 408A were amended by the Internal Revenue Service Restructuring and Reform Act of 1998, Pub. L. 105-206. On September 3, 1998, proposed regulations relating to Roth IRAs, sections 1.408A-1 through 1.408A-9, were published in the Federal Register (63 FR 46937). This notice incorporates definitions and terms used in those proposed regulations.

Section 408A(d)(3) of the Code and section 1.408A-4 of the proposed regulations prescribe rules for the conversion of an amount from a traditional IRA to a Roth IRA. Any amount converted from a traditional IRA to a Roth IRA is treated as distributed from the traditional IRA and rolled over to the Roth IRA and is generally includible in gross income for the year in which the amount is distributed or transferred from the traditional IRA (subject to a "4-year spread" for 1998 conversions, unless the taxpayer elects otherwise).

Section 408A(d)(6) of the Code and section 1.408A-5 of the proposed regulations prescribe rules for "recharacterizations" of IRA contributions, including Roth IRA conversion contributions. Section 408A(d)(6) provides that, except as otherwise provided by the Secretary of the Treasury, an IRA contribution that is transferred to another IRA in a trustee-to-trustee transfer on or before the date prescribed by law for filing the taxpayer's Federal income tax return, including extensions, (the "due date") for the taxable year of the contribution is treated as made to the transferee IRA and not the transferor IRA. The proposed regulations interpret section 408A(d)(6) to make its application elective by the taxpayer, permit the taxpayer to recharacterize most types of IRA contributions, and permit the taxpayer to recharacterize all or any portion of an IRA contribution.

TREATMENT OF RECONVERSIONS

The question has arisen whether a taxpayer who has converted an amount from a traditional IRA to a Roth IRA may not only transfer the amount back to a traditional IRA in a recharacterization but also subsequently "reconvert" that amount from the traditional IRA to a Roth IRA. The proposed regulations do not specifically address this question, and the Service and Treasury are considering whether final regulations should permit reconversions under any circumstances. However, effective as of November 1, 1998, the interim rules set forth below will apply for 1998 and 1999. Any future guidance that either prohibits reconversions or imposes conditions on reconversions more restrictive than those imposed under this notice will not apply to reconversions completed before issuance of that guidance.

If a taxpayer converts (or reconverts) an amount, transfers that amount back to a traditional IRA by means of a recharacterization, and reconverts that amount in a transaction for which the taxpayer is not eligible under the interim rules set forth in this notice, the reconversion will be deemed an "excess reconversion." However, any reconversions that a taxpayer has made before November 1, 1998, will not be treated as excess reconversions and will not be taken into account in determining whether any later reconversion is an excess reconversion.

A taxpayer who converts an amount from a traditional IRA to a Roth IRA during 1998 and then transfers that amount back to a traditional IRA by means of a recharacterization is eligible to reconvert that amount to a Roth IRA once (but no more than once) on or after November 1, 1998, and on or before December 31, 1998; the taxpayer also is eligible to reconvert that amount once (but no more than once) during 1999. (Any conversion of that amount during 1999 would constitute a reconversion because the taxpayer previously converted that amount during 1998.) This rule applies without regard to whether the taxpayer's initial conversion or recharacterization of the amount occurs before, on, or after November 1, 1998, and (as indicated above) even if the taxpayer has made one or more reconversions before November 1, 1998.

A taxpayer who converts an amount from a traditional IRA to a Roth IRA during 1999 that has not been converted previously and then transfers that amount back to a traditional IRA by means of a recharacterization is eligible to reconvert that amount to a Roth IRA once (but no more than once) on or before December 31, 1999. In determining whether a taxpayer has made a previous conversion for purposes of these interim rules, a failed conversion, as described in proposed regulations section 1.408A-4, Q & A-3 (that is, an attempted conversion for which the taxpayer is not eligible for reasons set forth in proposed regulations section 1.408A-4), will not be treated as a conversion.

Any excess reconversion of an amount during 1998 or 1999 will not change the taxpayer's taxable conversion amount (as defined in proposed regulations section 1.408A-8, Q & A-1(b)(7)). Instead, the excess reconversion and the last preceding recharacterization will not be taken into account for purposes of determining the taxpayer's taxable conversion amount, and the taxpayer's taxable conversion amount will be based on the last reconversion that was not an excess reconversion (unless, after the excess reconversion, the amount is transferred back to a traditional IRA by means of a recharacterization). An excess reconversion will otherwise be treated as a valid reconversion.

Any conversion, recharacterization, or reconversion of an amount under this notice must satisfy the provisions of section 408A and the proposed regulations. For example, a taxpayer making a conversion or reconversion must satisfy the $100,000 modified AGI limitation of section 408A(c)(3)(B)(i) and proposed regulations section 1.408A-4, Q & A-2, and a taxpayer transferring a contribution from one IRA to another IRA by means of a recharacterization must make the transfer on or before the due date for the taxable year of the contribution, as required by section 408A(d)(6) and proposed regulations section 1.408A-5, Q & A-1. In determining the portion of any amount held in a Roth IRA or a traditional IRA that a taxpayer is not eligible to reconvert under the interim rules set forth in this notice, any amount previously converted (or reconverted) is adjusted for subsequent net gains or losses thereon.

Example 1. On May 1, 1998, T converted an amount in a traditional IRA (Traditional IRA 1) to a Roth IRA (Roth IRA 1). T did not contribute any other amount to Roth IRA 1. On October 15, 1998, T transferred the amount in Roth IRA 1 to a traditional IRA (Traditional IRA 2) by means of a recharacterization. T is eligible to reconvert the amount in Traditional IRA 2 to a Roth IRA once (but no more than once) at any time on or after November 1, 1998, and on or before December 31, 1998. Any additional reconversion during 1998 would be an excess reconversion. This result would not be different if the recharacterization had occurred on or after November 1, 1998, instead of before November 1, 1998.

Example 2. The facts are the same as in Example 1, except that, on November 25, 1998, T reconverts the amount in Traditional IRA 2 to a Roth IRA (Roth IRA 2). After that reconversion, T may transfer the amount from Roth IRA 2 back to a traditional IRA by means of a recharacterization, but any subsequent reconversion of that amount to a Roth IRA before January 1, 1999, would be an excess reconversion. If T does transfer the amount from Roth IRA 2 back to a traditional IRA by means of a recharacterization, T is eligible to reconvert that amount once (but no more than once) during 1999. Any additional reconversion of that amount during 1999 would be an excess reconversion.

Example 3. The facts are the same as in Example 2, except that, on December 4, 1998, T transfers the amount from Roth IRA 2 back to a traditional IRA (Traditional IRA 3) by means of a recharacterization. If T does not reconvert that amount to a Roth IRA on or before December 31, 1998, T cannot use the 4-year spread available for 1998 conversions.

Example 4. The facts are the same as in Example 3. The value of the amount converted on May 1, 1998, was $X, and the value of the amount converted on November 25, 1998, was $Y. On December 8, 1998, T reconverts the amount in Traditional IRA 3 (which then has a value of $Z) to a Roth IRA (Roth IRA 3). Under the interim rules set forth in this notice, T is not eligible to make the December 8, 1998, reconversion, and that excess reconversion will not be taken into account for purposes of determining T's taxable conversion amount (although it is otherwise treated as a valid conversion). Instead, T's taxable conversion amount will be based on T's November 25, 1998, reconversion. Therefore, T's taxable conversion amount will be $Y. Because it is a 1998 conversion, the November 25, 1998, reconversion is eligible for the 4-year spread (unless T again transfers the amount from Roth IRA 3 to a traditional IRA by means of a recharacterization).

Example 5. The facts are the same as in Example 2, except that T's modified AGI for 1998 was $110,000. Therefore, T was not eligible to convert an amount from a traditional IRA to a Roth IRA in 1998, and T's attempted conversion (on May 1, 1998) and reconversion (on November 25, 1998) are failed conversions, as described in proposed regulations section 1.408A-4, Q & A-3. Therefore, if T transfers the amount of the failed conversion in Roth IRA 2 back to a traditional IRA by means of a recharacterization and converts that amount from the traditional IRA to a Roth IRA during 1999, T will be eligible to reconvert that amount once (but no more than once) on or before December 31, 1999. Any additional reconversion of that amount during 1999 would be an excess reconversion.

Example 6. On November 5, 1998, R converts an amount in a traditional IRA (Traditional IRA 1) to a Roth IRA (Roth IRA 1). On November 25, 1998, R transfers the amount in Roth IRA 1 back to a traditional IRA (Traditional IRA 2) by means of a recharacterization. R is then eligible to reconvert the amount in Traditional IRA 2 to a Roth IRA at any time on or before December 31, 1998. After that reconversion, R may transfer the amount back to a traditional IRA by means of a recharacterization, but any subsequent reconversion of that amount to a Roth IRA before January 1, 1999, would be an excess reconversion. If R does transfer the amount back to a traditional IRA by means of a recharacterization (whether before or after the end of 1998), R will be eligible to reconvert that amount once (but no more than once) during 1999. Any additional reconversion of that amount during 1999 would be an excess reconversion.

Example 7. On January 5, 1999, S converts an amount in a traditional IRA (Traditional IRA 1) to a Roth IRA (Roth IRA 1). S had not previously converted that amount. On February 17, 1999, S transfers the amount in Roth IRA 1 back to a traditional IRA (Traditional IRA 2) by means of a recharacterization. After the recharacterization, S is eligible to reconvert the amount in Traditional IRA 2 once (but no more than once) at any time on or before December 31, 1999. Any additional reconversion of that amount during 1999 would be an excess reconversion.

This notice is intended to clarify and supplement the guidance provided in the proposed regulations under section 408A and may be relied upon as if it were incorporated in those regulations. In accordance with the procedures for submitting comments on the proposed regulations, interested parties are invited to submit comments on whether final regulations should permit reconversions (and, if so, under what circumstances and conditions). Possible approaches to reconversions in final regulations might include providing that a taxpayer is not eligible to reconvert an amount before the end of the taxable year in which the amount was first converted (or the due date for that taxable year) or that a taxpayer who transfers a converted amount back to a traditional IRA in a recharacterization must wait until the passage of a fixed number of days (e.g., 30 or 60 days) before reconverting. Additionally, such approaches might include providing that an excess reconversion would be treated as a failed conversion that would be subject to the consequences described in proposed regulations section 1.408A-4, Q & A-3, and that could be remedied as described therein.

DRAFTING INFORMATION

The principal authors of this notice are Roger Kuehnle of the Employee Plans Division and Cathy A. Vohs of the Office of the Associate Chief Counsel (Employee Benefits and Exempt Organizations). However, other personnel from the Internal Revenue Service and the Treasury Department participated in its development. For further information regarding this notice, please contact the Employee Plans Division's taxpayer assistance telephone service at (202) 622- 6074/6075 (not toll-free numbers), between the hours of 1:30 and 3:30 p.m. Eastern Time, Monday through Thursday, or Ms. Vohs at (202) 622-6030 (also not toll-free).

References

The following are references that deal with the Roth IRA. We have included references on books, web sites and software.

A. Books on Roth IRA:

[1] Natalie B. Choate: *Life and Death Planning for Retirement Benefits*, 1998 Supplement, Ataxplan Publications, Boston Massachusetts, www.ataxplan.com

[2] Seymour Goldberg: *Pension Distributions: Planning Strategies, Cases and Rulings*, CPA Journal, New York City, 1998 sforbes@luca.com

[3] Seymour Goldberg: *How to Pay Less Tax on Your Retirement Savings*, 2nd Edition, J.K. Lasser, 1997. Available in many book stores.

[4] Robert S. Keebler, *A CPA's Guide to Making the Most of the New IRAs*, AICPA, 1997, www.aicpa.org

[5] Gobind Daryanani, *Market Report on Roth IRA Software*, 1998, DQI Inc. http://www.dqi-roth.com

[6] Ed Slott, *Your Tax Questions Answered*, 1998, slottcpa@aol.com Plymouth Press

[7] Lesser, Diehl & Kolojeski, *Roth IRA Answer Book*, Panel Publishers, 1998.

[8] Neil Downing, *Maximize Your IRA*, Dearborn Financial, 1998

[9] John Bledsoe, *Roth to Riches*, Legacy Press, 1998

B. Web Sites on the Roth IRA and related topics

http://www.rothira.com: Broad range of topics including news, calculators, links to articles in other newspapers and magazines, special feature articles.

http://www.fairmark.com: Good explanation of the rules for Roth IRAs.

http://www.senate.gov/~finance: The Senate Finance Committee site where all the Roth IRA rules originated. Includes information on Technical Corrections, source for information on Retirement Security hearings.

http://www.irs.gov: IRS publications and forms, Question and Answers on the Roth IRA wil be available here.

http://www.rothirabook.com: Updates on the Roth IRA Book by Gobind Daryanani

http://www.dqi-roth.com: Roth IRA Service Provider, provides a complete analysis for Roth Conversions using high-end software programs.

http://www.fidelity.com and http://www.vanguard.com for general information on the Roth IRA. Also see http://www.ml.com.

Roth IRA Software . This is a sample list. A detailed report is available from DQI Inc. http://www.dqi-roth.com, ask for the "*Market Analysis of Roth IRA Software*" report.

C1. Free Software Available on the Internet

http://www.strong-funds.com	lump sum
http://www.vanguard.com	lump sum
http://www.fidelity.com	lump sum
http://www.schwab.com	lump sum
http://www.prudential.com	fixed annuity
http://www.moneyinsider.com	tax calculations
http://www.quicken.com	fixed annuity

C2 Pay (not-free) Software

http://www.brentmark.com	minimum distributions, estate planning
http://www.moneytree.com	minimum distributions, tax calculations
http://www.roth.upi-net.com	fixed annuity
http://www.troweprice.com	fixed annuity, minimum distributions
http://www.rplanner.com	minimum distributions, estate planning
http://www.viga.com	fixed annuity
http://www.imagisoft.com	fixed annuity
http://www.adaris.com	eligibility, lump sum
http://www.rothirabook.com	minimum distributions, tax calculation and optimal conversion .. ***Roth Optimizer,*** 1-877-ROTH911

C3. Full Service Brokerage Companies
(these have internally developed software)

http://www.deanwitter.com   Dean Witter Reynolds Inc.

http://www.smithbarney.com   Salomon Smith Barney

http://www.ml.com   Merrill Lynch

http://www.painewebber.com   PaineWebber

D. Roth IRA Service Providers

Custom Analysis of Roth Conversion   http://www.dqi-roth.com

Consultations on calculators

need to send in a financial profile analysis (see back inserts of this book)

E. News Letters, Reports and Audio Tapes

Ed Slott's IRA Advisor, 100 Merrick Road, Rockville Center, NY 11570

Gobind Daryanani, "Market Analysis of Available Roth IRA Software Programs"

http://www.dqi-roth.com

Roth IRA Newsletter from www.rothira-advisor.com

Audio tape: Is the Roth IRA Right for You by American Century Investments (800-345-2021).

Index

Roth IRA Products and Services from

DQI (a division of Digiqual Inc.)

    http://www.dqi-roth.com

The following are offered by DQI Inc., a Roth IRA Service Provider:

1.   Custom analysis of Roth IRA Conversion for clients
       see web site for related financial profile questionnaire

2.   Seminars and consultations on the Roth IRA

3.   Information on the Roth Optimizer software used in Chapter 6

4.   Detailed report (300 pages) assessing currently available Roth IRA software

       "Market Analysis of Roth IRA Software" by Dr. Gobind Daryanani

DQI (a division of Digiqual Inc.)
P.O. Box 97
Bernardsville NJ 07924
http://www.dqi-roth.com
rothinfo@dqi-roth.com
1-877-ROTH911 (1-877-768-4911)

Visit our web site at

http://www.rothirabook.com

For the following:

- Questions on Roth IRA
- Reader's comments and suggestions on this book
- New articles and information on Roth IRA
- Downloadable pdf files of forms and statutes on the Roth IRA
- Permission to reprint tables or other information from this book

email at: info@rothirabook.com
toll free number: 1-877-ROTH911

Digiqual Inc.
P.O. Box 97
Bernardsville NJ 07924
http://www.rothirabook.com

"An outstanding text that should be bought by every professional who has a client considering the Roth IRA"

Seymour Goldberg, Professor Emeritus of Law and Taxation at Long Island University

"Dr. Daryanani's powerful insignt makes this an important tool in the library for every financial advisor"

Robert Keebler, CPA, MST, author of A CPA's Guide to Making the Most of the New IRAs

"Dr. Daryanani clearly presents a balanced approach to assessing the value of Roth IRAs in retirment planning: this book is a must for all advisors"

Gregory Kolojeski, editor of the Roth IRA Web Sit (www.rothira.com)